T0091376

WITCHES' CRAFT

A Multidenominational Wicca Bible

WITCHES' CRAFT

Bruce K. Wilborn

Skyhorse Publishing

Skyhorse Publishing books may be purchased in bulk at special discounts for sales promotion, corporate gifts, fund-raising, or educational purposes. Special editions can also be created to specifications. For details, contact the Special Sales Department, Skyhorse Publishing, 307 West 36th Street, 11th Floor, New York, NY 10018 or info@skyhorsepublishing.com.

Skyhorse® and Skyhorse Publishing® are registered trademarks of Skyhorse Publishing, Inc.®, a Delaware corporation.

www.skyhorsepublishing.com

10 9

Library of Congress Cataloging-in-Publication Data

Wilborn, Bruce K.
Witches' craft : a multidenominational Wicca bible / Bruce K. Wilborn.
p. cm.
Includes bibliographical references (p.) and index.
ISBN 978-1-61608-443-1 (pbk. : alk. paper)
1. Witchcraft. I. Title.
BF1566.W62 2011
133.4'3--dc22
2011025994

Printed in China

Contents

GRIMOIRE

SEASONAL RITES

APPENDICES

Acknowledgments

I would like to send my deepest thanks to everyone who contributed to this book in any way. Without the tremendous help and support of all these wonderful people, I wouldn't have been able to compile even one-tenth of this much information.

General thanks, however, are not sufficient to show my appreciation to everyone who helped make this book a reality. So, despite the fact that I might embarrass them with praise, I'd like to single out a few of my strongest supporters. My sincerest gratitude and thanks go out to Kristen Zagranski, Jennifer Koch, and Kim Olsen-Hinkley for helping me with things that I couldn't possibly have done by myself. Likewise, I can't say enough about the efforts of Lady Marlene, Richard, Alexander, and Julia. If it weren't for these people, this book would still be a tangled mass of scrap paper, handwritten notes, and incoherent thoughts. I'd also like to send sincere thanks to Dimple Aaron, Joyce Bridgeman, Ruth Leahy, and Brian Moore for everything that they've supplied me with over the years.

I'd also be remiss if I didn't thank my editor, Allan Wilson, and my publisher, Carole Stuart, for making this book possible. If it weren't for the fact that they decided to take a chance on this project, I would never have been able to share my intimate knowledge of the Craft with so many people.

Blessed Be!

Preface

Unlike many authors of books on witchcraft, I do not claim to have been a student of Gerald Gardner, Alex Sanders, or any of the other so-called "Great Witches" of our time. Instead, I'm a typical run-of-the-mill witch who's been deeply involved in the Craft for many, many years. But, it's precisely because of the fact that I'm an average Wiccan that I decided to write this book.

When I entered the Craft, my life changed in many ways. I enjoyed spiritual freedom, an understanding of who I was, and an appreciation for why I belonged. As a result of this newfound metaphysical rejuvenation, I became curious to learn as much as I could about every aspect of the religion. To this end, I began doing a lot of personal research into the areas of the faith that are often forgotten or overlooked. At the same time, I started to pump every witch that I could find for information about his or her individual practices, beliefs, and preferences. In a way, I guess that I had embarked on a quest to become the smartest witch that I could be.

However, as time passed, I recognized that the more I learned about witchcraft, the more there was to learn. I also realized that it was actually difficult to compare various aspects of different denominations because there wasn't a lot of precise information available. Sure, there were plenty of books on the subject; but they always seemed to leave out the intricate details. So, after being frustrated by one too many books, I decided that it would be a good idea to compile everything I'd learned into a single reference source. I hope the views, beliefs, and practices that I outline will help to shed some light on the difficulties that many people encounter when they attempt to understand the Craft of the Wise.

The following book contains a plethora of general information relating to most of the denominations in witchcraft. In addition, it also features specific material about the customs, practices, and rituals of five widely recognized Wiccan traditions. However, before you proceed to sort through the information contained in these pages, I'd like to take a moment to point out a few key details that I feel will make it much easier to digest the voluminous nature of this work. In the long run, I believe that this will help you gain a better understanding of the faith.

As a religion, Wicca is understanding, loving, spiritually fulfilling, nonjudgmental, and just about any other positive characteristic you can think of. Still, anyone who spends any amount of time studying the Craft eventually realizes that the secretive nature of the religion has created a quirky indecisiveness among the majority of its practitioners when it comes to deciding on a standardized way to perform spells, invocations, or even rudimentary rituals. In other words, even though most witches don't like to admit it, Wicca's one shortcoming is that its greatest asset, diversity, often leads to indecision.

The most amazing aspect of this phenomenon is that it occurs regardless of how long a person has been a witch. In fact, when faced with a peer whom they believe to be more knowledgeable on a given subject, even longtime witches seem a bit uneasy about their expertise. And, in these situations, one of two questions is inevitably asked: "How do you perform this?" or "Am I doing this correctly?" Oddly enough, the person they're asking is invariably asking the same questions of them. Thus, when discrepancies arise, the cycle of uncertainty usually continues because everyone assumes that the next person is correct.

Now, I'm sure that a lot of witches just scoff at the notion that they're uncomfortable about anything concerning their Craft; and, that's fine. But, whether they admit it or not, the truth is that a certain degree of insecurity exists. This occurs for two main reasons. First, unlike Christianity, Judaism, or Islam, each of which has a specific holy book, a set standard for individual practices, and even uniformity within various branches, the Wiccan religion is an eclectic conglomerate, which often appears very complicated because of its diversity.

If you doubt the veracity of this statement, think about the following example. Two Roman Catholic priests are holding Sunday mass. Regardless of whether one is in the United States and the other is in Australia, their words and actions are exactly the same because both are following a universal set of standards dictated by the Vatican. In comparison, two Gardnerian witches living twenty miles apart may be conducting the same rite on the same night; and they may even use the same wording. However, because there is no specific format that establishes the form or actions to be used, anyone viewing the two ceremonies would probably not realize that they were the same ritual. A second reason that usually compounds the situation is the fact that there are so many differing opinions that it's difficult to tell old from new, conventional from unconventional, or even right from wrong.

Although all witches and covens keep a religious diary, called a *Book of Shadows*, these books rarely match from one group to the next. Yet, without some type of standardized, step-by-step instruction, many people easily become intimidated by the complexities of the Wiccan rites. In addition, since society has shunned this religion for so long, thereby removing its unique phraseology from common usage, it's only natural that some of its eccentricities are difficult for the average person to grasp without a thorough explanation. After all, unless someone explains what to do, it's pretty hard to guess how to properly assume the Goddess Position, how to hold a wheel-dance, or what to do when a Brownie comes to your house.

Therefore, the purpose of this book is to familiarize everyone with the essentials of witchcraft. It will also endeavor to supply that ever-elusive, step-by-step breakdown of the rites and beliefs of some of the most widely recognized traditions. However, in order to accomplish this task, I first have to provide you with a basic explanation of the denominations themselves.

Gardnerian Wicca

Gardnerian Wicca, which has been assimilated into more modern denominations than any other branch of the Craft, has undergone a wide variety of modifications in the years since Gerald Gardner first popularized it. Yet, almost all of these changes can be attributed to just a few causes.

The foremost reason behind many of the alterations was that Gerald Gardner taught by example. And since he already knew what he was doing, there was no need for his personal *Book of Shadows* to be a clear-cut manual on how to be a witch. Unfortunately, this meant that unless you were among the lucky few who actually watched him as he performed his rituals, you ended up relying on secondhand information for every detail about his version of the Craft.

Naturally, this resulted in a multitude of minor variations concerning almost every aspect of every ceremony. To confuse matters even more, because the contents of Gardner's *Book of Shadows* could be copied only by hand, errors in copying allowed subtle changes to creep into the text. Although these small mistakes didn't mean a whole lot at the time, when the discrepancies were eventually noticed, the efforts made to restore them to their original form served to cloud the issue even more.

Finally, in fashioning his religious beliefs, Gardner had borrowed bits and pieces of information from a wide array of sources—Ceremonial Magick, Aleister Crowley, ancient texts, etc.—which some of his followers felt were either out of place or inappropriate. As a result, many parts of Gardner's original text were rewritten, revamped or removed. For instance, most modern versions of the *Charge of the Goddess* often exclude the phrase, "At her altars the Youth of Lacedaemon in Sparta made due sacrifice." Though the reasoning behind removing this sentence often varies, the fact remains that it's a perfect example of one of the ways that Gardner's original text was altered.

The point I'm trying to make is that it's very difficult to tell exactly which form of Gardnerian Wicca is authentic. For example, I once read two versions of the same invocation and discovered that they differed from one another. Yet both witches not only claimed that they knew Gerald Gardner, but that theirs was the original form. Since I had no way of knowing whether either one was really authentic, I disregarded both.

And that's my point. Because there was no way to be absolutely certain about the authenticity of any of the Gardnerian rites currently being practiced, the version I've given in this book is the one I was taught when I first entered the Craft. In certain places, such as the Charge, I've done my best to restore the text to the original form, though it's possible that there are still some inaccuracies. Also, in places where newer versions have become the accepted form, I've done my best to supply both versions.

Italian Wicca

The rites and practices of the Italian denominations share the same divergence problems as those of Gardnerian Wicca. However, the reason that the Italian rites are so diverse has more to do with the historical roots of the tradition than with its followers. Unlike Gardnerianism, which has only been around since the early 1950s, Italian Wicca's ancestry goes back thousands of years. Because of this long history, the various forms of Italian witchcraft altered according to the influences in their particular geographical regions. For instance, some areas absorbed a great deal of Roman and Greek culture and mythology into their beliefs, while the customs of other locations remained relatively unaffected by these two civilizations. In later centuries, Christianity, the Inquisition, and a variety of other factors also impacted beliefs.

The result is a collection of Wiccan subgroups that are categorized under the general heading "Italian"; and therein lies the first problem. Although all the subgroups are technically classified the same, there are often vast differences in their rites, practices, and beliefs.

A second difficulty that Italian witches face is trying to overcome incorrect translations of original passages. These usually occurred where the Italian language had multiple meanings for the same words and phrases. In these instances, separate translations often produced different versions of the same thing. For an example, refer to Charles Godfrey Leland's book, *Aradia: Gospel of the Witches.* In Leland's "The Conjuration of Meal," the following line appears: "Quando i segreti della terra io sapró." Leland translates this line to mean, "When Earth's dark secrets are known to me." In a recent translation in *Aradia or the Gospel of the Witches,* Mario and Dina Pazzaglini translate the same line to read, "When the secrets of the earth I will know." While these two translations are similar, Leland's use of the term "dark secrets" has the effect of conjuring up the image of wickedness. In addition to words with multiple meanings, regional slang also held different meanings from area to area. Therefore, because of outside influences and translation errors, various sects formed within the Italian Wicca tradition itself.

Since there is such a variety within the Italian denomination, the rites contained in this book are primarily based upon beliefs from the Tuscan region of west-central Italy, specifically around Florence, which have been handed down through one family for more than four generations. In order to properly present them in their original form, my friend, who is a hereditary Italian witch, supplied me with a complete English translation of her personal *Book of Shadows.* She also gave me full details on how she performs each ritual. Although certain portions have been slightly modified for modern practice, taking into account language, safety, and health issues, the information contained in these rites remains consistent with that of its source.

Saxon Wicca

In regard to Saxon witchcraft, there are a few basic issues that must be understood. First, many of the Saxon practices in use today are the result of efforts by the renowned witch Raymond Buckland to resurrect the denomination, although Buckland titled his version *Seax-Wica*. By outlining Saxon-based rites and beliefs in his book, *The Tree: The Complete Book of Saxon Witchcraft*, Buckland felt he was doing justice to the Saxon Craft. And in 1973, when he wrote it, he probably was.

Thirteen years later, in 1986, he published a far more comprehensive, though technically more generic, book titled *Buckland's Complete Book of Witchcraft*, which contained almost all of the text from his earlier work interwoven with elements of Gardnerianism. This book went on to become a best-seller in the category of witchcraft.

The trouble is that Raymond Buckland is, and always has been, a Gardnerian witch. Although he now claims to be eclectic, the fact remains that he was a student of Gerald Gardner. Yet a lot of people overlooked his original training and simply accepted that his version of Seax-Wica was, in a sense, the Saxon gospel. These same people also assumed that his 1986 book was merely a more "complete" version of the 1973 work. As a result, many of the witches who chose to follow this brand of "Saxon" Wicca ended up learning a blend of Seax-Wica and Gardnerianism.

Furthermore, over the past thirty years, witches that felt Buckland had done a disservice to the Saxon denomination reintroduced whatever elements of authentic Saxon customs they could uncover. Unfortunately, their material simply merged with Buckland's version and formed a new brand of witchcraft that is different from both its parents.

Armed with this knowledge, I did my best to locate someone who could help me unravel the complicated puzzle that would lead me to the authentic Saxon culture. As luck would have it, I located a pair of witches who were able to do just that. With their help and a number of historical texts, I was able to assemble the Saxon beliefs that I describe.

But, as I've noted, the Saxon denomination has undergone a great deal of change. Please keep in mind that the Saxon rites and beliefs contained in this book are those currently practiced by a modern coven located in the midwestern United States. While the standards may not be the same as everyone else's, and while they'll probably differ to some degree from the views expressed in Buckland's books, they do represent an accurate picture of the religious views of a present-day Saxon coven.

West Country Wicca

Although all denominations of witchcraft started in rural areas, some of them retained far more of their "country" roots than others. Of these,

North Country Wicca (originating in the area around Yorkshire, England) and West Country Wicca (originating in the areas around Devonshire and Cornwall, England) probably remained the closest to their roots. I chose to give details about these branches for several reasons.

While not much has been written about either branch, they actually have quite a significant following. And because they're so unheralded, these two denominations have escaped a lot of the scrutiny that the more publicized traditions encountered. This, in turn, has allowed their beliefs and practices to modernize with only minimal influence from cross-pollination, and without much outside pressure. I also found it very interesting that the beliefs of these two denominations mirror one another so closely. This aspect is so intriguing because it's difficult to find similarities between sects of the same denomination, much less different traditions.

But there's more to their inclusion than simple curiosity. Ultimately, I outlined these denominations because I felt that the effort needed to research the two traditions would be worthwhile simply to allow everyone to compare these unassuming rites to their Gardnerian, Italian, and Saxon counterparts. Along these lines, I'd like to point out that I have continually used the moniker "West Country" in this book although the information is a combination of both traditions. Since they are not completely identical, in instances where they differ on a particular point, I either footnoted it or listed both versions.

WITCHES' CRAFT

FUNDAMENTALS

History

Unlike Christianity, which began on the day of the resurrection of Jesus Christ, the humble beginnings of modern Wicca can't be narrowed down to a particular day. About the closest anyone can come is to say that Paganism is as old as mankind itself. Evidence of this claim can be seen throughout history.

Sometime between 30,000-25,000 B.C.E., ancient artisans carved a stone figurine, known as the Venus of Willendorf, to honor the Goddess of Fertility. Around the same time, the Venus of Laussel was carved on the wall of a rock shelter in Dordogne. Still other Venuses—of Sireuil and of Lespugne—prove that Willendorf and Laussel were not isolated coincidences. Between 30,000 and 12,000 B.C.E., Paleolithic cave art depicts images of a naked Goddess and a Horned God. Mankind had begun to plant the seeds of Paganism.

Within five thousand years after the last cave painting, around 7000 B.C.E., the first traces of Goddess cults, complete with Horned God consort, appeared as a recognizable religion. Three thousand years later, small farming communities were springing up in southeastern Europe, and for the first time in history, clay statuettes of a "Mother Goddess" started to appear regularly in households while clay tablets with magickal and ritualistic inscriptions became commonplace. But larger tributes were on the horizon.

Circa 3000 B.C.E., the first megaliths were built in Brittany to honor Pagan Gods and, shortly thereafter, Stonehenge was constructed on the Salisbury Plain in Wiltshire. Fourteen hundred years later, 1600 B.C.E., the sky disk of Nebra was designed and built in the Unstrut Valley, Germany. Much smaller than the megaliths, but of equal importance, the sky disk depicted the constellations of the night sky and showed an oared, night ship carrying the Sun God on his journey from darkness to dawn.

And for the first time in history, a motif that was common in ancient Egypt was suddenly transferred to Bronze Age Europe as a religious icon.

By 790 B.C.E., well-organized villages dotted the European countryside, and people paid homage to their Pagan Gods and Goddesses for bountiful harvests and successful hunts.

But the story of modern-day Wicca doesn't begin at Willendorf, Stonehenge, or even in the little country villages. It doesn't begin in 1899 when Charles Godfrey Leland published *Aradia: Gospel of the Witches* or in 1921 when Margaret A. Murray published *The Witch-Cult in Western Europe.* It doesn't even begin in 1949 when Gerald Gardner first brought witchcraft, as a religion rather than merely an occult practice, into the public spotlight with his book, *High Magic's Aid.*[1]

The events that shaped the religion began long before Leland, Murray, or Gardner were ever born. So that's just where this historical examination will begin, too. It will center on the events that caused the religion to fracture into so many different denominations, while focusing on the momentous historical circumstances that impacted the very roots of witchcraft, in an attempt to show the reasons that ultimately shaped the way witches practice their Craft today. However, while delving into the subject of ancient Wicca is important, it's just as crucial to understand things from a logical perspective.

The history of the Craft has been so muddied and diluted over time that it may be impossible for anyone to unravel the many lies from the few available facts in order to reconstruct an accurate picture of its ancestry. Time, jealously, and animosity have taken their toll on the truth. This predicament has been further exacerbated by three main things.

First, while there have been many historical accounts written on the topic of early Pagan beliefs, the vast majority of these were compiled from records that were kept by ancient historians. No matter how unbiased these ancient writers attempted to be, they were still writing from the perspective of that period.

Second, most of the records of ancient witches and their Craft are primarily contained in documents written about witchcraft prosecutions. Naturally, these facts are skewed in favor of the governing authority. Since the records of the Inquisition and later prosecutions were tempered to support the views of the prosecuting religion, a certain amount of skepticism must be automatically attributed to them. A perfect example of these warped ideas can be seen in allegations that witches were consorts of the

Devil. Despite the fact that Hell and the Devil are Christian beliefs, they were, nevertheless, linked to witches.

Third, because most witches of the past—discounting some sorcerers, ceremonial magicians, etc.—tended to be simple country folk, their level of formal education made it nearly impossible for them to keep accurate written accounts of their religious practices. And because the discovery of any such documents would mean death, the secrecy surrounding them through the centuries means no one can be absolutely certain about the actual history of the ceremonies and spells used by these early practitioners.

Therefore, in order to try to make sense of the events that molded Wicca into its current state, this inquiry will look at three specific occurrences—the causes of the Inquisition and the Malleus Maleficarum, the antiwitchcraft movement in post-Reformation England, and the Salem Witch Trials—which not only directly contributed to the decimation of early witchcraft practices, but also amassed a vast amount of written information on witches. I hope this will give a clear explanation as to how the religion became so diversified, and why modern Wiccan practices are so varied.

THE FIRST ANTIWITCHCRAFT LAWS

Since the earliest days of man-made law, there have been witchcraft prosecutions of one kind or another, but they were generally few and far between. For instance, the ancient Egyptians (1560–1080 B.C.), though themselves a Paganistic society, sporadically executed witches under extreme circumstances. The early Greeks and Romans also occasionally executed witches, even though their religions were Paganistic. Since witches were so feared in both societies, these episodes were very rare. Still, in Rome during the fifth century B.C., the Law of the Twelve Tables exposed the practitioners of black magic to capital punishment, but left those practicing white magic free to continue doing so without fear of persecution.

This odd distinction between black and white sorcery was due to the fact that Rome was filled with occultists who openly practiced their craft and who were welcomed into the highest circles. Emperors Augustus and Tiberius privately sought advice from astrologers and wizards concerning important matters, even as they publicly banished witches from their empire. These were not isolated examples, and witches enjoyed growing success and popularity.

Thus, by the time the Roman Empire began to crumble and Christianity gained a strong foothold over the civilized world, every form of Paganism was widely practiced. Unfortunately, even though Paganism was so common, there was a movement taking shape against witches and sorcerers, and the reasons behind this trend had nothing to do with the witches or their religious practices.

It is often difficult to separate true "witchcraft" from the perverted connotations that history has assigned to this term. What makes it so problematic is that witchcraft of the past was almost always linked to politics, feuds, or other situations that pitted powerful people against each other. Examples of this can be seen repeatedly throughout history and greatly contributed to the steady decline of the religion. A few of the most noteworthy instances are listed below.

- In 583 A.D., in France, King Chilperic's infant son was poisoned by Mummolus with poison he got from witches in Paris, prompting strict antiwitchcraft laws.
- King Kenneth I of Scotland (844-860 A.D.), passed several laws stating that all witches and sorcerers were to be burned to death after friction developed between the king and his political rivals over the use of sorcery.
- Starting in 924 A.D., and lasting for sixteen years, the laws of King Athelstan of France provided execution for any witch who cast a spell that resulted in death.
- In 968 when it was discovered that several witches had attempted to kill King Duffus by melting a waxen image of him, they were quickly burned at the stake, and antiwitch sentiment was reinforced with the introduction of new antiwitchcraft laws.
- In 1232, the Earl of Kent was accused of using witchery to gain favor with Henry III, thereby showing the need for more scrutiny of sorcery and witchcraft.
- In 1324, John de Nottingham was the central figure in a plot to kill Edward II through the use of witchcraft. After the plot was discovered, the participants were arrested. Nottingham died in prison awaiting trial. This plot prompted a renewed scrutiny of witches.
- Also during 1324, in Ireland, Dame Alice Kyteler and several accomplices were accused of plotting to kill her fourth husband, Sir John le Poer, through the use of witchcraft. Though Dame Alice escaped to England, her accomplices were convicted and sentenced to death.
- In 1419, Henry V prosecuted his own stepmother, Joan of Navarre,

for attempting to kill him through witchcraft. Joan was imprisoned for three years at Pevensey Castle until Henry's death, after which she was released and lived in semiexile at Havering-atte-Bowe.

- On May 30, 1431, Joan of Arc was excommunicated and condemned as a witch before being burnt at the stake in Rouen, France. This case is particularly telling since Joan was a strict Catholic who claimed to be following the word of God.
- On October 26, 1440, Gilles de Laval, the baron of Rais, a French knight and a commander of Joan of Arc's army, was convicted as an alchemist, witch, and practitioner of black magick, strangled and then burnt at the stake.
- In 1441, Henry VI faced a witchcraft-based plot to kill him in which several important people, including the Duchess of Gloucester, were accused and convicted.
- Richard III, who seized power in 1483, was a perfect example of a king using accusations of witchcraft to deal with his enemies. With simple accusations of witchery, he rid himself of his brother's wife and her supporters, as well as the Duke of Buckingham.
- In 1590, an enormous witchcraft conspiracy was uncovered in Scotland. It was discovered that on October 31 of the previous year, a coven of 200 witches, headed by Francis Stewart, the Earl of Bothwell, met at an old church in North Berwick in order to perform a ceremony aimed at wrecking the fleet that carried King James I.
- Even the papacy was not immune from witchery. In 1663, Pope Urban VIII was the target of attempted assassination wherein sorcery and poison were to be the weapons of choice. Although the plot was organized by the nephew of the would-be pope, the connection with witchcraft was not overlooked.
- Between 1679 and 1682, French authorities investigated more than 250 highly placed people for using witchcraft, poison, and sorcery to attempt to kill Louis XIV, the queen, the dauphin, and other high-ranking government officials.

With such a long line of malevolence associated with witches, it's no wonder that so much scrutiny was leveled against them. Laws were passed prohibiting witchcraft and a witch watch swept the land. But there were things that were far more damaging to witches than civil laws.

INTERVENTION OF THE CHURCH

Along with the assorted civil statutes aimed at wiping out witchcraft and sorcery, there were also a variety of ecclesiastical manifestoes handed down by the church. One of the first ever written, the Canon Episcopi,[2] was the official teaching of the Christian Church against witches and witchcraft. This is an interesting document because, although the Canon Episcopi denounces witches, it does not claim them to be in allegiance with the Devil. As a matter of fact, it wasn't until centuries later, when the church suddenly changed its policy towards witchcraft, that witches became the consorts of the Devil.

The Canon Episcopi does, however, make note that witches worship "Diana, the Goddess of the Pagans" and that witches are deceived into believing that they "ride upon certain beasts with Diana." In other words, this early proclamation declares that the church's official stance was that witches were nothing more than deluded heretics. Unfortunately, this position would dramatically change in the coming centuries.

Almost as soon as the church's attitude toward witches shifted gears, a new form of decree, the papal bull, became the instrument of choice against witches and sorcerers. In essence, these documents were proclamations from the pontiff, concerning a specific subject, directing that particular actions be taken in the name of the God and the church. Furthermore, these papal edicts sanctioned whatever action was necessary to accomplish the given task. And, although somewhat rare, bulls against witchcraft were written throughout history.

In 1233, Pope Gregory IX became the first pope to write a bull that specifically dealt with sorcery. Although this bull was mainly concerned with Luciferians who were practicing Satanism, it's credited with introducing the first papal Inquisition. But the success rate of witchcraft prosecutions was apparently not good enough for Pope Innocent IV because in 1252, he authorized the use of torture to gain confessions.

In December 1258, Pope Alexander IV issued a witchcraft-related bull to Franciscan inquisitors; and, in January 1260, he addressed a similar bull to Dominican inquisitors. According to Alexander IV's two bulls, inquisitors should only prosecute cases of witchcraft if heresy was involved, otherwise the prosecution was to be left to civil authorities. Yet, although on the surface Alexander's bulls seemed to offer a slight reprieve for witches, they actually promoted the belief that witchcraft and heresy should be continuously linked to one another.

Pope John XXII was even more adamant in his ill will toward witches, mainly due to the fact that he lived in personal terror of them. In 1317, in an attempt to crack down on beliefs in the "Philosopher's Stone" and the "Elixir of Life," he issued an edict banning all forms of alchemy; and in 1326, he authorized a renewed Inquisition.

Over the next 108 years, Popes Boniface VIII, John XXII, Benedict XII, Gregory XI, Alexander V, and Martin V all wrote bulls that denounced witchcraft and fueled the Inquisition, though none of these were particularly stunning in their overall effect. However, in February 1434, Pope Eugenius IV wrote the first of four bulls condemning black magic, which all had an impact on the Inquisition. And, in August of 1451, Nicholas V issued an antisorcery bull that was detrimental to Ceremonial Magicians.

In June of 1473, less than two years after assuming office, Pope Sixtus IV published his first declaration attacking witchcraft and identifying it with heresy. Five years later, in 1478, intent on spreading the church's influence across the whole of Europe, Sixtus IV authored two more bulls (in April and October) that specifically authorized the Spanish Inquisition—prior to these edicts, the medieval Inquisition had been restricted to mainly Italy and southern France.

Yet even though this long line of bulls had been handed down over centuries, there was one on the horizon that would prove cataclysmic to witches and do more to harm witchcraft than all the previous fires of the Inquisition.

WAR AGAINST WITCHCRAFT

The Inquisition had been underway for more than 250 years by the time Giovanni Battista Cibo became Pope Innocent VIII. Despite this fact, he was still determined to make his presence felt. On December 9, 1484, he signed a papal bull that was to become famous because of the impact that it would have on the future of the Inquisition, as well as on witchcraft prosecutions as a whole.[3] But this papal brief was only the first of a two-part series of actions by the pontiff. Along with his proclamation, Innocent VIII appointed two monks of the Order of S. Dominic—Fr. Heinrich Kramer and Fr. Jacobus (James) Sprenger—as general inquisitors for Germany and gave them far-reaching power in the prosecution of all matters relating to witchcraft. And he chose his inquisitors wisely. Frs. Kramer and Sprenger were not only well educated, highly motivated, and intelligent individuals, they possessed an unrelenting religious zealousness, which made them perfect candidates for the task that they were about to embark on.

So it was not surprising that within a short time after assuming their positions, the two monks produced a manuscript—titled the *Malleus Maleficarum* or *The Hammer of Witches*—that thoroughly scrutinized and denounced witchcraft. Upon its completion, this manual became the primary source of information used by nearly all inquisitors in witchcraft prosecutions. In fact, because it contained so much detailed information about aspects of witchcraft that were largely unknown, the *Malleus Maleficarum* gained widespread acceptance and became the undisputed authority for all judges, both Catholic and Protestant, in witchcraft cases.

Now, although laws punishing witchcraft had always been in effect, they were never enforced on a large scale until the fourteenth and fifteenth centuries. In earlier times, witches had to become a threat, nuisance, or get themselves noticed for authorities to take action against them. But the Inquisitions changed all that. For the first time in history, even country-dwelling witches—the forerunners of modern Wiccans—who normally went about their lives in relative anonymity, suddenly came under fire for their beliefs. Healers were lumped into the same category as practitioners of black magic, just as astrologers and fortune-tellers were branded alongside all forms of diviners. Practitioners of witchcraft, and virtually all Pagans with Wiccan-type beliefs, were vigorously persecuted in an effort to annihilate anyone who had knowledge of the ancient Paganistic traditions; the side effect was that the few remaining survivors were driven into deep hiding. And this increasing hostility was all due to the concepts set forth by Kramer and Sprenger.

A Manual for Witch-Hunters

The *Malleus Maleficarum* is a thorough treatise detailing the beliefs that the Catholic Church of the 1480s accepted as true. It is divided into three parts, further broken down into fifty-seven questions and twenty-two chapters. The first part—"Treating Of The Three Necessary Concomitants Of Witchcraft Which Are The Devil, A Witch, And The Permission Of Almighty God"—is divided into eighteen questions. The most telling of these (Question I) concerns Kramer and Sprenger's opinion that the belief in witches, and witchcraft, is an essential part of the Catholic faith. In other words, not to believe in witchcraft was considered to be heresy in much the same way as being a witch was heretical. This shows just how biased, and fearful, the authors were of witches. Yet, although they felt this way, they had to ensure that others would adopt their values and beliefs. Therefore, in order to assure that their opinions were readily accepted, the monks addressed subjects that were certain to frighten fellow inquisitors.

For instance, Question IX asks "whether witches may work some prestidigitory illusion so that the male organ appears to be entirely removed and separate from the body." After reading this passage—and keeping in mind that all inquisitors, bishops, and judges were men—it's highly unlikely that anyone would ever exonerate a witch. But Kramer and Sprenger didn't stop there.

In the second part—"Treating Of The Methods By Which The Works Of Witchcraft Are Wrought And Directed, And How They May Be Successfully Annulled And Dissolved"—they went on to discuss how witches "Prevent the Power of Procreation" and "Deprive Man of his Virile Member." These scare tactics definitely put the fear of God in the minds of men of authority and ensured that witchcraft prosecutions would proceed with vigor. Still, the pair weren't finished yet.

Since they didn't want to leave anything to chance, Kramer and Sprenger added the third part—"Relating To The Judicial Proceedings In Both The Ecclesiastical And Civil Courts Against Witches And Indeed All Heretics"—which covered the entire judicial process, as they saw it, that was to be used in witchcraft prosecutions. This section set forth every aspect of witchcraft prosecutions, including the sanctioned method of initiating a claim against a suspected witch, defenses that were acceptable against such an accusation, circumstances surrounding the reliability of witnesses, methods of torture to be used during interrogation, and the types of sentences to be pronounced after conviction. In short, the monks made absolutely certain that anyone reading their manual would fully condemn witchcraft and carry out the punishments that they decreed.

However, while it's safe to say that no single book has ever done more to harm a religion, the overall value of the *Malleus Maleficarum* should not be quickly dismissed. The main reason for this feeling is that, although they didn't realize it at the time, Kramer and Sprenger were providing future Wiccans with page after page of useful information about the beliefs of early witches. From the very beginning, the authors unwittingly supplied the careful reader with an enormous amount of interesting information, which can be plucked from the text. For example, they wrote about Diana and the belief that witches rode beasts across the nighttime sky with the Pagan Goddess. They described three kinds of witches—those who could injure but not cure, those who could cure but not injure, and those who could do both—and methods by which these feats were accomplished. They chronicled the infamous "witches' flying ointment," complete with the misconception that human flesh was needed for the concoction, and they made reference to feasts, waxen images, and even faeries. More importantly, they inadvertently described many ways that Catholic and Pagan religions readily intertwined.

So, although Kramer and Sprenger were trying to exterminate all witches, and the religion itself, they accidentally preserved valuable information for future generations that might otherwise have been lost forever.

Yet these two monks were not the last obstacles that witches would have to face. In other parts of the world, the stage was being set for the next chapter in the saga of witchcraft.

WITCHCRAFT IN ENGLAND

By the beginning of the fifteenth century, the Inquisition was in full swing and continental Europe was well on its way to being conquered by the power of the Roman Catholic Church. However, across a few short miles of ocean, England had not been consumed by this particular brand of systematic religious domination. Instead, the Reformation and Puritanism swept over the island nation. Unfortunately, these religions were no more tolerant of Pagans than their Roman Catholic counterparts. As a result, during the fifteenth and sixteenth centuries, England experienced an escalation in witchcraft prosecutions. These prosecutions lasted until the late seventeenth and early eighteenth centuries when they abruptly declined. And, although the English witch-hunts were not as bad as those on the Continent, nevertheless they set the stage for more and more persecutions.

English Witchcraft Laws

Although previous kings had instituted various decrees against witchcraft, the first English "statute" concerning witchcraft was enacted in 1542. Prior to that date, witchcraft prosecutions were carried out haphazardly, depending primarily on the ruling monarch's stance toward witchcraft and sorcery. However, as was the case everywhere else in the civilized world, organized religion eventually came to hold that Paganism should be exterminated.

The Witchcraft Act of 1542 was introduced to solve the problem of how to deal with the unwanted Pagans. By treating witchcraft as an ecclesiastical offense, which was punishable as a form of heresy, the government was finally able to exert control over witchcraft prosecutions. But five years later, in 1547, all the recently introduced Henrician statutes were repealed, including the witchcraft statute.

For the next six years the country would be left with no antiwitchcraft laws, just as it had been prior to 1542. This meant that, with the exception of ecclesiastic authority, English witches were relatively safe from prosecution. But in March of 1563, urged on by well-known Calvinistic Bishop John Jewel, Queen Elizabeth I passed the "Act agaynst Conjuracions Inchantments and Witchecraftes," which set forth the various witchcraft-related crimes and their punishments. In 1604, King James I (who authored the book *Daemonologie* in 1597) repealed the 1563 law and introduced his own version, which remained intact until 1736.

Though historians generally view the 1604 statute as being far more severe than that of 1563, the penalties mandated for a particular offense were actually only harsher in three crimes. It should also be noted that some "white witchcraft" offenses, such as "attempting to heal a person by magical means," remained solely within the jurisdiction of the ecclesiastical courts because they were never made part of the witchcraft statutes.

The table below shows the crimes and their punishments. With the exception of "Injuring people or property by witchcraft," "Fortune-telling," and "Taking dead bodies out of graves for witchcraft," the sentences in the two laws were identical.

Major Offenses:	**1563**	**1604**
Injuring people or property by witchcraft	1 yr/prison	Death
Using witchcraft to search for treasure	1 yr/prison	1 yr/prison
Causing death to a human being by witchcraft	Death	Death
Conjuring evil spirits	Death	Death
Fortune-telling	No penalty	1 yr/prison
Taking dead bodies out of grave for witchcraft	No penalty	Death
Lesser Offenses:		
Plotting to:		
Injure people or property by witchcraft	1 yr/prison	1 yr/prison
Cause death to a human being by witchcraft	1 yr/prison	1 yr/prison
Conjure evil spirits	1 yr/prison	1 yr/prison
Provoke a person to unlawful love by witchcraft	1 yr/prison	1 yr/prison

While these laws marked the official beginning of the English witch-hunts, there was still one glaring difference in the outcomes of English versus Continental prosecutions. The difference arose out of the fact that, unlike European or later American witchcraft cases, both the 1563 and 1604 laws safeguarded the rights of wives and successors of convicted witches. This meant that the land and belongings of an accused witch were not automatically confiscated.

A further difference between English and Continental prosecutions—which eventually carried over to America—was that when a person was convicted of witchcraft and sentenced to death, the punishment was by hanging unless petty treason had been committed, in which case the person was burned at the stake. However, this was a rare punishment in England and mainly seen as a carryover from medieval times.

Finger-pointing

Witches in England had always been viewed as different from their Continental or Scottish counterparts. For instance, people did not believe that English witches could fly. Tales of witches riding brooms, wild beasts, or using flying ointment did not abound in England. English witches were also not known to hold large sabbats, which relieved them of the "orgy" stigma that had been attached to many other Pagan religious gatherings. More importantly, there were very few profits to be made by witch-hunters. Since laws protected the rights of surviving family members, there were no great fortunes to be gained from confiscating the property of prosecuted witches. This fact meant that there were meager, if any, incentives for professional witch-hunters.

Finally, because the pope had no direct influence over England, the brutality of the Inquisitions that engulfed Europe could not be authorized. But this does not mean that no witch-hunters existed. In fact, some witchcraft indictments and prosecutions can be directly linked to instances where witch-hunters suddenly went on an offensive. A perfect example of this occurred in Essex County. From 1560 to 1680, court records show that the number of witch prosecutions remained relatively consistent. However, between 1644 and 1646, there was a sudden sharp spike in the number of people accused of witchcraft, as well as an increase in the amount of guilty verdicts handed down.

Not surprisingly, this is the same period that two witch-hunters, Matthew Hopkins and John Stearne, appeared in Essex. A self-appointed

"Witch Finder General," Matthew Hopkins was one of the few witch-hunters who actually made money from his efforts. Pretending to have a commission from Parliament, Hopkins made villages collect special taxes to pay his wages. Eventually, however, his exploits drew official condemnation, and Hopkins was forced out of business.

Another important point concerning the English witch-hunts is that, unlike witchcraft prosecutions in Italy, France, Spain, and Germany, blame cannot be placed on the Catholic Church. England had undergone the Reformation, as well as the rise of Puritanism. While the increase in religious activity in the 1580s and 1640s seems to have marked the highest periods of intolerance toward Pagans, it appears that religious fervor was not the main reason for most accusations. Instead, simple emotions such as fear, hostility, and revenge were the most prominent reasons for witchcraft charges and prosecutions. Evidence of this can be seen in the fact that most witchcraft accusations in England were made by people who lived within five miles of each other. Furthermore, many of these accusations were nothing more than the result of tension and jealousy between neighbors.

Examples of the petty differences that could lead one neighbor to denounce another are contained in the records of many counties. For instance, the Essex County records for 1582 show that Joan Robinson, Anne Herd, and Margaret Grevell were accused of witchcraft by their neighbors. Joan was accused because she refused to sell a pig to her neighbor and because she refused to rent out one of her pastures. Margaret's error in judgment was that she refused to give a hungry neighbor some mutton. And Anne simply made the mistake of removing a piece of wood that covered a muddy patch of ground in front of her house. But these minor misdeeds were enough to irritate their neighbors and have the women accused as witches. This became the fate of many innocent people and, from 1542 to 1736, slightly fewer than one thousand people were executed for witchcraft.[4]

Judging Witches

In order to find someone guilty of being a witch, evidence had to be produced showing that the person had engaged in witchcraft. Since most evidence tended to be unseen or seen only by the afflicted party, this was often difficult. Therefore, courts eventually adopted the acceptance of three degrees of evidence in witchcraft cases. There was "strong presumption" evidence, which when the presumptions were taken as a whole, might lead to conviction. Strong presumption evidence included being accused by a "white witch" or an accusation by a supposed victim of witchcraft combined with other proofs.

The second form of evidence was known as "sufficient proofs" evidence, which included an accusation by a confessed witch, an unnatural mark on the body allegedly caused by the Devil, a "witch teat" used to suckle a "familiar," or two witnesses who claim to have seen the accused make a pact with the Devil.

Finally, there was "conclusive proofs" evidence, which included failure to sink when immersed in water,[5] the discovery of pictures or images of a victim in the suspect's house, the bleeding of a corpse when touched by the accused, or cursing followed by an injury to the person cursed.

However, these are just a few examples of the various forms of acceptable evidence, as virtually anything an accused person did or said could be distorted and used against them. It should also be noted that, despite the fact that they were Protestant instead of Catholic, and although they didn't use it to the same extent as their Continental counterparts, English judges often relied on the *Malleus Maleficarum* as a judgment tool.

When charged with lesser degrees of witchcraft, "purging" was one way to prove innocence. This required the accused to produce three or more neighbors who were in good standing in the community to swear that the accused was not a witch. For this reason, it was important to have a good relationship with one's neighbors. But purging didn't always work because neighbors were often reluctant to assist even those they knew were falsely accused. In those instances, if the accused witch admitted the misdeed, a public penance was usually ordered as the punishment. After serving the penance, and paying a fine, the accused was then dismissed.

Besides jealousy and petty differences, illness also factored into witchcraft accusations. And while there were no specific ailments attributed to witchcraft, it seems that long-suffering maladies were more readily blamed on witchcraft than any other type of illness. However, even when a sickness was linked to witchcraft, one of the three types of evidence was still required for a conviction.

The Real English Witches

One of the more interesting observations of the English witch-hunts is that while the majority of the accused witches were probably nothing more than unfortunate people who irritated their neighbors, various types of true witches seem to have been everywhere. This observation is backed by several historical facts.

To begin with, it was common practice for average people to take precautions to avoid being bewitched. People surrounded themselves with magical objects, holy writings, magical plants, and even charms to ward off witchcraft. A common charm of the times was a form of Wiccan bottle magick whereby a bottle filled with magical objects was buried for protection. Animals, agricultural crops, or property, and even foods such as beer, wine, and butter were often protected by antiwitchcraft spells, too. In short, people used something they perceived as "white" magic to combat "black" magic. But in order to get these magical items and spells, they needed to seek the aid of a witch. The trouble with this solution was that because ecclesiastical law punished both black and white witchcraft—seeking the assistance of a witch was also condemned—this type of conduct placed many people in jeopardy. Yet its widespread acceptance proved that witches abounded.

The second point that tends to show that true witches existed—or at the very least that certain people possessed an intimate knowledge of witchcraft—comes from the fact that in order to prosecute a suspected witch in the early 1500s, a "cunning man," "witch-finder," "witch doctor," or "unbinding witch" was almost always consulted.

While it's obvious that some of these cunning men were nothing more than hired guns who profited from the political climate, they must still be classified as a type of "witch" due to their intimate knowledge and use of occult practices. Although they normally operated by using rumor, gossip, and other tricks of their trade to detect or defeat a witch, they also employed simple spells, charms, and various methods of divination—such as scrying mirrors or bowls of water—to help convince people of their effectiveness. Yet this fact means that they not only had a working knowledge of witchcraft, but that they used it. Eventually, ecclesiastical courts recognized that these people were witches and turned their attention on them, too. Nevertheless, until they were ultimately accused and prosecuted, these witches enjoyed quite a bit of success.

Finally, the vast array of ancient Pagan sites scattered across Great Britain conclusively proves that various Pagan religions flourished throughout England. Roman armies brought Celtic traditions with them to Britain; the Druids left remnants of their earth-based religion; and a steady influx of ancient people deposited their beliefs on the shores of the island nation. When these details are combined with the fact that the fifteenth- and sixteenth-century population was so familiar with witchcraft, a final analysis of the English witch-hunts proves that witchcraft was a prevalent aspect of early English life.

Compelling evidence of this is found in court records that contain case after case of average citizens seeking help from a witch. And some of these same documents show that run-of-the-mill people had their own limited knowledge of witchcraft, indicating that its usage was far more commonplace than originally thought.

Since it seems to have been so common, logic dictates that there had to have been a large contingent of true witches. This theory is further backed up by Margaret A. Murray in her book, *The Witch-Cult in Western Europe*, where she first promoted the idea that the witches of antiquity were a highly organized Pagan cult rather than a loose collection of undisciplined individuals. Although historians like to point out that many of Ms. Murray's ideas seem impossible because of the unorganized state of society at that time, the fact that the overall knowledge of witchcraft is so similar from area to area suggests an organized "witch cult" did exist.

As the years passed, the Inquisitions gradually died out in Europe, and the era of English witch-hunts slowly drew to a close. But across the Atlantic Ocean, a new chapter in the bloody history of witchcraft was set to unfold.

SALEM WITCH-HUNTS

Prior to the 1692 Salem Witch Trials, there were only five executions in Massachusetts that were based on the charge of witchcraft. Also, prior to 1692, most trials on this charge were considered fair and impartial and even favored the accused since it was difficult to prove witchcraft. Another important pre-1692 fact concerning witchcraft trials was that, even in a conviction, death was not the usual sentence. For example, in 1652, a man convicted of witchcraft was only fined, while another man, who was convicted a year later, was simply given spiritual counseling and released. These lenient punishments quickly became a thing of the past.

In late 1691, Salem, Massachusetts, was thrown into turmoil. Seemingly out of nowhere, several girls in the small community were suddenly struck by a mysterious illness unlike anything the Puritans had faced before. There was no cough or fever as with a normal cold, and traditional remedies offered no relief. Instead, the symptoms included uncontrollable violent muscular convulsions so strong that it took several full-grown men to hold down a teenage girl. Along with the convulsions, the girls experienced a prickling sensation in the skin, vertigo, headaches, vomiting, and diarrhea. They also experienced episodes of strong hallucinations. In some instances, victims reported having seen visions of wild animals or a black being with the body of a monkey, the claws of a rooster, and the face of a man.

When no worldly explanation could be found, the mysterious ailment was blamed on witchcraft. This not only panicked the Puritan community, it set off a series of accusations that resulted in the infamous Salem Witch Trials. During a nine-month period, 150 so-called witches were arrested and charged with being in allegiance with the Devil and bewitching people of the town. However, the first mention of witchcraft did not come from any of the afflicted girls.

In March of 1692, frustrated that there was no apparent cause for the girls' maladies, Mary Sibley, a neighbor of Samuel Parris—his daughter, Betty, and niece Abigail were both afflicted—instructed Parris's servant, Indian John, to make a "witch cake" in order to determine whether witchcraft was the cause of the girls' disorders.

Under her direct orders, Indian John made the witch cake using rye meal mixed with urine from the afflicted girls.[6] The cake was then fed to a dog. The process was performed under the assumption that the reaction of the dog would either confirm or disprove that witchcraft was to blame. Unfortunately, unknown to Mary Sibley, a fungus that had gotten into the rye meal, and which was also present in the urine of the affected girls, would cause the same effect in the dog as in the girls. Although no record of the dog's reaction exists, the likely outcome was confirmation of the belief that witchcraft was the problem.

Immediately after the introduction of the witch cake into the equation, the girls began stating that they were bewitched. They accused Tituba, a Caribe-Indian slave owned by Samuel Parris, Sarah Osborne, and Sarah Good of being witches and said that the three women were the cause of their ailments. On February 29, 1692, the three women were imprisoned, and by May 10, 1692, Sarah Osborne had died in prison without ever being tried or convicted of witchcraft. But this was only the beginning.

Within a short time, there was a group of ten "afflicted girls" of various ages who claimed to be bewitched.[7] Yet, while they all claimed to suffer from bewitching, not all the girls enjoyed the same status. Though not generally known, the group of afflicted girls was divided into two subgroups. The "inner circle" consisted of nine-year-old Elizabeth "Betty" Parris, eleven-year-old Abigail Williams, twelve-year-old Ann Putman, seventeen-year-old Elizabeth Hubbard, seventeen-year-old Mercy Lewis, and seventeen-year-old Mary Walcott. The "outer circle" was comprised of eighteen-year-old Susannah Sheldon, eighteen-year-old Elizabeth Booth, twenty-year-old Mary Warren, and twenty-year-old Sarah Churchill.[8] Even more surprising is that, despite the fact that she was only twelve years old at the time of the witch-hunts, Ann Putnam testified in twenty-one witchcraft cases and was considered by many to be the leader of the afflicted girls.

The worst aspect of the growing hysteria was that no one was safe from the accusations. George Jacobs Sr. was accused of witchcraft. Interestingly, prior to being accused, Jacobs was known to refer to the afflicted girls as "bitch witches." Since Sarah Churchill, one of the alleged victims, was a servant in the Jacobs house, she probably overheard this slander and passed it along to the group, thus sealing George Jacobs's fate. Simply put, Jacobs was likely singled out for speaking his mind. A former minister, George Burroughs, was not even living in the area—having moved to Maine—yet he was still accused.

And, in a strange twist, Samuel Wardwell initially confessed when accused. However, when he later recanted his confession, he was hanged for denying that he was a witch rather than for actually being one. It's also interesting to note that Mary Warren and Sarah Churchill were briefly imprisoned as witches themselves, but both were released when they continued to testify against others.[9] Thus, within a short time, the situation got so far out of hand that there was no way to tell who would be the next person accused.

On June 2, 1692, Sir William Phipps, the newly commissioned governor of Massachusetts, appointed the Court of Oyer and Terminer to deal with the mounting claims of witchcraft.[10] This court sorted through the cases of 150 men and women and passed sentence on those who chose not to confess. Although confessed witches were eventually set free after reaffirming their faith in God, accused witches were imprisoned, starved, and tortured until they confessed. The punishment for refusal to confess was death. Of all the people that were arrested, nineteen were taken to Gallows Hill and hanged, one was pressed to death because he refused to stand trial, and four died in prison. From June 2 through October 29, 1692, the court would be directly responsible for the deaths of twenty people.

In 1692, the following people were executed by order of the court:

Date	Name	Method
June 10	Bridget Bishop	Hanged
July 19	Sarah Good	Hanged
July 19	Rebecca Nurse	Hanged
July 19	Susannah Martin	Hanged
July 19	Elizabeth Howe	Hanged
July 19	Sarah Wildes	Hanged
August 19	George Burroughs	Hanged
August 19	John Proctor	Hanged
August 19	John Willard	Hanged
August 19	George Jacobs Sr.	Hanged
August 19	Martha Carrier	Hanged
September 19	Giles Corey	Pressed to death[11]
September 22	Martha Corey	Hanged
September 22	Mary Easty	Hanged
September 22	Alice Parker	Hanged
September 22	Mary Parker	Hanged
September 22	Ann Pudeater	Hanged
September 22	Margaret Scott	Hanged
September 22	Wilmot Redd	Hanged
September 22	Samuel Wardwell	Hanged

To this day, the debate still rages as to whether any of these unfortunate people were witches. Also, the Salem Witch Trials are especially interesting because it seems that the religious authorities were unconcerned with the fact that the native Indians were Pagans. That fact lends even more credibility to views that the Salem witch-hunts were politically and financially motivated. Although financial reasons did not trigger the events, they most likely sustained them since most, if not all, of the central figures behind the persecutions profited in one way or another.

For example, just prior to the witchcraft outbreak, there was a movement afoot to oust Samuel Parris from his position as minister. However, once the witch persecutions began, Parris gained extraordinary power and ample wealth. This was directly linked to the seizure of property from accused witches as well as innocent people who simply panicked when they were accused of being witches.

Philip English and his wife were arrested as witches, but escaped from prison. Their estate, estimated at approximately £1,500, was seized by Sheriff George Corwin. Following the arrest and conviction of Dorcas Hoar, her estate was confiscated and sold for as little as £8. Edward Bishop and his wife also escaped from prison, only to have their money, goods, and cattle seized by Sheriff Corwin and forfeited. In short, there was more going on than merely cleansing the area of suspected witches.[12]

Along with the executions, four accused witches died in prison while awaiting trial:

Date	Name	Result
May 10	Sarah Osborne	Died in prison; cause unknown.
June 16	Roger Toothaker	Died in prison of natural causes.
Dec. 3	Ann Foster	Died after twenty-one weeks in prison.
March 10, 1693	Lydia Dustin	Died in prison; cause unknown.

The cases of Ann Foster and Lydia Dustin are of particular note. On October 12, 1692, Sir William Phipps forbade any further imprisonment on the charge of witchcraft. His sudden change in policy came about after his wife, Lady Phipps, was accused of being a witch by the girls. Not only did he know the charge against his wife was false, but he was unwilling to have his status as governor jeopardized. Realizing that things had gotten out of hand, on October 29, 1692, Sir William formally dissolved the Court of Oyer and Terminer. But this meant that Ann and Lydia were still held in prison months after the court was disbanded. On May 25, 1693, a jury found Lydia not guilty of the charge of being a witch. Unfortunately, she'd died in prison two months earlier.

Still, the 300-year-old question remains: Why were the people of Salem so ready to believe in witchcraft? An examination of the evidence reveals that witchcraft was relatively fresh in everyone's mind. Although Puritanism was the predominant religion of the time, widespread Paganism was a fixture of the recent past. Beginning with the writing of the *Malleus Maleficarum*, witches were persecuted in Europe. In the 1500s, the persecutions escalated and crossed the English Channel. By the time the Puritans left England, the idea of witches and witch-hunts were already ingrained in their culture.

Yet, this was only the tip of the iceberg. At a time when church and state were closely joined, it was important to keep the population in line. As a leading politician and minister in Massachusetts, Increase Mather knew this all too well, and, along with his son, Cotton Mather, became a driving force behind the witch prosecutions.[13] And it was easy for the Mathers to make people blame witchcraft due to the presence of an unseen element that would remain hidden for hundreds of years.

Mysterious Illness

Much of the melodrama that took place in Salem was either exaggerated or faked, a point that was substantiated on more than one occasion.[14] However, there was also an underlying cause for the mysterious illness that went undiscovered for many centuries. It wasn't until 1976 that Linda Caporael, a behavioral psychologist, began to investigate the Salem witch trials, looking for something that would explain the source of the ailments and hallucinations that started the claims.

After a careful study of the records that still existed, including the actual witchcraft trial transcripts, Ms. Caporael saw a pattern emerging. Within a short time, she'd come up with the hypothesis that the Salem victims might have been suffering from ergot poisoning. But since this idea had never been explored, she had to start from scratch in order to prove that she was right. After exhaustive research, she finally pieced together several important points that seem to prove her theory.

Ergot is a parasitic fungus that grows on grain. The fungus grows in and around wet marshy areas and needs warm, damp conditions to reproduce. So Caporael's first mission was to determine if weather conditions during the 1691 growing season would support ergot growth. Although weather records weren't routinely kept, she was able to unearth a clerk's journal that established that the spring and summer of 1691 were unusually warm and damp. Furthermore, she discovered that several of the girls who made the original claims most likely ate rye grown in a group of particular fields; and these fields were bordered by swampy marshes. Since rye was a staple of the local diet, it was logical to assume that others within the town ate some of this tainted grain, too. This would account for how the poison became so widespread in the small community. In time, Linda Caporael pieced together enough data to theorize that the victims of Salem may have suffered from ergot poisoning. But this was not enough to end her search. She now had to find out if ergot poisoning would account for the strange symptoms that the Salem victims sustained.

There are two distinct forms of ergotism. The first, gangrenous ergotism, as its name suggests, is distinguished by a dry gangrenelike condition of the extremities that can result in the affected areas flaking away or even falling off the body completely. The second form, convulsive ergotism, is primarily characterized by violent convulsions and includes all the symptoms seen in Salem, along with episodes of mania, melancholia, psychosis, and delirium. Since the symptoms of convulsive ergotism matched the Salem symptoms so closely, Caporael decided that she was on the right track.

For the first time in history, the underlying cause of the witch-hunts had been discovered. On top of this, Caporael had stumbled upon an explanation for many of the witchcraft cases in Europe. In the course of her research, she uncovered evidence of other episodes in which a mysterious illness had been diagnosed as witchcraft. For instance, in the early 1580s, Alice Samuel, a woman in Warboys, England, was singled out as a witch after a young girl in the town became violently ill with convulsions, the sensation of crawling skin, and hallucinations—the same symptoms as found in Salem. When confronted with the allegations, Alice denied being a witch. However, after a year of prolonged torture, she finally confessed to the charges. As the law mandated, she was hanged for causing death to a human being by witchcraft. But now that ergot poisoning could be linked to the symptoms, an answer had been found that exonerated Alice, and other witches, from any wrongdoing.

Salem Witches: Fact or Fiction?

While ergot poisoning can explain the basic causes of the Salem trials, it also raises an important question: Was anyone at Salem a real witch? Although it's difficult to be absolutely certain, of all the people accused in 1692, Bridget Bishop was most likely a practicing witch; and she probably practiced her Craft along some of the same lines as modern-day Wiccans. The assumption that Bridget was a true witch is often made because she already had a reputation as a witch, and she'd already been accused once before.[15]

In 1680, Bishop had been brought before the Court of Assistants for witchcraft. At the time, she was acquitted of the charges. However, it's widely assumed that her acquittal only came about because of the influence of a local minister, John Hale, who spoke on her behalf. She was also rumored to have insinuated that she had some sort of occult powers, and on more than one occasion she'd made magical threats toward a neighbor.

Later, at her trial on June 2, 1692, John Bly Sr. and William Bly testified to finding several "popitts made up of Raggs And hoggs Brusells w'th headles pins in Them w'th the points out ward" hidden in holes in the cellar walls of a house that Bishop once owned. Since this is a form of magic that would have been used by a true witch, it's fair to assume that Bridget Bishop was, in fact, a practicing witch.

It is likely that Wilmot Redd was also a true witch. "Mammy," as she was known, had been the town witch of Marblehead for many years and was well known for her spell-casting prowess. So it was not surprising that she was eventually accused and convicted.

Similarly, on April 30, 1692, Dorcas Hoar was arrested and charged with witchcraft. And, like Mammy Redd, she was a practicing witch. Although Dorcas wasn't known as a spellcaster or a healer, she was renowned as a fortune-teller who based her readings on a combination of palmistry and observation of her subject's overall appearance. Yet, even though she'd been doing that for more than twenty years without incident, she was caught up in the hysteria of the time, and on September 9, 1692, she was convicted and sentenced to death. Dorcas, however, was not the only "witch-for-hire" around. Men such as George Burroughs and Roger Toothaker made money from their reputation for the occult and for being able to combat witchcraft with occult charms.

Bridget, Mammy, Dorcas, George, and Roger were all Puritans with money and property. But what about non-Puritans? Tituba was an admitted witch who was first accused along with Sarah Osborne and Sarah Good. Yet Tituba never had to worry about being hanged. As unbelievable as it sounds, the witch-hunters could find no valid motive to hang Tituba. Instead, they decided to keep her as a living example that witchcraft existed. Similarly, Candy, a Negro slave from Barbados who produced evidence that she'd been a practicing witchcraft since her mistress, Mrs. Hawkes, made her a witch, never faced the death penalty.

Another interesting point is that in the 1690s, a vast majority of the general population had some knowledge, however small, of witchcraft. The evidence confirming this basic knowledge of Craft practices can be found throughout the testimony of many witnesses as they allowed bits and pieces of this information to seep into their statements. For example, on June 1, 1692, in a deposition against several accused witches—including George Burroughs, Rebecca Nurse, Ann Pudeater, John Proctor and his wife, as well as others—Mary Warren stated that a "trumpet" was sounded and that the witches wanted her to go with them to a "feast" where they would eat "sweet bread" and drink "wine."

Throughout the witch trial, various accusers would repeat these statements over and over. Since it's highly unlikely that so many people would randomly guess the exact components of a sabbat, these testimonials seem to be vague references to early Wiccan ceremonies, complete with music (trumpet) and a feast with food and wine. Another interesting comment made by most of the accusers concerned a "book" that they were instructed to "touch" or "write in." Could these references to a feast and a book (of Shadows) be coincidental? Of course. But, at the same time, it's clear that there were at least a few practicing witches in Salem. And beyond that, it's even more obvious that the majority of people in Salem had some knowledge of witchcraft.

MODERN WICCAN REVIVAL

In the aftermath of centuries of witchcraft persecutions, the Wiccan religion was nothing more than a shell of its former self. Beyond the fact that so many innocent people had died, the worst side effect was the void of authentic Wiccan knowledge that survived. Centuries of ancient writings had been destroyed, temples and sacred sites had been demolished, oral histories had died with their possessors, traditions were forgotten or distorted, and age-old wisdoms had almost completely vanished. While bits and pieces of original witchcraft still existed in parts of the Old World—especially in the outlying areas of Italy—much of this lore was contaminated by aspects of Catholicism, Judaism, or religious beliefs brought by conquering armies. Mankind was on the verge of slowly forgetting its earliest religious roots. Fortunately, there were several people about to reverse this trend.

Saviors of Modern Wicca

- In 1824, Charles Godfrey Leland was born in Philadelphia. Fascinated by the occult, folklore, and magic, Leland moved to England in 1869 and began researching Gypsy culture in Britain. After living among the British Gypsies, he wrote several books on the subject of their language, folklore, and magic. In 1880, after becoming interested in witchcraft, Leland moved to Italy and spent the rest of his life in pursuit of knowledge of the ancient religion. By the time he died in 1903, he'd published more than seventy books. However, as far as witches are concerned, there are two books that rise above the rest. In 1892, Leland published his book, *Etruscan Roman Remains*. Up until then, no one even realized that witches still existed. Seven years later, in

1899, Leland published *Aradia: Gospel of the Witches*, which was to become the foundation for the reintroduction of Wicca. While this book did not fully ignite interest in witchcraft, it did have a lasting impact on a select few. More than that, it once again got people thinking about the religion of their ancestors.

- Margaret Alice Murray was born in Calcutta, India, in 1863. As an anthropologist, and later as an Egyptologist, Murray became interested in ancient Pagan religions. This fascination eventually led her to investigate witchcraft. After much research, Murray published her first book, *The Witch Cult in Western Europe*, in 1921. Although panned by scholars, the criticism did not daunt Murray. Instead, it seemed to fuel her determination to prove her theory correct, and in 1933 she published her second book about witchcraft, *The God of the Witches.* Murray's books served as a foundation for future research that helped propel witchcraft forward.

- Gerald Brosseau Gardner was one person who really took an interest in witchcraft. Born in northwestern England in 1884, legend has it that Gardner was initiated as a witch in September of 1939.[16] For the next ten years, he practiced and refined his views about witchcraft. In 1949, two years before the last Antiwitchcraft Act was repealed in Britain, Gardner published his first book, *High Magic's Aid*, which was supposedly a fictional account of witchcraft. After the law was repealed, Gardner went on to publish several more nonfiction books on witchcraft, including *Witchcraft Today* in 1954 and *The Meaning of Witchcraft* in 1959. But because of his passion for the occult, he would eventually contribute far more than mere books.

Gerald Gardner is the man widely credited with reintroducing witchcraft to the world, as well as introducing modern Wicca as a religion. The tradition of the Craft developed by Gardner, which is known as "Gardnerian Wicca," blends knowledge that he allegedly obtained from the New Forest coven, aspects of ancient witchcraft, and information that he gained from his friendship with the infamous Ceremonial Magician, Aleister Crowley, to form what we acknowledge today as modern Wicca.

Although Gerald Gardner is often seen as the father of Neo-Witchcraft, sometimes called the "Gardnerian Revival," there are many other people who have also been noteworthy contributors. For instance,

Alexander and Maxine Sanders were followers of Gardner until they decided to break away. They chose this path after forming the opinion that Gardner's tradition needed some changes he was unwilling to make. After leaving Gardner, the Sanders became the founders of "Alexandrian Wicca," which became widely recognized throughout Europe, though for some reason it never truly established itself in the United States to the same extent as Gardner's path.

Over the years, other Pagan denominations slowly came out of the shadows. Many of these have been aided by the emergence of new authors, such as Raymond Buckland (*Seax-Wica Tradition*), Laurie Cabot (*Science Tradition*), Janet and Stewart Farrar, Robert Graves, and Doreen Valiente,[17] while other branches have been helped along by noteworthy pre-Gardnerian authors such as Dion Fortune, Sir James G. Frazer, and S. L. MacGregor Mathers. These people have not only contributed to the vast amount of information on the subject of witchcraft, but they've left a lasting impact on the religion and the way modern Wiccans are viewed by society. They've also reintroduced long forgotten aspects, and pioneered new approaches, in an effort to rebuild the true essence of the religion.

Philosophy

It's extremely difficult to define all religions with a single thought because the values and concepts that make up one faith do not necessarily fall in line with another. There's also the problem of deciding what distinguishes a true religion from a stylish religious movement.

The only realistic way to define a true religion is to say that it's a spiritual path based upon ecclesiastical laws and ideas that serve as guidelines to mold and shape its practices and practitioners. These spiritual principles explain the customs and beliefs of the religion and show the responsibilities and objectives of its followers. Buddhism, Christianity, Islam, and Judaism fall within these boundaries. And as the oldest of the earth's religions, Wicca is no different. It has its own set of ethical laws, customs, and beliefs that form a foundation for its convictions and practices. In conjunction with these, its followers are bound by moral responsibilities and objectives that serve as blueprints for the religion. To fully understand Wicca, one must first examine it from a philosophical perspective.

RATIONALE

Emotion and intuition, along with the collective unconscious, is what kept witchcraft alive in the hearts and minds of its followers even when they could not understand its underlying rationale. And it's these motivating factors that combined to carry the beliefs into the twenty-first century. Without a coherent supporting rationale, the religion would have an increasingly difficult time attracting men and women of an educated society. Wicca is growing at a steady pace. So there must be something that's convincing educated people that this age-old faith is worthy of their loyalty and trust. But what?

Wicca, like all other religions, is based upon its own laws. While some witches say that there are as many as 162 of these, others feel that everything rests on a mere handful. And it's this divergence in opinion that critics usually point to as a fundamental flaw in the faith. This contention is silly because it's not the number of laws that is at issue, but rather the meaning of the word "laws." However, instead of arguing over the question of who's right and who's wrong, it's much simpler to examine both types of Wiccan law.

The Theories

The first type of laws is derived from Hermetic principles. Generally, this group consists of seven interwoven theorems that explain the workings of the physical and metaphysical worlds, as well as the interconnections between these worlds; different denominations believe in varying combinations of these principles.[1] As a whole, these laws illuminate the Wiccan philosophy, affirming each being's place in the natural order of the Universe.

The framework of laws consists of the following: Theory of Motion, Theory of Levels, Theory of Polarity, Theory of Gender, and Theory of Cause and Effect.

- **Theory of Motion**: In a nutshell, this theory states that everything, on every level, is constantly moving and vibrating at its own rate, and that nothing is ever at rest. The result of this movement is that all parts of all things are constantly active and thereby giving off energy. An interruption in this movement is a cause or remedy, depending on the circumstance.

  For instance, sickness is often the result of an imbalance in a person's energy field (aura), and healing is accomplished by altering the aura so that it returns to its normal rate of vibration and rotation. An understanding of this theory is important to witches because it's by manipulating this energy and motion that they're able to accomplish various tasks.

- **Theory of Levels**: From an early age, most of us have been taught to believe that reality exists on more than just the physical level. Different religions teach that reality exists on an ethereal, or heavenly, level. For instance, Christians, believe in the otherworldly concept of Heaven and Hell. The Wiccan Theory of Levels goes one step further. It states that a form of reality exists on many levels: physical, ethereal, astral, mental, and spiritual. In addition, while each of these levels has its own individual laws, the laws for all levels are compatible with one another. Their mutual and compatible resonance, or rate of vibration, thereby governs the interactions between levels.

Witches, like modern scientists, have proven in practice that there is interaction between the levels. We know of situations where the ethereal level interacts with, and acts on, the physical level, or the mental on the astral, and so on. Now, while each level is constantly affecting the others, there are areas of interaction, from occurrences of mutual resonance, which are particularly strong and sufficiently defined, to be used in the Craft. The understanding and ability to draw from these areas of strong interaction is what witches call "working through the levels." It's this action of using the interaction of levels in constructive workings that constitutes the operational side of Witchcraft. Thus, the ability to make constructive use of this interaction between the levels is the aim of witches.

- **Theory of Polarity**: This principle states that in order to exist, all form and force require the reciprocal action of opposing pairs—positive and negative, light and dark, masculine and feminine, etc. —and that the resulting output is defined by its constructive or destructive application. In short, the law basically means that everything is composed of opposing parts, a concept in contrast to most traditional religions. But the contradistinction occurs only because most modern religions view "polarity" as the struggle between "good" and "evil," and see everything as a product generated by the interaction of these two opposites. Witches see things differently. Wicca recognizes both good and evil, but unlike other religions, witches identify these opposites as components of a whole. Whether that whole then becomes a constructive or destructive application depends on its output rather than on one component conquering another.

- **Theory of Gender**: In a similar fashion, this theory states that all things contain a masculine and feminine component. Therefore, nothing is wholly masculine or feminine, but rather an equal combination of both genders. These dual forces, in continuous motion, constitute a creative force. This is an important concept for witches to understand. To become fully aware of the Universe and the forces within it, witches first need to become attuned to both their masculine and feminine components. Only after successfully mastering these dual elements are they able to factor masculine and feminine energies into creative work.

Although everyone possesses masculine and feminine properties, there is generally one characteristic that dominates while the other remains mostly dormant. This is not always true. Witches who can recognize and express the dual nature of their psyche are more likely to be creative (in the sense of the Craft) than those whose perspectives are limited by their physical gender.

Furthermore, even though one or the other component does not operate on the conscious level, a witch can learn to bring the unconscious component closer to conscious awareness. Then the unconscious component can act as a psychic guide for using the collective unconscious. Since all spells involve these principles, knowing how they operate, and being able to follow their guidance, can further a witch's ability in terms of the Craft.[2]

- **Theory of Cause-and-Effect**: The Hermetic principle that sets forth this theory is based on the premise that there is no such thing as chance that everything is caused by a preceding event, while at the same time being the cause of an event. In other words, there is no such thing as an individual who is unconnected to the rest of the Universe. And although it may not seem apparent on the surface, the actions of each person affect in the overall web of life, while the web simultaneously causes effects on the person.

The Wiccan Law

The second type of law (normally titled the "Law") is a series of fundamental axioms regarding the Craft that are alleged to have been written during, or immediately after, the Burning Times of the Inquisition.[3] Although most modern denominations disregard much of the contents as out of date or prejudicial, there is nevertheless a good deal of important information contained in its passages. In its entirety, the Law reads as follows:

> The Law was made and ordained of old. The Law was made for the Wicca, to advise and help in their troubles. The Wicca should give due worship to the Gods and obey their will, which they ordain, for it was made for the good of Wicca as the worship of the Wicca is good for the Gods. For the Gods love the brethren of the Wicca. As a man loveth a woman by mastering her, so the Wicca should love the Gods by being mastered by them. And it is necessary that the Circle, which is the

Temple of the Gods, should be truly cast and purified. And that it may be a fit place for the Gods to enter. And the Wicca shall be properly prepared and purified to enter into the presence of the Gods. With love and worship in their hearts, they shall raise power from their bodies to give power to the Gods, as has been taught of old. For only in this way may men have communion with the Gods, for the Gods cannot help men without the help of men. And the High Priestess shall rule her coven as the representative of the Goddess. And the High Priest shall support her as the representative of the God.[4] And the High Priestess shall choose whom she will, be he of sufficient rank, to be her High Priest. For, as the God himself kissed her feet in the fivefold salute, laying his power at the feet of the Goddess because of her youth and beauty, her sweetness and kindness, her wisdom and justice, her humility and generosity, so he resigned all his power to her. But the High Priestess should ever mind that all power comes from him, and it is only lent to be used wisely and justly. And the greatest virtue of a High Priestess be that she recognize that youth is necessary to the representative of the Goddess, so she will gracefully retire in favor of a younger woman should the Coven so decide in council. For a true High Priestess realizes that gracefully surrendering the pride of place is one of the greatest virtues, and that thereby she will return to that pride of place in another life, with even greater power and beauty. In the old days when witchdom extended far, we were free and worshipped in all the greater temples. But in these unhappy times, we must celebrate our Sacred Mysteries in secret. So be it ordained, that none but the Wicca may see our mysteries, for our enemies are many and torture loosens the tongue of men. So be it ordained that no Coven shall know where the next coven dwells or who its members be, save only the High Priest and High Priestess and Messenger. And there shall be no communication between them, save by the Messenger of the Gods, or the Summoner, and only if it be safe may the Covens meet in some safe place for the great festivals. And while there, none shall say whence they came, nor give their true names. To this end, any that are tortured, in their agony may not tell if they do not know. So be it ordained that no one shall tell anyone not of the Craft who be of the Wicca, nor give any names or where they abide, or in any way tell anything which can betray any of us to our foes. Nor may he tell where the Covendom be, or the Covenstead, or where the meetings be. And if any break these laws, even under torture, the Curse of the Goddess shall be upon them, so they may never be reborn on earth, and may they remain where they belong, in the Hell of the Christians. Let each High Priestess govern her Coven with justice and love, with the help and advice of the High Priest and Elders, always heeding the advice of the

Messenger of the Gods if he cometh. She will heed all complaints of all Brothers and strive to settle all differences among them. But it must be recognized that there will always be people who will ever strive to force others to do as they will. These are not necessarily evil, and they oft have good ideas and such ideas should be talked over in council. But, if they will not agree with their Brothers, or if they say, 'I will not work under this High Priestess,' it hath ever been the Old Law to be convenient for the Brethren and to avoid disputes. Any of the Third may claim to found a new Coven, but they need live over a league from the Covenstead, or that they are about to do so. Anyone living within the bounds of the Covendom, and wishing to form a new Coven, shall tell the Elders of their intention, and on the instant avoid their dwelling and remove to a new Covendom. Members of the old Coven may join the new one when it is formed. But if they do, they must utterly avoid the old Coven. The Elders of the old and new Covens should meet in peace and brotherly love to decide the new boundaries. Those of the Craft who dwell outside both Covendoms may join either, but not both. Though, if the Elders agree, all may meet for the Great Festivals if it be truly in peace and brotherly love. But splitting the Coven off means strife, so for this reason these Law were made of old, and may the Curse of the Goddess be on any who disregard them. So be it ordained.

If you would keep a book, let it be in your own hand of write. Let Brothers and Sisters copy what they will, but never let the book out of your hands, and never keep the writings of another. For if it be found in their hand of write, they may be taken and arraigned. Let each guard his own writings, and destroy them whenever danger threatens. Learn as much as you may by heart, and when danger is past rewrite your book if it be safe. For this reason, if any die, destroy their book if they have not been able to. For if it be found, 'tis clear proof against them. And our oppressors know well, 'Ye may not be a witch alone.' So all their kin and friends be in danger of torture, so destroy everything not necessary. If your book be found on you, 'tis clear proof against you alone, and you may be arraigned. Keep all thoughts of the Craft from your mind. If the torture be too great to bear, say, 'I will confess. I cannot bear this torture. What do you want me to say?' If they try to make you speak of the Brotherhood, do not. But if they try to make you speak of impossibilities such as flying through the air, consorting with the Christian devil, sacrificing children or eating men's flesh, to obtain relief from torture say, 'I had an evil dream, I was beside myself, I was crazed.' Not all magistrates are bad. If there be an excuse, some may show mercy. If you have confessed ought, deny it afterwards. Say you babbled under torture, say you knew not what you said. If you are condemned, fear not. The

Brotherhood is powerful, and will help you to escape if you stand steadfast. But if you betray any, there is no hope for you in this life or those to come. Be sure, if steadfast you go to the pyre, drugs will reach you and you shall feel naught. You go to death and what lies beyond; the ecstasy of the Goddess. To avoid discovery, let the working tools seem as ordinary things that any may have in their houses. Let the pentacles be of wax so that they may be broken at once or melted. Have no sword, unless your rank allows it. Have no names or signs on anything. Write the names or signs on them in ink before consecrating them, and wash it off immediately afterwards. Let the color of the hilts tell which is which. Do not engrave them lest they cause discovery. Ever remember, ye are the Hidden Children of the Goddess so never do anything to disgrace them or her. Never boast; Never threaten; Never say you would wish ill of anyone. If any person, not in the Circle, speaks of the Craft, say, 'Speak not to me of such, it frightens me. Tis evil luck to speak of it.' For this reason, the Christians have their spies everywhere. These speak as if they were well affected to us, as if they would come to our meetings, saying, 'My mother used to worship the Old Ones. Could I, I would go myself.' To such as these, ever deny all knowledge. But to others, ever say, 'Tis foolish talk of witches flying through the air. To do so they must be light as thistledown. And men say that witches all be blear-eyed old crones, so what pleasure can there be at a witch meeting such as folks talk on?' And say, 'Many wise men now say there be no such creatures.' Ever make it a jest, and in some future time the persecution may die and we may worship our Gods in safety again. Let us all pray for that happy day. May the blessings of the Goddess and God be on all those who keep these Laws. If the Craft hath any Appanage, let all guard it and help to keep it clear and good for the Craft. And let all justly guard all moneys of the Craft. And if any brother truly wrought it, 'tis right they have their pay, if it be just. And this be not taking money for the Art, but for good and honest work. And even the Christians say, 'The laborer is worthy of his hire,' but if any Brother work willingly for the good of the Craft without pay, 'tis to their greater honor. So be it ordained

If there be any quarrels or disputes among the Brethren, the High Priestess shall straightly convene the Elders and inquire into the matter and they shall hear both sides, first alone, then together. And they shall then decide justly, not favoring one side or the other, ever recognizing that there be people who can never agree to work under others. But at the same time, there be some who cannot rule justly. To those who ever must be chief, there is but one answer. Void the Coven, or seek another one, or make a Coven of your own, taking with you only those who will go. To those who cannot rule justly, the answer be, 'Those who cannot bear your rule will leave you.' For none may come to meetings with those with whom they are at variance. So, if either cannot agree, get hence, for the Craft must ever survive. So be it ordained.

In the olden days, when we had power, we could use the Art against any who ill-treated the Brotherhood. But in these evil days, we must not do so. For our enemies have devised a burning pit of everlasting fire into which they say their God casts all the people who worship Him, except it be the very few may be released by their priests spells and masses. And this be chiefly by giving moneys and rich gifts to receive His favor, for their great God is ever in need of money. But as our Gods need our aid to make fertility for man and crops, so the God of the Christians is ever in need of man's help to search us out and destroy us. Their priests ever tell them that any who get our help are damned to this Hell forever, and men be mad with the terror of it. But they make men believe that they may escape this Hell if they give victims to the tormentors. So for this reason, all be forever spying, thinking, 'If I catch but one witch, I will escape from the fiery pit.' So for this reason we have our hides, and men searching long but not finding, say, 'There be none, or if there be, they be in a far country.' But when one of our oppressors die, or even be sick, ever is the cry, 'This be witches' malice,' and the hunt be up again. And, though they oft slay ten of their own to but one of us, they still care not for they have countless thousands, while we are few indeed. So be it ordained.

That none shall use the Art in any way to do ill to any. However much they harm us, harm none; and in time many shall believe we exist not. That this Law shall ever continue to aid us in our plight. No one, however great an injury or injustice they receive, may use the Art in any way to do ill, or harm any. But they may, after consultations with all, use the Art to restrain Christians from harming us or our Brothers, but only to constrain them and never to punish. To this end, men will say, 'Such if one is a mighty searcher out and persecutor of old women whom they desire to be witches, and none hath done him harm, so it be proof they cannot, or more truly there be none.' For all know full well that many folk have died because someone had a grudge against them, or were persecuted because they had money or goods to seize, or because they had none to bribe the searchers. And many have died because they were but scolding old women, so much that many now say that only old women are witches. And this be to our advantage, for it turns suspicion from us. In England and Scotland, 'tis now many a year since a witch hath died the death. But any misuse of the power might raise the persecution again. So never break this Law, however much you are tempted, and never consent to its being broken in the least. And if you know it is being broken, you must work strongly against it. And any High Priestess or High Priest who consents to its breach must immediately be deposed, for 'tis the blood of the Brethren they endanger. Do good if it be safe, and only if it be safe; and strictly keep the Old Law. Never accept money for use of the Art, for money ever besmears the taker. 'Tis sorcerers and conjurers and priests of the Christians who ever accept money for use of their Arts, and they sell pardons to let men escape from their sins. Be not as these. If you accept no money, you will be free from temptation to use the Art for evil causes. All may use the Art for their advantage, or for the advantage of the Craft, only if you are sure you harm none. But ever let the Coven debate this use at length, and only if all be satisfied that none may be harmed may the Art be used. If it be not possible to achieve your ends one way, perchance the aim may be achieved by acting in a different way so as to harm none. May the Curse of the Goddess be on any who break this Law. So be it ordained.

'Tis judged lawful that if ever any of the Craft need a house or land and none will sell, to incline the owner's mind so as they be willing to sell, providing that it harms him not in any way and the full selling price be paid without haggling. Never bargain or cheapen anything while you live by the Art. So be it ordained.

'Tis the Old Law, and the most important of all Laws, that no one may do anything which will endanger any of the Craft, or bring them into contact with the law of the land, or any persecutors. In any disputes between the Brethren, no one may invoke any laws but the Laws of the Craft, or any tribunal save that of the High Priestess, High Priest and Elders. It is not forbidden to say as Christians do, 'There be Witchcraft in the land,' because our oppressors of old make it heresy not to believe in Witchcraft, and so a crime to deny it thereby puts you under suspicion. But ever say, 'I know not of it here. Perchance there may be, but it be far off and I know not where.' And ever speak of them as old crones consorting with the devil and riding through the air. But then say, 'How many men may ride through the air if they be not light as thistledown?' And the Curse of the Goddess be on any who cast suspicion on any of the Brotherhood, or who speak of any true meeting place or where they abide. So be it ordained.

Let the Craft keep books with names of all herbs which are good for men, and all cures, so all may learn. But keep another book with all the Bills and Apices and let only the Elders and other trustworthy people have this knowledge. And may the blessings of the Gods be on all who keep these Laws, and the curses of the God and Goddess be on all who break them. So be it ordained.

Remember the Art is the secret of the Gods and only may be used in earnest and never for show or glory. Magicians and Christians may taunt us saying, 'You have no power. Show us your power. Do magic before our eyes. Only then will we believe.' But they are seeking to cause us to betray the Art before them. Heed them not, for the Art is holy and may only be used in need. And the Curse of the Goddess be on any who break this Law. It ever be the way with women, and with men also, that they ever seek new love, nor shall we reprove them for this. But it may be found a disadvantage to the Craft, as so many a time it has happened that a High Priest or High Priestess, impelled by love, hath departed with their love, that they have left the Coven. Now if a High Priestess wishes to resign, she may do so before the full Coven, and this resignation is valid. But if she should run off without resignation, who may know if she may not return in a few months? So the Law is that if a High Priestess leaves her Coven, she shall be taken back and all be as before. In her stead, if she has a Deputy, that Deputy shall act as the High Priestess for as long as the High Priestess is away. If she does not return at the end of a year and a day, then shall the Coven elect a new High Priestess. And unless there be good reason to the contrary, the person who has done the work shall reap the benefit of the reward, Maiden and Deputy of the High Priestess. So be it ordained.

It had been found that practicing the Art does cause a fondness between aspirant and teacher, and it is the cause of better results if this be so. But if for any reason this be undesirable, it can easily be avoided by both persons from the outset firmly resolving in their minds to be as brother and sister, or parent and child. And for this reason a man may be taught by a woman and a woman by a man and women and women should not attempt these practices together.[5] So it be ordained.

Order and discipline must be kept. A High Priestess or High Priest may, and should, punish all faults. To this end, all the Craft must receive their correction willingly. All properly prepared, the culprit kneeling, should be told his fault and his sentence pronounced. Punishment should be followed by something amusing. The culprit must acknowledge the justice of the punishment by kissing the hand of the High Priestess on receiving sentence and again give thanks for the punishment received. So be it ordained.

Reincarnation

Beyond the views expressed by the theories and laws, there are two further principles—reincarnation and karma—that are just as important to Wiccan religious philosophy and which also require just as much explanation.

With a couple of exceptions, all Wiccans believe in reincarnation. This can be clearly seen in many instances, from the line in the Wiccan Creed that states, "immortal and ever-renewing," to the Charge of the Goddess which says, "Upon earth, I give the knowledge of the spirit eternal; and beyond death, I give peace, and freedom, and reunion with those who have gone before." They believe that death is nothing more than a single step in the process by which the soul progresses to a higher state of consciousness, and that the soul must undergo many experiences and lives before it can completely develop. Wiccans also believe that the human soul is made up of layers. These layers of the soul are further divided into two sections, Personality and Individuality, with each segment having distinct characteristics.

The first category, the Personality, consists of the lowest levels of human essence: Terrestrial or Physical, Lower Astral, Higher Astral, and Lower Psychic. This is the portion of the soul closest to actual consciousness. It's also specifically male or female, though not always in the conventional sense. The Personality is, therefore, the result of a single life experience. Its unique characteristics, mannerisms, and peculiarities are particular to each incarnation, and they do not usually carry over from one incarnation to the next. In other words, YOU will not reappear as yourself in the next life.

There may, however, be certain exceptions. A good example of just such an exception would be a child genius who may be the result of a past Personality that has carried over a significant portion of its accumulated knowledge. Déjà vu, which is best described as the unexplainable feeling of having been somewhere or done something previously, is more evidence that some piece of the Personality occasionally carries over. As a general rule of thumb, though, the Personality ceases upon physical death.

The second category, the Individuality, is the part of the soul that makes up the three highest planes: Higher Psychic, Lower Spiritual, and Higher Spiritual. But unlike the Personality, the three components of Individuality are eternal. In short, this is the piece of the human soul that outlives the physical body and is transferred to a newly conceived body upon reincarnation. Not surprisingly, this is also the portion of the soul that is bisexual, meaning it's composed of both male and female components in a balanced harmony. This dual-sexual premise can be further explained through the Theory of Gender and Theory of Polarity, but suffice it to say that the eternal portion of the soul needs to be both masculine and feminine in order to fully complete its development.

Now the above is merely a generalized theory of reincarnation, and almost every Wiccan denomination has its own specialized beliefs. For instance, in Celtic Wicca, the spirit goes to the Otherworld of Avalon[6] after death and remains there communing with the Goddess and God, and other spirits, and resting until its time for it to be reincarnated. Saxon Wicca holds to the belief that seven lives must be lived for the soul to fully develop and that there are seven dimensions—ultimate, divine, spiritual, astral, mental, elemental, and physical—that correspond to these lives. The Norse traditions believe in nine otherworldly planes, which are divided into three categories: Overworld or Celestial, Middleworld, and Underworld or Subterranean. These nine planes are named Asgard, Vanaheim, Lightalheim for the upper three planes; Midgard, Muspelheim, Nifelheim for the middle levels; and Swartalfheim, Hel, Jotunheim for the three lower planes.

Beyond the fundamental belief in reincarnation, Wiccans also believe in karma. But what is karma? When most people hear this Hindu word, they automatically think along the lines of reward and punishment. In reality, karma is much closer to cause and effect, or a cosmic system of checks and balances, than anything else. Another point that's often misunderstood is that there's not an instantaneous result from good or bad karma, but rather an accumulated effect. It's also worth noting that it's the upper levels of the soul that actually accumulate karma, and this occurs only as the soul progresses from life to life. Therefore, it's essential for the soul to advance from one life to the next, while at the same time trying to ensure that a balance is continually achieved. In terms of Wiccan philosophy, this simply means living each life to the fullest possible extent, without harming anyone else, while sampling the entire spectrum of life experiences possible.

ETHICS AND MORALITY

Regardless of the tradition—Gardnerian, Italian, Saxon, etc.—all witches try to live by a set of ethical and moral guidelines that cross all denominational lines. In fact, many of these people base their entire lives on these principles and adhere to them as closely as possible. The following is a brief discussion of some of these considerations.

There are eight simple words, known as the Wiccan Rede, that sum up the manner in which all witches attempt to live their lives: "And it harm none, do what you will." Along with this adage, witches also follow the Rule of Three. This tenet states that what you send out, whether good or bad, comes back to you threefold. Founded on the basic premise of karma, the Rule of Three simply means that if you do good you'll be rewarded three times over, but if you do bad, you'll suffer three times the harm you've caused. It's a fundamental "live and let live" creed that encompasses both social and environmental responsibilities, while at the same time establishing rewards for acceptable behavior or punishments for negative acts.

Along the same line, it's important to realize that Wiccan ethics are less about restrictions than other religions, and its morality is more concerned with ensuring personal freedoms than with insisting on prohibitions. This outlook differs greatly from religions such as Catholicism or Judaism in regard to liberties versus taboos. For instance, Catholicism teaches that homosexuality is contrary to the laws of God and Nature. It leaves no leeway for special circumstances, the unique potential of an individual, or for that matter, anything else. Therefore, in accordance with Catholic teachings, homosexuality as a whole is wrong. Wiccan ethics, on the other hand, not only teach acceptance, but stress the need to follow the path that Nature intended. In short, if you're heterosexual, then be heterosexual, if you're homosexual, then be homosexual. But either way, a person should be judged based on his or her own merit rather than solely on the basis of a religious bias.

A second part of this ethical theme concerns the fact that witches won't tolerate hateful acts such as bigotry, prejudice, or persecution. Wiccans also criticize perverted applications of the religious spirit (regardless of the religion involved), and they will vehemently oppose excuses to rationalize things such as cruelty or greed. For example, an evangelist growing rich pilfering donations collected for charity will always be challenged as wrong and action taken. If putting an end to the abuse requires crossing the ethical boundary of noninterference or nonviolence, then this line will be crossed without fear of ethical violation. This is because in situations where harm is being done, but it can be stopped, not acting is itself ethically wrong.

Witches also acknowledge the ethical standard of not harming anyone, although this should not be confused with total pacifism. In this world, there are very often situations in everyday life that require immediate and decisive actions. Although forgiveness is a nice virtue, it's not always a realistic approach to life. A wise witch recognizes this fact and acts accordingly. As such, the witch realizes that there may be a need for affirmative action and is willing to accept the responsibilities, and consequences, for the decisions.

Additionally, there are ethical and moral issues that must be considered in the use of the Craft, as there is a very fine line between assisting others and manipulating them. Healing, protecting, or resolving certain personal problems of someone who has requested assistance is acceptable; manipulation, in the form of interfering with a person's decisions or choice, is not. This distinct line also extends into other ethical territory. As a general rule, it is frowned upon for a witch to charge or accept payment for the use of the Craft. Not only does this belief stem from the human tendency to put on a show for the client's benefit, but it also takes into consideration the fact that even the most conscientious individual can be unwittingly corrupted by money. By not charging for their assistance, witches are not easily tempted to cross over ethical boundaries.[7] The main point is that witches should strive to maintain their ethical integrity when matters that affect others are at stake.

Up to this point, it's been all about the "do's" and "don'ts" of being a witch. But Wicca is about much more than laws and rationale. It's about joy, love, peace, and harmony. It's about beauty and compassion. It's about having a moral duty to discover and release the human potential, as well as that of the world around us. It's about self-development and the realization of one's unique gifts. In short, it's about the wonders of mankind, the Earth, Nature, and the Universe.

The only way to understand completely Wiccan ethics and morality is to start by acknowledging that Wicca is a pure and simple religion that celebrates the joys and wonders of Nature. After that, the rest is easy. There is a recognition that much of the actual contentment experienced by witches comes from their love of Nature and their interaction with the Universe; their understanding that life must be lived to its fullest; and an appreciation for all that the world has to offer.

Unfortunately, over the centuries, humanity has lost much of the closeness it once had with Nature. And that's one reason that Wiccans strive to be different. In this fast-paced and technologically advancing world, witches maintain their close ties with the Mother Earth. Wiccans take time out of their busy day to appreciate Nature by touching, smelling, and speaking to the Earth, trees, plants, and animals. Witches absorb the energy of the Mother Earth and her creations, and in return, share their own energies.

It's inevitable that some people will wonder whether all of this means that witches are nothing but "tree huggers" who go around talking to bushes. Nothing could be further from the truth. In reality, while Wiccans will readily hug a tree, they're more apt to fight to save a wetland or lobby against pollution. This arises from the fact that Wicca teaches ecological and environmental conservation. It promotes a way of life that does not conflict with Nature, and it instructs us all to be environmentalists. Basically, it all comes down to the fact that witches feel it's their personal obligation to protect the Earth, and it's this set of ethical and moral values that they try to pass on to future generations.

Perhaps the best way to sum up Wiccan ethics and morality is with this final thought: The true spirit of witchcraft comes from the hearts and minds of its practitioners and not from any book. If you watch a bird soar through the air or take the time to smell a flower, and you appreciate the majesty and beauty of what you are witnessing, then you will have learned more in that one act than I could ever write in these pages. If you plant a tree or pick up a piece of trash along the roadside, and you do it not because someone tells you to, but because you feel that it's your personal obligation to the Earth, then you will already have surpassed anything that anyone could ever say. And, in the end, it all comes down to the fact that while you can be told all there is to know about Wicca, only you can become a witch.

Deities

Although no one will ever know for sure, it's fair to assume that the first human beings to worship a Goddess or God probably had sacred names for their deity. Unfortunately, those names are lost in the mists of time. But as mankind developed and religion became a bigger and bigger part of everyday life, the names of Gods and Goddesses were etched in history. Isis and Osiris are but two names used by the Egyptians for their Goddesses and Gods. The Hindus called their deities Shiva and Shatki. The Christians prayed to Jesus and Mary. Yet these were by no means the only Gods of mankind, and along with these well-known religious figures, there were many names given to the deities of other faiths. Nowhere was this more prevalent than in the pagan religions.

In order to understand the way a particular denomination of witches practice their Craft, and the meaning behind some of their rituals, it's important to gain some amount of insight into the various characteristics that their God and Goddess share with each other. This is especially true when it comes to embracing and appreciating the subtle differences from one tradition to the next. Therefore, before going any farther, a short examination of the deities is required.

TRANSFORMATION OF THE GOD

Most religions, and almost all denominations of Wicca, follow a female/male or male/female theme, where one deity is slightly elevated over the other.[1] However, in the earliest beginnings of religion, the Mother Goddess—representative of the sun, moon, earth, and the elements of Nature—was generally accepted as the sole deity. She was the Goddess of Fertility, the Goddess of Nature, and the Great Mother of the Universe. Although she very quickly gained a male consort—the Horned God—she, nevertheless, remained the dominant figure in ancient theology.

One reason the Goddess enjoyed so much popularity was because early man knew nothing of the cycle of life. He saw the moon and sun and stars. He saw fire and water and earth. He saw the changing seasons. Yet he didn't understand any of it. About the only thing he did comprehend was that females were important because they were the bearers of new life, and this was enough for him to place his trust in a female Goddess.

Another reason for the early success of the Goddess was that she was represented by the sun.[2] She was the deity that ensured the proliferation of the tribe, and it was because of her fertility that the world was replenished. Later, with the introduction of farming and the domestication of animals for food, the fertility aspect of the Goddess was heightened even more as she suddenly became responsible for the success of crops and the herds. This newfound agrarian dependence also taught early man to appreciate the cycle of life, death, and rebirth; the changing seasons now had meaning.

Yet, as civilization spread across the planet, this matriarchal religious dominance slowly underwent a transformation. Some areas now saw a God begin to replace the Goddess as the dominant figurehead or, at the very least, to occupy an equal role. The religious hierarchy that was once ruled by a female deity was suddenly undergoing the same changes that were happening in society itself. As different cultures clashed and small tribes molded into larger civilizations, matriarchal communities were forced to convert to patriarchal societies. Considerations such as strength and stamina, both of which were essential for war, crept into communal life.

As this happened more and more often, the man evolved into a crucial asset of the tribe. Naturally, the status of the Goddess and God mirrored the lives of their worshipers. As the importance of woman diminished, so did the importance of the Goddess. The Horned God, the God of Nature, and the God of the Hunt became the tribe's protector. For the first time in history, the God was no longer considered a subordinate and took his place alongside the Goddess of Mother Earth. Then, as he assumed the attributes of the sun, he became the Sun God, the Fire God, or the Sky God. With this shift, the Goddess was consigned to the nighttime moon, the God adopted the power of the sun and fire, and matrilineal society gave way to a patrilineal hierarchy.

Along with these basic views of the supreme God and Goddess, ancient people were so awed by the forces of Nature that they assumed each of these powers must be controlled by a particular deity. They saw the wind as being regulated by a God or Goddess. Water and fire were each ruled by a God and Goddess. The trees, meadows, mountains, and animals all had their own protective deities. In other words, early people believed that a God or Goddess governed all aspects of life, death, Nature and the Universe.

GODDESSES AND GODS

Throughout the various denominations of Wicca, different names have been given to the same deities.[3] The following is a list of the names and characteristics associated with the different Goddesses and Gods, as well as information that will be useful in gaining a better understanding of the relationship each deity has with other Gods and Goddesses.

- **Abnoba**: A Gaul Goddess of the Hunt who presided over the forests and rivers.
- **Abundia**: Meaning "abundance," this is a name used for the Goddess Diana. (See Diana.) Also known as **Abundatia**.
- **Actaeon**: Italian Stag-horned God of the Forests. Very similar to the Celtic Horned God or the Great God Pan. In Greco-Roman mythology, Actaeon was a hunter who was turned into a stag by Diana and then torn to pieces by his own hounds.
- **Adsagsona**: Celtic Goddess of the Underworld.
- **Aed**: Irish Fire God.
- **Aine**: Irish Sun Goddess and Earth Goddess, especially of Midsummer.
- **Airmed**: Celtic Goddess of Herbs. Folklore says that a prayer to Airmed before cutting herbs increases their potency.
- **Amaethon**: Celtic God of Agriculture. As the Harvest King, he is often depicted holding a sickle or scythe.
- **Andraste**: Anglo-Saxon Warrior Goddess, also the Goddess of Victory.
- **Angus**: Celtic God of Love. Under the name **Aengus mac Og**, he is known as a healer of souls often associated with romance.
- **Aobh**: Matriarchal Goddess of Ireland, wife of Llyr, the Irish sea God.
- **Aphrodite**: Ancient Greek Goddess of Love and Beauty, also rules over lovers and marriage. Primary female deity in the Wiccan Love Craft Tradition.
- **Aradia**: The name frequently used for the Goddess by modern witches, it is derived from the legends of Tuscan witches as recorded by Charles Godfrey Leland in *Aradia: Gospel of the Witches*. She is the

daughter of Diana and Lucifer, and in Italian lore, she was sent to Earth as a witch to teach the magickal arts to witches before returning to the Overworld (Heaven).

- **Arawn**: Celtic God of Death and War. He is also the King of the Underworld.
- **Ardwinna**: Celtic Goddess of Nature, especially the woods and forests.
- **Arianrhod**: Welsh Goddess of the Moon, also a stellar Goddess. She also initiates the souls of the dead into the Otherworld. The name is often used by modern Welsh witches for the Goddess.
- **Artemis**: Greek Triple Moon Goddess. She is the ruler of the ebb and flow of psychic power, a Greek version of the Goddess Diana. Known by many other names, such as **Diktynna, Europa** ("the wide-glancing one"), **Kallisto** ("the beautiful"), and **Agrotera** ("the wild"). Artemis is the mother—or second—aspect of the trinity of the Goddess Diana. (see Diana).
- **Artio**: Celtic Goddess of the Animals, and especially the fertility of animals. She is important in ancient traditions for the prosperity of the herds.
- **Artisaeus**: The Horned God of Thessaly. In Italian lore, he is the father of Actaeon.
- **Aveta**: Celtic Goddess of Midwives and new mothers.
- **Badb**: Celtic (Irish) Goddess of War. On the eve of battle, she is believed to appear in the form of a giantess to warn soldiers. She is one of the three aspects of the Triple Goddess Morrigan and a Druidess of the Tuatha Dé Danann.
- **Banba**: Irish Goddess of Earth. In Irish lore, she is also a part of the trinity including Folta and Eriu.
- **Bebhionn**: Irish Underworld Goddess of Pleasure.
- **Bel**: Celtic Fire God and Sun God. He is a God of light and power, a purifying God associated with ritual cleansing. Also known as **Bael**, **Balar**, **Balor**, **Belenus**, **Bele**, and **Beli**. Celtic "Bel-Fires" are named in honor of the healing and purifying power of Bel.
- **Belisama**: Goddess of Fire with Italian lineage. She is the wife of Belenus, and as such, she inherits the sun's warmth. A Celtic version is **Belisana**, who is associated with the sun's healing effect on plants and animals.
- **Bormo**: Celtic God of Truth and Inspiration. As **Borvo**, he is often seen as a Celtic Apollo and a God of Fire/Water.

- **Branwen**: Welsh Goddess of Love. She is also called the "Venus of the Northern Sea."
- **Bres**: Celtic God of Agriculture and a God of Fertility.
- **Bridget**: Celtic Goddess of Fertility, Triple Muse-Goddess, and Goddess of the Sacred Fire. She is known by several names: **Banfile**, **Brede**, **Brid**, **Bride**, **Brigante**, **Brighid**, **Briget**, **Brigid**, and **Brigit**. She is the pre-Christian Celtic inspiration for St. Brigid's Day, a holy festival aimed at ensuring fertility.
- **Brigantia**: Celtic Goddess of Nature, she is often associated with rivers and valleys. She lends her name to the Celtic lands north of England.
- **Cailleach**: In pre-Celtic lore, she was the Mother Goddess who controlled the seasons and the weather. In ancient Irish lore, Caillech represented the crone aspect of the Goddess.
- **Camulus**: Celtic God of War.
- **Cerne**: In northern Britain, he was the Horned God and the God of the Hunt. In other areas, he was known as **Herne** or Herne the Hunter.
- **Cernunnos**: The name given to Cerne or Herne in southern Britain. Literally meaning "The Horned One," this is the name most widely used by modern Wiccans for the Horned God. He is also known as **Cerunnos** (Celtic Gaul), the Alexandrian tradition uses the name **Karnayna** instead of Cernunnos. A final interesting point is that the Celtic traditions held the belief that Cernunnos is the Ruler of Spirits and Ale. By itself, this view must have endeared him to many people.
- **Cilleac Bheur**: Scottish Winter Goddess. At Beltane, the Goddess Brigit deposes her.
- **Condatis**: Anglo-Saxon/Celtic God of Water and Rivers.
- **Cordemanon**: Celtic God of Wisdom. He is most often associated with knowledge, stone circles, and sacred sites.
- **Crom**: Celtic God of Lightning and Thunder.
- **Creirwy**: Celtic Goddess of Love and Beauty, daughter of Kerridwen.
- **Crone**: The third and final of the three stages of the Triple Goddess. This image signifies her life cycle nearing its end. In this aspect she's personified by the waning moon, and her characteristics represent wisdom and the completion of the cycle of life. As with all things nearing their end, the crone gradually withers until nothing remains. Thus, the waning moon gives an accurate depiction of the crone as it runs its course and fades away having completed its full cycle. Also known as the **Dark Goddess**.

- **Dagda**: The principle Irish God of Life, Death, and Wisdom. He is also known as the Father God, the Good God, and the Lord of Knowledge.
- **Dana**: Irish and Celtic Mother Goddess or the Goddess of Nature. In Celtic lore, she was said to be the mother of the Tuatha Dé Danann. Also known as **Anu, Ana, Anna, Ann, Danu,** and the Welsh **Don**.
- **Diana**: Celtic Great Mother Goddess, (Full) Moon Goddess. The most widely worshipped Goddess name. Diana divided herself into darkness and light with her son, Lucifer, becoming the light while she remained the darkness. Upon seeing the beauty of the light, she wanted it back in her darkness. But the light fled from her, thus creating day/night as dark chases light. As the Triple Goddess, she is Selene as the moon, Artemis as the Goddess of Woodlands, and Hecate as the Queen of the Otherworld. The name Diana means "divine," "brilliant," or "shining," and during the Middle Ages, she was sometimes referred to as Abundia (abundance) and Satia (satisfaction). The Druid priests of Tuatha Dé Danann were known as "the peoples of the Goddess Diana." In Italian witchcraft, Diana is the Goddess of all Witches and the Crescent Moon Goddess.
- **Dianus**: Italian Horned God of the Woods and consort of Diana.
- **Dionysos**: Greek Harvest God.
- **Dis**: Italian (Etruscan) God of the Dead.
- **Donn**: Irish God of the Dead.
- **Dunus**: Celtic God of Mountains and Grottos. (See Pan.)
- **Edain**: Celtic Goddess of Beauty. Also known as **Etain**. As Edain, she is one of the "White Ladies" of the Faeries.
- **Elayne**: Irish Warrior Goddess, also known as **Elen**.
- **Erie**: Irish Triple Goddess of Erin. When she is known as **Eriu**, she is part of the trinity with Folta and Banda.
- **Fana**: Italian Goddess of Forests and Wildlife.
- **Faunus**: Italian God of Forests and Wildlife. (See Pan.)
- **Februus**: Italian God of the Dead. Associated with February, the month of personal renewal and purification.
- **Fend**: Celtic Sea Goddess.
- **Findabair**: Celtic Goddess of the Otherworld.
- **Fliodhas**: Celtic Goddess of the Woodlands. Her association with forests is more on the lines of a protector of animals.
- **Folta**: Irish Earth Goddess, she is part of the trinity with Banda and Eriu.

- **Freya**: Old Norse Goddess of Love and Beauty, Goddess of Fertility. First (maiden) aspect of the Norse Triple Goddess with Frigga and Hel. This is also the name used in Seax-Wica for the Goddess.
- **Frigga**: Norse Mother Goddess and Queen of the Heavens. She is the second (mother) aspect of the Old Norse Triple Goddess along with Freya and Hel. In Saxon traditions she is also known as **Frig**.
- **Goibniu**: Celtic God of Magic. Also known as **Gobannon** and **Goibhnie**.
- **Grian**: Early Celtic Goddess of the Sun. As the sun gained a male perspective, this female deity faded away in many traditions.
- **Gwyn ap Nudd**: Irish/Celtic God of the Otherworld, God of the Wild Hunt.
- **Hecate**: Ancient Greek Goddess of witchcraft considered older than the Titans or classical Olympian Gods/Goddesses. In Greek and Celtic lore, she has many of the same basic characteristics as Diana. Hecate is the crone—or third—aspect of the trinity of the Goddess Diana. (See Diana.) In modern practice, she is often worshipped as a protectress of witches.
- **Hel**: Old Norse Goddess of Death and Queen of the Underworld. Third (crone) aspect of the Norse Triple Goddess along with Freya and Frigga.
- **Hellith**: Celtic/Norse God associated with the setting sun. He is also the protector of the souls of the dead.
- **Herodias**: This is the Christian name given to the Goddess of the Pagans in the Canon Episcopi and the *Malleus Maleficarum*. It is probably a mistaken use. In some traditions, it's another name given to Aradia.
- **Hertha**: Celtic Goddess of Rebirth. Also known as **Herdda**.
- **Hooded One**: The first of the three titles given to the God in Italian witchcraft. The Hooded One was the Green Man cloaked in greenery. He is a male equivalent of the "maiden" phase of the Goddess.
- **Horned God**: Generally, he is the God of woodlands and the hunt. (See Cernunnos, Pan.) In simple terms, the Horned God is the oldest God. Associated with death and rebirth, he is symbolized by the sun. Also known as the Keeper of the Gates of Life and Death, Lord of the Hunt, God of the Greenwood, and Ruler of the Underworld. He's a phallic God who represents the masculine side of Nature. Various races incorporate aspects of the Horned God into their religion, even

if not in the usual way. With the introduction of Christianity, the Horned God was perverted into the Devil.

- **Horned One**: The second of the three titles given to the God in Italian witchcraft. The Horned One was the Stag-horned God of the forests. He is a male equivalent of the "mother" phase of the Goddess.
- **Isis**: Ancient Egyptian Goddess of Fertility. She is associated with enchantment, the mysteries, and magick. Some modern Wiccans use this as their Goddess name.
- **Jana**: Italian Goddess of the Moon.
- **Janus**: Italian Sun God. He is also the God of all Portals between the worlds.
- **Kern**: Italian Stag-horned God of the Forest. Kern is the symbol of the waxing power of Nature.
- **Kernunnos**: Celtic God of Life, Death and Knowledge, another name for the Horned God. In various regions, he is known by names such as Cernunnos, Cerne, and Herne, or **Kairn** and **Kairnunos** in other locales.
- **Kerridwen**: Welsh Goddess of Wisdom and a fertility deity. Depicted as either the mother or the crone aspect of the Triple Goddess. Also known as **Cerridwen**, **Cerridwyn**, and **Ceridwyn**.
- **Letha**: Celtic Goddess of the Harvest at Midsummer.
- **Llyr**: Celtic God of the Sea. He is also known as **Lir**, **Lear**, **Leer**.
- **Lucifer**: Celtic Sun God, son/consort of Diana. Meaning "the light bringer," he was the father of Aradia. In later Christian theology, Lucifer took on the cloven-hoofed appearance of the Horned God/Pan and became the name of the Devil. Although Wiccans recognize Lucifer as a Sun God, they do not acknowledge him as the Devil because they do not believe in this Christian concept.
- **Lugh**: Primary Celtic Sun God, he is also known as **Lug**, **Lleu**, **Lleu Llaw Gyffes**, and **Llew**. Although sometimes also known as Lucifer, this name does not have the negative connotations that Christians associate with it.
- **Lupercus**: Italian Wolf God of Winter and the symbol of the waning power of Nature.
- **Macha**: A red-haired Celtic (Irish) Goddess of War and Battle. She was one of the three aspects of the Irish Triple Goddess Morrigan, and she was also a Druidess of the Tuatha Dé Danann.
- **Maiden**: The first of the three stages of the Triple Goddess. In this

facet she's embodied by the waxing moon. She's a young, virginal girl who becomes stronger and more powerful with each rising. At this stage, she displays the mystery of yet unseen beauty, as well as the beginning of her undiscovered power and growth. It's also during this period that she first stands for the fertility and birth of new life out of a barren void, and this, itself, is mimicked by the moon as it begins to appear out of an otherwise dark and empty sky. The maiden also has the distinction of being the Goddess of the Hunt, and many of the ancient depictions of her show a horn in her hand. Not only was this a reference to her prowess over the hunt, but it was also a symbolic representation of her in the crescent moon.

- **Math**: Welsh God of Magick.
- **Mei**: Primarily a Celtic Earth Goddess, she was also seen as a solar Goddess. Sometimes known as **Mai** or **Meia**.
- **Merlin**: Celtic God of Woodlands. The most famous associations of Merlin come from his connections with Druidic priests and the Tuatha Dé Danann.
- **Moon Goddess**: Generally, the "Goddess of the Moon" is the name given to the different Goddesses—Artemis, Diana, Isis, etc.—by many religions. Though each Goddess has her own particular traits, they all share the characteristics of fertility, enchantment, and mystery, as well as the waxing and waning cycles of power. With the moon as her sacred symbol, this depiction of the Goddess represents the secret powers of Nature and the occult.
- **Morgana**: Celtic Goddess of Death and War.
- **Morrigan**: The Irish Triple Goddess of War and Death, she is the mother of all Irish Gods. In Irish lore, this is the name given to the dark aspect of the Goddess. She mates with the God, Dagda, at the festival of Samhain. Her trinity consists of Macha, Badb, and Neman.
- **Mother**: The second of the three stages of the Triple Goddess. Throughout this stage, she is symbolized by the full moon. It's during this transformation (i.e., maiden to mother, symbolizing waxing moon to full moon) into the Great Mother that she fully exhibits the splendors of life, as well as her fertility and bounty. Because of this, the Goddess enjoys the distinction of being both the Goddess of the Hunt and the Queen of the Harvest. This is also the point at which the Goddess gives birth to the God who, like everything else, is born from the Great Mother.

- **Néit**: Irish God of Battle.
- **Neman**: Celtic (Irish) Goddess of War. Third (crone) aspect of the Goddess Morrigan. Sometimes known as **Nemon** or **Nemain**. She is also a Druidess of the Tuatha Dé Danann.
- **Nodens**: Celtic God of Dreams and Sleep.
- **Ogma**: Celtic God of Knowledge and Literature.
- **Old One**: The third of the three titles given to the God in Italian witchcraft. The Old One was the Elder, wise-one, or sage. He is a male equivalent of the "crone" phase of the Goddess.
- **Old Ones, The**: A catchall term used for all the Gods/Goddesses of the Old Religion. Also known as the **Ancients** in some paths. This label never refers to Elementals, Faeries, Demons, or the Christian Devil.
- **Ostara**: An ancient Gallic Sun Goddess associated with Spring, a Goddess of Fertility. Some modern Wiccans and Neo-Pagans honor her at the Spring Equinox.
- **Pan**: The Greek Horned God of Mountains and Forests. Literally meaning "All, everything," the "Great God Pan" was the goat-footed God of forests and animals, a positive influence on the life-force of the world, and the masculine side of Nature. He was also the patron God of shepherds and the protector of their flocks. Pan has the same attributes as Cernunnos, Dunus, Faunus, and **Sylvanus**. In the Welsh tradition, Pan is the name used for the God.
- **Persephone**: A Goddess of Greek, Roman, Italian, and Celtic lore. **Proserpine** was the Queen of the Realms of the Dead. A Goddess of Spring, the Spring Equinox marks her ascent from the Underworld. Also called **Proserpina** and **Liberia**.
- **Pwyll**: Celtic God of the Otherworld, usually depicted as accompanied by a pack of hounds. Similar to Lupercus, the Italian Wolf God.
- **Rhiannon**: A Celtic (Welsh) Mother Goddess; Queen Mother; wife of Pwyll. She is associated with the Underworld and ancient fertility rites.
- **Rosemerta**: Celtic Goddess of Bounty, wife of Lugh.
- **Sadv**: Pre-Celtic Goddess of Forests and Nature, often associated with deer.
- **Satia**: Meaning "satisfied," a name given to the Goddess. (See Diana.)
- **Selene**: The moon—or first—aspect of the trinity of the Goddess Diana. (See Diana.) Also the Guardian Goddess of practitioners of magick.
- **Sirona**: Celtic Astral and Solar Goddess.

- **Stag God**: Italian Forest God. (See Actaeon or Kern.)
- **Sun God**: Any male deity representative of the sun.[4] Also known as the **Sky God**. The Egyptian God **Rá** was the most prototypical Sun God recognized in history, though other deities—such as Bel, Janus, Lucifer, Lugh, Mercury, Osiris, etc.—have been likened to Sun/Sky Gods. In Pagan ideology, the Sun God undergoes death and rebirth at Yule (Winter Solstice) after having reached his peak during Midsummer (Summer Solstice).
- **Tagni**: Ancient Italian God of Witchcraft.
- **Taillte**: Irish Earth Goddess.
- **Tana**: Italian Goddess of the Universe, the Star Goddess.
- **Tanus**: Italian God of the Universe and consort to Tana; the Star God.
- **Taranis**: Celtic God of Storms. He is also the God that controls seasonal cycles.
- **Triana**: Celtic Triple Goddess—Sun-Ana, Earth-Ana, and Moon-Ana. As she is a triple-aspect Goddess, she retains the titles of Goddess of Fertility, Goddess of Healing, Goddess of Knowledge, and Goddess of Wisdom.
- **Triple Goddess**: The general Wiccan view of the Goddess is that she has a triple nature that encompasses all stages of existence in a single form. Because she is associated with the three periods of life, the Goddess is usually represented as having three faces with each depicting a different stage of life. This trinity mirrors the phases of the lunar cycle—waxing, full, and waning—and they are portrayed by the faces of the maiden, mother, and crone.
- **Uni**: Ancient Italian Goddess of Witchcraft. The earliest name given to the Goddess by Italian witches.
- **Viviana**: Celtic Goddess of Love, Goddess of Birth and Life. She is also known as **Vivian** and **Vivien**.
- **Woden**: Celtic God of the Waning Year. In Old Norse lore, Woden rode with the Waelcyrges (Valkyries) or "wild women" on a wild hunt. Also known as **Wodan**, **Wuotan**, **Nik**, and **Odin**. Woden is also the Saxon primary God, and this is the name of the God in Seax-Wica.
- **Wolf God**: Italian Forest God. (See Lupercus.)

Otherworldly Beings

Through centuries of misfortune, many of the beliefs of witches have changed time and time again. Because of this, it's usually difficult to pinpoint exactly how they finally settled into their current versions of certain religious views. Nevertheless, there are ways to ferret out information. And, despite the difficulty in unraveling some of these mysteries, it's sometimes important to know how or why a specific belief was adopted before deciding whether it's acceptable for a particular practice. One way to find the origin of many words and ideas that are in use today is to look back to the early Pagan religions. Through simple detective work, and a little conjecturing, these ancient beliefs often reveal useful information.

ELEMENTALS

Generally speaking, witchcraft recognizes the existence of the four Elements of Life. The elements are: Earth, Air, Water, and Fire.[1] Long ago, the Elements of Life were given names that associated them with the Spirits of Nature. These entities, or Elementals, are the spirits who channel the life-force into Nature, as well as the physical and nonphysical ingredients that constitute all the created materials of the Universe. As well as serving the building blocks of life, the Elementals took on individual forms that could then be used to accomplish specific tasks.

The Spirits of Earth, called Gnomes, took on a stout, rugged, human-like form and were seen as the "smart" or "knowing" spirits that dwelled in the Earth. They correspond to the north and symbolize strength, stability, form, fertility, and the tangible.

The Spirits of Water are the Undines. Commonly referred to as Water Nymphs, or the spirits of the waves, these beings represent the various aspects of water. They correspond to the west and symbolize life, subconscious, emotions, psychic powers, and the soul.

The Spirits of Air are known as Slyphs and are usually seen as beautiful transparent entities oftentimes having crystalline bodies with delicate gossamer wings like butterflies. They correspond to the east and symbolize freedom, conscious choice, communication, and the mind.

Finally, the Spirits of Fire are referred to as Salamanders. These beings are viewed as fire-lizards, or tiny dragonlike creatures, that dwell in the heart of all fires. They correspond to the south and symbolize energy, individuality, and personality.

The four elements, and their corresponding Elementals, also took on humanistic qualities, with air and fire becoming associated with masculine energy, while earth and water with feminine energies.

Although it doesn't seem apparent at first glance, it's important to point out that much of what modern witches know about the four elements is a result of influences from Ceremonial Magick rather than early witchcraft. This came about because ceremonial magicians, unlike witches, needed to conjure entities, or spirits, in order to command these beings to perform work for them. Since this magickal vocation needed specific spirits in order to operate, it made sense to classify these entities according to their function.[2] Therefore, because of specific needs, magicians took the idea of the Elementals to the next level and prompted the creation of more extensive beliefs.

Ancient ceremonial magicians believed that the elements, along with their Elemental inhabitants, belonged to places known as Kingdoms of the Spirits. These were the actual realms where the spirits dwelled when they were not visiting the mortal world and places where the spirits sometimes went in order to perform the tasks that they'd been given. Not only did magicians give these spirit kingdoms names, but they also named kings to rule them. The Kingdom of the Gnomes was ruled by the Earth King, Ghob, while the Kingdom of the Slyphs was ruled by the Air King, Paralda. The Fire King, Djin, ruled the Kingdom of the Salamanders, and Niksa, the Water King, ruled the Kingdom of the Undines.

Another interesting fact is that the belief in Elementals remained fairly consistent throughout the Pagan world. For instance, in Italian traditions, although the Elementals were given different names, their overall characteristics remained relatively consistent with those of their Celtic cousins. The Italian Elemental, Pala, the northern Spirit of Earth, was very much a gnomelike being. Similarly, Settiano, the southern Spirit of Fire, was a fire-lizard spirit, while Manii, the western Spirit of Water, and

Bellarie, the eastern Spirit of Air, mirrored the Undines and Sylphs.

The whole point is that the names modern witches use in connection with the four elements were most likely the by-product of an early intermingling between Paganism and Ceremonial Magick. Once this connection is recognized, it's easier to see why some Wiccan traditions blended aspects of the two disciplines into their current system of beliefs.

SPIRITS

In the Italian Wiccan traditions, there are several categories of spirits. These entities come in all shapes, sizes, and dispositions. However, while these spirits do have some unique attributes, they, nevertheless, greatly resemble Celtic Faeries.

The Lare are clan spirits who protect the homes and families of witches. Originally, they were the spirits of cultivated fields, but as individuals merged into villages, the Lare moved with them and became household entities. It soon became a common practice for Italian witches to erect small Lare shrines in their homes, and it was in these shrines that they made offerings of milk, honey, or wine to the spirits.

The Etruscan Lasa, although essentially just an earlier version of the Lare, were considered the first known spirits. Like the early Lare, the Lasa were beings of the fields and meadows. However, unlike the Lare, the Lasa were also the spirits associated with the Underworld. For this reason, offerings to Lasa were made in the west, while Lare offerings were made in the east.

Besides the Lasa and Lare, some of the most common spirits in Italian lore are the Folletti.[3] These are air spirits that travel on the wind, and they can be both playful and mischievous. In northern Italy, some Folletti are called Basadone, or "woman kisser," spirits. These playful beings are best known for their habit of stealing a kiss from a woman as they float by her on the wind.

In the regions of Tuscany, another type of spirit is known as the Linchetti. These entities are quite different than the Lasa, Lare, Folletti, or Basadone, as they are actually a category of Elf. In Italian lore, the Linchetti are the spirits of the night that are responsible for nightmares, and they are also the causes of strange or unsettling nighttime noises.

The Monachetti are gnomelike spirits along the same lines as the Linchetti. However, although somewhat similar, the Monachetti do not have the same bad reputation for causing unrest.

The Fata, along with the woodland Fauni and Silvani, are other types of Italian spirits. These gentle shape-shifters of the woods and water often appear in human or animal form and are very similar to Celtic wood/water Nymphs. Like Nymphs, Fata were always very grateful to anyone who was kind to them, and they often rewarded this kindness with gifts.

Finally, the Lauru is an elegant, finely dressed spirit with twinkling eyes and long curly hair. Their majestic appearance belies the fact that they are extremely mischievous beings that will go to great lengths to create havoc. However, if treated with respect, a Lauru may reveal hidden treasure. These traits make the Lauru appear very similar to Irish Leprechauns.

In Tuscan witchcraft lore, there are also many names for spirits—Alpena, Aplu, Dusio, Esta, Faflon, Fanio, Jano, Losna, Maso, Meana, Nortia, Pano, Silvanio, Spulviero, Termano, Tesana, Tituno, Turanna, and Verbio—and each of these spirits has a specific trait. For instance, Meana is the Spirit of Fate and Destiny, Losna is the Spirit of the Moon who aids in all magick, while Turanna is the Spirit of Love who has influence over all romantic matters. In short, each spirit has a special vocation. Tuscan witches also assign other traits to spirits. The north is believed to be the home of the Spirits of Destiny, while the Spirits of Life live in the east. The Spirits of the Overworld live in the south, and the Spirits of the Underworld live in the west.

WATCHERS

Most Wiccan denominations recognize a form of entity that acts as a Watcher. In some Celtic traditions, the Watchers are thought to be ancient Gods who stand guard at the Portals to the Otherworld.[4] Italian Wiccan traditions also recognize beings called the Grigori, whom they view as the Guardians of the Dimensional Planes. At one time, these beings were known as the Lesser Gods who watched over the heavens, but in truth they are actually somewhere between spirits and Gods.

Regardless of the names that they go by, whether Grigori or Watcher, these entities are the beings that protect the ritual Circle and are commonly invoked during the casting of a Magick Circle. These Watchers then oversee "towers" that guard the portals marking the Four Cardinal Points, thereby giving us the name "Watchtowers." So the Italian Grigori and the Celtic Watcher are simply the Guardians of the Four Cardinal Points. Watchers are also known by several additional names, including the Guardians of the Astral Realms, the Keepers of the Ancient Wisdom, the Watchers of the Quarters, and the Guardians of the Portals.

But witches were not the only religion to have a belief in Watchers. Hebrew cabalistic teaching portrays Watchers—which they also named Grigori—as angels and lists their names as Michael, Raphael, Auriel, and Gabriel. The Greeks believed in the Gods of the Four Winds, but categorized them more as Demigods than purely spiritual beings. Christianity acknowledges multiple forms of this guardian theme in angels, as well as the idea of Saint Peter standing guard at the gates of Heaven. In other words, most religions recognize a type of spiritual being that they perceive as a guardian of the gateway to another realm or dimensional plane.

FAERIES

Besides Elementals, Spirits, and Watchers, many Pagan traditions recognize a wide assortment of magickal beings. These beings, though often quite different from one another, are generally classified as Faeries. The witches who believe in these beings see them as inhabiting an invisible realm, known as the Otherworld or Faery World, which is on a different plane of existence than the mortal realm. While there are many names for Faeries, the most widespread are undoubtedly "Sidhe," "Good People," or "Little People."

It's also noteworthy to mention that although the Sidhe normally consist of a collection of magickal, mysterious beings that exist separate from human beings, there is quite a bit of interaction between the two races. Coincidentally, a good deal of this intermingling happens during the Pagan holy days.

In pre-Christian times, Faeries were believed to be the spirits of the dead. Much later, in post-Christian times, Faeries generally came to be known as fallen angels or Elemental spirits. However, as fallen angels started to take on negative connotations, Celtic races pulled away from the fallen angel beliefs, and Faeries steadily transformed into their own brand of mystical being.

Fundamentally, there are two main groupings of Faeries: the Seelie Court and the Unseelie Court. All good Faeries that are kindly towards humans belong to the Seelie Court, while all wicked Faeries that are harmful to humans are part of the Unseelie Court. These two types are then further subdivided into clan and solitary Faeries.

The first group, Clan Faeries, live in the magickal Realm of the Faery Otherworld where they have kingdoms, villages, and palaces that mirror those of the mortal realm. In short, whatever is found in one world has its reflection in the other. However, in the Otherworld of the Faery, time, space, energy, and form do not exist as they do in the mortal world. Appearance and reality are based on one's own perception, and these can shift from moment to moment. In layman's terms, the Realm of the Faery, and all that it contains, is magickal.

Solitary Faeries are the second group. Similar to Elementals, solitary Faeries are often associated with the earth, air, fire, or water; but they can also be linked to trees, forests, sacred sites, or even human households. For example, the Undine Faeries (e.g., Water Nymphs) live in water, while Earth Faeries (e.g., Dwarfs, Gnomes) live underground. Aside from the elemental classifications, there are also categories among the individual Faery races.[5]

Types of Faeries

The Elf, although technically classified as an order of earth spirit, is its own category of Faery. Though popularized in stories about Santa Claus as being short, happy toy makers with pointed shoes, storytellers such as J.R.R. Tolkien have given Elves a more correct image. In reality, Elves are tall, slender, genteel beings who live in well-lit forest settings. However, it should also be remembered that some traditions view Elves as an entire species of Faery and divide the group into two classes, Light Elves and Dark Elves, which equate to the Seelie Court and Unseelie Court. In these instances, Light Elves are friendly and kind, while Dark Elves are malicious and dangerous.

Besides the Elf Faery, there are other types of Faeries that fall within the Elf classification. For instance, the Ellyllon are tiny Welsh Elves that tend to be helpful to mortals. There are also Spriggans, which are the ghosts of old giants who generally act as guardians to Faeries of other castes. These beings are often found around castles, but they can also be seen anywhere that treasure is hidden.

Alongside these specialized Elves, there are several other types of Faery that are loosely classified as Elves. The Dwarf is a common example. A Faery that lives underground, the Dwarf is considered somewhat solitary, extremely loyal, and formidable. Sometimes called "Night Elves," they are difficult to befriend. However, once a Dwarf accepts friendship, he becomes a strong ally. These deep-forest-dwelling miners were popularized in the children's story "Snow White and the Seven Dwarfs."

A second type of woodland Faery, Gnomes, are also earth-dwelling entities. Much smaller than an Elf or Dwarf, (the Gnome only stands about one- to two-feet tall), Gnomes are shy and wary beings of the forest. Originally thought to treasure only gold, most Gnomes are generally fond of gems, beautifully polished stones, or any precious metal. The Leprechaun is a popular example of a Gnome. Made famous by Irish lore, the Leprechaun started out as a simple shoemaker before being transformed into his more commonly known form.

But not all Faeries are forest dwellers. There is an entire classification of spirits known as Hobs.[6] This type of Faery includes all domesticated spirits who live among mortals, providing that they work for their human hosts. The Brownie is an excellent example of a Hob. Like all Hob-Faeries, the Brownie is known as neat and fussy. After attaching itself to a particular household, these Faeries act as nighttime helpers while the host family sleeps. A Brownie will clean the house, wash the dishes, or do any other chore that it can find. In the Welsh tradition, the Brownie is known as a Bwbach or Bwca, while Scottish witches know them as Bodachs.

Another Hob, which is even more sought after than the Brownie, is the Kabold. Like the Brownie, the Kabold attaches itself to a particular household. Once established there, a Kabold will do some chores. At the same time, though, a Kabold will play pranks because it possesses a mischievous personality. Still, this Faery was cherished because it was known as an extremely loyal protector of its host family.

Nymphs are an entirely different category of Faery. Unlike an Elf, Dwarf, or Gnome, these Faeries are always gentle Nature spirits. Another important point about Nymphs is that they all possess the power of prophecy, and they are almost always kind toward human beings.

The Dryad, which is also called a Hamadryad, is a classic Wood Nymph. This Nymph conjoins itself to an oak tree—some people believe these Nymphs also bond with fruit trees—and becomes the tree's guardian. Though a Dryad is usually a gentle and friendly spirit, it's still capable of calling forth lightning to protect its host tree.

There is a second type of Wood Nymph called the Oakman. The unique aspect of the Oakman is that while most Nymphs take the form of beautiful females, the Oakman Nymph always assumes male form. Like the Dryad, the Oakman lives exclusively in trees, especially oak trees. However, while the Dryad is concerned with the well-being of its host tree,[7] the responsibilities of the Oakman tend to be more focused on guarding of animals.

Another Nymph, the Naiad, is a Water Nymph that usually dwell in lakes, rivers, streams, and fountains, but it can be found in virtually any body of water. Like their Undine counterparts, Naiads are most frequently seen only as trails that dance across the surface of calm water.

The Nereids are another species of Water Nymph. However, unlike the Naiads, the Nereids are Sea Nymphs and are almost never known to inhabit fresh water.

Oreads are a fifth type of Nymph. These mountain- and grotto-dwelling entities are often heard more than seen, and they account for many of the unusual noises of the forest. Although all Nymphs are said to be amorous beings who often take mortal lovers, Naiads, Nereids, and Oreads are believed to be the most sexually insatiable of all.

There are two other Faeries—Pixies and Sprites—who also dwell in forests.[8] While both of these Faeries share some qualities with Nymphs, they are generally much smaller than their Nymph cousins. Another important distinction is that Pixies and Sprites tend to live in much closer proximity to humans than Nymphs. Although they still live in wooded areas, they can get by with a single tree or a small garden patch. Also, both these Faeries tend to resemble human beings (though on a much smaller scale), with Sprites having the added feature of crystalline butterflylike wings. Beyond their general appearance, these Faeries also differ from their Nymph relatives in that they're very easily excited. This constant state of agitation regularly leads to uncontrollable bouts of mischief.

Unfortunately, not all Faeries are peaceful or benevolent. The Faeries of the Unseelie Court are not only dreaded, but some are quite dangerous. For instance, the Irish Banshee, or "Bean-Sidhe," is a solitary female Faery that can take on one of two different personalities. In Celtic lore, the Banshee is a prophet of death, and it was said that when a Banshee connected herself to a particular family or clan, her awful wailing became a forecaster of death or grave misfortune. There are also wild Banshees unconnected to a clan that prowl the woodlands trying to lure unsuspecting people to their death.

In Scottish lore, the Washer, or "Bean-Nighe," is a prime example of a harbinger of death.[9] As the name implies, it's said that the Bean-Nighe washes the shirt of someone who is about to die and then meets the person in order to give him his death shirt.

While not as feared as the Banshee or Washer, the Boggart[10] is another unwelcome Faery. More of a bothersome entity than one that does actual harm, the Bogart is characterized by his ability to torment a household using loud noises during the night or by committing mischievous acts that become annoying. A favorite trick of the Boggart is to place a nail, tack, or other small object where someone will step on it. Children's toys are also favorite objects for Boggarts to leave out. Boggarts go out of their way to make people stub their toes in the dark, even if this means moving pieces of furniture.

There is one Faery similar to and different from others of its kind. This being is called a Pooka. In Irish lore, the Pooka is a shape-shifting hobgoblin that can take both human and animal form, though it regularly appears as a black horse. At times, a Pooka can be very similar to a Brownie or Kabold, as its nature is to be extremely helpful to the household or person to which it has bonded. However, a Pooka can also be mischievous, so occasional antics should be expected. In Druidic lore, this being was feared because it was said to destroy crops that were left unharvested after Samhain.

But over time, the Pooka became more of a conditional being. Though generally defined as a Faery, in modern beliefs it's become a being that is specifically created with a purpose, life span, and disposition in mind. Think of it along the lines of an invisible companion in which every aspect of its existence is predetermined.

Traditions, Structure, and Offices

There are many misconceptions about witches. One of the most common is that all branches of witchcraft are exactly alike. But this couldn't be further from the truth. Modern Wicca, regardless of the tradition, bears little resemblance to its Pagan roots. From its early beginnings as an Earth-based religion, this once pure faith has been bombarded by the beliefs of numerous other religions. As a result, it absorbed Greek, Hebrew, Judeo-Christian, Egyptian, Roman, Cabalistic, and Druidic influences until it finally became what it is today.

In order to appreciate the many aspects of modern Wicca, it's important to realize just how many different traditions actually exist. There are denominations that favor a Celtic or Italian ancestry, and others that are purely male or female oriented. There are rituals that stretch from one denomination to the next, deities that seemingly appear in every tradition. Yet each path has its own concepts, beliefs, and practices. Another unique quality is the religion's rare ability to mold itself to an individual, rather than forcing the individual to reshape him or herself to fit the religion.

PAGAN TRADITIONS

To explain a little more about the various religious paths, the following is a partial list of some prominent traditions and a short explanation of the themes that they follow.

- **Alexandrian Wicca:** A path founded by Alexander and Maxine Sanders in England during the 1960s after they broke away from Gardnerian Wicca. Originally initiated into the Craft by Gerald Gardner, Alex Sanders felt that changes needed to be made in some of Gardner's beliefs. Gardner was unwilling to amend his practices. The Sanders founded a tradition that used a Gardnerian base, then combined Judeo-Christian elements, an extensive use of cords, and even more Ceremonial Magick. In this tradition, more emphasis is placed on the God than in the Gardnerian system.

- **American Celtic Wicca**: This path describes any of the Celtic-based traditions practiced in the United States. Under the name **American Order of the Brotherhood of Wicca**, this path was first promoted by Lady Sheba (Jessica Bell). It closely follows Gardnerian Wicca, except that its followers almost always work robed and the tradition also makes extensive use of Ceremonial Magick.
- **Anglo-Saxon Wicca**: A tradition that combines the practices of the Celtic people with the path of southern Teutons. (See Teutonic Wicca, Northern Way.) Seax-Wica is, in a sense, a more modern form of this tradition.
- **Aridian Wicca**: This is a modern Italian tradition that was originally established in the United States in 1981. Although technically an offshoot from the Italian Tanarric Tradition, it combines the entire spectrum of the Italian Triad Traditions into a workable path. Although originally it was derived from ancient teachings, elements of other Wiccan traditions have crept into Aridian practice. One aspect of this path is that the God and Goddess are viewed as equals, which is unique for a tradition with such old lineage. The forces of Nature play an essential part in the rites of this denomination, to the point where practitioners work robed during the dark months and skyclad during the light months.
- **Asatru Tradition**: See Northern Way.
- **British Traditional Witchcraft**: A path of Wicca that combines classic Celtic beliefs with newer Gardnerian practices to create a denomination that some consider to be just one more eclectic form of the Craft.
- **Britannic Wicca**: A path that combines Anglo-Saxon, Roman, and Celtic beliefs into a single tradition.
- **Caledonii Wicca**: A Scottish tradition that includes Roman beliefs.
- **Celtic Wicca**: The name given to traditions that incorporate elements of English, Scottish, and Irish witchcraft, along with Wiccan and Paganistic practices from continental Europe and Druidic faiths. Many different denominations exist within the realm of Celtic Wicca, and most modern traditions either have a Celtic lineage or incorporate Celtic practices within their system. Gardnerian Wicca is probably the most well-known Wiccan denomination that bases its beliefs and practices on Celtic origins.

- **Ceremonial Magick**: A post-Christian path that incorporates many ancient Paganistic beliefs and practices with elements of Judeo-Christian, Hebrew, and Cabalistic teachings to form a precise magickal vocation.[1]
- **Circle Wicca**: Founded in 1974 by Selena Fox and Jim Alan, this tradition is more attuned to American Indian Shamanism than European Wicca. Since the religion's inception, the Circle Network has become recognized as a nonprofit organization and a Neo-Pagan church.
- **Creabh Ruadh Wicca**: An Irish tradition that focuses on the male mysteries.
- **Deboran Wiccedom**: An eclectic path that attempts to reconstruct pre-Inquisition Pagan practices with the goal of restoring Wicca to what it was before Christian influences crept in. This tradition uses a degree system and stresses the balance between the God and Goddess, masculine and feminine, and the polarities.
- **Dianic Tradition**: This path was founded in the United States and stresses a Pagan religious base and practical magick applications. Also known as **Dianic Feminist Wicce**, all-female covens are the norm, though this is by no means a steadfast rule of the tradition; some mixed-gender covens do exist. However, a High Priestess is always the coven leader and must be present for any Circle.
- **Druidic Path**: The group of traditions based on Druidic philosophies and magickal practices. The following groups are contained within this general religious category. The **Druidiactos Tradition** is a path that specializes in the cultural and magical aspects of the Druid religion. The **Gwyddonic Druid Tradition** is a Welsh Druidic denomination based on the Concept of Oneness. This tradition also blends elements of Wicca into its practices. The **Order of Bards, Ovates and Druids** is another denomination that is based on Druidism, though this sect tends to adhere to post-Roman Druidic practices. The **Reformed Druids** are a tradition started in the United States in the early 1960s. This path incorporates ancient and modern Druidism with modern Celtic Wiccan practices. The **Ueleda Tradition** is an Initiatory Druidic path for women strictly based on the Druidesses of the Tuatha Dé Danann. There are no men admitted to this path. The **Dryad Tradition** is another feminist path that follows Druid principles and incorporates elements of Celtic Wicca and the Faery Tradition.

- **Eclectic Wicca**: Although not a specific path, this is a combination of traditions that is often followed by solitary witches. However, it's also quickly becoming popular with covens as new ideas and beliefs are blended into various denominations. The elements usually combined include Celtic, Druidic, Neo-Pagan, Faery, and Shamanism, though any Earth-based or Nature-based practices may be incorporated.
- **Egyptian Tradition**: A denomination based on the Gods and Goddesses of ancient Egypt. The spells and rituals of this path are elaborate, sometimes complicated, and are often compared to the complexities of Ceremonial Magick.
- **Eireannach Wicca**: A general term used for any of the Irish Wiccan denominations.
- **Faery Tradition**: This denomination is a blend of the Faery Tradition and Celtic Wicca. Containing folklore as well as Wiccan beliefs, it's thought to be one of the oldest traditions. The Faery Realm and Otherworld play a significant part in the beliefs.
- **Family Tradition**: A hereditary path in which the Old Ways have been orally preserved, it incorporates traditional witchcraft with superstition and folklore. To be admitted as a true "hereditary" witch, a person must be able to trace family roots within the Craft for at least 100 years[2] and must be initiated by a family member.
- **Frosts' Wicca**: A Welsh-based path founded by Gavin and Yvonne Frost in the early 1970s. After founding this sect, the Frosts went on to form the School Of Wicca, which is now located in Hinton, West Virginia.
- **Gaelic Wicca**: A general term used for any of the Irish or Scottish Wiccan denominations.
- **Gardnerian Wicca**: The most widely known and practiced tradition, it is named for Gerald Brosseau Gardner, who made its practices publicly known in the 1950s. The Gardernian path places emphasis on the Goddess over the God, and a High Priestess is almost always the coven leader, though she usually has a High Priest as her assistant. One of the first traditions is to install a degree system, this path usually favors working pairs, and skyclad practice is highly encouraged. Although Gardner claimed to have gained his knowledge of witchcraft after having been initiated as a witch in 1939 by an existing coven, skeptics continually allege that Gardner pirated ideas from the books of Charles Godrey Leland, James G. Frazier, and Margaret A. Murray,

then made up the rest of his tradition with the help of Aleister Crowley and Doreen Valiente. Regardless of the truth, there is a great deal of verifiable practices contained in Gardnerian Wicca.

- **Georgian Wicca**: A tradition founded in 1970 by George Patterson. In 1980, it officially became the Georgian Church. This path is primarily based on Alexandrian and Gardnerian Wicca, but it also incorporates various Celtic elements.
- **Hereditary Tradition**: See Family Tradition.
- **Hibernian Tradition**: A denomination traced back to the Middle Ages, it blends elements of Irish Wicca with Roman and ancient Christian beliefs.
- **Irish Wicca**: Another general term used for any of the Irish Wiccan paths. However, unlike the Eireannach or Gaelic traditions, Irish Wicca is predominantly pre-Celtic.
- **Love Craft Wicca**: A fairly recent denomination developed and founded by Gerina Dunwich that draws upon its basic teaching that "love is the law" and that love is the basis of all magick, healing, and other aspects of the path. This tradition relies upon a hodgepodge of bits and pieces of other denominations to form its underlying principles, but weeds out the overly strict or excessive requirements that many of these traditions frequently seem to use.
- **Maidenhill Wicca**: A denomination founded in 1979. This is a traditional path that begins with a Gardnerian foundation and then teaches novices to explore other traditions in an effort to blend as many beliefs as possible into their personal persuasion, very similar to Eclectic Wicca. However, regardless of the ultimate beliefs, the focus still remains on the Goddess and the Horned God.
- **Neo-Paganism**: This term technically encompasses any of the modern Pagan paths that combine pre-Christian beliefs and practices with modern concepts. Unfortunately, although this is a catchall term that can be used for just about everything from modern Wicca to the various branches of Occultism, negative connotations from the Left-Hand Path[3] are often associated with it and override its true neutrality.
- **Northern Way Wicca**: Founded in Illinois in 1980, this is a Celtic and Norse path that blends elements of the two traditions. Also called **Northern Tradition**, this path attempts to emulate authentic Norse beliefs and rituals.
- **Nova Wicca**: A tradition founded in the United States by two former

Gardnerians, this path has only slight variations from its parental Gardnerian roots.

- **Pecti-Wica**: A Scottish solitary path of the Pictish (pre-Celtic) people of northern Scotland. This tradition has been passed on by Aidan Breac to select students. The Pecti-Wica path is acutely attuned to solar and lunar changes, which translate to the balance between the God and Goddess. This tradition also incorporates elements of Ceremonial Magick, but these are of a very old variety.
- **Pictish Wicca**: A path based on Scottish Witchcraft that primarily focuses on the many magical energies associated with Nature. To describe this as a religion is stretching the definition of the word "religion" to its extreme, as this is more of a vocation along the lines of Ceremonial Magick.
- **Sacred Wheel Tradition**: Primarily a Neo-Pagan denomination, it is a Wiccan path that is partially based on a wide variety of Celtic beliefs.
- **Saxon Wicca**: See Anglo-Saxon Wicca.
- **Science Tradition**: A Wiccan (Neo-Pagan) path founded in the early 1970s by Laurie Cabot, the Official Witch of Massachusetts. This denomination is an eclectic path that is based on a wide variety of Celtic Wiccan beliefs, Ceremonial Magick, Hermetic principles, and theoretical science, with elements of Roman, Greek, and Egyptian influence mixed in.[4]
- **Scottish Wicca**: Another general term used for any of the Scottish Wiccan denominations. However, unlike the Gaelic tradition, Scottish Wicca is predominantly pre-Celtic. The Pictish tradition borrows extensively from this path.
- **Seax-Wica**: A tradition founded by Raymond Buckland in 1973. This path is based on Saxon Wicca, but was not intended to be—nor does it claim to be—a duplicate of original Saxon tradition. It's a democratic system wherein covens are led by a priest or priestess. One of the most open of all Wiccan denominations, at one time it was panned by critics as a joke. However, the critics were soon proven wrong, and it has achieved a strong following in the years since its inception.[5]
- **Stregheria Italiano**: Meaning "Italian Witchcraft." A catchall name often used for any Italian Wiccan tradition. Also called the **Strega Tradition**.
- **Teutonic Wicca:** All traditions based on Norse, or Viking, beliefs fall into this category. Scandinavian, ancient Icelandic, and even pre-

Christian Germanic customs, practices, and beliefs form the basis for all Teutonic paths, and old Norse deity names (Woden, Odin, Frig, Freya) are usually used. (See Northern Way.)

- **Triad Traditions**: There are three ancient Italian traditions that make up the collective "triad." These three paths are the Fanarra, Janarra, and Tanarra. The **Fanarra Tradition** (Keepers of the Earth Mysteries) occupies northern Italy. This path promotes the secrets of the Earth's powers, as well as the use of places and objects for directing this energy. The **Janarra Tradition** (Keepers of the Lunar Mysteries) occupies central Italy. This path focuses on lunar energy and its use in magick. The **Tanarra Tradition** (Keepers of the Stellar Mysteries) also occupies central Italy. This path concentrates on the secrets of stellar energy and their effects on Nature. It is not unusual for someone to learn one path, then move on to the others in much the same way that Druids move through three stages of learning.
- **Tuatha Dé Danann**: An Irish path based on the legends and lore of the Tuatha Dé Danann. This tradition incorporates some Celtic beliefs, though these most likely originated with the Tuatha anyway.
- **Welsh Wicca**: A collection of Wiccan paths that originated in the areas surrounding Wales. The most widely recognized example of this path is Frosts' Wicca (listed), though there are several lesser-known denominations under this general heading.
- **West Country Wicca**: A Wiccan path of the southwestern areas of England. This path celebrates only five festivals, rather than the eight of other traditions. **North Country Wicca** is a similar Wiccan path of the northern areas of England.
- **Witan Tradition**: A fertility-based (Earth) denomination, it blends aspects of Celtic, Scottish, and Norse into a single path. There is also a branch known as **Wittan**, which is a combination of old Irish, Scottish, and Norse.
- **Y Tylwyth Teg Tradition**: A Celtic/Welsh path founded by Bill Wheeler in Washington, DC, in 1967. Originally known as **the Gentle People**, it's based on the balance of Nature. The tradition also blends folklore, mythology, and the mysteries into its beliefs.

STRUCTURE AND OFFICES

Just as every tradition has its own Gods, Goddesses, and individualized beliefs, each one also adheres to a specific system of organization.[6] The following is a basic explanation of the different types of groupings and the various hierarchy of positions within the groups:

- **Assistant**: Pagan paths that employ a system with specific offices may include an Assistant, sometimes called a Maid(en), in their structure. Since most denominations that use this position are normally Goddess oriented and run by a High Priestess, this person is usually also a woman. Essentially, she is a High Priestess that acts as an assistant to the leader for ceremonial purposes. In some traditions, she will have the added duty of preparing the meeting area, assembling everyone prior to the Magick Circle, and even cleaning up afterwards. While this may seem like an unenviable position, many people welcome the tasks as a training experience for the time when they form their own coven.
- **Bards**: The first of the three stages of priesthood in the Druidic Order. The Bards preserve the oral wisdom of the faith through folklore, poems, and song. Typically, Bards were musicians, poets, and storytellers. Now, as in the past, they are trained to master the ways to make stories into incantations and use words as a method of divination. A Bard is also an oral historian of the denomination.
- **Circle**: In certain Pagan traditions, this is the term used for a small group of worshippers. A circle is simply a different name for a coven. Depending on the beliefs and construction of the individual path, a hierarchy may or may not exist within the circle. This should not be confused with the Magick Circle used by Pagans for rituals.
- **Clan**: A large Celtic Pagan group composed of an inner and outer court. The inner court is made up of circles, colleges, covens, or groves, and forms the actual clan. The outer court is composed of similarly minded people who associate with the clan, but are not actual members. The outer circle also serves a secondary purpose, as it's usually from the outer circle that new members are initiated into the various other bodies of the inner circle. This should not be confused with the clans of Scotland, as Scottish clans are family units consisting of members of the same bloodline, while the Pagan clan is only concerned with religious beliefs.
- **Coven**: A small independent group of Pagans, normally numbering no fewer than three and no more than thirteen, who meet on a regular basis to worship together. Though normally led by a High Priest or High Priestess, some covens operate with no specific leader. The per-

fect correlation within a coven of thirteen is six pairs of working partners, with the last position held by the coven leader. Admittance to most covens is often gained by initiation, and a degree system is usually the method of internal advancement. When the coven grows too large, an experienced High Priest/ess leaves to form a separate coven. If the coven has a Maid(en), this is often the person who forms the new coven. This process is known as "hiving off." Once a coven has had two new covens hive off from it, the coven leader acquires the distinction of being known as a Witch King or Witch Queen.

- **Covener:** A man or woman who is a member of a coven, although the name is also used for members of circles, clans, colleges, and groves. Only a Solitary Practitioner may not be referred to as a covener. In the Wiccan religions, this term is sometimes replaced by "coven witch."
- **Druid/ess**: A priest/priestess of any Druidic path. In ancient times, male/female Druids were not only powerful, but they were the most intellectual people around. Following in these footsteps, a modern initiate must pass through, and master, the Bard and Ovate stages of Druidism before attempting to master the Druid stage.
- **Druidic College**: A small- to medium-sized group of Pagans who adhere to Druidic beliefs and celebrate the eight festivals, along with rituals, feasts, and other spiritual occasions. Very similar to a Wiccan coven, though usually larger than a coven. A college is led by a High Priestess and High Priest who are elected by the other members of the college. There is a degree system in place, and practitioners strive to master the stages as Bards, Ovates, and Druids. A college is especially important to the teaching process of the faith, as this is the place where all learning occurs.
- **Grove:** An organized group of Pagans who come together to worship and meet for the eight festivals. A grove is primarily linked to the Nature-based denominations that practice their Craft almost entirely outdoors, especially in wooded areas. The most unusual aspect of a grove is that outsiders are always welcome to all rituals. This differs from many Wiccan traditions, which generally only open the sabbats to outsiders while reserving esbats for coven members.
- **High Priest**: In Pagan hierarchy, the High Priest is the male leader of most circles, clans, covens, and groves that contain both men and women.[7] In Goddess-oriented traditions, he's the person who assists in conducting rituals and helps with matters relating to the group. In

Wiccan paths that employ a degree system, this term may also apply to any second-degree or third-degree male witch.

- **High Priestess**: In Pagan hierarchy, the High Priestess is the female leader of most circles, clans, covens, and groves that contain men and women. In Goddess-oriented traditions, she's the person who conducts all rituals and oversees the other matters relating to the group.[8] In Wiccan paths that employ a degree system, this term can also apply to any second-degree or third-degree female witch.
- **Maid(en)**: See Assistant.
- **Novice**: In many Pagan traditions, newly admitted members fall under this general heading until they have reached a certain level of understanding or knowledge of their particular path. Some degree systems employ this term to describe a newly initiated priest/ess. Depending on the particular tradition, a Novice is also known as a **Neophyte**, **Postulate**, or **Initiate**. In the Seax-Wica tradition, a new member is known as a **Ceorl** (pronounced "cawl").[9]
- **Ovate**: The second of the three stages of priesthood in the Druidic Order. Simply put, the Ovates are healers. As in ancient times, modern Ovates are required to master the uses of herbs, plants, and minerals for healing and must also acquire basic medical knowledge. They are also required to understand and master the use of life energy in healing, as well as working with spirits. Also known as a **Vate**.
- **Priest/ess**: In any of the Pagan paths, a person who has been initiated is regarded as a priest or priestess. In paths with a degree system, this is sometimes the first-degree title before advancing to High Priest/ess.
- **Scribe**: A position within the Seax-Wica (Saxon) tradition that can be held by either a man or woman. A Scribe's job is to act as the coven secretary and record keeper. All entries in the Tree (i.e., Seax-Wica equivalent of the *Book of Shadows*) are made by the Scribe, and for this reason the person must have calligraphy skills or beautiful handwriting. Notification of meeting times and dates are handled by this person, as is all correspondence, record keeping, and note taking. Some other traditions often use an Assistant, or Maid(en) for these purposes.
- **Solitary Practitioner**: A person who practices any Pagan tradition alone. Although Solitaries may attend coven ceremonies from time to time, or may at some point be actual members of a circle, coven, college, or grove, as a rule they spend the majority of their spiritual time alone. However, a Solitary may be a member of a clan or tribe, even if

not regularly attending the clan/tribe meetings.

- **Thegn**: Pronounced "Thain," this is a position within the Seax-Wica (Saxon) tradition that may be held by either a man or woman, though a man is generally chosen. The focus of this position is primarily as a sergeant-at-arms who calls the coven together at the start of rites by blowing a hunting horn. Along with this duty, the Thegn acts as a ceremonial guard, carrying a spear and shield specifically for this ritualistic purpose.
- **Tribe**: A collection of clans or covens from a particular region, which share the same religious beliefs and practices. A close comparison can be made to the American Indian tribal system.
- **Vate**: See Ovate.

Tools of Witchcraft

As either a solitary witch or member of a coven, there's a short list of tools that you'll need to have. At the same time, there's also a short list of items that are highly recommended, although these are not absolutely essential. Without getting into too much minor detail, this list will provide fundamental information about each tool. Try to keep in mind that even though your tools don't need to be very elaborate or expensive, most of them are, nevertheless, quite important for practicing the Craft. Therefore, the first place to start is with a few bits of background information that apply to all tools.[1]

Because there are so many different traditions, with so many different tools, and so many different views, the five "Rules for Tools" should always be applied. These simple guidelines relate to all denominations and outline the basic principles necessary to properly obtain, consecrate, and use any tool.

RULES FOR TOOLS

- **Rule One**: The most important thing to keep in mind about any tool is that the owner/user (i.e., you) must feel comfortable using it. The reason behind this rule is simply that if you feel comfortable with your tool, you'll relax and concentrate on the task at hand. Conversely, if you're uncomfortable with an item, you'll expend more time and energy concentrating on the tool than on the purpose for which it is being used. This discomfort will then adversely affect your results, and it may actually be detrimental to your purpose.
- **Rule Two**: Ancient customs and practices maintain that the best, and the most appropriate, substances for making tools are those that once had a life-force of their own. For instance, wood is much better for making a wand than fiberglass, just as cords of silk, wool, or cotton

are always preferable to those made of synthetic material. Along these same lines, items that are personally handcrafted are always better than those bought from a store because personal energy is transferred during the construction process. However, since most modern witches are not master craftsmen, the use of store-bought tools is perfectly acceptable, especially if you are just starting out.

- **Rule Three**: Equally important to the success and effectiveness of your tools is that all of them should be consecrated inside the Circle immediately after your initiation. If you've been accepted into a coven, you'll be initiated using the coven's tools. Then you'll have plenty of help consecrating your own tools. If you plan on being a solitary witch, but happen to know someone who is already an initiated witch, this dilemma can easily be taken care of for you. However, if you're alone in your quest to become a witch, you'll have to consecrate your own tools after your self-initiation. While this is a slightly more difficult position to be in, it's not the end of the world.
- **Rule Four**: Never use any item that has an evil association or a checkered past. This is a steadfast rule designed to ensure that negative and/or evil influences do not attach themselves to you, your tools, or your rituals, as these influences can cause harm. The easiest way to avoid this problem is to be very careful when searching for items to use as tools. While antique shops, yard sales, and flea markets are favorite spots for witches to locate many useful items, extreme caution should be given to items such as daggers, swords, and anything with a military theme.
- **Rule Five**: Decide which tools you want to use, and then stick with them. While the number of tools you work with will largely depend on your particular tradition, changes can be made. If you feel particularly strongly about using a sword to cast a Circle, but your denomination doesn't employ a sword, simply add it to your personal repertoire. Although you won't use this item for group ceremonies, you will be able to use it during private rituals. You may also be able to slowly work it into the group setting. Keep in mind that some paths make extensive use of tools and others don't, and learning about different traditions can help in deciding if a tool is right for you. For example, Celtic Wicca uses a large number of different tools, while Saxon Wicca uses the fewest. Much of this can de directly attributed to the degree of influence that Christianity and Ceremonial Magick had on a particular tradition.

The following is a list of some of the tools and accessories used in the Craft and a short description of the purpose of each one.

Athame

The first, and most important, tool is the athame. This item is the true witch's weapon in all spiritual and magickal work. It has all the power of the sword and is used for casting the Circle as well as for controlling and banishing spirits. This tool is used in every Wiccan tradition, and it's usually the first tool to be consecrated by a new witch. Although it's usually known as an athame, it can also go by different names. For instance, in Saxon Wicca, the athame is called a "seax," Pecti-Wica calls it a "dirk," and the Aridians refer to it as the "spirit blade." Some Scottish and Italian paths use the term "dagger," while other traditions simply refer to it as the "black-handled knife." But regardless of its name, this tool is always considered to be an elemental tool, meaning that it's associated with one of the four Elements of Life.

The athame will most often signify the element of fire and be linked with the south cardinal point. However, there are some contrasting beliefs on this subject. Although somewhat rare, the athame (and sword) are sometimes associated with the element of air and the east cardinal point. In such a case, the wand then acquires the properties of the element of fire and becomes associated with the south. Instances of this usage are worth keeping in mind, even if they're so rare that they only require a passing mention.

The basic requirements for the athame are that the blade be two sided and that the handle be black; thus the name "black-handled" knife. But, the handle requirement can be altered. If you look back in time, you'll find that many witches believed that the magickal properties of natural substances, such as a deer antler or ram horn in their natural colors, were an appropriate alternative to a black handle. Since the athame is an extremely personal item, selecting one that is very elaborate can be just as appropriate as buying one straight from a hardware store or cutlery shop. Always apply Rule One in choosing the one that best suits your style and personality, and always be mindful of Rule Four.

It's also worth noting that most witches dull the blade and slightly blunt the tip for safety reasons, as this knife is almost always used exclusively for ritual gestures and not for actual cutting. However, since some witches don't use a "white-handled knife" (listed below), they tend to use their athame for everything, including ritual cutting, engraving,[2] carving, and cutting food during feasts.

Attire

For some reason, clothing tends to be a very neglected topic in most discussions about witchcraft. This has always struck me as rather odd, considering the fact that attire was so important to our Craft ancestors. Yet, as I've found out, even many longtime witches don't know why they wear certain clothing. Therefore, a short discourse on the basics of traditional attire is definitely needed.

The types of ceremonial robes that were worn by Pagans have changed throughout history. Prior to the onslaught of the Inquisitions and witch-hunts, most witches probably owned at least one elaborately decorated robe that they used exclusively for ceremonial purposes. Archeological evidence, such as the intricate multicolored silk and fine linen robes that have been found in the graves of Celtic priests, confirms this point. But as times became bad for witches, these flashy status symbols had to be modified into something less conspicuous.

Once the witch-hunts began to take their toll, witches recognized the need to conceal their identities. In doing so, they had to find a type of garment that was common enough not to stand out, yet practical enough to serve their purpose. It was this need for a functional disguise that prompted the custom of wearing dark-colored, hooded cloaks. An added benefit of this type of apparel was that it not only afforded them the ability to conceal their identity, but the dark colors allowed them to easily blend into the night.

Modern witches no longer have this fear of discovery, and the hooded cloaks, tunics, and ceremonial robes are now largely a matter of choice. Many people also practice their Craft skyclad, feeling that the nighttime sky is their ceremonial garb. So, even though a lot of people feel comfortable wearing special garments, it's not an absolute necessity, and the determining factor comes down to Craft custom or personal choice.

Assuming that you do want to wear a robe or tunic, what color is right? Well, as far as individual traditions are concerned, there is no truly established color scheme for clothing. There are a few traditions that do loosely follow a pattern, but even they're not too strict about it. For instance, Saxon Wicca tends to lean toward dark blue or dark green for the High Priest and High Priestess, while reserving light green or light blue for the coven. Seax-Wica prefers white for the priesthood and green or yellow for everyone else. Similarly, many Gardnerian covens prefer white, black, or earth tones.

In recent years, there has been a movement aimed at returning the past brilliance of the ceremonial robe, and this has resulted in exquisitely embroidered, multicolored garments once again becoming popular. When it comes to solitary practice, many witches seem to prefer colors such as white or black, but yellow, green, or brown are also fine.

Bell

It's unclear when the bell first gained widespread acceptance in the Wiccan religion. Although there are hints that it likely had pre-Christian roots, there's always the chance that it may have been added after appearing in Christian rites. But whatever the origin may be, the bell is now firmly a part of Wiccan ceremony.

Despite the fact that most witches feel that the bell is not a tool, many of them still use one at some point during a number of their rituals. They do this for two reasons. First, the bell is a feminine symbol, which is linked to the Goddess. Second, its frequency and tone are thought to have magickal properties. The vibrations can be used for everything from cleansing negative energy and calling deities to creating harmony and raising power.

In choosing a bell, the two most important points to keep in mind are tone and size. The tone of the bell should be clear, high pitched, and pleasant. Since cheaply made bells tend to produce a harsh sound, investing a few extra dollars in a quality bell will save you future headaches. In terms of size, a small, handheld bell, usually with a wooden handle, is probably best as it allows for both easy storage and usage.

Bowl

This item may seem like a no-brainer, but the bowl is actually an important tool that often goes unnoticed. Furthermore, these tools are an essential part of every Wiccan ritual.

Depending on location, the earliest versions of the bowl were large seashells or gourds; coastal regions used the shell, while inland areas used a wooden bowl or gourd. These shells/bowls held seawater that was used for purification purposes, offerings to the Goddess/God, or other items to be used in the rite. Several of the modern Italian denominations still refer to the bowl as the "spirit" bowl or shell.

There are also traditions that employ elemental bowls to hold the four elements. This is done by filling one with earth, one with water, one with smoking incense to represent air, and one with a candle to represent fire. Other bowls are used to hold consecrated water, bread/cakes, and items for the feast. Some paths also use a bowl filled with flammable alcohol—which is then lit—to represent the presence of the deity.

In modern practice, an assortment of materials has replaced the seashell and gourd. Wood, ceramic, glass, and metal are all commonly seen in Craft bowls; plastic is discouraged unless absolutely unavoidable. Customarily feminine in nature, the bowl is usually associated with the Goddess, although at times it can be identified with the God. However, regardless of its gender identity, it's always symbolic of rebirth or the renewed cycle of life.

Broomstick

Whenever anyone thinks of a witch's broom, the first image that automatically comes to mind is that of an ugly old hag with a pointed hat riding one across the night sky. Typical, but inaccurate. In point of fact, the broomstick is more of a symbolic object than an actual tool. Also known as a bune wand[3] or besom, the chief significance of the broom is as a fertility symbol. While it is used in a somewhat limited capacity in rituals like Handfasting, its usage is usually fertility related. The broom is also used by many, but not all, traditions for symbolically sweeping the Magick Circle clean of unwanted or negative energies. Another banishing aspect includes swinging the broom through incense smoke to "sweep" the air of negative energy.

There are two ways to obtain a broom. You can either purchase one from an occult shop, antique dealer, or craft store, or you can build one yourself. Although buying one is the easiest, constructing a besom is not difficult. When it comes to actually making a broom, there are far too many different views on this subject for me to discuss in detail; i.e., the use of specific trees for certain parts, when to cut the parts, and so on. Therefore, just use your best judgment and a little common sense.

Basically, if you want to make your own broomstick, you really can't go wrong with a hardwood—oak is preferable—handle and a birch twig brush. Other fine choices for the brush are pine boughs, any of the ornamental grasses, scented herbs such as lavender, rosemary, etc., or even long-stemmed flowers.[4] If you're adventurous, or a skilled craftsman, try adding willow for the binding. Just remember that you're the one who has to use it, so design it with yourself in mind.

Candle

The candle is another self-explanatory item, and very little needs to be added to what you may already know. However, there are a few points that should be touched upon. First, candles are associated with the elements of fire and air. Second, they are almost always used on the altar as the Watchtowers of the Circle and in certain types of magick. And third, they are regularly used to represent the Goddess and God. In addition to these associations, candles of specific colors are generally used for specific purposes. Symbols and inscriptions are often placed on candles to highlight or boost their effectiveness.

When it comes to selecting candles, your imagination is the only thing standing in your way. If you intend to use candleholders, make sure the candles fit. Otherwise, a wide-based candle will probably be your best bet. The only other factor to consider is the colors, if any, that your particular traditions follows; i.e., many witches use green (fertility) for the Goddess, red (strength) for the God, and white (purity) for spirit.

Cauldron

Of all the things in Witchcraft, the cauldron is one of the most recognizable items that a witch will ever own.[5] Visions of Shakespeare's witches standing around a boiling cauldron come to mind at even the slightest mention of the word. In reality, the cauldron is a very useful tool with extensive historical roots. Although it's infrequently used for its original purpose these days, the cauldron began its existence as the household cooking pot. Since witches were healers, they used their cauldrons to boil medicinal concoctions and brew elixirs. This is how the cauldron came to be associated with witches.

The cauldron, like the chalice, is normally feminine in nature and therefore associated with the Goddess, though it too can be identified with the God. Regardless of its gender identity, it's always symbolic of rebirth. In ritual use, the cauldron is a fertility symbol and jumping over it, instead of the broomstick, is common practice at some rituals. For indoor rituals, it's often used to hold either water or fire, but many things can be placed inside it.

The design of the cauldron is fairly simple and really hasn't changed significantly over time. It is most commonly made of cast iron, with three small feet, a cover, and a handle. You can also use a large copper or brass kettle as a substitute since there really is no strict rule governing its design.

For a witch just starting out, a regular cooking pot will do nicely in a pinch. However, if you decide to use a kitchen pot, remember to consecrate it first, then don't use it to cook with after that until you are completely finished with it as your cauldron.

Censer

The censer is the tool used for holding burning incense. It may be anything from a small brass bowl, preferably with legs, to an expensive objet d'art. Since incense is used at all rituals, the censer will be used often. Therefore, it's important to choose one that you're comfortable with, as well as one that suits your needs. Some witches prefer to have the censer sit on the altar, while others have one that hangs from a chain. The design of the censer is less important than the incense you use, but considerations such as cost, convenience, availability, or space requirements may force you to choose one type over another.

For finding a censer, a religious supply store is usually a good place to start since these stores carry a large variety of incense burners from which to choose. Also, because there's no real difference between the incense burners used by any of the major religions, including Wicca, one type will work just as well as the next. On this note, if you visit one of these stores looking for supplies, don't pass up a perfectly good item just because it wasn't specifically made for witchcraft. There are also mail-order catalogs and occult shops that carry a full line of these products, or you can construct your own censer rather than buying one. However, if you decide to make one, be sure to fashion it out of a material that will not burn or line it with a nonflammable substance to ensure that it doesn't accidentally catch on fire.

It's impossible to examine the censer without looking at the incense itself. The incense smoke carried by the air obviously belongs to the element of air, and ancient legends say that it's this smoke that carries prayers and invocations to the God and Goddess. The scents are also a pleasing sacrifice to the deities. Furthermore, incense smoke is welcoming and encouraging to good spirits, and it can aid in banishing evil ones. The whole trick is to pick the correct scent for the task at hand. Scents of all kinds have a swift and varying influence on the senses, and each one is intended to assist in creating an atmosphere that is right for a specific task. For this reason, most witches like to have a wide selection on hand, and some even mix their own combinations.

Chalice

Known as the cup, grail, or "Vessel of the Goddess," the chalice is one of the many tools used in witchcraft. As another of the elemental tools, it symbolizes water and the fertility that is associated with the Goddess. Like the cauldron and bowl, the chalice is almost always feminine in nature.

The biggest use for the chalice is as a ceremonial cup to hold the consecrated wine (or sometimes water), which is then shared in honor of the Goddess. Other than this, the chalice doesn't play a significant part in the rituals.

Although it has many eloquent names, the chalice can be something as simple as a plain metal cup or as elaborate as a jewel-encrusted antiquity. Most often, a hand-worked metal version is used, although glass or ceramic varieties are also popular.

An interesting historical side note is that, in early times, the chalice was not presented, or even spoken of, with the other tools. This was because Christians considered any mention of it to be a parody, or mockery, of the Catholic Mass, and the mere suggestion of it would immediately lead to torture if discovered. This may seem quite absurd by today's standards, but it nevertheless happened. What made it even worse is the fact that the act of sharing food and wine was originally a Pagan custom that far predates even the earliest Christian rites.

Cords

The cords are nothing more than lengths of ceremonial rope. In fact, they don't need to be actual rope and can be made from any type of material. Every witch in a coven should own a set of three cords, and the coven should have a set of its own. The cords should be nine feet long—length is measured from knot to knot—and the ends should be knotted to stop them from fraying. In addition, a coven should have a set of two initiation cords that are four and a half feet long. There are also some paths that require cords to have knots at the four-and-half-, six-, and seven-foot marks.

There are many uses for cords, but the three most prevalent are ritual binding during initiation, cord magick, and, in denominations with a degree system, they're often used to designate advancement. Cords are also used to measure and draw a Magick Circle.

In regard to magick, the cords being used will be different colors. Although there is no standard color scheme required, if at all possible, the color should match the work being done. A few examples of colors and their associated symbolism are: White = Purity; Yellow = Sun; Brown = Earth; Green = Nature; Silver = Moon; Red = Life; Black = Limitation; and Blue = Sky. This is only a small sampling of color symbolism and further research is necessary if you'd like to know more.

There are two things that you should keep in mind when selecting material for cords. First, they are for ritual binding, like during the Initiation Ritual. Since they will come in contact with your skin, make sure the material you select is not too rough, or it's likely to irritate your skin and leave abrasions. Second, try to use a material that once had its own life-force, such as silk, wool, or cotton. These materials will not only fulfill the requirements of my earlier suggestion, but will be far better for storing psychic energy than synthetic materials.

Finally, cords are sometimes used to signify the rank of a coven witch. Alexandrian Wicca, for example, uses differently colored cords to differentiate between the degrees of its practitioners. But this is more of an exception to the rule, and cords are primarily used in rituals or for magick.

Drum

The drum is a tool that some Wiccans use and others don't. More magickal than practical, it's often associated with the element of air, though it isn't unheard of for it to be associated with the element of earth, too. As far as usage goes, some Celtic paths employ this tool as a bridge to the Otherworld, while others use it only during chanting as a way to enhance and focus the process of gathering psychic energy. As with the bell, the drum's vibrations and tone play an essential part in its usefulness.

Horn

There are several uses for animal horns (including deer antlers) throughout Wicca. First, when placed on the altar, this item is used as a symbol of the God in place of a God-statue or a God-candle; e.g., Science tradition. Second, some denominations use the horn as a drinking vessel in place of the chalice; e.g., Saxon/Seax-Wica. And third, a number of traditions also use a hunting horn, made from a bull horn, as a ceremonial item to call the coven members together; e.g., Seax-Wica. The only problem seems to be finding an authentic horn. Keep in mind that plastic reproductions are hard to distinguish from real horns. Although this will not matter if the horn is only to be used as a calling device, it will completely diminish the item's effectiveness in the other two instances.

Nanta Bag

In Italian traditions, there is an item known as the nanta bag, which must be classified alongside tools. Shamanism uses a similar spirit bag. While not specifically a conventional tool, the nanta bag is, nevertheless, important to Italian practice. The bag is designed to keep wearers in balance with Nature while at the same time ensuring that they can perform their rituals anywhere. In short, it's both a source of protective energy and a portable Craft kit.

To put together a nanta bag, obtain a small cloth or leather bag that is just big enough to hold the following items: small stone (earth), feather (air), match (fire), vial of water (water), thimble (cup), coin with five-pointed star (pentacle), twig or small dowel (wand), needle or pin (athame), small seashell (Goddess), acorn or pine cone (God), salt, incense, vial of oil, tinfoil (to form a bowl), birthday candles, and a nine-foot piece of string. Once you have these items, place them in the bag, tie the end shut, and then consecrate it as you would any other tool. After that, keep it with you as a positive energy source or for the rare occasion when you need an emergency Craft kit.

Pentacle

The pentacle is another of the essential tools used by most witches. But it's also another tool that witchcraft borrowed from Ceremonial Magick, and not all traditions have adopted it. Regardless of this, it's widely used.

One of the Elemental tools, the pentacle is the primary earth symbol. As the centerpiece of the altar, all items are consecrated before it. Most pentacles are generally made of metal, heat-resistant ceramic, or marble and come in various sizes and colors. However, there is a growing trend among witches today to shift back to the old ways where the pentacle was carved from wood. For safety reasons, there was also a time when they were even made of wax so that they could easily be destroyed by throwing them in a fire, although this is hardly necessary anymore. The average size of the disk, or plate, is usually six to seven inches in diameter, though personal preference has led to nine-inch disks that are easier to work with. Like most of the tools mentioned, you can find a wide assortment of these items at any occult shop or mail-order catalog. You can also make your own very easily out of any number of readily available materials.

A pentacle will always have symbols on the disk face, which can be painted or engraved. The central marking is the upright pentagram, which is the symbol of the Craft. The Horned God symbol is usually placed on the middle-lower left side (when looking at the pentagram, this would be under the left "arm"), and on the right are the waxing and waning crescent moons of the Goddess. Furthermore, a coven pentacle will almost always contain a symbol that represents the coven or symbols that are specific to the coven's particular tradition.

Finally, some witches, especially solitary practitioners, add their initials, zodiac signs, gems, or other symbols that mean something special to them to personalize their pentacle. As with all the other tools in Witchcraft, the pentacle should represent you, and you should be comfortable using it.

Scissors

While scissors are only used by a handful of Wiccan denominations, they are still worth mentioning because they are another common household item that has been adapted to religious (magickal) use by shrewd witches. In modern Wicca, scissors are primarily used as a method of severing magickal connections and breaking spells. By holding the scissors in the air and cutting, a witch can symbolically shear through the ties that bind a spell. Other uses include cutting through objects used in magick, such as pictures or parchment. The only rules governing scissors is that they must not have been used for any evil purpose and they must be consecrated before use. Beyond that, any type will work.

Scourge

Like many of the other tools, the scourge has more than one use, and there are divided versions of its symbolism. The most common belief is that the scourge is a symbol of severity, though at times, it represents power and domination, or even purification and enlightenment.

In ancient times, the scourge (or a form thereof) was used to punish those who broke the coven rules. Today, since this violent practice is no longer enforced, the scourge serves mainly as a tool that is used for symbolic flagellation during the Initiation Ritual, as well as at other appropriate times. As with some of the other tools, the scourge is not used by all traditions. It's mainly used by Gardnerians and Gardnerian offshoots. Even among these traditions, the scourge is used infrequently.

Traditionally made of nut wood, the scourge is approximately fifteen to eighteen inches long. Fastened to one end are several lengths of knotted material. The number of lengths and the number of knots in each length will vary slightly depending on tradition. While the most common number of strands is eight, there can be anywhere from five to nine. Also, the number of knots in each strand is normally five, but this, too, can vary considerably. Silk, cotton, rope, or leather are a few types of materials that are often used. If necessary, synthetic materials will serve the purpose, but these should only be used as a last resort.

Shield

This ceremonial item is used in Saxon/Seax-Wica traditions. In Saxon Wicca, it is one of three items (shield, spear, and hunting horn) used by the Thegn, or ceremonial watcher, to guard the Circle and the coven.

The shield is an ornamental object that traces its roots back to ancient times. About two feet in diameter, the shield is usually circular in design and made of wood with a handle on the back. In ancient times, the wood was likely the strongest available, but modern shields are usually constructed of the lightest wood possible. Most shields are also covered with leather and decorated with the coven's coat of arms or seal.

Spear

This is a purely ceremonial tool used in Saxon/Seax-Wica traditions. In Saxon Wicca, it is the weapon of the Thegn, or ceremonial watcher, used to guard the Circle and the coven. In Ceremonial Magick, the spear is also known as a Short Lance.

Since the spear is not actually used for anything other than ornamental purposes, its construction is straightforward and simple. The spear's height is normally six feet with a metal head. The shaft is almost always wooden and usually made from oak or maple. Other than these basics, there are no special requirements.

Staff

Yet another type of Elemental tool, the staff was borrowed from Druidic practice by early Celtic Wiccans and used to represent authority. As a symbol of the element of earth, the staff combines power and knowledge into a single tool.

In buying or building a staff, there are several factors that must be considered. The first factor is height. Historically, the staff was measured by taking the height of the magician (or witch) and adding the length of his or her wand to get a final staff length. However, in more modern times, witches have modified these lengths to include staffs that are only shoulder high.

The second factor that is always considered when preparing a staff is the type of wood to be used.[6] In some Pagan faiths, trees are thought to be Middleworld bridges between the Overworld and the Underworld. They have their own life-force and share their bounty (i.e., fruit) with humans. Beyond that, trees have spirits that live within them (i.e., wood nymphs), as well as deities that they shelter (i.e., the Horned God, Pan, etc.). In other words, trees are very important to the Earth, its creatures, and the Gods. So deciding which tree to use becomes a big step. For this reason, most Wiccan traditions have their own recommendations concerning the type of wood to use for a staff. Although nut wood seems to be the most popular choice for a wand or scourge, many witches tend to favor rosewood, elder, or willow for staffs. In the absence of these varieties, a hardwood such as maple is also acceptable.

The third factor in preparing a staff is the cutting process. While the actual procedures differ from tradition to tradition, the most common belief involves cutting a virgin tree[7] during the waxing moon cycle and then allowing the wood to cure for an entire lunar cycle. Some denominations (such as Aridian and Italian) believe the curing process only needs nine days, though they have additional requirements for consecration.

Sword

While it may seem that the uses of some tools overlap, there are, nevertheless, distinct purposes for each. And the sword is no different. As previously pointed out, the sword is interchangeable with the athame for almost all ritual purposes such as casting the Magick Circle, banishing unwanted spirits, or for cutting the Handfasting cake.[8] Since it's so interchangeable with the athame, it's not an essential tool, and most witches do without a personal sword.

The sword, like the athame, is one of the Elemental tools that represents air or fire, depending on a tradition's beliefs, and virtually every path uses a sword for one reason or another.[9] Most covens like to have a sword as a symbol of coven identity and power, while reserving the athame as a symbol of the individual identity of each witch. At the same time, most solitary witches don't have a sword because of its cost and the fact that the athame serves just as well.

The design of the sword is completely a matter of personal choice, but a straight, narrow blade (often known as a gentleman's sword or dress blade) is probably the most suitable as it's light and easily maneuvered within the Magick Circle. In regard to the handle, black is the most appropriate color, but any dark color will do. It's also a good idea to keep the sword, like the athame, slightly dull and blunted for safety reasons. Also, if you decide to get a sword, remember that you'll need a scabbard and sash (or belt) to go with it since the sword is usually worn for ritual purposes.

Now, assuming that any sword you get will have been purchased, you should take the time to personalize and charge it. Simply engraving personal symbols or inscriptions is a good idea. If it's a coven sword, have everyone add something special.

Wand

The wand is another of the Elemental tools. Although it normally represents the element of air, some traditions view the wand as representing the element of fire and the athame the element of air. These two distinctly different views can be directly attributed to the amount of influence that Ceremonial Magick has had on each tradition, as a wand is customarily a magician's tool. Though less common, there are also some Wiccan denominations, such as Saxon Wicca, that use a staff instead of—or along with—a wand. These staffs share all the same characteristics as the wand, and in reality, the two are used for the same purposes.

A typical wand is approximately eighteen inches long, or the length of the forearm from elbow to fingertip. However, since this distance is not the same measurement on everyone, wands range in length from about fifteen to twenty inches. Regardless that the size is a personal choice, most people are comfortable with a wand between seventeen to eighteen inches long.[10] Many witches also add a precious or semiprecious gemstone to the wand's tip. Nowadays, many of the wands sold in occult shops have quartz or crystal tips, but these are really no better than the wooden ones.

While custom varies on just about every detail of making a wand, there are a few age-old practices that are fairly universal. First, the type of wood is very important. Most traditions suggest using a nut wood. Hazelnut seems to be the most popular, but walnut and chestnut are acceptable substitutes. In the absence of a nut wood, any fruit-bearing wood such as cherry or apple is fine. This is not to say that a hardwood such as maple, mahogany, or teak can't be used, but these varieties should be last resorts. However, all of these are just suggestions, and you can even make a wand by using a dowel from your local hardware store.

The second suggestion is about acquiring the wood. Along with the tips already given (see Staff), there is a practice that says the wood for a wand should be taken from a branch that has a fork in it; the symbolism being a representation of the human arm. In order to collect the wood, simply follow the recommendations concerning the best time and manner. If this is all too much for you, a fine selection of wands can be purchased. And, by buying a wand, you open up the range of materials to include metal and stone, which are both natural substances that more than serve the purpose.

The third suggestion—whether to engrave your wand with markings—is a matter of personal choice. If you decide to add engraving, try to use symbols that mean something special or somehow represent you. For instance, witches typically inscribe zodiac symbols to represent themselves and their family members, personal initials, names, and magickal symbols. Although this is all very simple, it's the little personal touches that make a wand special to its owner and therefore more comforting to use.

White-Handled Knife

There's a second knife frequently used by witches called the white-handled knife. In some Celtic traditions, this knife is also called the bolline.[11] Like the athame, this knife is another product of the influence that Ceremonial Magick has had on witchcraft. However, unlike the athame, this knife is not merely used for ritual purposes. Instead, this is the tool used for actual cutting, such as carving, inscribing, and engraving. Another difference between the two knives is that the white-handled knife can only be used inside the Magick Circle, and the blade must be kept sharp at all times. On the other hand, the athame can be used outside the Magick Circle, and its blade is usually kept dull. In place of the white-handled knife, some witches use a tool called a burin. This is nothing more than an engraving awl used for marking symbols.

While there is no standard for this knife other than having a "white" handle, it's best to use a smooth-edged, culinary-grade, kitchen knife. This type of knife has a stiff blade, cuts cleanly, and stays sharp even with heavy use. Cutlery shops have a wide variety of knives, and you'll probably be able to purchase your athame, white-handled knife, and sword at the same time. An interesting note is that as the revival of Earth-based religions has grown, some cutlery stores are carrying matching sets of these items, which are specifically designed with Pagan religions in mind.

In case you can't get a white-handled knife right away, you can use a kitchen knife as a substitute. However, you'll have to consecrate the knife before using it. Once it is consecrated, simply keep it separate from your other kitchen utensils as long as it's in use.

Altars

Regardless of the religion, the altar is the central point of every religious ceremony. In Wicca, it's the place where tools and accessories are kept, where items are purified, and where offerings are made to the Gods. Although a Wiccan altar may be nothing more than a table, a tree stump, or even a large stone with a flat top, its importance as the focal point within the Circle is not diminished.

Since there are differences in the basic altar setups used by various denominations,[1] the diagrams in this section will show examples of the proper placement of tools and accessories. These layouts will be the same for each ceremony, except that occasionally there will be an extra item or two added for a specific ritual. Comparing and contrasting the layouts will give you an idea of features that you may want to corporate into your own ceremonial setup.

Beyond tool placement, there are other points to keep in mind. While all witches know that it's important to be comfortable with their working tools, the significance of the altar itself should not be taken for granted. It's just as important to find a proper altar as it is to find a comfortable sword. Therefore, before settling on any old table, take a minute to consider practical needs. For instance, if you are trying to decide between using a coffee table or an antique piece of furniture, think about which one offers the most advantages. Drawers or shelves are helpful for storage, and they offer the advantage of having everything close at hand in case you forget something while setting up. Also, there are times when people may be kneeling in front of the altar while performing a rite. If the altar is too high, something to kneel on is needed.

When selecting an altar, a second point to keep in mind is: Don't use a piece of furniture that has negative energy stored up in it (a table used for food preparation where meat was cut, a desk where angry letters may have been written; etc.). Although it would be somewhat rare for the altar to have a considerable negative impact on a ritual, it can happen. Always remember that the altar is no different than any other tool. Just as you'd ensure that your personal athame wasn't used to butcher animals, you should do everything possible to ensure the neutrality of the altar.

ALTAR ARRANGEMENT

Before laying out a single tool, the first issue is to decide where the ceremony is going to be conducted. Once that's settled, select the location for the altar, then clear the area around this site. Remove any extra items, such as chairs and lamps, that are not going to be part of the ceremony.[2] Remember that the Magick Circle itself is usually nine feet in diameter, so make sure a large enough space has been cleared. Theoretically, the altar can be placed anywhere inside the Circle. Some witches use the northern edge, some use the southern edge, and some use the center. If the altar is placed in the center, arrange it so that everyone is facing north or east when working at it. Also keep in mind that you need enough room to walk completely around the altar without breaking the Circle.[3] This last point is an important one that many newer witches invariably seem to forget.

Altar cloths are also recommended. These coverings can be anything from a plain white sheet to a special ceremonial cloth, but natural materials such as cotton, silk, or wool are best. Depending on the tradition, some colors are used more than others. For instance, Celtic denominations generally prefer red or green cloths, while Aridian/Italian traditions prefer black because they feel that it symbolizes the darkness of procreation. It's also common to embroider, paint, or draw symbols and pictures on the cloth.

Perhaps the most important part of setting up the altar is the correct arrangement of tools and accessories. The diagrams (Figures 7.1–7.6), show that the denominations that employ a pentacle usually place it in the center of the altar, then set everything else within easy reach. This layout allows for the easiest access to all the items.[4] Similarly, Goddess/God statues and candles are normally positioned at the head of the altar. The rest of the items can be arranged in any convenient location, although a general pattern should be followed.

For instance, in Celtic Wicca the left side of the altar is devoted to the Goddess, and the items placed there are equated to her nurturing aspect. The right side is devoted to the God, and the items on this side reflect the God's power aspect. But other denominations do things differently.

The Science Tradition[5] devotes its altar layout to directing the flow of energy by using black/white candle placement and quartz protection crystals to establish conduits to properly channel the energies. On the other hand, Gardnerians adhere to a pattern that places tools in a location that offers the easiest access.[6] Therefore, individual altar layout will depend on a tradition's beliefs, or on the beliefs that a coven adopts.

In addition to the tools and accessories on the altar, there are several other items needed. These can be placed on a small table or, if the altar has drawers, kept inside. The following is a partial list of some of the most commonly used items:

- Cassette Player or CD Player (with music)
- Charcoal Incense Ring (for Censer)
- Flowers (with or without vase, depending on ritual)
- Four "Watchtower" Candles with Holders (only for traditions following this belief)[7]
- Herbs (depending on ritual requirements)[8]
- Incense (several scents)
- Libation Dish (only necessary for indoor rites)[9]
- Matches or Lighter
- Pen, Paper, Bottle, Candle, etc. (for spells, magick)
- Tapers (to light candles and for ritual use)

CELTIC TRADITION

Fig. 7.1

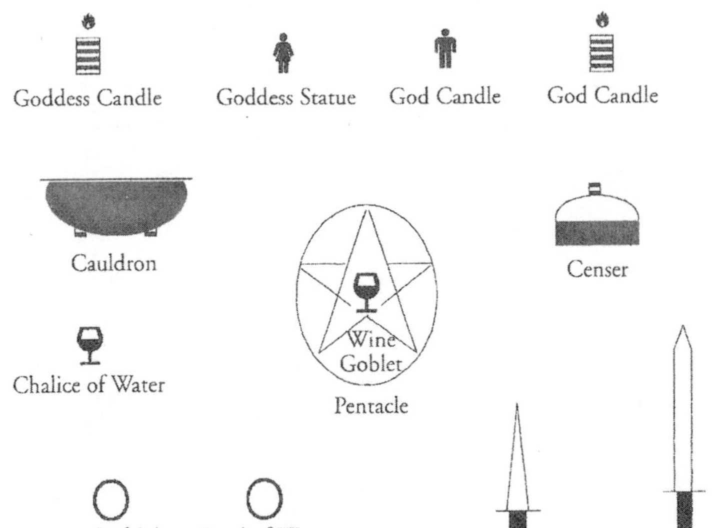

GARDNERIAN TRADITION

Fig. 7.2

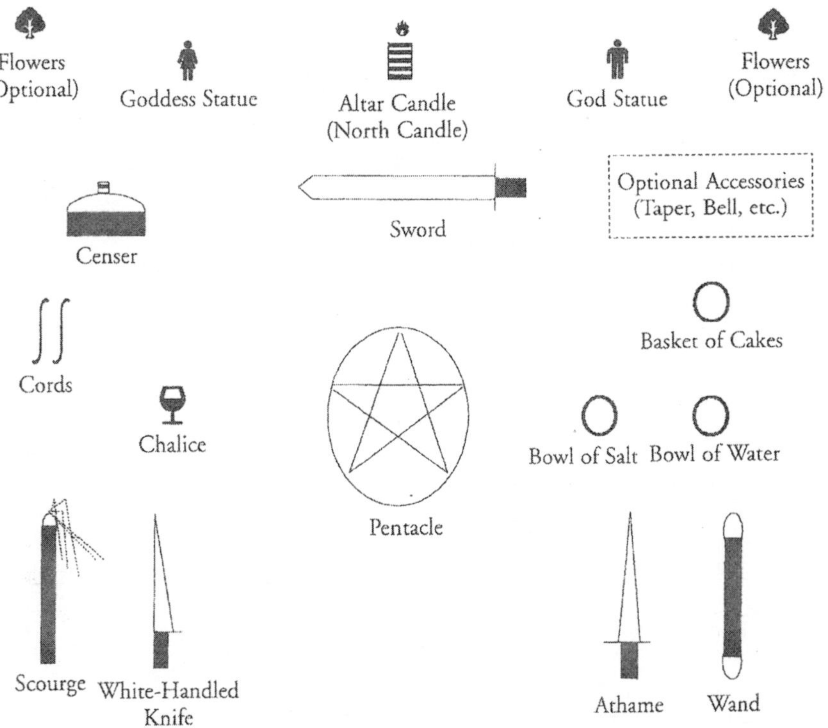

ITALIAN TRADITION *Fig. 7.3*

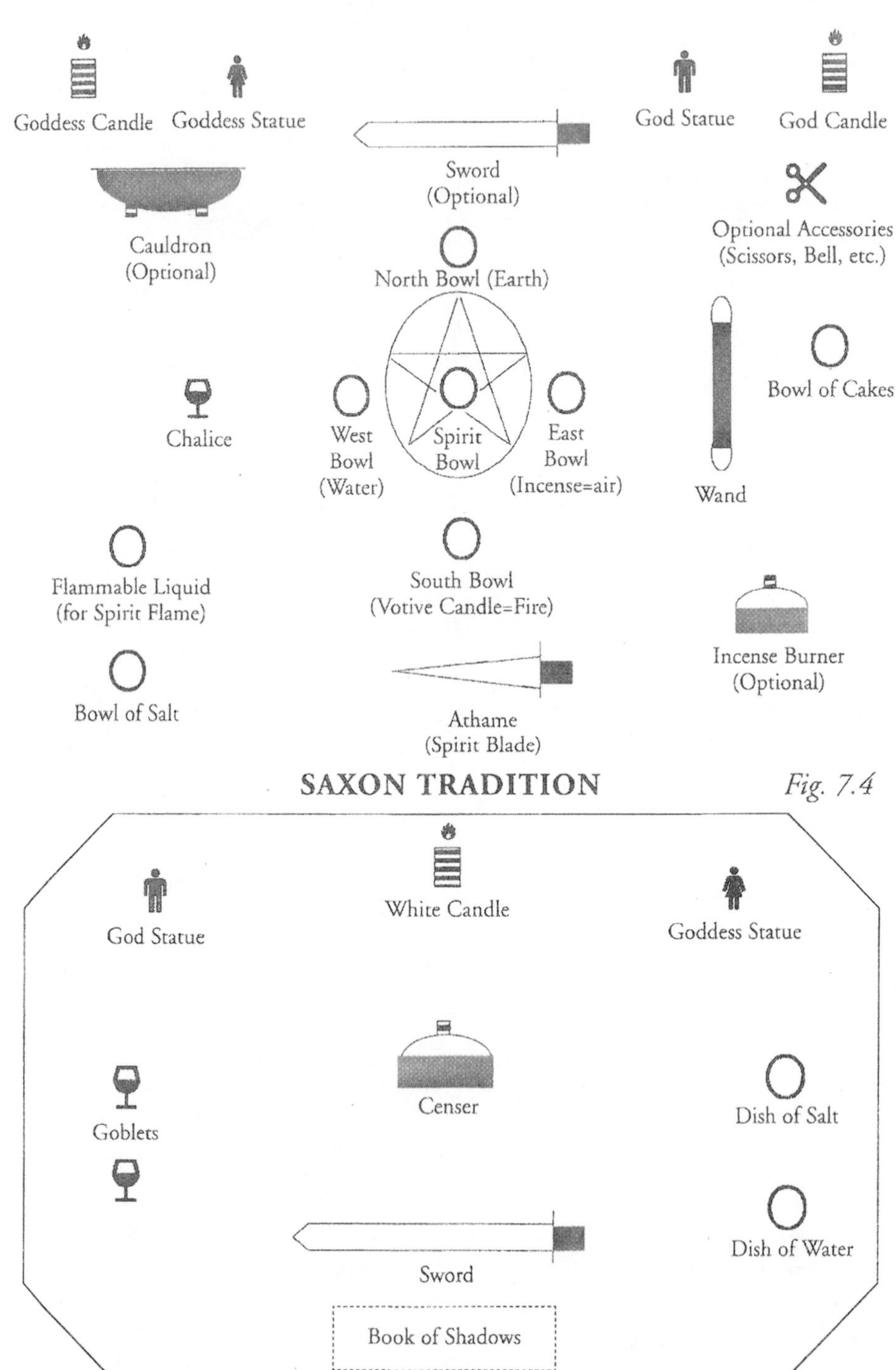

SCIENCE TRADITION

Fig. 7.5

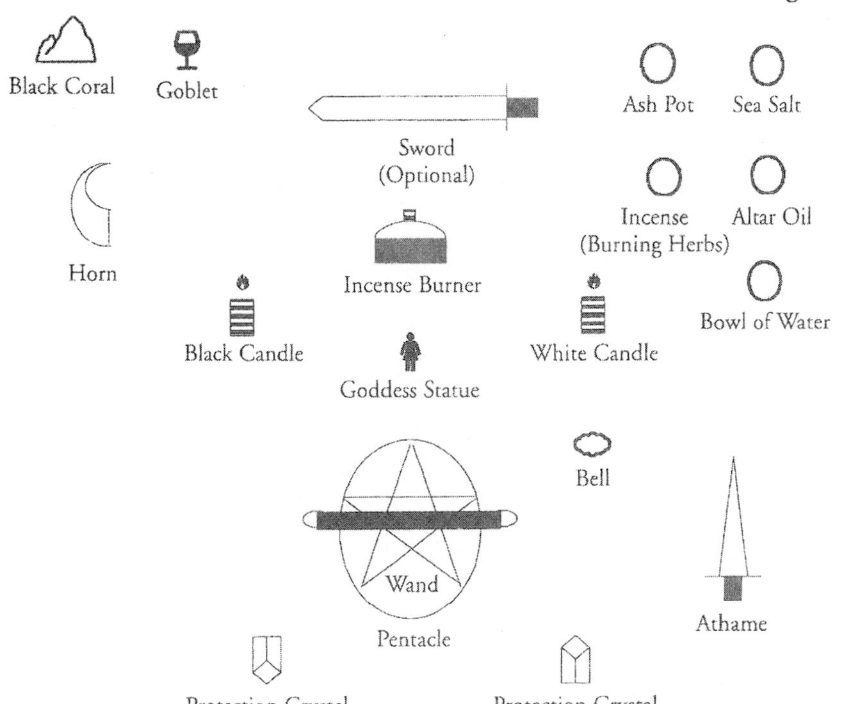

COUNTRY TRADITION

Fig. 7.6

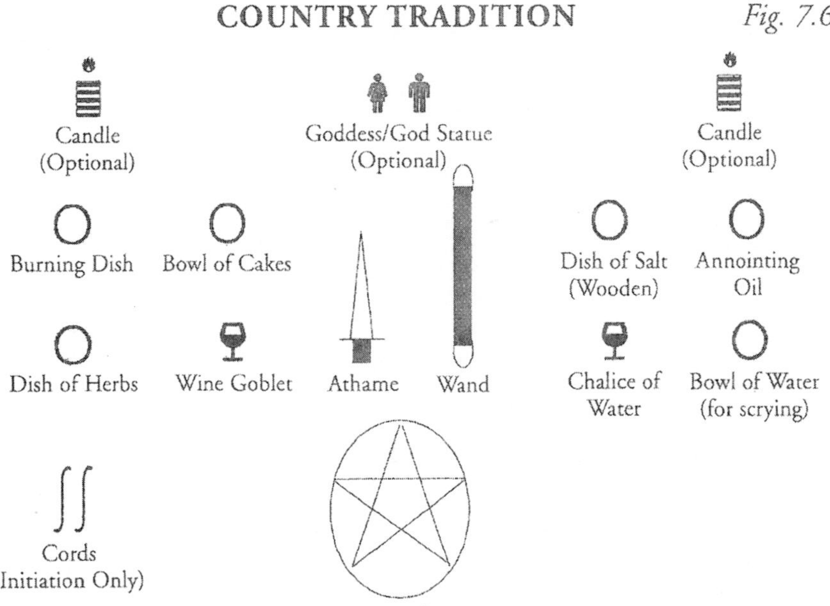

RITUALS

Magick Circle

Trying to list all the uses and meanings of the Magick Circle throughout the ages would open the floodgates of nonessential information. Still, a brief lesson on the Circle is insightful and necessary.

For nearly as long as mankind has been around, the Magick Circle has been used as a protective measure. It was used by many early cultures, from the ancient Greeks, Romans, and Norse to inhabitants of the Middle East, to protect them from sickness, harm, or to keep unwanted spirits away. Due to this widespread usage, and its place in Ceremonial Magick, the Circle became so deeply ingrained in Pagan practices that all modern traditions use it extensively.

In most Wiccan denominations, a standard-size Magick Circle is nine feet in diameter.[1] While this measurement is by no means a steadfast rule, it's usually large enough for a small coven or small enough for a solitary witch. Although the actual boundaries of the Magick Circle are defined during the casting ritual, it's commonplace to have a Circle outline painted, drawn, or etched on the floor. The outlines for outdoor Circles are usually just scratched in the ground.[2] Some witches create a more elaborate Magick Circle by drawing a second ring—one foot in diameter larger—around the outside of the first. Pentagrams are then drawn at the four quarters in the space between the two Circles—east, south, west, north—and a candle is placed on each pentagram.[3]

The Magick Circle, in both Wicca and Ceremonial Magick, has two purposes. First, it protects from malevolent outside forces, thereby allowing witches or magicians to control their surroundings. Second, it establishes a sacred space that acts like an invisible cover, serving to concentrate the power raised within its confines. This concentration of psychic energy creates the Cone of Power, which is a buildup of energy that allows a witch to perform spells. It's because of this that witches view the Magick Circle as the only place where spiritual and magickal work can be conducted, as well as a psychic sanctuary. Basically, it's the sacred spot that witches create to invite the Goddess and God to join them and a protected location where they can safely channel celestial and terrestrial energies.

CASTING THE CIRCLE

For most practicing witches, their earliest days in the Craft were probably spent trying to absorb as much as possible about the religion. All the tools, spells, incantations, and the wide assortment of concepts and beliefs most likely blended together. But if they were to think back to the beginning, there's a strong probability that one of the very first things they learned was how to cast a Magick Circle. And this holds true for anyone just starting to explore Wicca. Before anything else, it's essential to know how a Circle is cast. Therefore, the ritual known as Casting the Circle, Erecting the Temple, or simply the Opening Ritual, is the first step to becoming a witch.

Setup

At every esbat or sabbat, casting the Circle takes place before anything else. It's through this act that the sacred space is created. But there's more to properly casting a Magick Circle than simply running out and drawing a ring in the dirt. In fact, setting up to cast a Circle requires the same degree of preparation as any other rite.

First, the altar must be put in the proper location. This may differ slightly for different ceremonies. Once this is done, lay out all necessary tools and accessories on the altar according to the diagrams given in this book or by following the layout of a particular denomination. The Watchtower candles should also be ready since they're important for the Circle ritual. And depending on the tradition, the following items must also be on the altar: (1) the sword to cast the Circle; (2) the athame (seax, spirit blade, etc.) to consecrate the bowls of water and salt, or as a substitute for the sword; (3) the pentacle; (4) the censer with incense; and (5) the altar candle or a ceremonial candle. Only when this is prepared should the ceremony begin.

Gardnerian[4]

The rite begins with the High Priestess and High Priest kneeling before the altar with the pentacle directly in front of them and the bowls of water and salt close by. The High Priestess places the bowl of water on the pentacle and extends the tip of the athame into the water. She then recites the following words:

I exorcise thee, O creature of water, that thou cast out from thee all the impurities and uncleanliness of the spirits of the world of phantasm; in the names of Aradia and Cernunnos.[5]

The High Priestess puts down her athame and picks up the bowl with two hands and holds it in front of her. She closes her eyes and momentarily visualizes her energy extending out and purifying the water. Once she opens her eyes, the High Priest places the bowl of salt on the pentacle and puts the tip of the athame in the salt. He then recites the following words:

Blessings be upon this creature of salt; let all malignity and hindrance be cast forth hencefrom, and let all good enter herein; wherefor I bless thee, that thou mayest aid me, in the names of Aradia and Cernunnos.[5]

The High Priest puts down the athame and pours the bowl of salt into the bowl of water that the High Priestess is holding. (Optional: He then uses the tip of the athame to stir the water and salt until the salt is totally dissolved in the water. While stirring the water and salt mixture, the pair recite the following words: *In the names of Aradia and Cernunnos, I bless this water and salt, which has been cleansed and purified, that it will aid me in my task.*) The High Priestess places the bowl of water on the altar and picks up the sword (or the athame if there is no sword). Starting at the northernmost point, she begins drawing the Circle by walking deosil (in a counterclockwise direction) around the circumference with the tip of the sword/athame pointing at the ground where the Circle's edge should be. As she walks she recites the following words:

I conjure thee, O Circle of Power, that thou shalt be a meeting place of love and joy and truth; a shield against all wickedness and evil; a boundary between the world of men and the realms of the Mighty Ones; a rampart and protection that shall persevere and contain the power that is raised within thee. Wherefore do I bless thee and consecrate thee, in the names of Aradia and Cernunnos.

The coven members are then brought into the Circle by the High Priestess, who designates three witches to assist her. Each witch is given a task. The first witch takes the bowl of water/salt and walks deosil around the Circle sprinkling a few drops of water as he/she goes. Back at the starting point, the witch sprinkles the entire coven and places the bowl back on the altar. The second witch picks up the smoking censer, walks deosil around the Circle (if the censer is on a chain, it should be swung back and forth to disperse the smoke), then puts it down. The third witch picks up the altar candle and carries it around the Circle. When this procession is completed, the High Priestess leads the coven in setting the Watchtowers.

The coven members hold their athames and face east while reciting the following words:

> *Lords of the Watchtowers of the East, Lords of the Air, we summon and call you up to witness our rites and to guard this sacred Circle.* (Additional wording when Watchtower candles are used: *As this temple is lit in the East, so it shall be filled with the sacred Element of Air.* Then the candle is lit.)[6]

The High Priestess takes her athame and draws the Invoking Pentagram of Earth[7] in the air in front of her, kisses the tip, and presses it to her heart. (Figure 8.1.) The High Priest and the coven follow along with the High Priestess and mirror her movements.

INVOKING PENTAGRAM OF EARTH *Fig. 8.1*

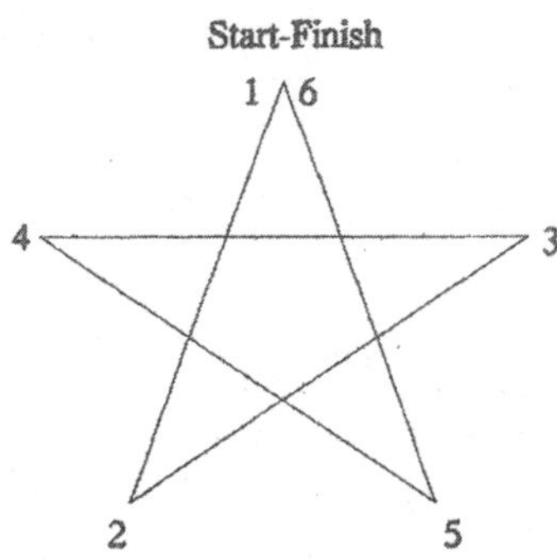

The High Priestess and coven turn to the south and repeat the process, reciting:

> *Lords of the Watchtowers of the South, Lords of Fire, we summon and call you up to witness our rites and to guard this sacred Circle.* (Additional wording when Watchtower candles are used: *As this temple is lit in the South, so it shall be filled with the sacred Element of Fire.* The candle is lit.)

The High Priestess and coven, turn to the west and repeat the process, reciting:

> *Lords of the Watchtowers of the West, Lords of Water, Lords of Death and Initiation, we summon and call you up to witness our rites and to guard this sacred Circle.* (Additional wording when Watchtower candles are used: *As this temple is lit in the West, so it shall be filled with the sacred Element of Water.* The candle is lit.)

The High Priestess and coven turn to the north and repeat the process, reciting:

> *Lords of the Watchtowers of the North, Lords of the Earth, guardian of the Northern portals, powerful God and gentle Goddess, we summon and call you up to witness our rites and to guard this sacred Circle.* (Additional wording when Watchtower candles are used: *As this temple is lit in the North, so it shall be filled with the sacred Element of Earth.* The candle is lit unless the altar candle is doubling as the North Watchtower, in which case it's already lit.)

The coven members put away their athames. The Circle is now complete.

Italian

Most Italian denominations begin by marking the circumference of the Circle, setting the white Grigori (Watchtower) candles in place, and purifying the area with consecrated water.[8] This technique differs greatly from Wiccan traditions, which make the salt/water purifying aspect a major part of the rite. After the area is purified, the altar is laid out.

The ceremony commences when the High Priest/ess lights the spirit bowl. S/he then lights the altar candles and recites:

Diana, Goddess of the Moon; Dianus, God of the Sun, we gather together and call your holy names.

The High Priest/ess rings the bell over each Elemental bowl, beginning with the north, and recites:

I conjure you, Spirits of the Earth . . . (Air, Fire, Water). Grace us with your presence within this sacred Circle and grant us unity with your powers.

The spirit blade (athame) is touched to each Elemental bowl three times then drawn through the spirit flame. The goal of these actions is to charge the spirit blade with the Elemental powers. Once this is done, the High Priest/ess walks along the edge of the Circle, with the spirit blade pointed at the Circle's border, visualizing the spirit flame projecting from the blade's tip. As s/he walks, the following words are recited:

I conjure this Circle to become a vessel to contain the power which shall be raised within, and which shall serve to protect the rites held within its confines as we honor the Old Gods; Diana and Dianus.

A procession now takes place. A witch takes a taper and uses it to light the Grigori candles; the taper is lit from the spirit flame.[9] A second witch carries the censer and passes it back and forth (three times) in front of each quarter. After the last pass, a third witch rings the bell (a hunting horn can also be blown) three times. As each series occurs, the High Priest/ess recites:

We call upon you, the Ancient Ones who dwell in unseen realms of glory. Come! Hear our call! Come forth and aid us by granting us the use of your endless powers.

The High Priest/ess taps the wand on the altar three times. The Circle is cast.

Saxon

After the Circle is marked out, unlit candles are placed at the cardinal points as follows: yellow to the east, red to the south, blue to the west, and green to the north. The altar is set up in the center of the Circle facing east. If so desired, two white altar candles may be used instead of one. The Priestess and Priest (coven leaders), with the coven trailing behind, enter the Circle from the east and stand facing the altar. The Priest lights the altar candles then hands one to the Priestess. Customarily, the Thegn says the next passage, but the Priest can also do it. The Thegn recites:

The Temple is about to be erected. Let all within this Temple be here of their own free will and accord in peace, love and harmony.

The Priest and Priestess take the altar candles and starting in the east, move deosil to the first candle. The Priestess uses her altar candle to light the East Watchtower. She recites:

I bring light and air into this Circle at the east to illuminate the temple and give it a breath of life.

The pair proceeds to the south point where the Priest lights the candle and recites:[10]

I bring light and fire into this Circle at the south to illuminate the temple and bring it warmth.

They proceed to the west point where the Priestess lights the candle and recites:

I bring light and water into this Circle at the west to illuminate the temple and cleanse it.

The pair ends at the north point where the Priest lights the candle and recites:

I bring light and earth into this Circle at the north to illuminate the temple and give it strength.

The Priest and Priestess return the candles to the altar. The Priestess takes the sword and walks deosil around the Circle's circumference with the tip pointed downward tracing the baseline; it doesn't have to actually touch the ground. Once she's completed an entire revolution, she returns to the altar. She takes her seax and places the tip in the dish of salt and recites:

Salt is Life. Let this salt be pure and let it purify and cleanse our lives, bodies and spirits as we use it in these rites which we dedicate to Woden and Frig.

The Priestess dips her seax into the salt and transfers three portions (whatever amount stays on the blade) into the bowl of water. She uses her seax to stir the water while reciting:

Let the Sacred Salt drive out any impurities in this water that it may be used throughout these rites as we honor and service Woden and Frig.

The Priestess puts down her seax and picks up the bowl of water. In the same pattern that she followed with the sword, she walks around the Circle sprinkling drops of the consecrated water. She returns the bowl to the altar and repeats the process with the smoking censer.

When this is completed, she places the censer in its place and returns to stand next to the Priest. She dips her fingers into the water and anoints the Priest's chest with a pentagram, then the two kiss. The Priest repeats the process to the Priestess. When both are consecrated, the Priest calls forth the male witches one at a time. As each witch approaches the altar, the Priestess dips her fingers into the water and anoints the witch's chest with a pentagram. The two kiss, and the next witch steps forward. Once all the male witches have completed this process, the Priestess calls forth the female witches, and the Priest anoints them in the same manner. When the entire coven has been consecrated, the Priest recites:

Let us now invite Woden and Frig to our Circle to witness these rites that we are about to hold in their honor.

The Priestess holds the sword in front of her while the coven hold their seaxes; all face the center of the Circle. She recites:

Lord and Lady; God and Goddess; Mother and Father of all life; we invite you to join us in our rites. Guard us within this Circle and guide us in all that we do in your honor. So be it.[11]

Coven repeats: *So be it.*

Everyone kisses the blade of his or her seax and then sheaths it. The Priestess kisses the blade of the sword and places it on the altar. The Priest and Priestess pick up the goblets and spill a few drops of the wine into a libation dish or directly onto the ground if outdoors. As they make the offering, the pair recites:

Hail to Woden and Frig.

The Thegn (or Priest) then recites:

The Circle is cast and the temple is erected. Let none leave but with good reason until the Gods have been thanked and the temple has been cleared. So be it.

Coven repeats: *So be it.*

West Country

The West Country rite is so similar to the Gardnerian version that there's no need to list the two separately. However, this close resemblance raises two interesting questions. Did one tradition copy the other? Did both denominations originate from the same ancient source?

Solitary Rite

This is a Gardnerian-based Circle casting ceremony that was originally designed to deal with the problem of pre-initiation[12] ritualistic space for a person who wanted to become a witch, but didn't have access to a coven. With minor variations, a slightly modified version is used by many "initiated" solitary witches.

Mark the Circle, set up the altar, put the Watchtower candles in place, then light the altar candle. Use a taper lit from the altar candle to light each Watchtower. As the east candle is lit, recite:

Lords of the Watchtowers of the East, Lords of the Air, I beckon you to bear witness to these rites, and to watch over me as I venture forth for the first time and cast this sacred Circle. As my temple is lit in the East, so it shall be filled with the sacred Element of Air.

As the south candle is lit, recite:

Lords of the Watchtowers of the South, Lords of the Fire, I beckon you to bear witness to these rites, and to watch over me as I venture forth for the first time and cast this sacred Circle. As my temple is lit in the South, so it shall be filled with the sacred Element of Fire.

As the west candle is lit, recite:

Lords of the Watchtowers of the West, Lords of the Water, I beckon you to bear witness to these rites, and to watch over me as I venture forth for the first time and cast this sacred Circle. As my temple is lit in the West, so it shall be filled with the sacred Element of Water.

As the north candle is lit, recite:

Lords of the Watchtowers of the North, Lords of the Earth, I beckon you to bear witness to these rites, and to watch over me as I venture forth for the first time and cast this sacred Circle. As my temple is lit in the North, so it shall be filled with the sacred Element of Earth.

Return to the altar and place the bowl of water on the pentacle. (Since you don't have consecrated tools, you'll have to use substitutes to purify the water and salt, as well as to actually cast the Circle. Your index finger will work fine for the time being in place of the sword, athame, or wand. The key to this substitution is visualizing your inner power coursing through your body, down your arm, and projecting from the tip of your extended finger.) Place the tip of your index finger into the water. Recite:

I cast out from these waters all that is unclean of spirit, and all that I know to be impure, and I bless the purity that remains in the name of the Goddess, and in the name of the God.[13]

Using your other hand, pick up the bowl of water, close your eyes, and visualize your inner energy extending down your arm and into the water. Put the bowl of water down and place the bowl of salt on the pentacle. Place your index finger in the salt and recite:

I cast out from this salt all that is unclean of spirit, and all that I know to be impure, and I bless the purity that remains in the name of the Goddess, and in the name of the God.

Repeat the process of picking up the bowl of salt and visualizing your energy purifying it. Put down the bowl of salt, and return the bowl of water to the pentacle. Pour the salt into the water, and use the tip of your finger to stir the water/salt. Stir the mixture and recite:

In the names of Goddess and God, I bless this water and salt, which is cleansed and pure, that it will aid me in my task.

You're now going to draw the Circle. Using your index finger like a pointer, begin walking deosil around the circumference of the Circle with the tip of your finger pointing at the ground where the rim should be. Start at the northernmost point and end at the same point, remembering to make certain that the Watchtowers are situated on the boundaries, yet not breaking the plane. As you begin to walk, recite:

I conjure forth the Circle of Power, that it shall protect me from harm; that it shall shield me from wickedness and evil; that it shall provide me a sanctuary of love, joy, and serenity; that it shall bring me into the realms of the Old Gods; and that it shall contain and channel the powers that I raise within. I bless and consecrate this Circle in the names of the Goddess and the God.

Pick up the bowl of water/salt and walk deosil around the Circle sprinkling a few drops of water as you go. When you get back to the point where you started, sprinkle yourself with a few drops of the water. If you have a censer, carry it around the Circle, then take the altar candle and repeat the pattern. The Circle is now complete.

BANISHING THE CIRCLE

If Casting the Circle is the first ritual that all witches learn, banishing the Circle is the second. That's because it's just as important to banish the Magick Circle as it is to cast it. Also known as the Closing Ritual, or Clearing the Temple, this is the last step at every esbat or sabbat. The sole purpose of this rite is to dissipate the sacred space, and its energy, which was created when the Circle was erected.[14]

While there's no special requirement for this rite, since the Magick Circle is already erected, there are a few things to keep in mind. First, it's wise to be careful with any newly consecrated items (e.g., tools, jewelry) when banishing the Circle.

In a coven, the High Priest/Priestess will instruct one of the members to carry the newly consecrated objects and remain safely behind him/her as the banishing is conducted. This isn't possible for a solitary witch. Therefore, Solitaries must remember to keep the items behind, or directly beneath, them at all times during the rite. The main goal is to stop the Banishing Pentagram from having any adverse or neutralizing effect on the consecrated objects.

Second, during indoor ceremonies when offerings (cakes and wine) to the Mother Earth are saved, they must be kept away from the banishing effects in the same manner as other consecrated items.

Third, far too many witches get to this point and then just breeze through this rite as if it were an inconvenience or afterthought. Remember, every rite is an act of reverence to the Goddess and God and should be treated as such.

Gardnerian

The rite begins with the High Priest and High Priestess facing east. The coven lines up in an arc behind them.[15] There is a designated witch[16] who is ready to blow out the Watchtower candles as each is banished. The High Priestess recites:

> *Lords of the Watchtowers of the East, Lords of the Air, we thank you for attending our rites and protecting our Circle. As you depart to your pleasant and lovely realms, we bid you hail and farewell.*

The High Priestess, using her athame, draws the Banishing Pentagram of Earth (Figure 8.2)[17] in the air; kisses the tip of the athame, and presses it to her heart. The High Priest and the coven mirror her movements. When the last stroke of the Banishing Pentagram is completed, all recite: *Hail and Farewell.*

BANISHING PENTAGRAM OF EARTH *Fig. 8.2*

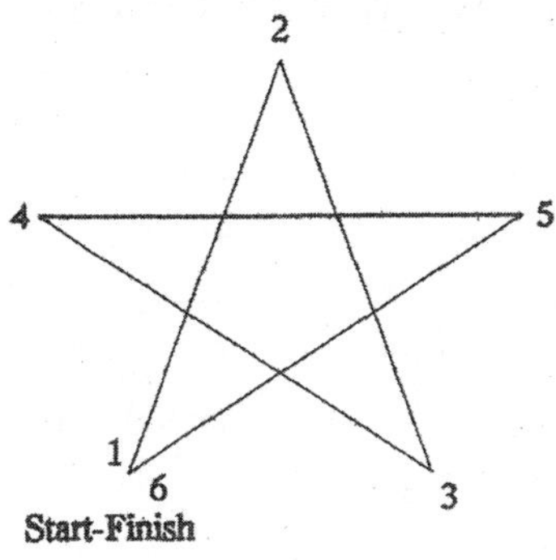

The Maiden blows out the east candle. The entire congregation proceeds toward the south Watchtower. They repeat the process, and the High Priestess recites:

> *Lords of the Watchtowers of the South, Lords of Fire, we thank you for attending our rites and protecting our Circle. As you depart to your pleasant and lovely realms, we bid you hail and farewell.*

Again, the Banishing Pentagram is drawn, the athame is kissed, and the coven recites, *"Hail and Farewell."* The Maiden blows out the south candle, and everyone moves to the west Watchtower where the process continues:

Lords of the Watchtowers of the West, Lords of Water, Lords of Death and Initiation, we thank you for attending our rites and protecting our Circle. As you depart to your pleasant and lovely realms, we bid you hail and farewell.

The gestures are repeated a third time, and the west candle is blown out. Finally, the coven proceeds to the north Watchtower candle. The same process is repeated, and the following words are recited:

Lords of the Watchtowers of the North, Lords of the Earth, guardians of the Northern portals, powerful God and gentle Goddess, we thank you for attending our rites and protecting our Circle. As you depart to your pleasant and lovely realms, we bid you hail and farewell.

The Maiden blows out the north candle.[18] The High Priestess lowers her athame (or places it on the altar), turns to face the coven, and recites:

The Goddess and God have gone, the Lords of the Four Quarters have departed, and this rite is done. All may now leave in peace, joy, and love.

The Circle has been banished. Tools can be put away and the area cleaned. If the ceremony was held outdoors, make absolutely certain that there are no smoldering ashes or coals left if you had a bonfire. Also, don't forget to also make sure that the charcoal ring in the censer is extinguished. Finally, if cakes/wine were saved as an offering, now is the time to take the offering outside.

Italian

While the Gardnerian banishing ritual is fairly complex, the Italian rite is quite simple. The ritual begins with the High Priestess in the Position of Power (Figure 8.3).[19] She stands facing the north quarter, spirit blade in her right hand, wand in her left, and arms held straight out approximately shoulder high. With the coven gathered behind her, the High Priestess recites:

Hear me, Diana and Dianus, as we honor and praise you for attending our Circle. We bid you now to depart for your secret realms, that you may again come when we call. With peace and love, we say; Ave, Vale.

The coven repeats: *Ave, Vale.*

POSITION OF POWER *Fig. 8.3*

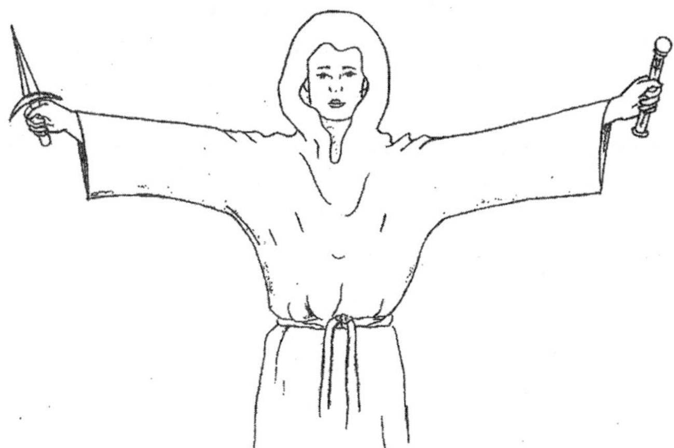

At the other three cardinal points, the same line is repeated. Once this is done, the High Priestess takes the spirit blade and retraces drawing the Circle. However, this time she envisions the spirit flame being drawn back into the spirit blade. She then goes to the altar and places the tip of the spirit blade into the spirit flame, thereby allowing the blade to discharge the flame back into the spirit bowl. After a moment or two, she takes the spirit blade and passes it over the Elemental bowls (three times) to dissipate the elements.

The ritual is completed. Blow out the Watchtower candles, the altar candles, and extinguish the spirit flame. The Circle is banished.

Saxon

This denomination has the briefest banishing ritual of all Wiccan traditions. Despite its brevity, it still possesses the same general qualities of more lengthy rites. In order to accomplish a successful banishing using a far less complex ceremony, Saxon witches understand the key lies with the individuals. To this end, they accept that each witch must remain extremely focused on the goal of releasing the energy that was raised, dispersing the sacred space, and thanking the Gods.

The rite begins with the Priestess standing with her back to the altar facing the coven. The coven is fanned out in an arc facing her. She recites:

The time has come for us to part. Let the love that we have shared go with us until we come together once more in this Circle.

The Priestess turns to face the altar. She picks up the sword and holds it in front of her; the hilt should be at eye level. The coven stands in an arc behind her and copies her movements with their seaxes. The Priestess recites:

We give thanks to Woden and Frig for guarding over us, and for guiding us in our rites. As we leave this Circle and go our separate ways, we shall be mindful that Love is the Law, and Love is the Bond.

Coven repeats: *Love is the Law, and Love is the Bond.*

The Priestess lowers the sword, and the coven lower their seaxes.[20] The Thegn steps forward, blows out the altar candle, then recites:

The Temple is now cleared. So be it.

The Circle is banished and the rite is over.

West Country

Because the banishing rite of this denomination is very similar to the Gardnerian ceremony, there's no need to repeat the procedure. But it again raises questions about the roots of the two traditions.

Invoking the Gods

To ensure Divine assistance in workings, rites, or any religious matter, it's essential to invite the Goddess and God into the ritual area. This is accomplished by asking the particular deity being invoked to descend into a willing human receptacle, the High Priest or High Priestess. However, the process of invoking is a request to the deity and should not be confused with the act of evoking, or commanding, a spiritual being appear. Higher beings are invoked, lesser beings are evoked.

DRAWING DOWN THE MOON

In many Wiccan denominations, the ritual of Drawing Down the Moon, or Invoking the Goddess, is an important part of the Opening ceremony. This rite involves the process by which the High Priest invokes the spirit of the Goddess into the High Priestess, who then acts as a conduit for the Goddess to enter the Circle. While this wasn't always something that all witches accepted, in modern Wiccan practice, it's become fairly popular due to its widespread usage. Still, not all traditions celebrate this rite. For those that do, under normal circumstances, the rite is performed as part of the Opening. Therefore, no special setup is required. But, like anything else, there are exceptions to everything.[1]

Gardnerian

Once the Circle is cast and the Watchtowers set, the rite starts with the High Priestess standing in front of the altar facing the coven. The coven should be spread in an arc along the opposite edge of the Circle. The High Priestess should be holding a wand in her right hand and a scourge in her left.[2] Her arms are crossed against her chest, and she crosses the shafts of the wand and scourge in order to form the Osiris Position (Figure 9.1).[3] The High Priest then kneels at her feet.

OSIRIS POSITION *Fig. 9.1*

The High Priestess opens her arms to receive the Fivefold Kiss (Figure 9.2),[4] and the High Priest begins by kneeling in front of the High Priestess. He kisses her on the right foot, then the left foot, the right knee, then the left knee, the womb, the right breast, then the left breast, and finally on the lips while the two embrace. After each series of kisses (feet, knees, etc.), the High Priest recites:

Blessed be your feet, that have brought you down this path.
Blessed be your knees, that shall bend before the sacred altar.
Blessed be your womb, without which we would not be.
Blessed be your breasts, formed in beauty.
Blessed be your lips, that speak the names of Aradia and Cernunnos.

FIVEFOLD KISS *Fig. 9.2*

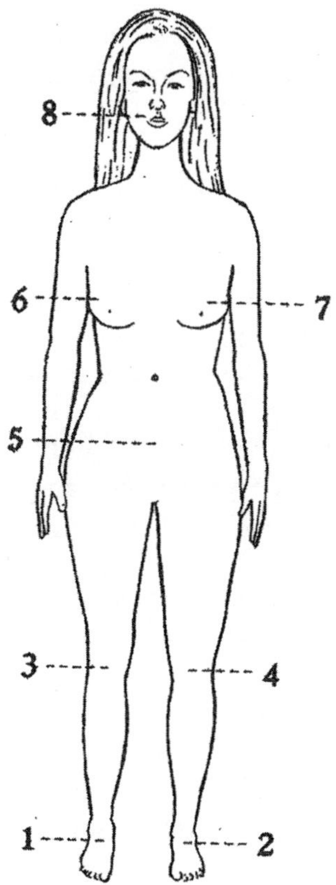

After the kisses, the High Priest returns to his knees before the High Priestess; she must shift her right foot slightly forward. The High Priest begins the invocation by reciting:

> *I invoke and call upon thee, O' Merciful Goddess, Mother to us all, bringer of all fruitfulness; by seed and root, by bud and stem, by leaf and flower and fruit, by life and love do I invoke thee to descend unto the body of your servant that stands before me. Come to us, O' Merciful Goddess Aradia, and bless us with your presence.*

The High Priest uses his right index finger and touches the High Priestess on the lips, then on the left hip, then the right breast, then the left breast, the right hip, and finally back to the lips, thus creating the Invoking Pentagram of Earth.[5] The High Priest repeats this sequence two more times. Next, the High Priest spreads his arms outward, with his palms facing the High Priestess, and continues the invocation by reciting:

> *Hail, Goddess Aradia. I bow before you* (The High Priest kneels and continues) *as your divine presence fills this sacred Circle with overflowing love.*

The High Priest kisses the right foot of the High Priestess and continues:

> *My lips upon your foot show my devotion that you may know the love I have for you; that you may see that I am lost without your guidance; and that you may come to aid me at this special time.*[6]

The High Priest stands, bows slightly, and takes a step back from the High Priestess. She takes her wand and draws the Invoking Pentagram of Earth in the air between herself and the High Priest, and recites:

> *I come in answer to your call. Look now upon me and see the love that I bring to you. With this sign, I charge you and lend my aid to your Circle.*[7]

The High Priestess turns and puts the wand and scourge on the altar. Once these items are on the altar, the rite is complete, and the Charge follows immediately. An exception to this sequence would be the rite of Drawing Down the Sun. If this ritual were also being conducted, the Charge is administered after its completion.

Italian

This denomination does not perform the Invocation of the Goddess at every esbat, instead reserves the act for special occasions. Because of its infrequent usage, the rite is far less complex than its Gardnerian counterpart. Also, the rite is known as Calling Down the Moon. The process of "drawing down the moon" is something entirely different. This discrepancy results from the fact that "Calling" refers to invoking the Goddess, while "drawing" refers to absorbing the power (or light) of the moon. The difference exists because the moon is a symbol of the Goddess, but it's not actually the Goddess. At the same time, however, the moon has its own power.

The ritual begins with the High Priestess standing at the altar facing east. Her arms are by her sides, but her palms are turned forward. The High Priest, with a wand in his right hand, kneels in front of the High Priestess. Using the wand, he lightly touches the High Priestess on the right breast, left breast, pubic area (womb), and right breast again.[8] The High Priest then recites:

Diana, Goddess of the Moon, Queen of the Heavens, hear me at this time of need. I call upon you to come into this Circle. Appear before me, lovely Diana.

The High Priestess now raises her arms, palms pointed upward, and looks upwards. The High Priest recites:

Diana, Goddess of beauty and love, as your Priestess welcomes you with upraised arms, I invoke you to descend upon us and lend your power to this rite.

The High Priest bows his head. Silence is observed for a moment while the High Priestess receives the Goddess. At this point in most Wiccan ceremonies, the Fivefold Salute would be given. However, the Italian tradition does not follow this pattern, and no salute is used. Instead, after the moment of silence, the High Priest simply stands up, and the ceremony progresses onto the sabbat rituals or the working portion of the esbat.

West Country

Although this tradition practices a short Drawing Down rite, its method of invoking the Goddess is, nevertheless, uncommon. The Priest must first draw the God into himself before invoking the Goddess into the Priestess.[9] Beyond that, the basic objective of the rite itself is held in higher esteem than in other denominations. While most traditions believe that Drawing Down the Moon brings the power of the Goddess into the Circle and gives the Priestess wisdom and insight, West Country witches maintain that this ritual channels the Goddess through the Priestess so that she becomes a conduit for the Goddess to actively participate in the ceremony. The difference is that the West Country rite doesn't just aim at invoking the essence of the Goddess, but rather strives to invoke the Goddess herself.

To begin the rite the Priestess should stand facing south.[10] The Priest stands in front of the Priestess, facing her. He raises his arms and silently invokes the God. Once he feels the God's presence, he places his hands on the shoulders of the Priestess and recites:

O' Gracious and loving Goddess, behold thy daughter (Priestess' name) *who comes forth to receive thy blessing. Descend upon her, that she may share thy power and knowledge. Join with her now, that she may see the mysteries which are hidden, and that she may know the wisdom of the ages. Come; enter thy Priestess* (name)*; and grace us with thy presence.*

The Priest kneels in front of the Priestess (if the dish of water is there he moves it) and proceeds to give her the Fivefold Salute. He kisses the Priestess on each foot, each knee, above the pubic area (or on the womb), each breast, and finally on the lips.[11] After the series of kisses, the pair embraces, and the Priest recites:

I salute you with blessings upon your body and spirit.

After the embrace, the pair reverses positions, and the Priestess gives the salute to the Priest. When this is done, the rite is complete. A chant and dance usually follow.

DRAWING DOWN THE SUN

Drawing Down the Sun, or Invoking the God, is similar in many respects to Drawing Down the Moon, except the essence of the God is now being invoked into the Priest.[12] As with Drawing Down the Moon, this is not a rite that all traditions follow. In recent years, this, too, has become fairly popular because of a heightened interest in balancing the male and female polarities. However, this rite should not be confused with the Gardnerian "Invocation to the Great God Cernunnos," as it is not a substitute.

Gardnerian

This rite starts with the High Priest standing with his back to the altar, facing the coven, which is spread in an arc along the opposite edge of the Circle. The High Priest should be holding his athame with a two-handed grip.[13] The athame should be pointing upward, and the hands should be positioned in the middle of the chest.[14]

The High Priestess kneels in front of the High Priest and begins to give him the Fivefold Kiss. The sequence of kisses are: the right foot, the left foot, the right knee, left knee, the area above the public region,[15] the right breast, left breast, and finally on the lips while the two embrace. After each series of kisses (feet, knees, etc.), the High Priestess recites:

Blessed be your feet, that have brought you down this path.
Blessed be your knees, that shall bend before the sacred altar.
Blessed be your phallus,[16] *without which we would not be.*
Blessed be your breasts, formed in strength.[16]
Blessed be your lips, that speak the names of Aradia and Cernunnos.

After the kisses, the High Priestess returns to her knees before the High Priest and begins the invocation by reciting:

As the Goddess calls upon the God to strengthen her, so do I call upon your servant and Priest to strengthen me.

The High Priestess then uses her right index finger and touches the High Priest on the lips, the right hip, the left breast, the right breast, the left hip, and finally back to the lips, thus creating the Invoking Pentagram of Fire.[17] This sequence is repeated two more times. The High Priestess spreads her arms outward, palms facing the High Priest, and continues the invocation by reciting:

In the name of the Goddess Aradia, I invoke and call upon thee, O' Mighty God Cernunnos, Father to us all. Come in answer to my call. Descend unto thy servant and Priest, that he may share your power and strengthen this sacred Circle.

The High Priestess stands and takes a step backwards. The High Priest takes his athame and draws the Invoking Pentagram of Fire in the space between himself and the High Priestess. After drawing the Invoking Pentagram, the High Priest raises his arms and recites:

I come in answer to your call. Look now upon me and see the strength and love that I bring with my divine presence. With this sign, my Spirit lights the way. Let there be light.[18]

The High Priest turns and puts the athame on the altar. This is the completion of the rite. In the traditions that perform the rite, the Charge follows immediately after its completion.

West Country

As seen in Drawing Down the Moon, this denomination invokes the God into the Priest prior to him invoking the Goddess into the Priestess. But unlike traditions that have a specific ritual for this purpose (i.e.,

Gardnerian, Alexandrian), West Country does not have a set rite. Instead, the Priest invokes the God into himself by silently reciting a short prayer (or invocation) in which he asks the God to join with him. The words used for this invocation are usually very simple, and the Priest often makes up the prayer on the spot rather than reciting a prepared verse.

Declamations

Wiccans have two general speeches that are given after the Goddess or God have been invoked. One address is given by the High Priest and another by the High Priestess. These speeches are known as the Charge of the Goddess and the Invocation of the God.

CHARGE OF THE GODDESS

In the denominations that use it (Gardnerian, Italian, etc.), the Charge is the Goddess' speech to her followers. The uniqueness of this oration is that it's administered by the High Priestess after Drawing Down the Moon, when the spirit of the Goddess has been invoked into her. In other words, the High Priestess' address takes on a divine aura due to the presence of the essence of the Goddess.

Gardnerian

The Charge begins after Drawing Down the Moon.[1] The High Priestess faces the coven; if she's still holding the wand and scourge, she places them on the altar. The High Priest stands next to the High Priestess and recites:

> *Listen to the words of the Great Mother, she who of old was called among men, Artemis, Astarte, Dione, Melusine, Aphrodite, Cerridwen, Diana, Arianrhod, Isis, Bride, and by many other names. At her altars, the youths of Laceademon in Sparta made sacrifice.*[2]

The High Priestess takes over the recitation and begins the Charge:

> *Whenever ye have need of anything, once in the month and better it be when the moon is full, then shall ye assemble in some secret place and adore the spirit of me, who am Queen of all Witcheries. There shall ye assemble, ye who are feign to learn all sorceries who have not yet won my deepest secrets. To these will I teach that which is yet*

unknown. And ye shall be free from slavery, and as a sign that ye be really free, ye shall be naked in your rites; and ye shall dance, sing, feast, make music and love, all in my praise. For mine is the ecstasy of the spirit, and mine is also joy on earth. For my law is love unto all beings. Keep pure your highest ideals and strive ever towards them. Let none stop you or turn you aside. For mine is the secret door which opens upon the Land of Youth; mine is the Cup of the Wine of Life and the Cauldron of Cerridwen, which is the Holy Grail of Immortality. I am the Gracious Goddess who gives the gift of joy unto the heart of man. Upon earth I give the knowledge of the spirit eternal, and beyond death I give peace, and freedom, and reunion with those that have gone before. Nor do I demand sacrifice. For behold, I am the Mother of all things, and my love is poured out upon the earth.

The High Priest recites:

Hear ye the words of the Star Goddess. She, in the dust of whose feet are the Hosts of Heaven, and whose body encircles the Universe.

The High Priestess resumes her address:

I who am the beauty of the green earth, and the white Moon among the stars, and the mystery of the waters, and the desire of the heart of man, call unto thy soul. Arise and come unto me. For I am the soul of Nature, who gives life to the Universe. From me all things proceed, and unto me all things must return. Before my face, beloved of Gods and of men, let thine innermost divine self be enfolded in the rapture of the infinite. Let my worship be within the heart that rejoiceth. For behold, all acts of love and pleasure are my rituals. Therefore, let there be beauty and strength, power and compassion, honor and humility, mirth and reverence within you. And thou who thinkest to seek for me, know thy seeking and yearning shall avail thee not unless thou knowest the mystery that if that which thou seekest thou findest not within thee, thou wilt never find it without thee. For behold, I have been with thee from the beginning, and I am that which is attained at the end of desire.[3]

Italian

The Charge used by this denomination is extremely similar to the Gardnerian version. This familiarity relates solely to the fact that Gerald

Gardner borrowed extensively from the works of Charles Godfrey Leland. Since Leland received the information for *Aradia* from Italian sources, the two denominations are bound to overlap in some areas; and this is one such example. The Italian Charge of Aradia is recited to the coven by the High Priestess as follows:

> *When I shall have departed from this world, whenever ye have need of anything, once in the month, and when the moon is full, ye shall assemble in some deserted place, or in a forest all together join, to adore the potent spirit of your queen, my mother, the Great Goddess Diana.*
>
> *Ye who fain would learn all sorcery yet has not won its deepest secrets, to them my mother will teach in truth all things as yet unknown. And ye shall all be freed from slavery, and so ye shall be free in everything. And as the sign that ye are truly free, ye shall be naked in your rites, both men and women also.*
>
> *And thus it shall be done: all shall sit down to the supper naked, and the feast over, they shall dance, sing, make music and then love in the dark, with all the lights extinguished, for it is the Spirit of Diana who extinguishes them, and so they dance and make music in her praise.*
>
> *And it came to pass that Diana, after her daughter, Aradia, had spent her time on earth, gave her the power to gratify those who conjured her by granting them success. Whatever thing should be asked from the spirit of Aradia, should be granted unto those who merit her favor. And thus they must invoke her.*[4]

Saxon

Saxon Wicca does not have an address to the coven known as the Charge. However, it does have the same type of speech, with the same type of language, used in the same type of context.[5] So, while the Saxon declamation is not the exact equivalent of the Gardnerian Charge, it nevertheless has some very similar qualities. For example, the High Priest sets the stage with a short recitation proclaiming the greatness of the Goddess, then the High Priestess addresses the coven from the perspective of the Goddess. In effect, this is the same basic formula used in the Gardnerian and Italian Charges.

The Saxon address begins after the Temple has been erected. After the High Priest kisses the High Priestess, he recites a short introduction:

Let us join together to remember the Gods. For the Lord and Lady shape our lives and lead us on our paths; they watch over us and bestow their gifts upon us; and, when we are in need, they provide for us. It is only right that we thank and honor them.

To set the stage for her speech, the High Priestess takes over and gives the following generalized recitation:

When man was a child, the Gods watched over him. The Goddess Frig was his mother; the Great God Woden his father. From the God and Goddess, man learned all. He was taught that he would be rewarded when he did right, but would receive nothing when he did wrong. He learned that when he gave of himself, his love, his life, it would be returned to him. Yet, when greed or malice drove him on, he would suffer for his actions. For the Gods are just and fair. Please them and be rewarded. Yet, as we need them, they need us. Our love is theirs, and theirs is ours. Let us therefore live and love together, always knowing that Love is the Law, and Love is the Bond.[6]

The High Priest resumes speaking:

During this time, when the moon is full, and the Great Mother is at her most glorious, bless us with your love. Hear us and answer our call, as we honor you. Lovely Lady Frig, at different times and different places, you have been known by many names to many people; Aphrodite, Arianrhod, Cerridwen, Diana, Isis. Through these names, and many more, you have been adored. Yet it is as Frig that we know you, and it is by this name that we worship you.[7]

The High Priestess takes over and addresses the coven:

Hear me, honor me, and love me, now and for all time. For I am the beginning of life and I am its end. I am the one who watches over you. I am the Maiden, the Mother, the Crone; I am all of this and much more. In strength and love, I am the one you seek. Yet whenever you have need of me, look no farther than yourself and know that I am always here; for I abide within you. And as you would be true to yourself, so you shall be true to me. Do this, and I shall be your strength, love and desire; your guide and guardian; your beginning and your end.

At this point a prayer to Woden is often added. On the other hand, if a normal esbat ritual was performed, this isn't necessary since the invocation was included in the dialogue. But if reference to the God was omitted (as in the above passages), then the following must be recited by the High Priest:

> *Mighty God, we honor and praise you. Let us know and love you. For you are the consort of Frig; you are the father of all; and you are strength. As our Lord, you guard us from harm and guide us in our lives. Bless us that we may be worthy of your love.*[8]

If any working has been scheduled to take place (magick, healing, etc.), a power-raising chant usually occurs at this point to increase the energy. Other than that, the cakes and ale are consecrated.

West Country

When it comes to the Charge, this denomination is different from a lot of the others in that it doesn't have its own version. Although the full reason behind West Country's lack of a Charge is unknown, at least part of it seems to involve the Charge being deeply rooted in Italian Wicca and only becoming widely known after Gerald Gardner incorporated it into his rites. Because West Country is a pre-Gardnerian tradition, the Charge was simply unknown to it. But, the fact that it's not original to their denomination doesn't mean that modern West Country witches don't use it. In today's practice, the Gardnerian version of the Charge is sometimes used at both esbat and sabbat ceremonies. On those occasions, it's always used in the same manner and location as in Gardnerian Wicca.

THE GOD INVOCATION

Throughout Wicca there are a wide range of prayers and invocations specifically designed to honor the God. While they can technically be recited almost anywhere within a rite, most of these prayers take place immediately following the Charge or any invocation to the Goddess.[9] This is because the Goddess is often viewed as the principle figure, while the God occupies a slightly subordinate role. Therefore, dedications to the Goddess almost always take precedence over prayers to the God. The Gardnerian tradition is a perfect example of this.

During a normal Opening Ritual, this denomination (which holds the Goddess in more esteem than the God), performs the rites of Drawing Down the Moon and the Charge before reciting the Invocation to the

Great God Cernunnos.[10] Furthermore, while the invocation to the Goddess involves both actions and elaborate wording, the prayer to the God calls for nothing more than a hand gesture and short recitation. But Gardnerians are not alone in this; many other denominations follow the same pattern. The following are a few examples of the ways that the God is honored through various invocations and prayers.

Gardnerian

At the conclusion of the Charge of the Goddess, and prior to beginning the Witches' Rune, a short prayer to honor the God is recited by the High Priest. After the coven call, the High Priest and High Priestess face each other and make the Horned God Sign (Figure 10.1).[11] The High Priest then turns toward the coven and recites[12]:

> *O' Mighty One who hast created all things; Who knowest all things and from Whom nothing is hidden; Who knowest that we perform not these ceremonies to tempt Thy power, but that we may arrive at an understanding of secret things, of whatever nature they may be, by Thine aid. O' Lord, be Thou unto me a strong tower of refuge and come quickly and without delay into our presence from every quarter and every climate of the world wherein ye may be, in the Great Name of Cernunnos.*

HORNED GOD SIGN *Fig. 10.1*

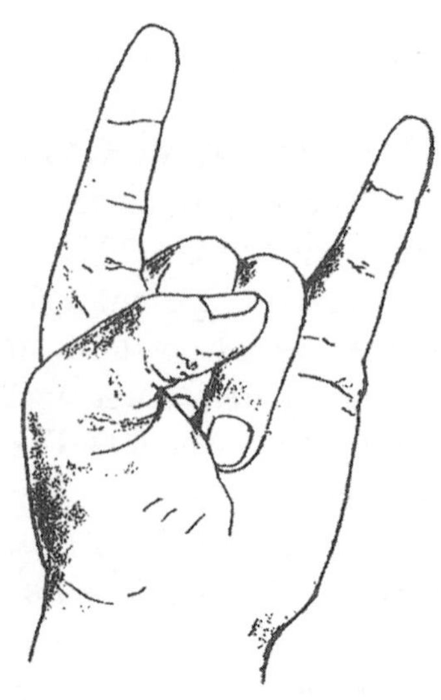

Italian

Like Gardnerian Wicca, this denomination employs a number of invocations dedicated exclusively to the God. However, these prayers are made primarily at the sabbats and are somewhat dictated by the season. For instance, during Samhain there's an actual Charge of the God given, while at other times the speech is reduced from an address by the God to a short verse or prayer. In deciding on a prayer or invocation, the time of year is also taken into consideration. During winter (God) months, an invocation is recited, but during the summer (Goddess), months none are given. This winter/summer pattern also holds true on the rare occasion that a God invocation is used at an esbat.

The Charge of the God takes place immediately after the Circle is cast and the Fivefold Kiss given. It begins with the High Priestess reciting a few words welcoming the God. The High Priest then takes over and recites:

I conjure thee, O' Lord, as thou canst ne'er
Have rest or peace until thou shalt be freed
From the sun where thou art prisoned, and must go
Beating thy hands and running fast meanwhile:
I pray thee let me know my destiny;
And if 'tis evil, change its course for me!
If thou wilt grant this grace, I'll see it clear
In the water in the splendor of the sun;
And thou, O' Lord, shalt tell by word of mouth
Whatever this my destiny is to be.
And unless thou grantest this,
May'st thou ne'er know peace or bliss![13]

Saxon

When it comes to a Charge of the God, the Saxon tradition is a little different than other denominations. This branch of Wicca does not have an invocation dedicated to the God nor does it have an individual prayer for this purpose. Yet, as was seen with the Charge of the Goddess, it does have a fair amount of language devoted to praising the deities. So even though the Saxons don't have the exact equivalent of the Gardnerian or Italian Charges, the denomination still has a method of honoring the God, which employs many of the same sentiments. For example, during the esbat ritual about half of the wording is directed at glorifying the God, while the other half honors the Goddess.

The following is a typical prayer to Woden:

> *Mighty God Woden, Lord of Life and Death, we gather on this night, beneath the stars in the heavens, to honor and praise you. For you are the consort of the Goddess Frig; you are the Father of all that is and ever will be; you are strength and you are power. Let our love call you to us in times of need that you may guard us from harm and guide us in our lives. Great Lord Woden, bless us that we may be worthy of your love.*[14]

West Country

As previously discussed, this denomination doesn't have its own version of a God or Goddess Charge. Although this can be partially explained by West Country beliefs that shun several modern Wiccan customs (the observance of eight sabbats, the policy of particular coven leaders, etc.), it, nevertheless, seems odd for a denomination that has so many specific male rituals. But as with the Charge of the Goddess, just because the tradition doesn't have an invocation devoted to the God doesn't mean that modern West Country witches don't use one.

Consecration

In Wicca, all items must be ritually purified by subjecting them to a process known as consecration before they are used for religious purposes. This is true of tools, jewelry, water, salt,[1] wine, cakes, or just about anything else that becomes a part of a witch's spiritual life. Witches believe that this special rite serves a dual purpose, and it's important to understand this concept.

First and foremost, the goal of consecrating an object is to purify it spiritually in order to enhance its natural magickal properties. Ultimately, this process charges the item with greater power. A second function of the act is to produce a psychological effect on the user that strengthens confidence in the object's ability to accomplish its intended task while validating its sanctity. This affects the user's psyche, thereby achieving the desired results.

Since this rite will take place during a normal esbat or sabbat, there really aren't any extra requirements necessary. However, a widely accepted rule of thumb holds that it's important to keep all newly consecrated tools or jewelry to one's self for a complete full moon cycle. If the items are to be gifts, they should be given to the new owner with instructions not to lend them out for a month.[2] The reasoning behind this practice stems from the belief that keeping the tool away from contact with anyone else gives the consecrated item a chance to bond with its owner and absorb some of his/her energy (i.e., aura).

ATHAME/SWORD CONSECRATION RITE

Not all Wiccan denominations have purification rituals for individual items, and most traditions simply consecrate everything using the same wording and ceremony. But among those that do have a special rite, there's usually a ritual with the sole purpose of cleansing the athame and sword.

The following two traditions, Gardnerian and Saxon, offer excellent examples of particularized consecration rites for the sword and athame.

Gardnerian

Begin by casting a Circle and conducting the Opening Ritual. During this process the water/salt will be consecrated and used to consecrate the athame.[3] When ready to consecrate the athame, place it on the pentacle. If at all possible, have an already consecrated Elemental tool (sword, wand, etc.) sitting on the altar next to the pentacle. Sprinkle a few drops of the consecrated water/salt on the athame.[4] Pick up the censer, and pass it over the pentacle, making sure that the smoke drifts down onto the athame. If it doesn't, lift up the athame, and pass it through the smoke. Now pass the tip of the athame through the flame of the altar candle. Place the athame back on the pentacle. Lay your hands on the athame (if there are two of you, both people lay one hand on the athame) and recite:

> *I conjure thee, O Athame, by these Names, Abrahach, Abrach, Abracadabra, that thou servest me for a strength and defense in all magical operations against all mine enemies, visible and invisible. I conjure thee anew by the Holy Name Aradia and the Holy Name Cernunnos; I conjure thee, O Athame, that thou servest me for a protection in all adversities.*[5]

The athame is again sprinkled with consecrated water and the censer passed over it. With it on the pentacle, the two witches lay their hands on it again and recite:

> *I conjure thee, O Athame of steel, by the Great God Cernunnos and Gentle Goddess Aradia, by the virtue of the heavens, of the stars and of the spirits that preside over them, that thou mayest receive such virtue that I may obtain the end that I desire in all things wherein I shall use thee, by the power of Aradia and Cernunnos.*[6]

If a consecrated athame/sword is on hand, it should be laid across the athame (sword) being consecrated before the newly consecrated blade is touched. Assuming that the rite was performed by a male and female witch, the witch who isn't the owner of the newly consecrated item should give the other person the Fivefold Kiss. The owner should then pick up the athame and hold it against his/her chest. This rite is finished.

Saxon

In the Saxon tradition, a witch consecrates his or her individual seax when first admitted into a coven.[7] The ritual begins after the Temple has been erected. The new witch stands at the altar between the Priestess and Priest. The witch, holding the seax with both hands, raises it high in the air and recites:

> *Lord and Lady; God and Goddess; Woden and Frig, here is my seax, my weapon that I shall use in your honor. Purify it for me and help me to keep it pure in your service.*

The witch places the seax on the altar between the censer and the sword. After dipping his/her fingers into the consecrated water, he/she gently sprinkles the seax, turns it over, and sprinkles the other side. The witch then passes the seax through the smoke of the censer, turning it several times. Next, the witch passes the seax over the altar candle, turns it over, and completes another pass. When this is done, he/she raises it high in the air once more and recites:

> *Again I present my weapon, which has been washed in holy water, bathed in the smoke of incense, and cleansed by the warmth of the flame. In all things that I use it, let it always be pure in your service and let it always guard me from harm. So be it in the names of Woden and Frig.*

The Priest/Priestess and coven repeat: *So be it.*

The rite is complete. As with anything else, only the owner should initially handle the newly consecrated seax. Also, it should be kept on your person for the first twenty-four hours and then kept under your pillow for three more days.

WORKING TOOL CONSECRATION RITE

The purpose of this ritual is to consecrate the other tools (i.e., wand, chalice, scourge) that are used by witches. As with the athame/sword consecration rite, not all denominations have a specific ceremony for working tools. Among those that do, the Gardnerian tradition has one of the most intricate rituals, while the Italian tradition has one of the simplest.

Gardnerian

Start this rite the same way as the last, by casting your Circle and conducting the Opening Ritual. Take the item to be consecrated (in this case a wand), and place it on the pentacle.[8] Both witches place their right hands on the object and recite:

Most Holy, Aradia and Cernunnos, deign to bless and to consecrate this wand, that it may obtain the necessary virtue through thee.[9]

The man sprinkles a little of the consecrated water onto the wand, then the woman bathes the wand in the incense smoke. The wand is placed back on the pentacle, and the pair recites:

Aradia and Cernunnos, bless this instrument prepared in your honour, so that it may only serve for a good use and end, for your glory.[9]

The wand is again sprinkled with water and passed through the incense smoke. If a consecrated athame/sword is on hand, it should be laid across the item being consecrated before the newly consecrated item is touched. The person who isn't the owner of the newly consecrated item should give the other person the Fivefold Kiss. The owner should then hold the item against his/her chest. This rite is finished.

Italian

The consecration rite must be performed on the night of a full moon to take advantage of the moon's power. A Circle is cast, and a normal ceremony proceeds up to the point where the consecration is to take place. Using consecrated water, bathe the item (again a wand will be used as an example), and dry it with a white cotton or wool cloth. Face the east quarter, present the wand, and recite:[10]

I proclaim that this is to be my wand of magick, which shall have the power over the Element of Air.

Now comes the important part. If the Circle is outdoors or if moonlight shines into the Circle, the second blessing now takes place. Otherwise, cut a doorway in the Circle, and go outside into the moonlight.[11] With moonlight shining down upon the wand, hold it high, and recite:

Lady Diana, Great Moon Goddess, ruler of the heavens, bless and charge this wand which has been cleansed in your honor. I do consecrate and dedicate this wand to your service. In the name of Diana, so be it.

The item is consecrated and ready to use. Unlike other traditions that feel the item must be kept with the owner for days or weeks, the Italian denomination believes that it may be pressed into service immediately.

CAKES AND WINE CONSECRATION RITE

At every esbat and sabbat, the wine and cakes must be purified before they can be shared. Like the water and salt, this is probably the only other consecration rite that will be performed on a regular basis. This being the case, you'll not only become very familiar with this ceremony, but you'll most likely feel the need to adapt it to your own style after a very short time.

Unlike consecrating tools, every denomination has a ceremony to consecrate the cakes and wine.[12] Although the wording is different, each tradition holds this rite after the worship portion of the ceremony is completed. For instance, Gardnerians hold the consecration rite as the last act before the coven relaxes and celebrates.[13] Likewise, the Saxon tradition waits until the veneration segment is finished before beginning the cakes and ale rite. In both cases, the rite serves as a link between the working and social aspects of the ceremony.

Gardnerian

When the working portion of the ceremony is finished, you've reached the point for consecrating the wine and cakes. Start with the wine first. The High Priest holds the chalice containing the wine in front of him while he kneels before the High Priestess.[14] The High Priestess, holding her athame, lowers it into the chalice until the tip breaks the surface of the wine. The High Priest recites:

> *As the athame is to the male, so the chalice is to the female. Together, they become one.* (If not used as part of the Great Rite, the Priest continues.) *This wine is blessed and consecrated as a symbol of devotion to the Goddess and God.*

The High Priestess removes the athame from the wine and sets it on the altar. The High Priest remains kneeling. After kissing the High Priest (either on the lips, cheek, or forehead), she takes the chalice from him and takes a sip of the wine.[15] The High Priest stands up and receives the chalice. He takes a sip and with a kiss, passes it on to the next female, who takes a sip and passes it to the next male. This continues until the whole coven has had a sip of wine. Return the chalice to the altar.

The cakes are now consecrated. Begin as you did with the chalice:

High Priest kneeling in front of the altar holding the basket of cakes, High Priestess holding her athame. The High Priestess uses her athame to draw the Invoking Pentagram of Earth over the basket of cakes. As she does, the High Priest recites:

> *Great Goddess Aradia, bless these cakes that we are about to take into our bodies. Allow this food to bestow health, strength, joy, love and peace upon us, and grant us the fulfillment which is perfect happiness.*

The High Priestess lays her athame on the altar, kisses the High Priest, and takes a cake. He takes a cake and with a kiss, passes the basket on to the next female, who takes a cake and passes it to the next male. This continues until the whole coven has taken a cake. The rite is done.

Italian

This denomination is slightly different from the others in the timing of the cakes and wine blessing and in the fact that the High Priest or High Priestess is the one to conduct the rite depending on the season.[16] Following the rite of Drawing Down the Moon and the recitation of the Veglia, the Priest/ess stands before the altar, hands held out over the cakes and wine in gesture, and recites:

> *Blessings upon this food and drink that was provided to us. Blessing upon the earth which has grown the grain for these cakes and the vines which produced this wine. We gather now to give thanks to Diana and Dianus, for it is by their divine mysteries that we receive these gifts.*

The High Priestess gestures over the wine and recites:

> *By the power of this act may this wine be blessed by the Great Goddess, Diana.*

The High Priest gestures over the cakes and recites:

> *By the power of this act may these cakes be blessed by the Great God, Dianus.*

The pair turns to the coven and together recites:

> *Through these cakes and wine, may you be blessed by the God and Goddess. May this gift give you strength, joy, vision, and inner peace.*

And, may each that partakes in this bounty become one with Diana and Dianus.

The coven members come forward, and each one takes a sip of wine while offering a silent tribute to the Goddess. However, as with other denominations, the cakes and wine portion of the ceremony doesn't come until working has been finished. Therefore, eating the cakes is put off until the working is completed. At that time, the cakes, and more wine, are shared with everyone.

Saxon

The goblets are filled with ale by the Scribe. He/she is also responsible for keeping them refilled as they're passed around. The Priest and Priestess, standing in front of the altar, each hold a goblet and face the coven. They raise the goblets in salute, and the Priest recites:

As the Gods give to us, let us share with them. Let this ale represent the drink of life, and let us give thanks for all the goodness that they pour out upon the earth. Thanks be to the God and Goddess.

The coven repeats: *Thanks be to the God and Goddess.*

An offering is made to the Gods by the Priest/Priestess as each pours a few drops of ale onto the ground or into a libation dish if indoors. The pair takes a sip of ale and passes the goblets around. Once everyone has taken a sip, the goblets are placed back on the altar. The Scribe hands the bowl of cakes to the Priestess. She raises the bowl and recites:

We give thanks to the God and Goddess for the food they provide. Let us share with one another, and let us always be certain to share with those who have nothing. Thanks be to the God and Goddess.

The coven repeats: *Thanks be to the God and Goddess.*

An offering is made to the Gods by the Priest/Priestess as each takes a cake and crumbles a few pieces of cake onto the ground or onto a dish if indoors. The pair passes the bowl so that everyone may take a cake. The Priest recites:

Let us enjoy this bounty that we have been given. But let us never forget that we owe all that we have to the God and Goddess. So be it.

The coven repeats: *So be it.*

The rite is finished, and the cakes and ale shared. The coven relaxes and socializes until it's time to banish the Circle.

West Country

Employing modest practices, this denomination has one of the shortest cakes and wine (or ale) rites of all the branches of Wicca. However, because it's a simple ritual, doesn't mean it's any less valid.

The rite begins when the working portion of the ceremony is completed. A Priest and Priestess usually perform the rite together. The Priest holds a goblet of wine while the Priestess dips her athame into the wine. The Priestess recites:

Blessings be upon this cup of wine, that has flowed from the seed planted in the earth. As we drink, we give thanks for what we have received.

The Priest puts down the goblet and picks up the plate of cakes. The Priestess pushes the tip of her athame into one of the cakes and recites:

Blessings be upon this food, which has come from the earth's bountiful womb. As we eat, we give thanks for what we have received.

The rite is finished. The wine and cakes are shared.

PERSONAL ITEM CONSECRATION RITE

The purpose of this ritual is to consecrate personal items, such as jewelry, so they're cleansed and blessed. However, this rite can also be used for items that have ceremonial use (candles, herbs, taper, etc.) even though they aren't actually considered tools. Also, as this is primarily a Gardnerian rite, only a few other denominations have a similar ceremony.

This is a very simple rite that will normally take place at an esbat after the Circle has been cast and the full Opening Ritual completed. When you're ready, the owner of the item to be consecrated places it on the pentacle.[17] The Priest/Priestess lay their right hands on the item and recite:

By the power of the Element of Earth, we consecrate this (item name).

The High Priest/ess sprinkles a little of the consecrated water/salt onto the object, and the pair recites:

By the power of the Element of Water, we consecrate this (item name).

The High Priest/ess passes the censer over the pentacle (or the item through the censer smoke), and the pair recites:

By the power of the Element of Air, we consecrate this (item name).

The High Priest/ess picks up the object and passes it over the flame of the altar candle. If the item is metal, it is passed through the flame. The pair recites:

By the power of the Element of Fire, we consecrate this (item name) *in the names of Aradia and Cernunnos.*

The High Priest/ess takes the item and with a kiss, hands it to the owner. The consecration is complete. Move on to the next item. However, before beginning, consider using a shortcut for multiple items since an item-by-item method can be very time consuming. To accomplish this, simply conduct the ritual with all the items at once, rather than consecrating them one by one. The coven leaders perform the consecration after the items are placed on the pentacle by their owners. At the point when individual attention is paid to an item (passing it through the censer smoke, passing it over the altar flame), simply do one item at a time.

Saxon

This denomination is one of the few that recognizes the need for personal items to be consecrated. But the actual rite for doing so is nothing more than a modification of the seax/sword consecration ritual.

The consecration begins with the owner of the item standing at the altar between the Priestess and Priest. The owner, holding the item with both hands, raises it high in the air and recites:

Lord and Lady; God and Goddess; Woden and Frig, here is my (item name). *I present it to you for your blessing. Purify it for me and help me to keep it pure.*

The witch places the item on the altar between the censer and the sword. After dipping his/her fingers into the consecrated water, he/she gently sprinkles the item, turns it over, and sprinkles the other side. He/she passes the item through the smoke of the censer, turning it several times. The item is passed over the altar candle, then turned over, and another pass is completed. When this is done, he/she raises it high in the air once more and recites:

> *Again I present my* (item name*) which has been washed in holy water, bathed in the smoke of incense, and cleansed by the warmth of the flame. Let it always be pure.* (For a talisman or charm add: *and let it always protect me from harm*; for a necklace, add: *as it represents the eternal circle of life*; for a ceremonial object such as a candle, add: *that it may aid in your service.*) *So be it in the names of Woden and Frig.*

The Priest/Priestess and coven repeat: *So be it.*

The rite is complete. As with anything else, only the owner should initially handle the newly consecrated item. Also, personal items should be kept on your person for the first twenty-four hours and then kept under your pillow for three more days. Other items (candles, etc.) may be used immediately.

Wiccan Chants

The Witches' Rune is a Gardnerian term for a power-raising chant accompanied by a ring-dance. Although this name originally referred exclusively to the Gardnerian version, over the years other denominations adopted the term to describe their own chants.[1]

Probably the best definition of a witches' chant is that it's a technique used by witches to build psychic energy within the confines of the Magick Circle in an effort to erect and strengthen the Cone of Power.[2] Normally conducted as part of the opening ceremony to set the tone for the rituals to follow, this method of power-raising is composed of two separate components: rhythmic chanting and ring-dancing.

The chant itself usually consists of very basic wording, which is formed into an invoking rhyme and set to a rhythmical beat. Although there is no specific content required, references to the God and Goddess, the elements, and the four quarters are common. The ring-dance is set to the same rhythmic beat as the chant and often involves the coven holding hands while its members dance around a central point. When combined, these two parts raise power by forming a group consciousness.

Naturally, all of this is done for a reason. First, in a coven, the rhythmic chant produces a mesmerizing effect on the participants, which allows a collective consciousness to form. As the chant is repeated over and over, the participants' individual psychic patterns unite into one harmonious collection, thus generating a centralized buildup of power. Second, the rhythmic ring-dance produces the effect of coming together as one continuous body that's acting in unison. This uninterrupted harmony induces a mild hypnotic state, which produces a power-raising atmosphere.

There are several versions of the chants that are commonly used. Of these, the most popular is undoubtedly the Witches' Rune practiced by both the Gardnerian and Alexandrian traditions. Although developed by

Gerald Gardner and Doreen Valiente many years ago, it has become so widely used among other denominations that it rarely retains the "Gardnerian" moniker anymore. There are also less well-known renderings, as well as chants that are preferred by individual traditions. However, none of these compares with the popularity of the Gardnerian version.

In order to decide which wording suits your personal (or coven) style, it's best to try different versions. This comparison will ensure that the correct results are achieved. To make matters easier, the original Gardnerian Witches' Rune is included, along with a modernized version and a common solitary version.

Gardnerian Witches' Rune

Eko, Eko, Azarak,
Eko, Eko, Zomelak,
Eko, Eko, Cernunnos,
Eko, Eko, Aradia.[3]
Darksome night and shining moon,
Hearken to the Witches' Rune;
East, then South, West, then North,
Hear! Come! I call thee forth;
Earth and water, air and fire,
Work your will by my desire;
Power of the witch's blade,
Come ye as the charge is made;
Wand and pentacle and sword,
Hearken ye unto my word,
Cords and censer, scourge and knife,
Waken all ye into life;
Queen of Heaven, Queen of Hell,
Lend your aid unto my spell;
Horned Hunter of the night,
Work my will by magick rite;
By all the power of earth and sea,
Be obedient unto me;
By all the light of moon and sun,
As I do will, shall it be done.
Eko, Eko, Azarak,
Eko, Eko, Zomelak,

Eko, Eko, Cernunnos,
Eko, Eko, Aradia.

Celtic Chant

When the wheel turns, and the time is right,
We gather to dance, in the dark of night . . .
First East, then South, then West, then North,
Our chanting calls the Old Gods forth . . .
With Earth below and Air above,
We ask that Thee return our love . . .
As Fire burns, and Waters run,
We pray to Thee, that our will be done . . .
With wands and swords, with cups and knives,
We pledge to Thee our spiritual lives . . .
For as we dance, and sing to Thee,
We call Ye forth, for all to see . . .
Queen of Dark, and Lord of Light,
Come to us on this special night . . .
Goddess and God, Mother and Son,
As we do will, shall it be done.

Modern Wiccan Chant

Lord and Lady,
Lady and Lord;
Lord and Lady,
Lady and Lord;
Lord and Lady,
Lady and Lord.[4]

Under dark of night, and shining moon,
We come to chant, our joyous tune;
East, South, West, North,
Hear our call, and hurry forth;
Water, Air, Earth, Fire,
Our will is strong, with one desire;
With wands or swords, or by athames,
We use our tools, to praise your names;
Symbols are cut, with sacred knives,
To bring you forth, to enrich our lives;
Woman to woman, man to man,

The Old Gods will help, as only they can;
Frig is here, so ring the bells,
She blesses us, and aids our spells;
Woden is with us, on this night,
To work our will, by magick rite;
The power of moon, the power of sun,
We sing and chant, that our will be done;
The vigor of land, the force of sea,
As we do wish, so mote it be.

Great Rite

This rite has partially different meanings to the various denominations that practice it.[1] Some older traditions view the Great Rite solely as a type of fertility rite aimed at ensuring that crops be bountiful. While there is a basis for this belief in ancient custom, the references tend to indicate a connection more along the lines of sex magick than deity worship. On the other hand, modern denominations have taken a slightly different outlook regarding the ritual. Instead of just accepting its fertility aspect, contemporary Wiccans use it to honor the God and Goddess.[2]

Under either premise, the purpose of the rite is to celebrate the opposite attractive characteristics of the forces of Nature and the Universe, as well as the properties of male/female polarity. And through the Great Rite, witches are able to share in this experience. Something else to keep in mind is that all men and women inherently have male/female traits, and it's these opposite characteristics that are the balancing point of an individual's psyche. Nature and the Universe are similarly composed of these female/male parts, and it's the combination of these opposites that keep things in balance. In short, everything has an opposite (male/female, light/dark, up/down), and balance is achieved through this natural pairing of complementary opposites.

The Great Rite can be performed in two ways. First, the rite can be "actual," meaning that the couple enacting the rite engages in actual sexual intercourse as part of the ceremony. Since this usually takes place in a coven setting, everyone in the coven, except the couple, is asked to leave the Circle (and the room) before the sexual aspect of the rite. They will not return until called back by the couple. It's also strongly recommended that the couple performing the "actual" version of the rite be married—legally or by Handfasting—and that unpaired "volunteers" never be used due to the possibility that an uncomfortable situation could arise in the future.[3]

Second, the rite can be "symbolic," meaning that no sexual intercourse takes place and everyone can remain and participate.[4] This practice is not only far more common among the denominations that conduct the Great Rite, but it allows the entire coven to experience the completeness of the act.[5]

Gardnerian (Symbolic Rite)[6]

To enact this rite, a silver or white veil approximately one square yard is needed. For this version, the coven members are positioned around the perimeter of the Circle; if possible they should alternate man-woman, man-woman. The cauldron, which is normally kept in the center of the Circle, is moved out of the way. The wine is unconsecrated.[7] After the sabbat ceremony, the rite begins.

The High Priest and High Priestess face each other in the center of the Circle; her back is to the altar. The High Priest gives her the Fivefold Kiss. The High Priestess then lays on her back in the center of the Circle; her head is pointed toward the altar and her arms and legs are extended to form the pentagram (Figure 13.1).

PENTAGRAM POSITION *Fig. 13.1*

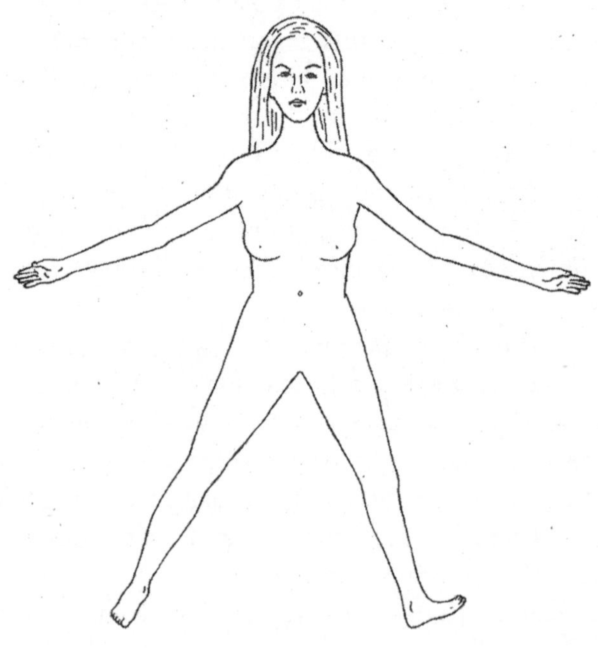

The High Priest retrieves the veil and covers her with it. He then kneels at her feet. Two predesignated witches (a man and woman) go to the altar and get the athame and chalice. The man, carrying the chalice, stands to the east of the High Priestess; the woman, carrying the athame, to the west.[8] Once the two witches are in place, the High Priest begins the invocation by reciting:

Assist me to erect the ancient altar, at which in days past all worshipped, the Great Altar of all things. For in old times, Woman was the altar. Thus was the altar made and placed, and the sacred place was the point within the center of the Circle. As we have of old been taught that the point within the center is the origin of all things, therefore should we adore it. Therefore whomever we adore we also invoke, by the power of the Lifted Lance. O' Circle of Stars, whereof our father is but the younger brother, marvel beyond imagination, soul of infinite space, before whom time is bewildered and understanding dark, not unto thee may we attain unless thine image be love. Therefore by seed and root, by stem and bud, by leaf and flower and fruit, do we invoke thee, O' Queen of Space, O' Mist of Light, continuous One of the Heavens. Let it ever be thus, that men speak not of thee as One, but as none; And let them not speak of thee at all, since thou art continuous.[9] *For thou art the point within the Circle which we adore; the fount of life without which we would not be. And in this way are erected the holy twin pillars of Boaz and Jachin.*[10] *In beauty and in strength they were erected, to the wonder and glory of all men.*

The High Priest removes the veil from the High Priestess;[11] she kneels to face him. He hands the veil to the woman and takes the athame from her. The High Priestess is handed the chalice. The High Priest recites:

O' secret of secrets that art hidden in the being of all lives, not thee do we adore, for that which adoreth is also thou. Thou art That, and That am I. I am the flame that burns bright in the heart of every man. I am both life, and the giver of life. Therefore, with the knowledge of me is the knowledge of death. I am alone, the Lord within ourselves, whose name is Mystery of Mysteries.

The High Priest leans forward and kisses the High Priestess and continues:

Make open the path of intelligence between us, for these truly are the Five Points of Fellowship (The following lines are best suited only for the actual rite: *Foot to foot, knee to knee, Lance to Grail, breast to breast, lips to lips. Let the light course through our bodies, fulfilling of us resurrection. For there is no part of us that is not of the Gods.*) *In the name of Aradia, by the power of Cernunnos, encourage our hearts.*

The High Priestess holds the chalice in front of her and the High Priest lowers the tip of the athame into the chalice until it penetrates the wine.[12] He hands the athame back to the woman, places both his hands on top of the High Priestess' hands so that both are holding the chalice, and the pair kiss. The High Priestess takes a sip of wine, followed by the High Priest. The pair kisses again, then stand up.

The High Priest takes the chalice and passes it to the closest female witch[13] with a kiss. She takes a sip and passes it to the next male witch with a kiss. This process is done until all have taken a sip of wine. The chalice is returned to the altar. The rite is complete. The cakes are now consecrated in the usual way.

Gardnerian (Actual Rite)

This version follows the above ritual all the way to the end of the first invocation, (i.e., "wonder and glory of all men"). At this point a female witch[14] uses her athame to open a doorway in the Circle. The coven leaves the Circle and the room.[15] The Circle doorway is sealed by the High Priest. The invocation is continued, and the sexual act replaces the symbolic athame/chalice joining. When the private portion of the rite is done, the High Priest cuts a doorway in the Circle and summons the coven. After the coven enters the Circle, the doorway is sealed. The cakes and wine are then consecrated.

West Country

In recent years, very few practitioners of the modern form of this denomination still use the Great Rite. One reason for its sudden decline is that the ritual was mainly performed to ensure the fertility of crops. Since modern farming practices and technology have made this unnecessary, the rite lost some of its importance. But there's a far more important reason that the rite faded into obscurity.

As a rural religion, its original practitioners had no hang-ups about sexuality. Because of this, the tradition only had an "actual" version. To those ends, the rite was carried out at crossroads for fertility or between a newly initiated witch and the Priest/ess initiating him/her. While this may have been acceptable at one time, by current societal standards, both situations would be more than a little out of place. Therefore, the rite has largely become a thing of the past.[16]

Esbat

Of all the ceremonies celebrated by witches, the esbat is by far the most commonly practiced religious ritual. Yet even though every denomination practices this ceremony, it doesn't mean that they all follow the same pattern.

An esbat is the regular monthly (or sometimes weekly) meeting of a coven where rituals are performed and where other activities usually take place. Whenever possible, the esbat should be held during the full moon or as close as schedules permit. Since there are thirteen full moons during the course of each year, this means that there are also thirteen Full Moon Esbats. Many witches also attempt to meet around the time of the new moon, and a ceremony held at this time would be called a New Moon Esbat.[1] Beyond this, there are a few other things to keep in mind.

Perhaps the most interesting characteristic of esbats is that there's no strict formula to follow. Owing to the flexibility of Wiccan practice, all covens have their own rites that they perform at their esbats. It's this basic concept of nonuniformity that makes each gathering unique.

There are still some general practices that are common among different covens and even among the different traditions. For the most part, though, since Wicca does not have a rigid structure like that of the Catholic religion, there's nothing set in stone dictating that an esbat must be conducted a specific way. Therefore, even though a loose motif for the ceremony exists, it'll vary from coven to coven or denomination to denomination.

Even so, all esbats will begin with an opening ritual that will contain a rite to erect a Circle and will end with a closing ritual that serves to banish the Circle. Likewise, there will always be a consecration rite for wine and cakes, a ritual to welcome and honor the Goddess and God, and an assortment of other rites aimed at raising power or giving thanks. Another facet familiar to all esbats is that they're normally events that the coven celebrates alone, unlike sabbats where many covens may come together.[2]

In the case of the Full Moon Esbat, there's an additional benefit derived from holding the ceremony at this time of the month. With psychic powers at their strongest around the full moon, esbats held during this lunar phase are considered an excellent opportunity for any psychic or magickal work. This is the reason why many witches set aside time at the esbats to be specifically used for spell-casting, as this is one of the few times that spells can be effectively worked because of the unusually high psychic energy.

The esbat is also the time when babies are presented to the Old Gods during the rite of Wiccaning and the time when couples are ritually joined together through the rite of Handfasting. Rites are performed to seek spiritual help for such tasks as healing, and new tools or other personal items are usually consecrated at these ceremonies. While these rituals can technically take place at a sabbat, they're much more frequently held during the esbat simply because of the far more intimate nature of the occasion. It has also become customary for novices to be formally initiated during the esbat, especially in covens that prefer their initiates to be skyclad.

With all of this emphasis on things that a coven does during an esbat, some people might be thinking that a solitary witch is missing out by practicing alone. This type of thinking is just nonsense. In reality, the Full Moon Esbat Ritual is much more important to a solitary witch than to a coven. This stems from the simple fact that a solitary practitioner needs all of his/her ability to create a link with the Goddess and God. Without the luxury of the combined psychic energy of a coven, a solitary witch must rely solely upon his/her own capability. Therefore, during the full moon, when the psychic flow is at its peak, a sole practitioner can take advantage of the extraordinarily strong psychic currents and perform work that he/she may not otherwise be able to accomplish alone. This increased capacity to carry out spells makes this ritual essential to solitary witches.

FULL MOON ESBAT

During the time of the full moon, the general esbat ceremony is slightly modified to incorporate the differences in the ebb and flow of the psychic currents, and the objective of the ceremony shifts to an "increase" mode. Initiation, Handfasting, Wiccaning, and healing are only a few examples of events that take place at this time. Consequently, during the New Moon Esbat, which occurs in the "decline" phase of the moon, the objectives shift into a decrease mode. Handpartings and funerals are examples of events during this lunar phase. In order to distinguish between the two rituals, keep in mind the differences between the phases of the moon, the symbolism associated with the cycle of the moon, and the characteristics of the psychic energy.

The thirteen full moons of the year are named:

Wolf Moon (first full moon after Yule)	Mead Moon
Storm Moon	Wort Moon
Chaste Moon, Pure Moon	Barley Moon
Seed Moon; Fertile Moon	Wine Moon; Spirit Moon
Hare Moon	Blood Moon
Dyad Moon	Snow Moon (last full moon of year)[3]

BASIC ESBAT SETUP

All denominations start with their own basic altar layout, except that the Goddess figurine should be moved into a more prominent spot near the center of the altar.[4] Items to be consecrated, or anything needed for a specific working, should also be added to the setup. In short, except for the placement of the figurine, there's no special preparation for this ceremony. This differs from the sabbats, which each have their own theme and require special layouts.

There are, however, a few points that should be incorporated into the preparations. Assuming that the ritual is not being held outdoors, it's wise to adjust the altar position to a spot where moonlight can shine on it, or at the very least, moonlight should fall on a part of the Circle. It's also traditional to conduct the ceremony as close to the height of the full moon as possible, preferably near midnight when the moon is believed to be at its peak.[5] But, if this is too late, perform the ceremony whenever practical.

There's one final esbat custom that seems to traverse denominational lines, even if it's not practiced by everyone. Many witches, especially Solitaries, like to incorporate "13 stones" into their rite by placing the stones around the inside circumference of the Circle at even intervals. The size of these stones can vary greatly, but as a general rule, they are usually somewhere between a baseball and a cantaloupe in size. Furthermore, while this was obviously adopted from Druidism, and then adapted to Wiccan practice, it's nevertheless become more and more common.

Gardnerian

The Gardnerian version of the esbat adheres to a fairly uniform pattern, and there's basically no new wording. This is just as true for a Full/New

Moon Esbat as it is for a weekly ritual. The benefit of this standard format is that by using the same rites time and time again, a level of familiarity builds up that allows the participants to focus on the spiritual aspect of the ceremony rather than worrying about terminology or design. And while modifications can still be made to the ritual (e.g., to compensate for lunar phases), the underlying uniformity is beneficial for its consistency.

Once the altar's set up and everything's in place, conduct the ceremony as follows:

1. Consecrate the salt/water and cast the Circle
2. Perform the rite of Drawing Down the Moon complete with the Fivefold Kiss[6]
3. Recite the Charge[7]
4. After the Charge, the High Priest recites a rallying call as follows:

   Eko, Eko Azarak[8]
   Eko, Eko Zomelak
   Eko, Eko Aradia
   Eko, Eko Cernunnos
   Bagabi laca bachab,
   Lamac cahi achabab,
   Karrelyos
   Lamac lamec bachalyas
   Cabahagy sabalyos
   Baryolos
   Lagoz atha cabyolas
   Samahac et famyolas
   Harrahya! (All repeat.)
5. Perform the Witches' Rune
6. Stage the Great Rite[9] (when appropriate)
7. Perform all working (healing, spell casting, etc.)[10]
8. Consecrate the wine and cakes
9. Private time for instruction or socializing
10. Banish the Circle

Italian

In the Italian traditions, the Full Moon Esbat follows a pattern that is both different than that of Gardnerian Wicca and at the same time, quite similar. This scenario evolved because Gerald Gardner based many of his rites on information taken from Charles Godfrey Leland's book, *Aradia: Gospel of the Witches*, which was, itself, based upon ancient Italian practices. The foundations of the two traditions thus began with a common origin, but diverged after Gardner's modifications.

The Italian ceremony opens with the water/salt being consecrated and the Circle being cast. The High Priestess, or High Priest, gives a short prayer to the Goddess Diana. After the prayer, the coven stands (or sits) in a circle with the chalice of wine in the center. The High Priest/ess begins a chant,[11] and the rest of the coven joins in. After one or two verses, the chant is halted by the leader. The High Priest/ess takes a sip of wine and then passes the chalice to each witch to take a sip. This is the symbolic act of joining the coven. Each witch now goes to the west quarter, one at a time, and makes an offering of wine to the Goddess. The following sequence of rites then takes place:

1. Drawing Down the Moon
2. The Veglia[12]
3. Blessing of the wine and cakes[13]
4. The Charge of Aradia[14]
5. The High Priest/ess then recites a closing prayer[15]

At this point, the formal ceremony is complete. Healing, tool consecration, initiation, or anything can be done. After that, the wine and cakes are consecrated and shared. When the entire ritual is completed, the Circle is banished.

Saxon

In contrast to the complexity of the Gardnerian esbat, this denomination holds a fairly modest ceremony. Part of the reason behind this simplicity is that the Saxons do not have the numerous rites of other denominations. Yet, although uncomplicated, the esbat still serves its purpose.

The ritual begins with the Circle being cast. The coven is arranged in a semicircle facing the altar. The Priest and Priestess are at the altar. The Priest raises his arms in the Welcoming Gesture (Figure 14.1), takes a half-step forward, and addresses the coven. He recites:

> *We come together on this night to honor the God and Goddess, and to join in worshipping Woden and Frig. Let us give thanks for all that we have, and for the love and joy that we share with each other.*

WELCOMING GESTURE *Fig. 14.1*

The Priest steps back, and the Priestess raises her arms, steps forward, and takes over the recitation:

> *Let us join together to remember the Gods. For the Lord and Lady shape our lives and lead us on our paths; they watch over us and bestow their gifts upon us; and, when we are in need, they provide for us. It is only right that we thank and honor them.*

The coven responds: *So be it.*

A moment of silence follows while each witch gives silent thanks to the Gods. The moment of silence ends when the bell is rung three times by the Thegn. The Priest again steps forward and recites:

> *When man was a child, the Gods watched over him. The Goddess Frig was his mother; the Great God Woden his father. From the God and Goddess, man learned all. He was taught that he would be rewarded when he did right, but would receive nothing when he did wrong. He learned that when he gave of himself, his love, his life, it would be returned to him. Yet, when greed or malice drove him on, he would suffer for his actions. For the Gods are just and fair. Please them and be rewarded. Yet, as we need them, they need us. Our love is theirs, and theirs is ours. Let us therefore live and love together, always knowing that Love is the Law, and Love is the Bond. So be it.*

The coven responds: *So be it.*

This is the end of the standard esbat. The Full Moon portion takes place at this point. If there's no full moon rite, the ceremony moves to the cakes and ale consecration and ends with the Circle being banished.

During a Full Moon Esbat, the following would be added.[16] The Priest and Priestess take out their seaxes and hold them in the air. The Priestess recites:

> *Lord and Lady; Woden and Frig. During this time, when the moon is full, and the Great Mother is at her most glorious, bless us with your love. Hear us, and answer our call, as we honor you.*

The coven responds: *So be it.*

The Priest lowers his seax and kneels before the Priestess. He then recites:

> *Lovely Lady Frig, at different times and different places, you have been known by many names to many people; Aphrodite, Arianrhod, Cerridwen, Diana, Isis. Through these names, and many more, you have been adored. Yet it is as Frig that we know you, and it is by this name that we worship you.*[17]

The Priestess lowers her seax. The Priest stands and kisses the Priestess. She kneels before him and recites:

> *Great Lord Woden; consort of Frig. Let us know you that we may give you our love. Guard us and guide us in our lives that we may be at one with the Gods.*

The coven responds: *So be it.*

The Priestess stands and kisses the Priest.[18] If there is any working (healing, spells, consecration, etc.) scheduled, this is the time to do it. When everything is finished, move on to the cakes and ale rite. After this, relaxation and social time should be concluded by banishing the Circle.

West Country

Of all the Wiccan traditions that have survived into the twenty-first century, the esbat rites of West Country are undoubtedly the most basic.[19] This denomination employs a modest ceremony that dispenses with some of the frills that other traditions use, while still keeping the essential components of the rite alive. Beyond the simplicity of the actual ritual, a unique aspect of the West Country is that the coven members take turns conducting the ceremony. Unlike other traditions, this denomination does not establish coven leaders in the conventional sense. Therefore, the witches in the coven usually rotate leading the esbats.

As a folksy tradition, West Country practitioners have to make a decision about the Circle layout prior to the ceremony. If there's going to be a bonfire lit in the center, the altar is set up in the north. If, however, there's no fire, such as indoors, the altar is usually placed in the center. A shallow pan of water is also placed on the ground somewhere within the Circle.[20] When that's done, the ceremony is conducted as follows:

1. The Circle is cast
2. A short power-raising chant is sung by the coven[21]
3. The Lord and Lady are welcomed to the Circle, and Drawing Down the Moon, with the Fivefold Kiss, is performed
4. A second power-raising chant, with ring-dance, is carried out[22]
5. Any working is performed
6. Cakes and ale are consecrated and shared
7. The Circle is banished

First-Degree Initiation

For most people who decide to enter the Craft, the process of becoming a witch will likely involve an association with and membership in a coven. These witches are affectionately referred to as coven witches, though some denominations prefer the terms grove members or coveners. Any of these names are appropriate.

Naturally, in order to become a coven witch, you'll have to be accepted into a coven. But don't worry because, while this may sound like a daunting task, it's actually a fairly simple process.

The first step is to find an established coven. Now you may be wondering how to go about finding a coven, since up until this point, you've probable never heard of one in your area. Well they're really not that difficult to locate if you know what you're looking for.

Perhaps the best place to start searching for contacts in your area would be an occult bookstore or New Age shop. If you live in a rural locale, where something like this might be rare, you will likely need to go to a midsize city to find one. However, don't be too discouraged. There are some Wiccan organizations, which are out in the open, that will be glad to assist you in this process. There are also some publications that regularly run advertisements and personal ads from a wide variety of witches trying to meet other witches, as well as covens looking for new members. Two such publications are Circle Network News, P.O. Box 219, Mt. Horeb, WI 53572; and Llewellyn's New Times, P.O. Box 64383, St. Paul, MN 55164-0383. Each will send you one free issue, each has a yearly subscription rate, and both are well worth the small cost.

Regardless of how you locate a coven, the most important point is that you look for one that you not only feel comfortable with, but one that complements your personality. Remember, not all covens, or witches, worship in the same way. For example, some covens practice skyclad, and this is definitely not for everyone. There are same-sex covens, lesbian and gay covens, etc., and any one of these may not be for you. If you were to join a coven in which you weren't comfortable, it might taint your entire experience and possibly drive you away from the religion altogether. It is, therefore, crucial for your spiritual development to select a coven that you feel comfortable with.

Also keep in mind that you are bringing something new into the lives of the other members of any coven you join. That's why it's important to make sure you really want to become a coven witch, otherwise it may be unpleasant for everyone. The best advice is that you should simply try to find a coven that's accepting new initiates. Since covens try to select only people that are suitable, there's a good chance that you'll fit in if they ask you to join.

Once you are formally accepted into a coven, the next step will be for the coven to hold an Initiation Rite, where you'll be initiated as a witch. Many traditions, such as Gardnerian, utilize a degree system and will view you as a "first-degree" witch after initiation. For all practical purposes, this will make you an equal member of the coven, though you'll have more limited obligations than the other witches. However, even with limited duties, you'll still participate in all future ceremonies and rituals and almost anything else that the other coven members do.

Depending on the denomination, you'll also adopt a witch-name[1] at initiation. This custom was originally started to conceal the identity of witches and their families from persecution, but it has carried over into modern practice. Today, a witch takes on a new name as a symbol of rebirth into the Craft, rather than out of necessity. In short, the witch-name is the functional equivalent of a Catholic taking a name at confirmation, and it's also something practiced by most religions of the world in one form or another. In choosing a suitable name, witches will try to find one that best expresses something about them or their personality. But, the only important thing is that the name means something to the witch.

After becoming more knowledgeable in the Craft, you'll be initiated again as a second-degree witch. This act essentially elevates you to High Priest/ess. You'll have more responsibility, play a more active role in rituals, and generally have a much greater awareness of your own powers and limitations, as well as those of the other witches in the coven. On top of that, you'll also be able to initiate others as witches, but only to an equal or lesser degree than yourself.

Some denominations (e.g., Gardnerian) have one more step in the initiation process. Once a witch is emotionally and spiritually ready, he/she is elevated to a third-degree witch. At this point in their spiritual development, witches answer only to their own conscience and the Gods. Although they're probably not going to be the leader of their coven, they are nonetheless capable of forming or running their own coven.[2]

The final type of initiation is Self Initiation. As its name suggests, this involves nothing more than a solitary rite combined with a true belief in the philosophies of Wicca. Reasons for becoming a solitary practitioner range from unavailability of a convenient coven to personal preference for spiritual freedom and self-sufficiency.

While such a decision may seem a little out of character, especially considering the Wiccan doctrines of love and caring, it must be remembered that most witches of antiquity were Solitaries. History has taught us that witches were secretive and cautious by necessity. Add to this fact the sheer difficulty involved in travel several hundred years ago, common sense dictates that a certain amount of solitary practice was inevitable. The point is that becoming a solitary witch has always been a part of the Craft and should not be considered better or worse than coven practice.

SETUP

First initiations almost always take place during an esbat rather than a sabbat for the simple reason that the smaller venue usually offers greater intimacy and a more relaxed atmosphere, which helps put the Neophyte at ease. Other reasons may include the fact that the Novice is usually skyclad while being initiated, or that there are often nonwitches invited to sabbats. But since everything will already be in place for the esbat, setting up for an initiation is quite easy. The only additional items needed are:

- Blindfold (color is unimportant)
- Anointing oil
- Three cords (one nine-feet long and two four-feet)[3]
- Novice's personal tools and jewelry to be consecrated after initiation
- Horned Helmet[4]
- Spool of twine (Gardnerian/Alexandrian only)

Gardnerian

With the exception of Alexandrian Wicca,[5] this denomination has the most intricate initiation rites of any tradition. And because there's such a vast difference between this rite and the versions used by less formal denominations, it seems logical to assume that the complexity was the result of Gerald Gardner adding elements of Ceremonial Magick to the rite in an attempt to enhance it. But this isn't necessarily a bad thing. In fact, many witches feel that the elaborate style of the Gardnerian ritual lends a certain degree of historical ambiance to the occasion.

The initiation usually begins before the Circle is cast.[6] The Novice stands outside the Circle area. If the northeast sector is available, this is where he or she should wait. The Novice is blindfolded and bound with the cords[7] as follows (a man is initiated in this example): The Novice places one arm behind his back (Figure 15.1), and the center of the nine-foot cord is tied around the wrist. The second hand is brought behind the back, overlapping the other wrist, and the cord is used to bind the wrists together (Figure 15.2). The ends are looped loosely around the neck (Figure 15.3) and tied[8] (Figure 15.4). Next, one short cord is tied around the right ankle (Figure 15.5) while the High Priestess recites:[9]

Feet neither bound nor free.

A second short cord is then tied around the left knee (Figure 15.6).

Fig. 15.1

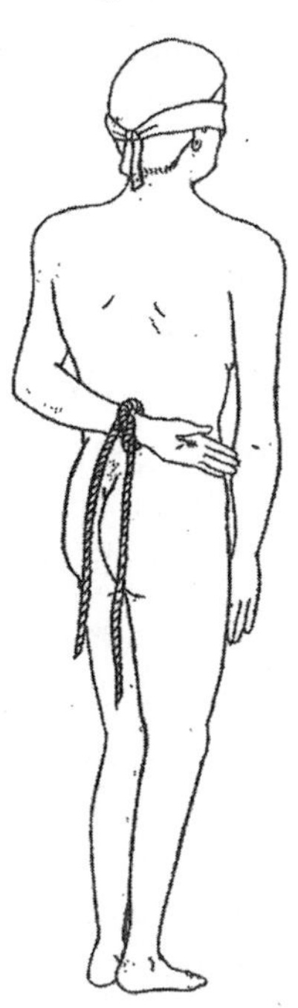

Fig. 15.2

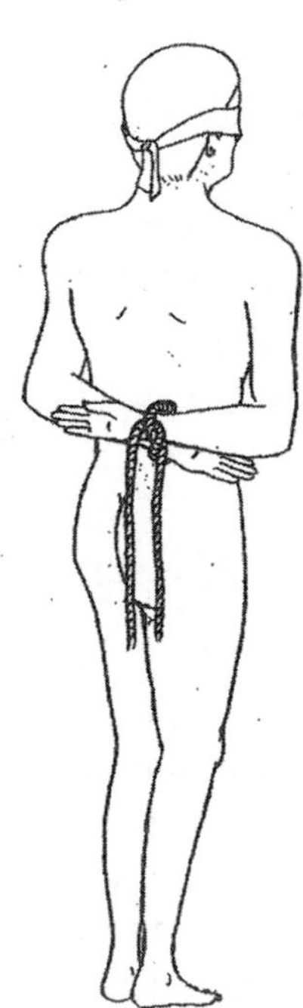

Fig. 15.3

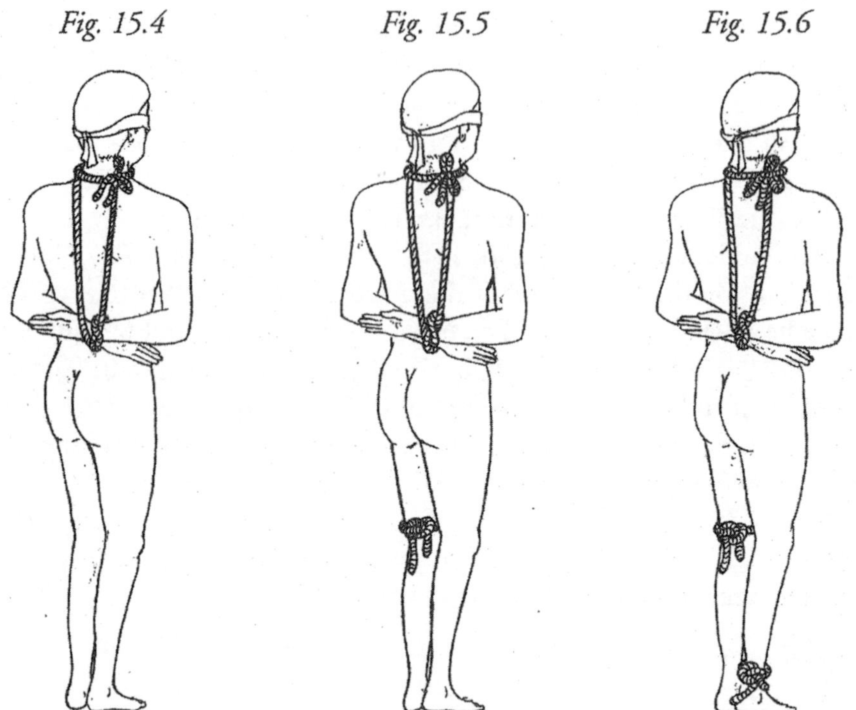

The Circle is cast, and the coven enters, leaving the gateway open. One witch stays behind with the Novice. The normal Opening Ritual proceeds through Drawing Down the Moon. If a female is being initiated, Drawing Down the Sun should also be enacted. However, the Charge is saved until later.

The High Priestess gives the Sign of the Cabalistic Cross[10] as follows: Touch forehead and say, *ATEH* (thou art). Touch breast and say, *MALKUTH* (the Kingdom). Touch right shoulder and say, *VE-GEBURAH* (and the Power). Touch left shoulder and say, *VE-GEDULAH* (and the Glory). Clasp hands in front and say *LE-OLAM* (forever). Next, the Witches' Rune is enacted, then the High Priestess and High Priest face the Novice and recite the Charge. After this is completed, the High Priest takes a step backward, and the High Priestess recites:

> *Thou who stands on the threshold between the pleasant world of men and the dread domains of the Lords of the Outer Spaces, hast thou the courage to make the trial?*

The High Priestess places the tip of the sword (or athame) lightly against the Novice's chest, directly over his heart, and she recites:

For I say to thee now that it is better to hurl thyself onto my blade and perish, than to attempt the trial with fear in thy heart.

The Novice answers:

I have two passwords. Perfect love for the Goddess, perfect trust in the Goddess.

The High Priestess recites:

All who have such are doubly welcome. I give thee a third, a kiss (pauses to give Novice a kiss) *to pass through this dread door.*

The High Priestess hands the sword to the High Priest. She goes behind the Novice, wraps her arms around him, and guides him into the Circle. The High Priest follows them into the Circle, closes the doorway using the sword, and places it on the altar. The High Priestess leads the Novice around the Circle, stopping at each cardinal point. At each Watchtower the High Priestess recites:

Take heed, ye dread Lords and gentle Goddesses of the East (South, West, North) *that* (insert Novice's name) *is properly prepared to be initiated as a priest* [priestess] *and witch.*

After the High Priestess has taken the Novice to all four cardinal points, she leads him into the center of the Circle and steps away. The coven holds a ring-dance around the Novice. The High Priestess and High Priest usually participate in the dance, but they can refrain. The coven chants the opening of the Witches' Rune as they dance:

Eko, Eko, Azarak
Eko, Eko, Zomelak
Eko, Eko, Cernunnos
Eko, Eko, Aradia

This chant continues until the High Priestess calls for it to stop. She then turns the Novice so that he's facing the altar, while the High Priest rings the handbell three times. The High Priestess recites:

In other religions the novice kneels while the priest towers above him. But in the Magickal Art we are taught to be humble. Thus I kneel to welcome him.

She proceeds to give the Fivefold Kiss. Once this is completed, the High Priest retrieves the twine and white-handled knife and brings them to the High Priestess. He motions for a female witch[11] to assist the High Priestess and steps out of the way.

The High Priestess says, *We are now going to take your measure.* With the Maiden's help, the twine is stretched from the floor to the top of the Novice's head, then cut with the white-handled knife. The High Priestess takes the cut piece of twine, measures around the Novice's head and ties a knot. The same procedure is repeated around his chest (heart) and around his waist (pubic area). When the three knots are made, the twine is wound and placed on the altar. This can be done by the High Priest.

The Maiden helps the Novice kneel down. Once kneeling, he bows his head. The High Priestess and Maiden then use cords (already tied to his right ankle and left knee) to bind his ankles and knees together (Figure 15.7). When this is done, the Maiden retrieves the scourge and gives it to the High Priestess, who is standing above the Novice.

The High Priest rings the handbell three times and says, *Three.* The High Priestess uses the scourge to give the Novice three lashes.[12] The High Priest rings the bell seven times and says, *Seven.*[13] The High Priestess gives seven lashes. The High Priest rings the bell nine times and says, *Nine.* The High Priestess gives nine lashes. The High Priest rings the bell twenty-one times and says, *Twenty-one.* The High Priestess gives twenty-one lashes.

Fig. 15.7

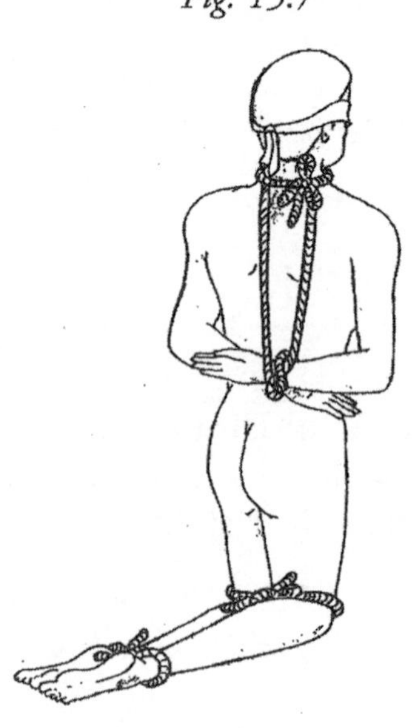

Following the last lash, the High Priestess says:

Thou hast bravely passed the test. Art thou ready to swear that thou will always be true to the Craft?

The High Priestess asks:

Art thou always ready to aid, protect, and defend thy brothers and sisters of the Craft?

The Novice answers: *I am.*

The High Priestess lays a hand on the Novice's shoulder and instructs him to repeat after her. She then recites:

I (Novice inserts name*) in the presence of the Mighty Ones, do of my own free will and accord most solemnly swear that I will ever keep secret and never reveal the secrets of the Craft, except it be to a proper person, properly prepared within a Circle such as I am now in; and that I will never deny the secrets to such a person if he or she be properly vouched for by a brother or sister of the Craft. All this I swear by my hopes of a future life, mindful that my measure has been taken; and may my weapons turn against me if I break this my solemn oath.*

The Maiden helps the Novice stand up while the High Priest retrieves the anointing oil and the chalice of wine from the altar. The High Priestess dips her index finger into the oil and says:

I hereby consecrate thee with oil.

The High Priestess uses her finger to anoint the Novice with the oil, forming the inverted triangle, the Sigil of First Degree (Figure 15.8). She anoints him in the following pattern: above the pubic region, the right breast, left breast, and again above the pubic region.

When this is completed, she takes the chalice, dips her finger in the wine, and repeats the pattern by saying: *I hereby consecrate thee with wine.* After forming the triangle with the wine, she says: *I hereby consecrate thee with my lips as a priest and witch.* Once again she forms the triangle using her lips to kiss the points. The High Priestess removes the Novice's blindfold while the Maiden unties the cords. As soon as he is unbound, the coven files past, and each member greets him with a kiss.

SIGIL OF FIRST DEGREE *Fig. 15.8*

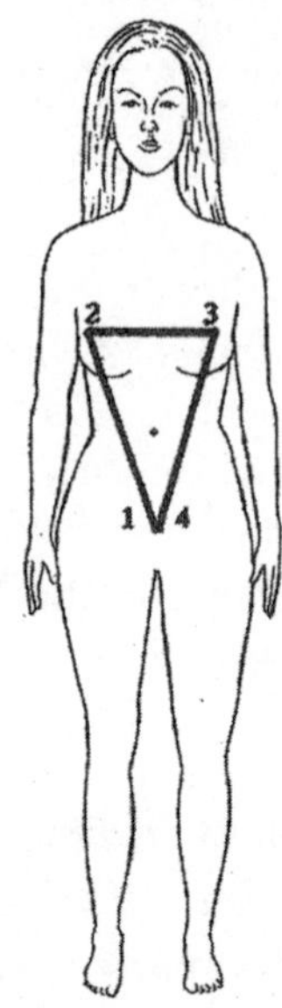

Once coven members have returned to their places, the High Priest retrieves the working tools, one by one, from the altar and hands each item to the newly initiated witch. The High Priestess recites:

I now present to thee the working tools of the Craft. In your hand you hold the Magick Sword. With this, as with the Athame, thou canst form all Magick Circles, subdue and punish all rebellious spirits and demons, and even persuade good spirits. With this in thy hand, thou art the ruler of the Magick Circle.

The High Priest takes the sword and hands over the athame. The High Priestess recites the next verse:

Next, I present the Athame. This is the true witches' weapon, and it has all the powers of the Magick Sword.

The High Priest takes the athame and hands over the white-handled knife. The High Priestess recites the next verse:

Next, I present the White-Handled Knife. Its use is to form all instruments used in the Art. It may only be used within the Magick.

The High Priest takes the white-handled knife and hands over the wand. The High Priestess recites the next verse:

Next, I present the Wand. Its use is to call and control certain Genii to whom it would not be mete to use the Magick Sword or Athame.

The High Priest takes the wand and hands over the pentacle. The High Priestess recites the next verse:

Next, I present the Pentacle. This is for the purpose of calling up the appropriate spirits.

The High Priest takes the pentacle and hands over the censer. The High Priestess recites the next verse:

Next, I present the Censer of Incense. This is used to encourage and welcome good spirits and to banish evil spirits.

The High Priest takes the censer and hands over the scourge. The High Priestess recites the next verse:

Next, I present the Scourge. This is a sign of power and domination. It is also used to cause purification and enlightenment. For it is written, "To learn thou must suffer and be purified." Art thou willing to suffer to learn?

The witch answers: *I am.* The High Priest takes the scourge and hands over the cords. The High Priestess recites the next verse:

Next and lastly, I present the Cords. They are of use to bind the sigils in the Art; and also the material basis; and also they are necessary in the Oath.

The High Priest takes the cords. The High Priestess now recites:

I salute thee in the names of Aradia and Cernunnos, newly made Priest.

The High Priestess now presents the new witch to the Watchtowers. She begins in the east by reciting:

Hear Ye, O Mighty Ones of the East (South, West, North), (Witch's name) *has been consecrated a Priest and witch.*

At this point the witch is fully initiated. The ceremony can now continue as usual. For a first working, the new witch may consecrate his/her tools or be allowed to assist with the rest of the ritual.

Italian

When it comes to becoming a Strega or Stregone, this denomination relies heavily upon ancient custom. As a result, the ritual used for coven initiation and self-initiation are virtually the same. The good thing about this is that a solitary witch and coven witch have both gone through the same initiation process and are, in a sense, interchangeable. In a solitary rite, the prospective witch will simply modify the wording to first person and perform all the actions.

Unlike Gardnerian, there are no special tools needed for this ceremony. There are, however, a few requirements. First, if at all possible, the rite should be held in an open field or a clearing in the woods at the height of the full moon. It's also preferable to have a stream, pond, or other body of water in the field or beside the clearing. Second, water, wine, and salt must be brought along, plus a bowl in which these ingredients can be mixed and a drinking cup.[14] Third, fire must be introduced into the rite. This can be done using a candle or small bonfire. Finally, a circlet of flowers (for a woman) or holly (for a man) should be worn by the Novice.

The ritual begins at midnight during a normal esbat meeting. The Circle is cast with the Novice outside it. Even if the coven wears clothing, the Novice is usually skyclad for initiation, but this custom can be waived. After casting the Circle, the High Priestess pours the water and wine into the bowl, then adds a little salt while reciting:

In the name of Diana, I consecrate this water and wine with the purifying goodness of this salt.

The Novice (again male) is now ushered into the Circle by a female witch. She leads him to the High Priestess and positions him in front of her. The High Priestess dips her fingers into the bowl and anoints the Novice with the Invoking Pentagram of Earth: forehead, right breast, left shoulder, right shoulder, left breast, forehead. She hands the bowl to an assistant, places her hands on the Novice's shoulders, and guides him to his knees. She recites:

You have come before us, beneath the Moon and stars, in the presence of the Old Ones, in the hope that you may learn the secrets of the Old Religion.

The Novice, kneeling at the feet of the High Priestess, bows slightly. She places her hands on his head and recites:

> *Hear me, Diana, Goddess of the Moon. As the full moon shines down upon this Circle, I call upon you to receive your child, who kneels before me, into your graces. Bestow the gifts upon* (Novice's name) *who has come forth on this night to honor and worship you.*

The High Priestess dips her fingers in the water/wine mixture (the assistant should have remained close by) and anoints the Novice again. After each stroke, she recites:

> *Diana, Goddess of Beauty and Queen of all the Witches, let the power of Earth* (forehead to right breast) *the power of the Air* (right breast to left shoulder) *the power of Fire* (left shoulder to right shoulder) *the power of Water* (right shoulder to left breast) *and the power of Spirit* (left breast to forehead) *be a blessing upon this, your servant, as we welcome him into the Old Religion. So be it.*

The newly initiated witch stands and dips his own fingers in the bowl. He anoints himself in the same Invoking Pentagram pattern and recites:

> *In the name of Diana, I swear my allegiance to the Old Gods, and pray that I may be worthy of being known as Stregone. So be it.*[15]

The rite is over. It's customary for the newly initiated witch to be asked to assist with the remainder of the esbat.

Saxon

This is one of the few traditions in which, regardless of the sex of the Ceorl (i.e., the person being initiated), the Priest performs most of the initiation. Besides the Priest, the Thegn, Scribe, and Priestess all participate, as does the Ceorl's adviser.[16] Another interesting aspect of this denomination is that the rite takes place immediately after the Temple is erected. No blessings, offerings, or other rites are enacted until the initiation is completed. In modern practice, this immediacy appears to be unnecessary, though it likely owes its roots to an attempt to keep the secrets of the Saxon tradition from the uninitiated. However, consecrated water is needed for the rite, so this must be prepared in advance.

The ceremony begins with the Ceorl (again a male) outside the Circle.

A coven that normally wears clothing should do so, but the Ceorl should be skyclad. The Temple is erected in the usual fashion. The Thegn then says:

> *The Temple is erected and the Circle cast. None shall be allowed to leave but for good reason.*

Coven recites: *So be it.*

There are two slightly different schools of thought at this point. The first holds that the Priest puts on the Horned Helmet only if the Ceorl is a woman, while the second says he puts it on regardless of the Ceorl's gender. In either case, the Scribe then recites:

> *Here, written in the book* (or "*in The Tree*" instead of the book) *is the progress of* (Ceorl's name) *the one who seeks to join us.*

Priest asks: *Who presents him to us?*

Advisor answers: *I do. For I have shown* (Ceorl's name) *the way.*

Priest replies: *Then bring him forth that he may join us to worship the Mighty Ones.*

The Thegn, carrying the spear and hunting horn, goes to the edge of the Circle and cuts a doorway for the Ceorl. After blowing the horn three times, he motions for the Ceorl to enter, then uses his spear to close the Circle. The Thegn remains by the doorway as a guard while the Ceorl approaches the altar. The Priest faces him and recites:[17]

> *I am the one who speaks for Woden. You have come before us being known as* (Ceorl's name) *but no longer shall this be your name.*

The Priest dips his fingers in the consecrated water and anoints the Ceorl on the forehead, heart, and above the pubic area. He then recites:

> *In the names of Woden and Frig, I cleanse you with the sacred water. As it has been purified, so it shall drive out all impurities. May you now be filled with love for all things.*

The Priest embraces and kisses the Ceorl on both cheeks.[18] He places his hands on the Ceorl's shoulders, guides him to his knees, and asks a series of questions:

> *To be counted among us, you must have certain knowledge of our ways. Only then can we be sure that your desire is true. What are the names of the Gods?*

Ceorl answers: *We know them as Woden and Frig.*

Priest asks: *Are these the Gods that you accept as supreme?*

Ceorl answers: *Yes.*

Priest asks: *Will you promise to faithfully attend the rites held in their honor, to keep their names sacred, and defend the faith?*

Ceorl answers: *I will.*

Priest asks: *And will you promise to love, honor, and protect your brothers and sisters of the Craft, aid all who are sick or in distress, and forever be true to the Oath that you hereby swear?*

Ceorl answers: *I will.*

Priest says:

> *Then I give you this name by which you shall always be known to your brothers and sisters.* (Priest stands and holds out his hand to the Ceorl.) *Arise* (insert new name) *and be counted among us in this Circle, for now we are equal not only in the eyes of Woden and Frig, but in all things. Know now that Love is the Law and Love is the Bond, and keep this as your secret Oath.*

Ceorl repeats oath: *Love is the Law, and Love is the Bond.*

The Priestess steps forward, embraces, and kisses the Ceorl, and says: *You must now meet your brothers and sisters.*

She then leads him around the Circle, and each coven member welcomes him with an embrace and kiss. The Thegn is omitted as he is still guarding the doorway. Once everyone has greeted the Ceorl, the Priestess guides him back to the altar where the Priest is waiting with the goblet of ale in his hands. The Ceorl faces the Priest as an offering of ale is poured onto the ground (or into a libation dish). The Priest recites:

> *You are now and forever a Gesith, and from this moment forth you shall always be one of us. So be it.*[19]

Coven: *So be it.*

The Priestess retrieves clothing for the new Gesith, unless the coven is skyclad. It's customary for the Priest to present him with a seax. The Scribe then brings the coven book (The Tree) and says:

> *You are now a member of this coven, and I ask that you place your name next to those of your brothers and sisters.*

Once the new Gesith signs his new name in the book, the ceremony moves on to the normal esbat ritual.

West Country

This denomination has the simplest initiation ritual of all the branches of Wicca. In fact, it's so easy that there's absolutely no difference between the wording of a coven and solitary rite. But there are two things that are slightly different from other denominations. First, in ancient times, the rite always took place at the entrance to a cave so that the Inductee could emerge from the depths. This was a symbolic gesture used to signify emergence from the earth.

Today, however, the cave has been replaced by a less intrusive requirement (i.e., crawling on the ground). Second, whether or not they normally work clothed, the entire coven is skyclad during the initiation. This is mandatory. Although this may not be for everyone, ritual nudity is important to establish trust and remove any shame, within the coven. Other than that, the rite is very short.

Prior to the Circle being cast the Inductee is blindfolded and bound with cords around the legs and wrists. Unlike the Gardnerian custom of tying the arms behind the back, this denomination keeps the arms in front. The Inductee is always skyclad. A witch stays with the Inductee, away from where the Circle will be held, until after it's been cast. The Inductee is escorted to the edge of the Circle where a gateway has been opened, then he/she is told to get down onto hands and knees. Urged on by the other witches, the Inductee crawls into the Circle.[20] Once the Inductee enters the Circle, he/she stands, is unbound, and the blindfold is removed. The Inductee is anointed with a mixture of warm oil and water[21] by several members of the coven and then given his/her own athame. The Inductee recites:

> *In the name of the Lady and Lord, I swear to harm no one, either by word or deed. I further swear that I shall not reveal the secrets of the Faith, except to one that I know to be a follower of the Goddess. From this time forward, I shall be known as* (witch name) *to all who share my path.*

The witch who acted as an escort walks the Inductee around the Circle to be greeted by the other coven members. After all have greeted him/her the coven recites:

Welcome (witch name) *blessed are you now and for always as you travel along the path with the Lady and Lord.*

This is the end of the initiation. If the coven normally works robed, everyone may dress before the ceremony resumes.

Second-Degree Initiation

There are only a few denominations that have an advancement system of initiation. Of these, the Gardnerian tradition is, without question, the most complex.[1] In order to advance to the next degree, a Gardnerian witch is expected to be emotionally prepared to deal with the rigors of added responsibility, knowledgeable enough to handle the duties of Craft practice, and secure enough to confront any irregular circumstances that might arise.

The only additional items needed for a second-degree initiation are:

- Blindfold (color is unimportant)
- Anointing oil
- Three cords (one nine foot; two four-and-a-half foot)
- A new white candle
- Mask[2]
- Assorted items (veil, jewelry)[3]

Gardnerian

The ceremony follows a normal esbat format through the Invocation to the Great God Cernunnos. At this point, the coven members position themselves in an arc around the inner perimeter of the Circle while the Initiate stands in the center to be bound and blindfolded. The partial binding is the same as in the first-degree rite.[4] The High Priestess leads the Initiate around the Circle, stopping at each cardinal point. At every Watchtower, the High Priestess recites:

> *Hear, ye Mighty Ones of the East (South, West, North) that (insert Initiate's name) being a duly consecrated Priest and Witch is now properly prepared to be made a High Priest and Magus.*[5]

After the High Priestess has taken the Initiate to all four cardinal points, she leads him back to the center of the Circle, faces him toward the altar, and steps away. The coven joins hands and holds a ring-dance around the Initiate. The High Priestess and High Priest always participate in the dance.[6] After the dance, the Initiate is fully bound and helped to his knees. The High Priestess steps forward and recites:

To attain to this degree, it is necessary to suffer and be purified. Art thou willing to suffer to learn?

Initiate answers: *I am.*
The High Priestess responds:

I purify thee to take this Oath rightly.

The High Priest rings the handbell three times and says, *Three*. The High Priestess uses the scourge to give the Initiate three lashes.[7] The High Priest rings the bell seven times and says, *Seven*.[8] The High Priestess gives seven lashes. The High Priest rings the bell nine times and says, *Nine*. The High Priestess gives nine lashes. The High Priest rings the bell twenty-one times and says, *Twenty-One*. The High Priestess gives twenty-one lashes. Following the last lash, the High Priestess says:

I now give thee a new name (insert witch name) *that shall only be known to your brothers and sisters of the Art.*

She instructs the Initiate to repeat after her:

I (insert witch name) *swear upon my mother's womb, and by my honor among men, and by my brothers and sisters of the Art, that I shall never reveal any of the secrets of the Art, except it be to a worthy person, properly prepared in the center of a Magick Circle, such as I am now in. This I swear by my hopes of salvation, my past lives, and by my hopes of future ones to come, and I devote myself to utter destruction if I break this, my solemn Oath.*

The High Priestess kneels next to the Initiate, places her left hand under his knee and her right hand on his head.[9] She says, *I will all my power into thee*, while concentrating in an effort to direct her power into the Initiate. When finished, she stands and motions for the High Priest to bring the chalice of wine and the anointing oil. The Initiate is helped to stand, and his feet and legs are untied, his wrists remain tied, and the blindfold is left on.

The High Priestess says, *I consecrate thee with oil.* She then anoints the Initiate to form the Sigil of Second Degree as follows: throat, right hip, left breast, right breast, left hip, and throat (Figure 16.1).[10]

Once this is completed, she takes the chalice, dips her finger in the wine, and repeats the pattern, saying, *I hereby consecrate thee with wine.* Next she says, *I hereby consecrate thee with my lips* and kisses the same points *as High Priest and Magus.*

SIGIL OF SECOND DEGREE (AMERICAN) *Fig. 16.1*

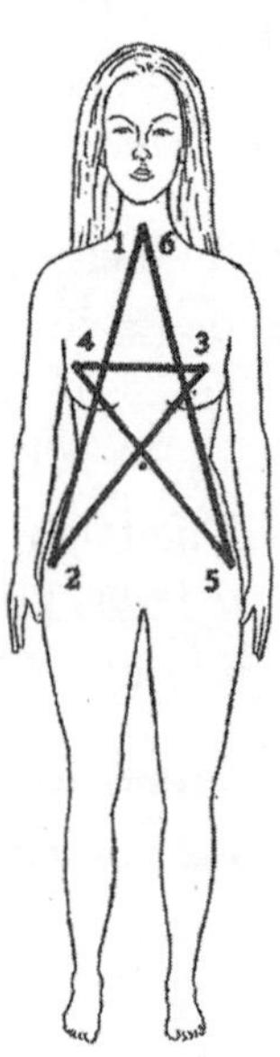

The High Priestess removes the Initiate's blindfold while another witch unties the last cord. As soon as he is unbound, the coven files past, and each member greets him with a kiss. The coven members return to their places while the High Priest retrieves the first working tool from the altar and hands it to the Initiate. The High Priestess recites:

You will now use the tools in turn. First, the Magick Sword. Recast the Circle with it.

The Initiate silently recasts the Circle. The High Priest takes the sword and hands over the athame. The High Priestess recites the next verse:

Second, the Athame. Recast the Circle with it.

Initiate silently recasts the Circle. The High Priest takes the athame and hands over the white-handled knife. The High Priestess recites the next verse:

Third, the White-Handled Knife. Inscribe the candle.

The Initiate uses the white-handled knife to inscribe a pentagram on the white unlit candle.[11] The High Priest takes the white-handled knife and hands over the wand. The High Priestess recites the next verse: *Fourth, the Wand.*

The Initiate takes the wand and waves it in the direction of all four cardinal points. The High Priest takes the wand and hands over the pentacle. The High Priestess recites the next verse: *Fifth, the Pentacle.*

The Initiate takes the pentacle and holds it toward the four cardinal points. The High Priest takes the pentacle and hands over the censer. The High Priestess recites the next verse: *Sixth, the Censer of Incense.*

The Initiate takes the censer and walks around the Circle. The High Priest takes the censer and hands over the cords. The High Priestess says: *Seventh, the Cords.* With the assistance of the High Priest, the Initiate binds the High Priestess the same way he was bound. She is made to kneel facing the altar.[12] The High Priest retrieves the scourge and gives it to the Initiate. The High Priestess then recites:

Eighth, the Scourge. Learn that in Witchcraft thou must ever give as thou receive, but ever triple. Where I gave thee three, return nine; where I gave seven, return twenty-one; where I gave nine, return twenty-seven; and where I gave twenty-one, return sixty-three. (Optional line: *Now take up the scourge and return to me what I deserve.*)

The High Priest says, *Nine*, and the Initiate gives the High Priestess nine light strokes with the scourge. Next, the High Priest says, *Twenty-One*, and the Initiate gives the High Priestess twenty-one light strokes with the scourge. The High Priest says, *Twenty-Seven*, and the Initiate gives the High Priestess twenty-seven light strokes with the scourge. Finally, the High Priest says, *Sixty-three*, and the Initiate gives the High Priestess sixty-three light strokes with the scourge. The High Priestess then says:

Thou hast obeyed the Law. But mark well, for when thou receivest good, so equally art thou bound to return good threefold.

Initiate and High Priest help the High Priestess to her feet and unbind her. The High Priestess now presents the Initiate to the Watchtowers. She begins in the east by reciting:

> *Hear Ye, O Mighty Ones of the East* (South, West, North) *that* (witch's name) *hath been elevated to Second Degree and duly consecrated High Priest and Magus.*

At this point, there are two completely different schools of thought. One version holds that the Magickal Legend of Aradia[13] is enacted now. A second belief is that this rite is finished, and the Magickal Legend of Aradia occurs during the Third-degree ceremony. Without having access to Gardner's original text, it's impossible to be sure which is correct. My experience, though, has been that it belongs in the next initiation phase. So that's where it'll remain. However, it can just as easily be added here.

West Country

Apart from the Gardnerian and Alexandrian branches, most Wiccan traditions do not have more than one stage of initiation. For instance, in Italian and Saxon Wicca, a witch is a witch. Once initiated into these denominations, there can be a promotion to coven leader, but no other formal spiritual advancement.

While there are varying reasons behind these single-initiation beliefs, the most prominent seems to be that an initiated witch is already blessed by the God and Goddess. Therefore, the only possible explanation for a second initiation ceremony would be to gain a higher degree of blessing from the Gods. This, in effect, would imply that a first-degree witch is spiritually beneath a second-degree witch in the eyes of the God and Goddess. Since this notion is totally against the beliefs of Wicca, a single initiation keeps everyone on the same spiritual footing. Advancement within the coven merely puts a witch on a different footing in regard to Craft knowledge.

West Country, however, does have a second form of initiation. And, while it does appear to elevate the Initiate to a higher spiritual plateau, the difference may be due to mislabeling after the beginning stage. In short, it would probably be better to call the person a "novice" after the first initiation and a "witch" after the second.

This distinction makes sense for two reasons. First, a novice is still learning how to connect to the Gods, while a witch already knows. Since no Drawing Down the Moon (or Sun) takes place at the first initiation, this is a good indication that the Initiate is too inexperienced to handle a direct connection with the Gods. Second, the final initiation cannot be held until one year and one day have passed. During this time, the new witch is not allowed to practice alone and is taught the knowledge needed for the future. Thus, both reasons lend credibility to the novice theory.

Regardless of the reasoning, West Country does have a second initiation stage. Further, this denomination holds a Circle specifically for this initiation. In other denominations, the rite is part of the esbat ceremony.

In West Country, the rite begins with the Initiate robed and blindfolded. Even if they usually work clothed, the entire coven is skyclad during the initiation. The Priestess performing the initiation (assuming a man is being initiated) dons a mask and veil to conceal her identity. Then, with the Initiate present, the Circle is cast and a power-raising chant conducted. The Priestess and Initiate refrain from participation. When the chant ends, the Initiate is brought before each quarter by the Priestess and introduced using his witch name:

I present (witch name) *to the East* (South, West, North*) for blessing.*

He's then led back to the center of the Circle where he reaffirms his initial oath:

> *In the name of the Lady and Lord, I swear to harm no one, either by word or deed. I further swear that I shall not reveal the secrets of the Faith, except to one that I know to be a follower of the Goddess. I am now prepared to accept the power and wisdom that shall be bestowed upon me.*

Following this speech, a doorway is cut in the Circle, and the coven files out, usually leaving the immediate area. The Priestess removes the robe and blindfold from the Initiate and instructs him to lie on the altar, which the coven cleared prior to leaving. Sometimes the Initiate is disrobed and laid on the altar before the coven exits. The Great Rite now takes place between the Initiate and the Priestess.[14] Once this act is completed, Drawing Down the God (or Moon) is performed. The coven is then summoned back to the Circle. Upon entering, the coven restores the altar.

With the coven arranged in an arc, facing the altar, the Priestess and Initiate consecrate the wine (or ale) and apple slices[15] using the following words:

In the name of the Lady and Lord, witnessed by all on this hallowed night, may blessings be upon this bounty of the Earth, and may those who partake of it share in its sanctity.

The Initiate distributes a piece of apple to each coven member, saving a piece for himself. He takes the cup, dips his piece of apple into the wine, and recites:

On this night, within this Circle, I have joined with the Goddess (or God*) just as this fruit enters the cup. Through love and deed, I prove myself worthy of being counted among the children of the Lady and Lord.*

The Priestess says: *If any have reason to doubt this man, speak now.* The coven answer: *We find him worthy.* The Initiate responds, *I am*, and takes the cup, presenting it to the coven members so that they can dip their piece of apple in the wine. After this, the cup is returned to the altar and the Priestess recites:

Another has been added to the fold. He is now and forever a Keeper of the Mysteries. Let him always be welcome within this Circle.

The coven recites: *We will always welcome him.* With this statement, the rite is over. The Circle is now banished.

Third-Degree Initiation

The Gardnerian and Alexandrian denominations are the only branches of Wicca that have a three-prong system of initiation. In order to advance to the last degree, a Gardnerian witch must successfully complete the first two phases and be adept in virtually all fields of Wiccan knowledge and Craft practice. Along with having accumulated wisdom, they must be mature enough to handle the enormous emotional commitment and have sufficient self-control to act appropriately. The rationale behind this is based on the fact that a third-degree witch has no superior in the Craft. He or she is, in effect, only accountable to the God and Goddess. Therefore, it's merely sound judgment to ensure that this tremendous responsibility is only passed on to those individuals who are properly prepared.

The additional items needed for this initiation depend entirely on the version that's practiced. If the Magickal Legend of Aradia is going to be enacted (assuming it was not performed during the second-degree rite), a crown, veil, and jewelry are necessary; otherwise, only the veil is required. The location for the Great Rite (whether actual or not) is the center of the Circle, but the surface it is to take place on needs to be determined. Since the Priestess[1] will need to lie down for a portion of the rite, most covens simply clear the altar and move it to the center. The Priestess can then lie across it. In this case, a small table is usually set up so that the tools can be placed on it. Other than that, a place needs to be prepared (swept, blanket laid down, etc.) and a chair set in the center. No chair is necessary if the altar is moved as the Priestess can sit directly on the altar.

The ceremony follows a normal esbat format through the Invocation to the Great God Cernunnos. At this point, the coven members position themselves in an arc around the inner perimeter of the Circle, while the Priestess sits on the altar (or chair) with her back to the north. She is skyclad, unbound, and in the Osiris Position. The High Priest kneels in front of her, kisses her knees, and bows his head. (If the Great Rite is going to be symbolic, the following athame/wine portion is moved until later in the ritual. In that case, skip to consecrating the cakes). He stands, retrieves the chalice, kneels before the Priestess again, and holds the chalice up to her. The Priestess holds the athame with both hands and lowers the tip into the chalice until it penetrates the surface of the wine. She recites:

As the athame is male, so the cup is female. Conjoined, they bring blessedness.

The Priestess kisses the athame and lays it down, takes the chalice from the High Priest, and drinks from it. She gives the High Priest a kiss as she hands it back to him. The High Priest stands, drinks from the chalice, and passes it to a female witch with a kiss. This continues woman to man until all have partaken. The chalice is returned to the altar. The High Priest brings forth the cakes to be consecrated. He presents them to the Priestess, who picks up the athame and touches the tip to the cakes one at a time. While moving the athame from cake to cake, she recites:

O' Queen most secret, bless this food unto our bodies, bestowing health, wealth, strength, joy, and peace, and that fulfillment of Will, and Love under Will, which is perpetual happiness.

The Priestess takes a cake, kisses the High Priest, and then eats the cake. He takes a cake and passes the rest to a female witch with a kiss, and so on until everyone has one to eat. When the cakes are consumed, the High Priest stands facing the Priestess and asks:

Dare I proceed with this sublime rite, I must beg purification at thy hands.

The Priestess takes the red cord and binds the wrists of the High Priest behind his back, draping the ends over his shoulders. She uses these ends to lead him around the Circle. The High Priest then kneels facing the altar, and the Priestess takes the scourge and gives him several light strokes. After putting down the scourge, she unties the High Priest, and the process is reversed. He ties her and gives her several light strokes with the scourge. The High Priest leads the bound Priestess around the Circle and presents her to each Watchtower by saying:

Hear, ye Mighty Ones of the East (South, West, North) *the twice consecrated and holy* (Priestess' name) *High Priestess and Witch Queen, is properly prepared, and will proceed to erect the Sacred Altar.*

Once all four quarters have been called, the High Priest leads the Priestess back to the altar and unties her. He then says: *I again beg purification.* The Priestess binds him once more and leads him around the Circle. After the scourging, the High Priest is untied. He turns toward the coven and says: *I must reveal a great mystery.*[2]

The Magickal Legend of Aradia is performed. The following roles should have been assigned prior to the ceremony: the Narrator, the Goddess (usually portrayed by the Priestess herself), the Lord of the Underworld (usually portrayed by the High Priest), and the Guardian of the Portals.[3] The Narrator now stands behind the altar while the Lord of the Underworld (hereafter referred to simply as the "Lord") stands in front of the altar with his back to it. The Goddess stands with her back to the south, while the Guardian of the Portals (hereafter referred to simply as the "Guardian") stands facing her. The coven sits facing the center of the Circle. Once everyone is prepared, the Narrator begins:[4]

In ancient times, our Lord, the Horned One, was as He still is, the Consoler, the Comforter; but men knew him as the Dread Lord of the Shadows, lonely, stern, and just. But our Lady, the Goddess, would solve all mysteries, even the mystery of death; and so she journeyed to the nether lands. The Guardians of the Portals challenged her . . .

The Goddess steps forward, and the Guardian challenges her with his athame.

Strip off thy garments, and lay aside thy jewels. For naught mayest thou bring with thee into this, our land.

The Goddess removes her veil and jewelry and places them on the floor. The Guardian removes the red cord from his waist and binds the Goddess with it. The cord is tied around her wrists behind her back, the ends draped over her shoulders and tied around her neck, with the loose ends hanging down her chest.

So she laid down her garments and her jewels and was bound, as all living must be who seek to enter the realms of Death, the Mighty Ones.

The Guardian leads the Goddess (by the loose ends of the cords) forward until she is facing the Lord. The Guardian releases her and steps aside.

Such was her beauty that Death himself knelt and laid his sword and crown at her feet . . .

The Lord kneels and lays the sword at the feet of the Goddess, then removes the crown and lays it with the sword. He kisses the feet of the Goddess (right then left).

Blessed be thy feet, that have brought thee in these ways. Abide with me, but let me place my cold hands on thy heart.

The Lord stands and holds his hands above the Goddess' heart.

And she replied: "I love thee not. Why dost thou cause all things that I love and take delight in to fade and die?"

The Lord moves his arms downwards, palms facing the Goddess.

"Lady," replied Death, "tis age and fate, against which I am helpless. Age causes all things to wither; but when men die, at the end of time, I give them rest and strength so that they may return. But thou art lovely. Return not; abide with me." But she answered: "I love thee not."

The Lord stands and retrieves the scourge. He returns and faces the Goddess.

"Then," said Death, "an thou receive not my hands upon thy heart, thou must kneel to Death's Scourge." (Goddess kneels) *"It is fate, better so," she said, and she knelt. And Death scourged her tenderly.*

The Lord gives the Goddess three, seven, nine, and twenty-one light strokes with the scourge.

And she cried, "I know the pangs of love."

The Lord lays down the scourge and helps the Goddess to her feet. He kneels.

And Death raised her and said, "Blessed be." And he gave her the Fivefold Kiss, saying "Thus only may thou attain to joy and knowledge."

Without reciting the wording, the Lord performs the Fivefold Kiss. He stands and unties the Goddess.

And he taught her all the mysteries and gave her the necklace which is the circle of rebirth.

The Lord retrieves the necklace and puts it on the Goddess. She picks up the crown and places it on his head.

And she taught him the mystery of the sacred cup, which is the cauldron of rebirth.

The pair moves to the altar. The Goddess should be on the left (west) and Lord on the right (east). The Goddess picks up the chalice, then the Lord puts his hands over hers.

They loved and were one, for there be three great mysteries in the life of man; and magic[5] *controls them all. For to fulfill love, you must return again at the same time, and at the same place, as the loved ones, and you must meet, and know, and remember, and love them again.*

The Lord removes his hands, and the Goddess puts down the chalice. The Lord picks up the sword and scourge, faces the coven, and assumes the God Position (Figure 17.1). The Goddess faces the coven and assumes the Pentagram Position.

GOD POSITION *Fig. 17.1*

But to be reborn, you must die and be made ready for a new body. And to die, you must be born; and without love you may not be born. And our Goddess ever inclineth to love, and mirth, and happiness, and guardeth and cherisheth her hidden children in life: And in death she teacheth the way to her communion; And even in this world she teacheth them the mystery of the Magick Circle, which is placed between the worlds.

The Legend is completed. All items are removed, and the rite continues. The Priestess stands in front of the altar and assumes the Osiris Position (with athame and scourge), and the High Priest gives her the Fivefold Kiss. When this is completed, the Priestess puts down the athame and scourge and lies on her back (on the altar or whichever place has been arranged); her head should be to the east and her feet to the west. The High Priest stands (kneels if she's on the ground), beside the Priestess and starts the Great Rite. His kisses form the Crowned Pentagram (Figure 17.2).[6] He begins the invocation by reciting:

Assist me to erect the ancient altar, at which in days past all worshipped, the Great Altar of all things. For in old times, Woman was the altar. Thus was the altar made and placed, and the sacred place was the point within the center of the Circle. As we have of old been taught that the point within the center is the origin of all things, therefore should we adore it (first kiss). *Therefore whomever we adore we also invoke, by the power of the Lifted Lance. O' Circle of Stars* (second kiss) *whereof our father is but the younger brother* (third kiss) *marvel beyond imagination, soul of infinite space, before whom time is bewildered and understanding dark, not unto thee may we attain unless thine image be love* (fourth kiss). *Therefore by seed and root, by stem and bud, by leaf and flower and fruit, do we invoke thee, O' Queen of Space, O' Mist of Light, continuous One of the Heavens* (fifth kiss). *Let it ever be thus, that men speak not of thee as One, but as none; And let them not speak of thee at all, since thou art continuous. For thou art the point within the Circle* (sixth kiss) *which we adore;* (seventh kiss) *the fount of life without which we would not be* (eighth kiss). *And in this way are erected the holy twin pillars of Boaz and Jachin* (ninth kiss). *In beauty and in strength they were erected, to the wonder and glory of all men.*

The High Priest removes the veil from the Priestess[7] and recites:

O' secret of secrets that art hidden in the being of all lives, not thee do we adore, for that which adoreth is also thou. Thou art That, and That am I. I am the flame that burns bright in the heart of every man. I am both life, and the giver of life. Therefore, with the knowledge of me is the knowledge of death. I am alone, the Lord within ourselves, whose name is Mystery of Mysteries.

The High Priest kisses the Priestess (tenth kiss) on the lips. In a symbolic Great Rite ceremony, he would lay himself on top of, or directly over, the Priestess.

SIGIL OF THIRD DEGREE *Fig. 17.2*

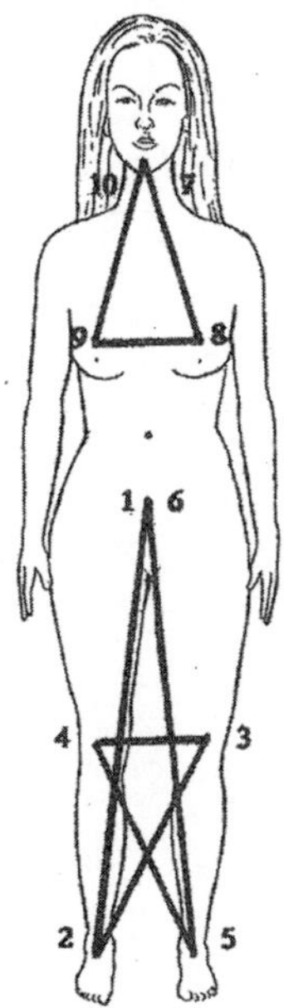

After the last kiss, he continues:

Make open the path of intelligence between us, for these truly are the Five Points of Fellowship. Foot to foot, knee to knee, Lance to Grail, breast to breast, lips to lips. Let the light course through our bodies, fulfilling of us resurrection. For there is no part of us that is not of the Gods. In the name of Aradia, by the power of Cernunnos, encourage our hearts.

If the rite is symbolic, the High Priest stands, helps the Priestess up, and proceeds to the Watchtowers. If the rite were actual, the High Priest would call back the coven and readmit them to the Circle. Then he'd lead the (High) Priestess to the cardinal points and recite:

Ye Lords of the Watchtowers of the East (South, West, North) *the thrice consecrated High Priestess greets and thanks you.*

The rite is completed.

Handfasting

The ritual of Handfasting is simply a witch's wedding. Although it's very often part of a legal marriage, it can also be conducted without the marriage being lawfully sanctioned. In short, this rite is a basic spiritual commitment to a life-partner. It's this aspect of the rite that is extremely popular with gay and lesbian couples, especially those who live in intolerant states that do not officially sanction same-sex marriages.

There are two basic beliefs as to the best time to perform this rite, and both are based primarily on symbolism. The first school of thought holds that Handfasting should be conducted during the new moon, as the symbolism between the "new moon" and the "new marriage" is unique. The second belief holds that a Handfasting should take place only during the waxing phase of the moon, since the "waxing moon" is symbolic of increase, growth, and the beginning of a new cycle.

While both of these philosophies offer acceptable justification for following them, the second belief tends to be favored because of the particular symbolism associated with the waxing moon. However, since Wicca is not a rigid religion, this rite is wide open to variations and only limited by one's own imagination. Therefore, don't feel inescapably bound by any set of rules when it comes to the Handfasting.

SETUP

This occasion is supposed to be far more festive than most, and the best way to exhibit this feeling is by using a lot of flowers. Coincidentally, all denominations not only follow this theme, but they adhere to it in similar fashion.

The first unique thing about the Handfasting is that the Circle itself is outlined with flowers. Because of this, there needs to be enough flowers on hand to overlay the nine-foot Circle perimeter. Additionally, flowers are needed to fill the cauldron, to decorate the altar and the general area around the altar, and to assemble a Wand of Flowers. This can be substituted by merely covering the coven wand. It's also traditional for the bride to have a small bouquet.

The couple to be joined may dress as they please as there is no specifically traditional manner of dress required. A coven that normally worships skyclad may, however, want to be clothed for this ceremony. This is especially true if noncoven members are in attendance.

It's also customary for the couple to have a small symbolic gift for each other, and each item should be placed on the altar before the ritual. Along with the gifts, the couple will need wedding rings to exchange. Since the rings are blessed during the rite, they should be placed on a small plate and set on the altar.

Finally, depending on the denomination, the following actions are also required:

- The altar is placed on the eastern side of the Circle.
- Incense that has a flowery scent, such as rose, is used.
- Two unlit white candles are placed on the altar.
- A Wand of Flowers is needed.[1]
- A broomstick is placed near the altar.[2]
- Wedding cords (white and red) are needed.

Gardnerian

This denomination does not have a universally accepted Handfasting ceremony. Although this may seem strange given the extent to which Gardner covered less important subjects, it's nevertheless the case. Therefore, when Gardnerian witches decide to marry, they tend to follow one of three paths. First, if they're fortunate enough to belong to a well-established coven, the coven will likely have its own particular version of the rite that they can use. Second, they can adopt the rite of another denomination. Since most Handfastings are remarkably similar, this is a commonly accepted practice. Third, the couple can compose their own rite.

The rite begins with a normal Opening Ritual, except that a gateway is left in the northeast for the couple to enter the Magick Circle. The circle of flowers is also left open at this gateway, with the extra flowers to close the circle placed next to the opening. It's also customary to exclude the couple from the Opening Ritual, and they are usually made to wait outside the Magick Circle until summoned.

After Drawing Down the Moon, the Charge is skipped, and the Invocation to the Great God Cernunnos recited next. Once this is completed, the High Priestess leaves the Circle and retrieves the groom. She welcomes him to the Circle with a kiss. When they return, the High Priest goes out and leads the bride into the Circle in the same way.[3]

After the bride and groom have entered, the High Priestess will symbolically close the gateway with the Wand of Flowers, and the High Priest will follow this by closing the gateway with the Sword. The High Priest and High Priestess return to the altar and stand with their backs to it. The couple should be facing them with the coven (and guests) assembled in a semicircle.

The High Priest takes the two unlit white candles from the altar, and the High Priestess lights them using the altar candle. The white candles are handed to the couple. The High Priest raises his arms and recites:

I call upon the Goddess Aradia and the God Cernunnos to bear witness to this sacred rite, that they may bless this ritual of love. Come forth, you who are to be joined.

The couple takes a step forward. The High Priestess then asks the groom:

Have you (name) *come here of your own free will to be joined to* (bride's name) *before these witnesses?*

An answer is given. The High Priest asks the bride:

Have you (name) *come here of your own free will to be joined to* (groom's name) *before these witnesses?*

An answer is given. The High Priestess says:

We welcome you both into this sacred Circle, that you may be joined before all assembled, in the presence of the Goddess and God.

The couple step backwards into the center of the Circle, and the coven performs the Witches' Rune, focusing on the couple standing in the center. The ring-dance should revolve around the pair. When this is completed, the couple returns to their places facing the altar. The High Priest and High Priestess stand in front of the couple with their backs to the altar, and the coven again takes its place around the edge of the Circle. The High Priest picks up the wand and recites:

With this Wand as a symbol of Life, I call upon the Element of the Air to tie tightly the bonds that bind these two together. Know that you are from here on bound closely, so that you become as one.

The High Priest puts down the wand and picks up the sword (or athame). He then recites:

With this Sword as a symbol of Light, I call upon the Element of Fire to bestow true love upon these two that we join together, that they may know the heat of ever-consuming passion, and always feel bound as one.

The High Priest puts down the sword, and the High Priestess picks up the chalice and recites:

This Chalice is a symbol of Love, in which I hold the Element of Water, and I call upon the Water to confer richness of life and spirit upon the two that are here before us, that they may always be closely bound as one.

The High Priestess puts down the chalice, picks up the pentacle, and recites:

This Pentacle is a symbol of Understanding, which I hold to call the Element of the Earth, and ask that it bring strength and power to this union, that the two here before us shall be steadfast and always be closely bound as one.

The High Priestess puts down the pentacle. At this point the Charge is usually recited. Once the Charge is completed, the High Priestess raises her hands and recites:

O' Merciful Goddess Aradia, O' Mighty God Cernunnos, we ask that you look favorably upon these two people before us and that you give your blessings, your love, and your protection, to this union. Blessed Be!

Coven repeats: *Blessed Be!*

The High Priest then picks up the wand, onto which the two wedding rings have been slipped. Holding one end, he hands the other to the High

Priestess. The rings should be kept as close as possible to the center of the wand. They extend their arms so that the wand is between them and the couple, then the High Priest recites:

Place your hands over these rings, as they symbolize the circle of your never-ending love for each other, as well as the full Circle of Life.

The High Priestess joins the High Priest in reciting the following words:

Before us are two who wish to become as one. As is our tradition, we pass to them these words of wisdom. Always keep your love strong, that it shall forever shine like the stars above; Be free and giving to each other, and understanding in all matters, that each shall possess the warmth and love to forgive the other; And, for however long this union lasts, always be faithful to one another.

The couple holds hands and extends their arms in front of them to be bound. Retrieving the cords from the altar, the High Priestess binds the wrists of the pair. Once bound, the bride repeats after the High Priest:

I call upon thee, Mighty Mother of us all, bringer of all fruitfulness; by seed and root, by bud and stem, by leaf and flower and fruit, by life and love do I invoke thee to bless this holy union.[4] *I* (name) *wish to become one with this man. As these Cords bind our hands, so shall my love bind me to him for life. In the names of Aradia and Cernunnos, I proclaim my undying love, now and for all times.*

The High Priestess now instructs the groom to recite:

I call upon thee, Mighty Mother of us all, bringer of all fruitfulness; by seed and root, by bud and stem, by leaf and flower and fruit, by life and love do I invoke thee to bless this holy union. I (name) wish to become one with this woman. As these Cords bind our hands, so shall my love bind me to her for life. In the names of Aradia and Cernunnos, I proclaim my undying love, now and for all times.

The High Priestess unties the cords binding the couple while the High Priest removes the rings from the wand and hands one to the bride. He holds on to the other ring until it's the groom's turn to present it. The bride places the ring on the groom's finger and recites:

In the presence of our brothers and sisters who have come to bear witness, I (name) *give you* (name) *this symbol of my love. As it represents the eternal Circle of Life, so shall it embody our endless love.*

The groom takes the ring from the High Priest, places it on the bride's finger, and recites the same verse. The High Priestess then recites:

Hear ye, Hear ye, all who have come. Let it be known that we have witnessed (name) *and (name) joined together, under the watchful gaze of the Old Gods, with the moon and stars shining as a veil across the heavens. By these rites, this couple is now blessed by the Goddess Aradia, the Great God Cernunnos, and all who have chosen to attend. Blessed Be!*

Coven recites: *Blessed be!*

The High Priest takes the broomstick and lays it on the ground in the center of the Circle. Hand in hand, the couple jumps over it. It's then customary for the High Priestess, High Priest, coven, and any non-Wiccan guests to also jump over the broomstick as a sign of luck and well-being toward the marriage. At this point, some covens enact the Great Rite, normally the symbolic form. But, this is not a steadfast custom, and it's often omitted. If the Great Rite is excluded, the couple proceeds to consecrate the wine and cakes together.[5] After that, the ritual is complete. There's usually a wedding festival held now. And, since the Circle is too confining, it can be banished first.

Italian

Like the Gardnerian tradition, this denomination has several versions of this rite. However, there are a few characteristics common to all the variations: (1) The couple must prepare a wedding cake, which symbolizes their willingness to work together, an important quality in ancient times. The cakes will also serve as an offering to the Old Gods and an offering of food to each other. (2) Wedding rings, or suitable "circular" substitutes such as necklaces, are needed. (3) White and red cords, for binding the wrists, are needed. The white represents the aspects of love and purity, while the red represents the aspects of passion and power. (4) A small handbasket of rose petals for each coven member.

The inner perimeter of the Circle is ringed with flowers. With the exception of the High Priestess, the entire coven waits outside the Circle area, arranged in a procession consisting of male/female pairs,[6] High

Priest, then the bride and groom. The High Priestess casts the Circle, leaving a gateway in the northeast. She then redraws it using a bunch of flowers in place of the athame. Once she's drawn the Circle a second time, she leaves the Circle and takes her place beside the High Priest, keeping with the male/female sequence.

The ritual begins with the coven procession proceeding to the Circle gateway. The coven members form a line on each side of the gateway and toss rose petals as the High Priest and High Priestess lead the bride and groom into the Circle. As the bride and groom pass, the coven members swing in line behind them.[7] The Circle remains open.

The High Priestess takes her position in front of the altar facing the couple. The High Priest should retrieve the wedding cake from wherever it's being kept and hand it to the bride and groom. They then step forward and hand it to the High Priestess with the following words:

We present this as an offering to the Old Gods, that they may find us worthy to grant their blessings to this marriage.

The High Priestess takes the cake and places it on the altar. One variation has her present it to the north quarter before putting it on the altar, while another has her present it to the north quarter and then hand it back to the couple. Although presenting it to the north quarter doesn't create a problem, giving it back to the couple will make it difficult for them to continue the rite. The High Priestess recites:

Hear me, all who have come to bear witness to these rites, and know that I speak in truth and love. We gather now in this Sacred Circle so that (bride's name) *can be joined to* (groom's name) *before the Goddess and God, in the presence of their new and forever family.*

High Priestess turns to address the bride and asks:

Have you come here of your own desire?

Bride answers: *I have.*
High Priestess turns to address the groom and asks:

Have you come here of your own desire?

Groom answers: *I have.*
The High Priest retrieves the wedding cake and white-handled knife

(sword or athame can also be used during Handfasting) from the altar and holds it out to the couple. The bride takes the knife and makes a cut in the cake, then hands it to the groom, who also cuts the cake. The couple each takes a piece of cake, and the High Priestess recites:

> *As you prepared this cake together, it became a symbol of your love for each other and your desire to be united as one. Now, as you share this cake, you give the gift of life.*

The bride and groom feed each other a small piece of cake. The High Priest brings forth the wedding rings. These should be on a cloth-covered plate. The High Priestess lays her hands on top of them and recites:

> *By the power of the Goddess Diana, and her Consort Dianus, I bless these rings as a symbol of love, life and union. Let them forever symbolize the love that you have for each other, the Circle of Life upon which your paths now cross, and the everlasting power of this holy union.*

The High Priest hands one ring to the bride and instructs her to place it on the groom's finger. She then recites:

> *This ring is a symbol of my love for you. Wear it always that I may be with you in spirit.*

The High Priest hands the other ring to the groom, who places it on the bride's finger and repeats the same verse. The couple now holds one another's hands while the High Priestess binds them around the wrists with the white, then red cords. Using the wand, she touches the bride on the head, then the groom, while reciting:

> *Bound to the God, bound to the Goddess, and bound to each other. In the name of Diana and Dianus, I bless this union and ask the Lord and Lady to grant you prosperity, love and happiness. You must now seal this union before the Old Ones, and all who have gathered.*

Coven repeats: *Seal this union.* Once the bride and groom kiss, the rite is over. The Circle is banished, and a wedding celebration is held.

Saxon

When it comes to the actual rite, this denomination is very similar to others. For instance, the ceremony is held during the waxing moon, the altar and Circle are decorated with flowers, and wedding rings are exchanged. However, the Saxon rite has two significant differences. First, the bride, groom, coven (and any guests) are all inside the Circle when it's cast. Second, it's customary for the bride and groom to be skyclad, even if the coven is not. Although this requirement may have been acceptable in times past, it's a bit out of proportion with today's practices. While other traditions don't specifically forbid couples from being skyclad, they do discourage it due to the frequent presence of non-Wiccans at Handfasting ceremonies.

Once everyone's assembled in the Circle area, the ceremony begins with the Temple being erected. When this is completed, the Priest and Priestess kiss. The Thegn leads the bride and groom to the altar. The couple stand facing the Priest and Priestess; bride in front of the Priest, groom in front of the Priestess. The Thegn positions himself on one side, and the Scribe steps to the other side. The Priest asks:

For what reason do you bring this man and woman before us?

Thegn answers: *They wish Handfasting.*
Priest asks the bride: *Are you* (name) *here of your own free will?*
Bride answers: *I am.*
Priestess asks the groom: *Are you* (name) *here of your own free will?*
Groom answers: *I am.*

The Priestess takes the sword and raises it. A popular variation is to hold it slightly over the couple. She recites:

Mighty God Woden, Merciful Goddess Frig, before me stand two people who have come of their own free will to be made as one. We call you to bear witness to that which they now declare.

After the Priestess has placed the sword on the altar, the Priest takes his seax and gently lays the tip against the bride's chest (over her heart). The bride repeats after the Priest:

I (name) *have come here of my own free will, to be joined to* (name) *in wedlock. I come with love and heartfelt sincerity, wishing only to become one with my chosen partner. I will always strive to give* (name) *happiness and honor, and I will defend him with my life. And, if I am not sincere in my pledge, may the seax plunge into my heart. This I declare in the names of Frig and Woden, that I may gain strength from them to be true to my vows. So be it.*

Priest lowers his seax, and the coven repeats: *So be it.*

The Priestess raises her seax and gently lays the tip against the groom's chest (over his heart). The groom repeats after the Priestess:

> *I* (name) *have come here of my own free will, to be joined to* (bride's name) *in wedlock. I come with love, adoration and sincerity, wishing only to become one with my chosen partner. I will always strive to give* (bride's name) *peace, happiness and joy, and I will defend her with my life. And, if I am not sincere in my pledge, may the seax plunge into my heart. This I declare in the names of Woden and Frig, that I may gain strength from them to be true to my vows. So be it.*

The Priestess lowers her seax, and the coven repeats: *So be it.* She then consecrates the wedding rings with water, incense smoke, and fire,[8] and then hands them to the couple. The Priest now recites a poem.[9] When he finishes, the Priestess recites:

> *The time has come to exchange the gifts. As you do, always remember that as you give joy, so shall you receive it; as you give strength, so shall you receive it; and as you give love, so it shall be given. For even as the Law guarantees that you receive what you give, so too shall your partner always grant return.*

Priest recites: *Be true to each other, and the Gods shall be true to you.*

Coven recites: *So be it.*

The couple exchange rings and kiss. They consecrate the cakes and ale, feed each other, and then the rest is shared with the coven. The ritual is complete. If extra room is needed for a celebration, the Circle can now be banished.

West Country

Curiously, this denomination really doesn't have a fixed standard to define the components of its Handfasting ceremony. Instead, the West Country ritual depends largely on an individual coven's own interpretation.

Even with this lack of uniformity, there are a few things that remain the same throughout the tradition. For instance, the Circle is always eighteen feet in diameter for Handfasting. This is primarily to accommodate a larger number of people, especially if guests are invited to attend. The Circle and altar are also fully decorated with flowers, including herb leaves and flower petals scattered on the ground.

A second custom is that the couple wears crowns, or simple circlets, made by intertwining flowers. These flower crowns represent the couple's connection to the bounty of the Earth and Nature. Also, rather than using cords, the couple is bound with a wreath of flowers. This wreath is usually made by attaching flowers to a length of rope, or a large hoop, but it can also be formed entirely of flowers.

Finally, near the end of the rite, the couple must leap over fire, which is essential because it represents purification of the marriage. When indoors, the altar candle is used for this purpose, while a bonfire is always used outside.

As for specific dialogue, this is another area that is widely diverse.[10] The tradition follows a basic pattern that includes a vow of love and equality between the bride and groom, but the wording tends to center more on the couple than the Gods. Along with this, some West Country witches seem to favor old-fashioned language, while others lean toward modern vocabulary. Although this doesn't appear to make much difference as far as general content, it does have an effect on the overall ability of a coven to borrow passages from another.

Handparting

Since witches are no different from anyone else, not all marriages last forever. Because of this, witches need a way to terminate a failed marriage. For this purpose, witches have the ritual of Handparting.

As the name suggests, this is simply the method that witches use to dissolve the union created at Handfasting. It can be done following a divorce in a civil marriage, or if no such legal marriage took place, it can be conducted to end the spiritual commitment of life-partners.

The Handparting rite, like Handfasting, also holds two basic beliefs concerning the appropriate time to perform this ritual. One belief is that the ceremony should take place "one year and one day" after the couple was joined, or if more than a year has elapsed, the time shifts to the next anniversary of this day. The second belief is that Handparting should take place only during the waning phase of the moon since the waning moon is symbolic of decrease and the decline of the life cycle.

While both of these philosophies offer acceptable justification, most witches tend to follow the second belief for two reasons. First, they specifically like the particular symbolism associated with the waning moon and the ending of the Handfasting union. Second, they frown upon the idea of timelines that force people to make monumental decisions just to meet a deadline (i.e., the one year and one day anniversary) because this invariably leads people to regret the hasty decisions they've made. Luckily, the religion permits the freedom of choice, which means that either belief is perfectly acceptable.

There are, however, a few things that are unavoidable. For instance, if this ritual is not part of a legal divorce, then there may be monetary and property issues that arise between the couple, such as the division of items that they purchased together. While this is legally not the responsibility of the coven, it's a good idea to inquire about this in advance so that such issues are not brought up during the ceremony. At the same time, if one of the partners is not present (for whatever reason), someone may substitute for this person. A witch from the coven who is willing may act as a surrogate to represent the missing partner so that the ritual may be performed. However, it is the duty of the coven leader to make certain that the absent individual really does not want to be present.

SETUP

Unlike the preparation required for Handfasting, this rite requires very little work. In fact, with one or two exceptions, the preparation for a normal esbat is usually more than sufficient.

To properly conduct the rite, two unlit white candles (similar to the ones used during Handfasting) are needed. These candles are held by the couple and lit just before the ceremony starts. There are witches who feel the candles should be black instead of white since they represent the termination of the Handfasting. Like many other things, however, this matter is best left to personal discretion. Also, the altar is customarily set up on the western edge of the Magick Circle for this rite, whereas it was on the eastern edge for Handfasting.

Gardnerian

Much of the Handparting rite is the exact opposite of Handfasting. The rite begins with a normal Opening Ritual except that a gateway is left in the northwest, instead of the northeast, for the couple to enter the Magick Circle. The couple, each carrying an unlit white candle, will remain outside the Circle until called. If practicable, the pair should be holding hands. Once again, the Charge is omitted, but the Invocation to the Great God Cernunnos is recited.

Following this, the High Priest exits the Circle through the gateway and then leads the couple in. After the couple has entered, the High Priest seals the gateway with the sword and takes his position next to the High Priestess in front of the altar with the couple facing them. The coven should already be spread out in an arc along the edge of the Circle behind the couple.

The High Priestess raises her arms and recites:

I call upon the Goddess Aradia and the God Cernunnos to bear witness to these sacred rites, that they may know that this union has ended. Come forth you who are one, that this union may be parted.

The couple takes a step forward. The High Priest then asks one of the couple:

Have you (name) *come here of your own free will to be parted from* (partner's name) *before these witnesses?*

An answer is given.[1] The High Priest asks the other partner:

Have you (name) *come here of your own free will to be parted from* (partner's name) *before these witnesses?*

An answer is given. The High Priest then recites:

You have come to this sacred Circle to stand before the Goddess, the God, and all who are present, to freely dissolve a partnership that was willingly formed. Let us now proceed, remembering that we are ever in the presence of the Old Gods and these witnesses.

The couple moves to the center of the Circle, and the coven performs the Witches' Rune. However, this time the ring-dance revolves "widdershins" (counterclockwise) around the couple. Once this is complete, the couple returns to its place in front of the altar, facing the High Priestess and High Priest. The coven members again take their places along the edge of the Circle. The High Priestess picks up the wand and recites:

With this Wand I call upon the Element of the Air to break the bonds that bind these two people together. Know that from this time forward you are no longer viewed as one.

The High Priestess puts the wand on the altar, picks up the sword (or athame), and recites:

With this Sword I call upon the Element of Fire to sever the bonds that bind these two people together. Know that from this time on the passion that you had for each other is no more.

The High Priestess puts down the sword, picks up the chalice, and recites:

In this Chalice I hold the Element of Water, and I call upon the Water to wash away the bonds that at one time bound you both so closely together that you were as one.

The High Priestess puts down the chalice, picks up the pentacle, and recites:

I hold this Pentacle to call the Element of the Earth, that it may forever end this union. You both freely stand here to be absolved from these bonds, and so it shall be. But in doing so, you must know now that this union is over and you are no longer one. So mote it be.

The High Priestess puts down the pentacle. The couple is now asked to repeat the following:

I (name) *come here of my own free will, before the Goddess and God, and all who are present, to dissolve my bonds and union with* (partner's name). *From this time forth we are no longer bound to each other, nor are we as one. We may now freely go our separate ways, secure in the knowledge that we shall always be respectful of each other, and thankful to the Old Gods for granting us this time together. So mote it be.*

Coven repeats: *So mote it be.*

The couple releases hands and blows out the candles that each is holding. They then take off their wedding rings and hand them to the High Priestess. Holding one ring in each hand, the High Priestess recites:

O' Merciful Goddess Aradia, O' Mighty God Cernunnos, we ask that you allow these two people to go their separate ways, and that you help them to find love and happiness in the future. So mote it be.

The High Priestess opens her hands, and the High Priest sprinkles the rings with a few drops of consecrated water to cleanse them. Then he recites:

With this water I cleanse these rings. No longer are they a symbol of the love that bound these two people together. So mote it be.

The High Priestess recites:

Hear ye, Hear ye, all who have come, let it be known that we have witnessed the rings cleansed, and all ties that once bound these two people together are now broken. In the presence of the Goddess Aradia, and the Great God Cernunnos, these people are now Handparted and may go their separate ways, stronger and wiser for the time they have spent as one. Blessed Be!

The coven repeats: *Blessed be!*

The High Priestess returns the rings, and the couple may do with them as they please. Once the rings are returned, the couple joins the rest of the coven around the Circle. The ritual is complete.

Italian

This denomination, like many paths that were born in a rural setting, technically had no Handparting rite since people in the country rarely divorced. However, as the tradition made its way into modern times, the need for such a ritual arose. Therefore, Italian witches were forced to create a rite to break the Handfasting. Today, several versions of this rite exist.

The rite begins with the High Priestess casting the Circle. She leaves a gateway in the northwest. During this, the entire coven waits outside the Circle area arranged in a single-file procession[2] with the High Priest and the couple at the end. As soon as the casting is completed, the High Priestess leaves the Circle and takes her place in front of the High Priest. Once she's in place, the coven procession proceeds to the Circle gateway. Unlike in the Handfasting, the coven members file straight into the Circle and take up places along the edge of the Circle. The gateway remains open.

The High Priestess takes her position in front of the altar facing the couple. The High Priest should be next to her. The High Priestess recites:

Hear me, all who have come to bear witness to these rites, and know that I speak in truth and sadness. We gather now in this Sacred Circle so that (man's name) *can be released from his bonds to* (woman's name) *before the Goddess and God, in the presence of their brothers and sisters.*

High Priestess turns to address the woman and asks:

Have you come here of your own desire?

Woman answers: *I have.*

High Priestess turns to address the man and asks:

Have you come here of your own desire?

Man answers: *I have.*

The High Priest holds out his hands, and the couple gives him their wedding rings. He turns and presents them to the High Priestess, who lays her hands on top of them and recites:

By the power of the Goddess Diana, and her Consort Dianus, I receive these rings as a symbol that your love and union are no longer. Let this act forever symbolize that your paths no longer lead to the same destination. Where they once crossed, they are now parted; and where the everlasting power of your holy union was strong, it has now been dissolved.

The High Priest hands one ring to the man and the other to the woman. Using the wand, the High Priestess touches the man's forehead, then the woman's, while reciting:

Where once you were bound by the God and Goddess, and bound to each other in holy union, now those bonds are severed. In the name of Diana and Dianus, I release you from your vows and ask the Lord and Lady to grant you freedom to find new prosperity, love and happiness. The bond is broken. Go in peace.

Coven repeats: *The bond is broken. Go in peace.*

The man and woman take their place with the coven and the rite is over.

Saxon

When it comes to divorce, this denomination is one of the few that has a set standard. Although this is likely a twentieth-century addition, it nevertheless fills a much-needed void and is a welcome augmentation to a potentially awkward situation.

However, before any rite can take place, a few matters must be cleared up. First, the couple must present the coven leader with a written document dividing up any joint property. For items with substantial value (house, car, investment portfolio, etc.), this document must be legally binding and signed by both parties. In the case of children, all custody and visitation issues must be settled with a legally binding agreement.[3]

A second matter to consider is the timing of the ritual. The ceremony itself is always held during the waning phase of the moon to signify the decline of the marriage. If something were to prevent using this lunar phase, the new moon is also acceptable as a neutral time. The new moon would also signify the rebirth of the couple back into single life.

While on the topic of symbolism, it's also important to point out that Saxon Handparting has two aspects that differ greatly from those of other traditions. First, the Priest, Priestess, couple, and coven are all inside the Circle when it's cast. Second, while it's customary for a bride and groom to be skyclad during Handfasting, even if the coven is not, the divorcing couple must be robed. Then, upon being separated, they remove their robes to again become skyclad. This act signifies the rebirth of the man and woman.[4]

Once everyone's assembled in the Circle area, the ceremony begins with the Temple being erected. When this is completed, the Priest and Priestess kiss. The Thegn calls the couple to the altar. The couple stands facing the Priest and Priestess with the woman in front of the Priest and the man in front of the Priestess. The Thegn positions himself on one side, and the Scribe steps to the other side. The Priest asks:

For what reason do you bring this man and woman before us?

Thegn answers: *They wish Handparting.*
Priest asks the woman: *Are you* (name) *here of your own free will?*
Woman answers: *I am.*
Priestess asks the man: *Are you* (name) *here of your own free will?*
Man answers: *I am.*
Either the Priest or Priestess asks the Scribe:

Has a settlement between this man and this woman been reached and duly recorded in the Book?

Scribe answers: *It has.*

The Priestess takes the sword and raises it. A popular variation is to hold it slightly over the couple. She then recites:

Mighty God Woden, Merciful Goddess Frig, before me stand two people who have come of their own free will to break the bonds that made them as one. We call you to bear witness to that which they now declare.

After the Priestess has placed the sword on the altar, the Priest takes his seax and gently lays the tip against the woman's chest (over her heart). The woman repeats after the Priest:

I (name) *have come here of my own free will to break the vows which I declared to* (husband's name) *in this sacred Circle. I come with honesty and sincerity, wishing to end my partnership so that I shall be once again free of restraint. In the presence of Woden and Frig, and with my brothers and sisters as witnesses, I hereby declare that I release all that tied us as one. May* (husband's name) *go in love and friendship. So be it.*

Priest lowers his seax and the coven says: *Hand Part.*

The Priestess raises her seax and gently lays the tip against the man's chest (over his heart). The man repeats after the Priestess:

I (name) *have come here of my own free will to break the vows which I declared to* (wife's name) *in this sacred Circle. I come with honesty and sincerity, wishing to end my partnership so that I shall be once again free of restraint. In the presence of Frig and Woden, and with my brothers and sisters as witnesses, I hereby declare that I release all that tied us as one. May* (wife's name) *go in love and friendship. So be it.*

The Priestess lowers her seax and the coven says: *Hand Part.* The couple removes wedding rings and hands them to the Priestess. She cleanses them with water, incense smoke, and fire during which she says:

I cleanse these rings in the name of Woden and Frig.

The Priestess hands the rings back to the couple. The man and woman return to stand with the rest of the coven as the Priestess recites:

You are now parted. Go in peace, always mindful of the time you were joined as one; and always remember that you are bound by the Law.[5]
So be it.

Coven recites: *So be it.*

The Handparting is complete. The cakes and ale are consecrated by the Priestess and Priest, then shared with the coven. If there is nothing else scheduled, the Circle can now be banished.

West Country

Like many country-based denominations, this tradition has absolutely no ritual for Handparting. This obviously stems from the fact that during the early days of the denomination, people in rural areas rarely, if ever, divorced. So there was never a rite developed to deal with divorce. Modern witches have solved this problem by formulating their own versions of Handparting, but there is no central pattern or theme followed. In short, when West Country witches want to divorce, unless their particular coven already has a ceremony in place, they pretty much have to make it up as they go along.

Wiccaning

Just as Christians introduce their children to their God through the rite of christening, Wiccans also present their children to their Gods through a ritual known as Wiccaning. Although at first glance it would appear that the two religions share the same belief when it comes to inducting their children into their respective faiths, this is clearly a misconception.

During Wiccaning, parents are seeking to invoke Divine intervention in order to protect the physical and metaphysical body of their child, while at the same time introducing a new member into the hierarchy of the clan (coven). Through this process, they hope that their child will receive the blessings of the God and Goddess, as well as their coven's unconditional love and acceptance.

Further, while the act does introduce the child to the Wiccan religion, it does not attempt to lay claim to the child's ultimate spiritual well-being nor automatically induct him or her into its ranks. Christening, on the other hand, though similar in regard to invoking Divine intervention for the child's protection, also places demands on two aspects of the child's future. First, the responsibility for the child's soul and eternal salvation now falls squarely on to the shoulders of Christianity. Second, the ultimate goal of the rite is to commit the child to the religion. In short, the act of christening is intended to remove the child's religious freedom of choice. And this is the reason the two religions diverge since Wiccans allow their children to choose their own spiritual path.

SETUP

There really isn't much that needs to be done for this rite other than a few simple decorating preparations, and these follow a central theme associated with the introduction of new life. In keeping with this idea, it's customary to decorate the Circle and altar with young flowers (unopened buds or buds that are just opening) and pine boughs with new growth. This symbolizes the inclusion of Nature and new life, as well as decorating the general area.

Along with adding flowers and greenery, some witches (from various denominations) have a potted sapling at the altar.[1] The seedling is representation of the child and presented to the Gods as a symbol of the child's inclusion into the Tree of Life. It's also supposed to be a symbol of the child's ecological awareness and respect for Nature.

For traditions that use a cauldron, it's always placed in the center of the Circle and decorated with flowers and greenery.

Lastly, anointing oil and a very mild incense are needed. Also, since non-Wiccans are often allowed to attend this ceremony as guests of the parents, the ritual is performed robed, even by a normally skyclad coven.

Gardnerian

At the beginning of the ceremony, the parents and child are outside the Circle area with the High Priest,[2] while the coven stands along the inside of the perimeter opposite the altar. The High Priestess casts the Circle in the usual way, leaving a gateway in the east (birth). As soon as she's finished, the High Priest leads the parents into the Circle. The mother should be carrying the child if it's a boy and the father if it's a girl.[3]

After entering the Circle, the mother, father, and baby stand in front of the cauldron facing the altar, while the High Priest takes his position beside the High Priestess. The opening ritual is now performed up to the conclusion of the Invocation of the Great God.[4] Normally the Witches' Rune is enacted at this point, but it can be excluded if it's determined that it might frighten the baby. The High Priestess then recites:

> *Hear Ye! Hear Ye! The time has come for us to gather close. Come forth and stand round the Womb,*[5] *that we may lend our powers on this night as* (mother's legal name) *and* (father's legal name)[6] *present their child* (child's name) *to the Goddess and God.*

As a whole, the coven steps forward and forms a half-circle around the cauldron. All members should still be facing the altar. The High Priestess continues:

> *It is our belief that no one shall force their will upon another. So on this night, we do not seek to pass on our will, but rather to pass on our blessings and ask that the Great God Cernunnos, and Gentle Goddess*

Aradia, protect this child and watch over his life until such time as he is grown and able to choose his own path.

Coven repeats: *Grant him joy, happiness and health.*
The High Priest recites:

Come forward (mother's witch name) *and* (father's witch name) *that the love and blessings of the Goddess and God may be placed upon your child.*

At this prompting, the parents step forward until they're close to the altar. The High Priestess holds out the bowl of anointing oil so the High Priest can dip his finger in it. He anoints the baby's forehead with the Invoking Pentagram of Spirit (Figure 20.1) and recites:

I anoint and mark you with the Spirit, which shall bring the Earth, Air, Fire, and Water with it.

INVOKING PENTAGRAM OF SPIRIT *Fig. 20.1*

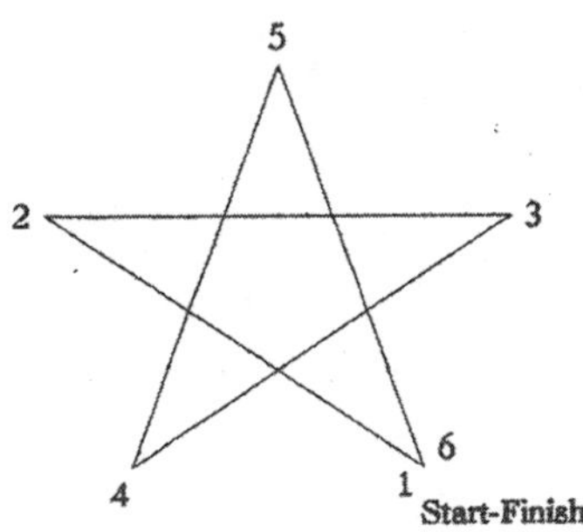

The High Priestess puts down the bowl of oil and holds out the chalice of wine. The High Priest dips his finger in it. He anoints the baby's forehead again and recites:

I anoint you with consecrated wine in the names of Aradia and Cernunnos, and ask that they protect and bless you.

Lastly, the High Priestess holds out the consecrated water, and the High Priest dips his fingers into it. He anoints the baby's forehead a third time and recites:

I anoint you with this consecrated water that it's cleansing powers may guide you safely through life until such time as you are wise enough to choose your own path.

With the anointing finished, the High Priest leads the group (mother, father, and child) to the Watchtowers. The High Priestess remains at the altar. At each cardinal point, the group stops, and the High Priest recites:

> *Ye Lords of the Watchtowers of the East* (South, West, North) *Lords of the Air* (Fire, Water, Earth) *I call you to bear witness that* (child's name) *has been marked with the Spirit and duly blessed with wine and water, in the names of Aradia and Cernunnos.*

The High Priest returns to the altar with the parents, and everyone takes their original place. The High Priestess raises her arms, palms outward, and recites:

> *O' Gracious Goddess Aradia, bless this child and give him the gift of love, health, and happiness.*

She lowers her arms, and the High Priest repeats the posture while reciting:

> *O' Mighty God Cernunnos, bless this child and grant him the gift of Strength, power and wisdom.*

The High Priest lowers his arms and motions for the parents to turn around and face the coven.[7] (This is the act of presenting the baby to the clan.) All the witches hold hands and repeat after the High Priest:

> *You have been blessed by the Goddess and God, and your name has been spoken to the Lords of the Watchtowers. We welcome you into this, our sacred Circle, that it may protect you. So mote it be.*

At this point the rite is complete. If by chance there's working to be done (which is rare at a Wiccaning), it takes place now. The cakes are then consecrated and passed around with the already consecrated wine. Gifts may now be given, a small party held, or whatever else is planned, and then the Circle is banished.

Italian

Although the Strega, like all other witches, do not try to force their religious beliefs on anyone, the rite they use to bless a child makes it almost seem as if they do. Yet this is nothing more than an ancient practice being misconstrued in relation to today's standards. In reality, this ceremony is an introduction to the community rather than an induction into the religion. It stems from a time in history when Italy was filled with rural villages, and children rarely moved away from these remote locations. And because children were integral to the success or failure of the village, they were ceremonially adopted into the communal clan. Naturally, the Strega were called upon to bless the children in order to protect them from harm. So this rite was created. Further, the facts do not support the contention that this ritual forces religious beliefs on the child because, if it were so, then there'd be no reason to hold an initiation if the child wishes to enter the Craft.

The ritual, itself, follows a normal esbat pattern. After the Charge of Aradia, the High Priest leads the parents (mother holding baby) to the altar where the High Priestess is waiting. She dips her fingers in consecrated oil,[8] anoints the baby's forehead, and recites:

> *We call upon the Lord and Lady, the Grigori, and the spirits of our departed ancestors, to bear witness to these rites. I anoint your head in the hopes that this mark may bring you the wisdom and knowledge that you shall need throughout your life.*

She dips her fingers into the oil again and anoints the baby's palms:

> *I anoint your hands that they may be strong in all the tasks that they must perform throughout your life.*

She dips her fingers into the oil a third time and anoints the soles of the baby's feet:

> *I anoint your feet that they may carry you down the path of honor and glory throughout your life.*

She addresses the parents:

> *You have brought this child to join with us and receive our blessings. But none here know his (her) name.* (Mother responds with the child's name.) *From this time forward, let all present welcome* (child's name) *into their homes and their hearts.*

The coven recites: *We welcome him (her).*

At this point, the High Priest steps forward and leads the parents to the four quarters to present the child. While there is no specific dialogue, the child's name is usually spoken at each cardinal point. The mother and child then approach the altar where the child is given milk.[9] Custom dictates breast-feeding, though this really isn't necessary; bottle-feeding is a perfectly acceptable alternative. After the child is given milk, the coven may come forward, one by one, and give small tokens of affection and offer a wish or blessing for the child's future. Once everyone has passed, the High Priestess recites:

> *May the Old Ones bestow their gifts of health, happiness, strength and love upon you, and protect you all the days of your life. In the names of Diana and Dianus, Uni and Tagni, or any other names by which the Lady and Lord are known, may you always be blessed.*

The coven recites: *Blessed be.*

This is the end of the ceremony. The Circle is now banished.

Saxon

There's a tossup between this denomination and West Country as to which has the least complicated birth rite. And although simplicity isn't necessarily a good quality in terms of a religious ceremony, in this instance, it actually seems to be beneficial to the underlying purpose, that of protecting the child until the child can protect him or herself.

Special preparation is not required, though flowers or other decorations may be added to the Circle and altar areas. If gifts, charms, talismans, etc., are being given to the child, they should be placed on or near the altar to be cleansed. Also, it's very important to use incense that will not irritate the baby. Lavender and rose are popular choices, but any mild scent is acceptable.

Begin the ceremony as if a normal esbat was being held.[10] The Priest and Priestess stand with their backs to the altar, and the coven is arranged in an arc on the opposite side of the Circle facing the altar. The parents (mother holding the child) are on the eastern edge of the Circle. The Scribe stands with them. After the temple is erected, the Scribe leads the parents to stand before the Priest and Priestess. He recites:

> *I bring* (child's name*) who is the son* (or daughter) *of* (mother's name) *and* (father's name) *to be an addition to our number. Let us give* Together, the Priest and Priestess recite: *We welcome you with love.*

The Priestess retrieves the consecrated water from the altar and anoints the baby's forehead. A second version says forehead and heart. The Priest retrieves the censer and then passes it by the baby so that the smoke drifts over the child. The mother may also move the baby into the smoke. Finally, the Priestess takes the altar candle and brings it close enough for the light to shine on the baby.[11] The parents (mother still holding the baby) follow the Priest around the Circle as he presents their child to the four quarters. They stop at each cardinal point, but no words are spoken. When the group returns, the Priestess recites:

May the Great Goddess Frig, and her Horned Consort Woden, guard you from harm and guide you down the path of enlightenment. From this day forward, may you ever know what is right, and avoid that which is wrong. And may the Goddess and God bestow their blessings upon you. So be it.

Coven repeat: *So be it.*

The cakes and ale are now consecrated and shared. If an esbat is being conducted, it continues as normal. Otherwise, the Circle is banished, and the ceremony is over.

West Country

Although this tradition probably has the simplest of all Wiccaning ceremonies, it's still a meaningful rite that should be extended to all children. On top of that, because of its simplicity, there's no reason not to conduct it.

Other than some flowers to decorate the Circle and altar, the rite doesn't require any special preparation. It is, however, a good idea to have a small bowl on hand that can be used to mix water, wine, and oil. This mixture is used to anoint the child in one pass, thereby alleviating the need for more than one anointing; again, a sign of simplicity.

The ceremony begins with the Circle being cast. The Priest, Priestess, parents, baby, and coven are all inside prior to the casting. After the Circle is cast, the Priestess anoints the baby's forehead with the water/wine/oil mixture, making the Goddess Crescent Moon Sign (Figure 20.2), and then recites:

I anoint you (child's name) *with the sign of the Goddess that she may watch over and protect you.*

GODDESS CRESCENT MOON SIGN *Fig. 20.2*

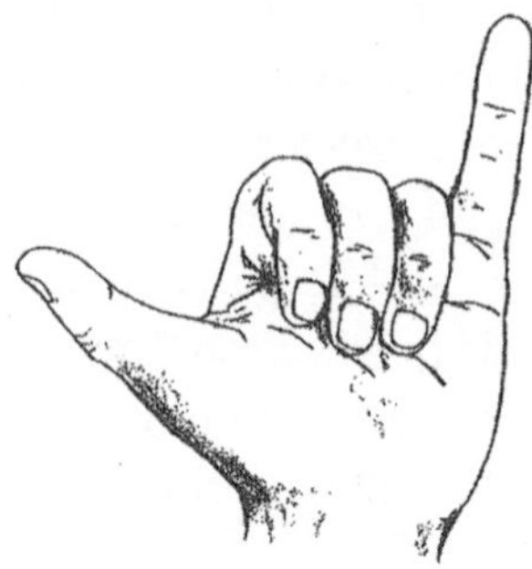

A female witch takes the altar candle and passes it around the baby. It's usually best to ring the mother, too. The witch recites:

May this flame bring the warmth of the Goddess upon you.

Another female witch waves burning incense pass the baby so that the smoke drifts onto the child, or the mother can pass the child into the smoke. The witch recites:

May your name be on the wind, and the Goddess ever close to you.

Starting in the east, the child's name is spoken to the quarters. The baby, however, does not need to be physically presented. After this, the wine and cakes are consecrated, and an offering of wine is poured on the ground. The wine and cakes are then shared with the coven. The rite is completed once the Circle is banished.

Funerals

Witches are by no means afraid of death even if they're not particularly fond of it. Their view is that death, like life, is a natural part of the life cycle. But this cavalier attitude does not represent callousness toward life or a fatalistic approach to living. Instead, it symbolizes a positive outlook about death that is based on a thorough understanding of the principles of reincarnation. As a result of this point of view, witches do not mourn their dead in the same manner as many other religions.

Wiccans have a specific belief concerning the act of sending the soul of a friend or relative to the Summerland. However, the ritual for this purpose varies immensely from denomination to denomination and even from coven to coven. For instance, Gardnerian witches hold an elaborate funeral ceremony called the Requiem. Although the exact components of the ritual often change from coven to coven, the basic structure remains the same. At the opposite end of the spectrum, the Saxon rite of Crossing the Bridge is a fairly simple affair. And despite the fact that it has none of the complexities of the Gardnerian Requiem, it produces the same results.

There are, however, a few points common to all traditions. First, unlike the burial rites of most religions, a Wiccan ceremony doesn't focus solely on the death, but rather promotes death as a part of eventual rebirth. Second, the atmosphere of the gathering is not dismal. While there is a natural degree of sadness associated with the death of a friend or relative, there is virtually no despondency. Instead, the rite embraces a festive tone that is designed to reinforce the belief that the departed soul has gone to the Summerland to await rebirth. Third, the ritual contains interaction so that everyone in attendance can participate in sending the soul on its way. This group involvement lets each person contribute his or her own particular energy to the deceased's spirit, thereby allowing them to be a small part of the reincarnation cycle.

SETUP

Each coven seems to have its own ideas about the appropriate preparation for this ceremony, and specific denominations don't appear to have a strong influence on the outcome. Some witches like to use colorful and festive decorations on the altar, and even around the Circle, because they look past the death of the person in order to appreciate the joyousness of eventual rebirth.

Other witches, while understanding the death/rebirth aspects, still feel that the rite should reflect a somber tone. Because of these conflicting opinions, the decor of the Circle becomes a coven/personal choice.

Depending on denomination, there are a few other preparations required. For instance, in the Gardnerian and Italian traditions, the Magickal Legend of Aradia (Descent of the Goddess) is performed. This role-playing requires a veil, jewelry, and a crown.

It's also customary to bury or cremate a witch's personal Craft items with the witch. The items most frequently included are initiation cords, measure, wand, athame, and chalice, though metal items should be excluded from cremation. The *Book of Shadows* is another matter altogether. During the time of the Inquisitions, including this item for burial meant taking an unwise risk. However, it's now perfectly acceptable to add the *Book of Shadows* to the list.

When a witch is to be buried instead of cremated, a black candle is used in place of the cremation. Although the exact significance of this custom was lost over time, three theories for its use are generally advanced. First, cremation is an act of purification meant to release the soul from its lifeless shell (the body), send the spirit on its way, and return the body to the elements. A second interpretation is that this practice originated during the years of the Black Plague. This view suggests that witches, though not knowing the cause of the plague, realized that the bodies were contaminated and required cremation. The third theory is that witches of antiquity chose to be cremated because the alternative was Christian burial.

Finally, burial cords[1] are sometimes included as part of the rite.

Gardnerian

The manner in which this rite is conducted will depend on whether the deceased's body is present. If the wake is held in a private home (or in the unlikely event that a funeral parlor would allow it), the rite will center around the deceased witch. If, however, the deceased's presence is not possible, the ritual takes on a second form.[2]

The ceremony begins with the Circle being cast.[3] Following this, the opening remains until the end of the God invocation. The High Priest[4] takes the black candle to the center of the Circle, and the coven performs the Witches' Rune. In this version, the ring-dance becomes a slow inward spiral. During the dance, each witch focuses on the candle. Then all lay a hand on it at the end of the spiral.[5] Once the Witches' Rune is completed, the High Priest carries the candle to the west quarter while the High Priestess recites:

We come together to lend our powers to our departed friend (deceased's name) *as he leaves this world for the next. May this funeral pyre*[6] *light the way.*

The High Priest lights the black candle from the flame of the altar candle. The west Watchtower can also be used. Once lit, he places the black candle on the ground and recites (facing west):

Lords of the Watchtowers of the West, Ye Lords of Death, we light this fire in the West that it may brighten the path between worlds so our departed friend may find his way.

A moment of silence follows. The High Priest returns to the altar and takes his place next to the High Priestess, while the coven spreads out in an arc along the eastern edge of the Circle, and all raise their athames in salute. Raising the sword (or her athame), the High Priestess recites:

We have gathered on this night to pay tribute to our beloved friend. Though his (her) passing brings momentary sadness, it also brings joy in the knowledge that this is but the next step on the path of enlightenment. For while he (she) has left this world, he (she) shall return; while he (she) has died, he (she) shall be reborn; and while we shall not see him (her) again in this life, we shall surely meet again. Yet we cannot bid farewell without knowing that the Goddess and God are at the portal to greet him (her). For it is under the guidance of Aradia and Cernunnos that he (she) shall find his (her) way to the Summerlands; it is by their blessings that he (she) shall find peace; and it is by their will that he (she) shall be reborn. We must therefore honor the Goddess and God, for it is in their care that we now commit his (her) spirit.

The coven members lower their athames and recite: *Praise be, Aradia and Cernunnos!*

At this point the Magickal Legend of Aradia is performed in its entirety. Although not mandatory, a good way to enhance the experience for as many people as possible is to have the High Priestess and High Priest refrain from participation. The following roles should have been assigned prior to the ceremony: the Narrator, the Goddess, the Lord of the Underworld, and the Guardian of the Portals.[7] The Narrator now stands behind the altar while the Lord of the Underworld ("Lord") stands in front of it with his back to the Narrator. The Goddess stands with her back to the south, while the Guardian of the Portals ("Guardian") faces her. The coven sits facing the center of the Circle. Once everyone is prepared, the Narrator begins:[8]

> *In ancient times, our Lord, the Horned One, was as He still is, the Consoler, the Comforter; but men knew him as the Dread Lord of the Shadows, lonely, stern, and just. But our Lady, the Goddess, would solve all mysteries, even the mystery of death; and so she journeyed to the nether lands. The Guardians of the Portals challenged her . . .*

The Goddess steps forward, and the Guardian challenges her with his athame:

> *Strip off thy garments, and lay aside thy jewels. For naught mayest thou bring with thee into this, our land.*

The Goddess removes her veil and jewelry and places them on the floor. The Guardian removes the red cords from his waist and binds the Goddess with it. The cord is tied around her wrists behind her back, the ends draped over her shoulders and tied around her neck, with the loose ends hanging down her chest.

> *So she laid down her garments and her jewels and was bound, as all living must be who seek to enter the realms of Death, the Mighty Ones.*

The Guardian leads the Goddess forward by the loose ends of the cords until she is facing the Lord. The Guardian then releases her and steps aside.

> *Such was her beauty that Death himself knelt and laid his sword and crown at her feet . . .*

The Lord kneels and lays the sword at the feet of the Goddess, then removes the crown and lays it with the sword. He kisses the feet of the Goddess (right then left).

Blessed be thy feet, that have brought thee in these ways. Abide with me, but let me place my cold hands on thy heart.

The Lord stands and holds his hands above the Goddess' heart.

And she replied: "I love thee not. Why dost thou cause all things that I love and take delight in to fade and die?"

The Lord moves his arms downwards, palms facing the Goddess.

"Lady," replied Death, "Tis age and fate, against which I am helpless. Age causes all things to wither; but when men die, at the end of time, I give them rest and strength so that they may return. But thou art lovely. Return not; abide with me." But she answered: "I love thee not."

The Lord stands and retrieves the scourge. He returns and faces the Goddess.

"Then," said Death, "An thou receive not my hands upon thy heart, thou must kneel to Death's Scourge." (Goddess kneels.) *"It is fate, better so," she said, and she knelt. And Death scourged her tenderly.*

The Lord gives the Goddess three, seven, nine, and twenty-one light strokes with the scourge.

And she cried, "I know the pangs of love."

The Lord lays down the scourge and helps the Goddess to her feet. He kneels.

And Death raised her and said, "Blessed be." And he gave her the Fivefold Kiss, saying "Thus only may thou attain to joy and knowledge."

Without reciting the wording, the Lord performs the Fivefold Kiss. He stands and unties the Goddess.

And he taught her all the mysteries and gave her the necklace which is the circle of rebirth.

The Lord retrieves the necklace and puts it on the Goddess. She picks up the crown and places it on his head.

And she taught him the mystery of the sacred cup, which is the cauldron of rebirth.

The pair move to the altar; the Goddess should be on the left (west) and the Lord on the right (east). The Goddess picks up the chalice, then the Lord puts his hands over hers.

They loved and were one, for there be three great mysteries in the life of man; and magic controls them all. For to fulfill love, you must return again at the same time, and at the same place, as the loved ones, and you must meet, and know, and remember, and love them again.

The Lord removes his hands, and the Goddess puts down the chalice. The Lord picks up the sword and scourge, faces the coven, and assumes the God Position. The Goddess faces the coven and assumes the Pentagram Position.

But to be reborn, you must die and be made ready for a new body. And to die, you must be born; and without love you may not be born. And our Goddess ever inclineth to love, and mirth, and happiness, and guardeth and cherisheth Her hidden children in life: And in death she teacheth the way to her communion; And even in this world she teacheth them the mystery of the Magick Circle, which is placed between the worlds.

The Legend is complete. With the High Priestess accompanying him, the High Priest takes the black candle and moves it from the west (death) to the east (rebirth). The pair returns to the altar, and the High Priestess recites:

The cycle of life is again set to continue, and we must now move forward, secure in the knowledge that we have opened the pathway from this world to the next, and from that world to this. We bid farewell to our beloved friend, and give thanks to Aradia and Cernunnos for their blessings. Blessed Be Aradia; Blessed Be Cernunnos.

Coven repeats: *Blessed Be Aradia; Blessed Be Cernunnos.*

The rite is over. Typically, the consecration and sharing of wine and cakes occurs now to celebrate the departed soul. When this is completed, the Circle is banished.

Italian

In the Italian denominations, this ritual is known as the Journey of the Spirit or the Passage of the Soul. Since it's customary for Italian witches to cremate their dead, the ceremony was traditionally performed moments before the actual cremation. But due to modern cremation practices, this is nearly impossible. Therefore, the ritual may be held whenever the opportunity arises.

Since the body is to be cremated, the *Book of Shadows* is always placed with the deceased witch. Other items usually included are ceremonial robe (often worn); wand (only if wooden); personal initiation cords; altar cloth.[9] It's also customary for each witch to offer a small token of remembrance. Appropriate items include flowers, sprigs of herbs, or poems and prayers handwritten on paper or parchment.

The rite begins with the High Priestess casting the Circle. A gateway is left in the west. After entering single file, the coven members arrange themselves along the west side of the Circle, leaving a break in their formation at the point where the Watchtower sits.[10] As soon as everyone is positioned, the High Priest closes the gateway. The High Priestess picks up the altar candle, walks over to the west portal, and holding it chest high with both hands, extends it outward toward the west. (See Endnote 10.) The High Priest now recites:

> *We have come here to send* (deceased's name) *on the sacred journey to the Realm of the Old Ones. Once again, the Mystery of Life and Death is before us. The Lord and Lady call our brother* (*sister*), *and the spirit dance begins. Let us wish our friend love, peace and happiness as he* (*she*) *is guided by this light to the beautiful realms beyond. Blessed Be.*

Coven repeats: *Blessed Be.*

The Myth of the Descent of the Goddess[11] is performed. When the Myth is completed, the High Priest and High Priestess return to the altar, and the coven turns to face them. The High Priest recites:

> *O' Great Lord and Merciful Lady, the time has come for us to call upon you to accompany our friend on his* (*her*) *journey. Grant him* (*her*) *the peace and joy that come to all who walk the path of your*

enlightenment, and upon his (her) return to this world, grant him (her) the health and prosperity that he (she) deserves.

In an ideal situation, the cremation would take place at this point. However, since that's unlikely, each person is now given the opportunity to say a few words in memory of the deceased. After speaking, they present their offering. Once everyone has finished, a funeral prayer is recited. The coven then recites:

Until we meet in the next realm, the next life, or somewhere along the way, we bid you farewell, dear friend.

Unlike with other denominations, there is no consecration of cakes and wine or other rites. The ceremony concludes when the Circle is banished. After cremation, it's customary to scatter the ashes into the wind or onto a body of water.

Saxon

The Saxon ceremony of Crossing the Bridge is the simplest of all Wiccan funeral rites. To begin, the Temple is erected in the normal manner. The Thegn then blows the hunting horn (or rings a bell, bangs a drum, etc.) and announces:

The horn (bell, drum, etc.) has been sounded for (deceased's name). *So be it.*

Coven repeats: *So be it.*
The Priestess recites:

For the first time (deceased's name) *is not with us in the Circle. Though this saddens us all, let us try to remember that he (she) is now free to move on. Let us also remember that we shall meet again. And when we again meet, it will mark a time for celebration.*

The High Priest says:

Let us send forth our prayers and power to usher him (her) over the Bridge.

At this point in the rite, one of two versions is followed: (A) Led by the Priestess, the coven members point their seaxes at the west portal and envision the deceased's spirit exiting the Circle. The coven's focus is on sending their love and energy with the spirit to accompany it on its journey. After a few moments, the Priestess lowers her seax and moves on to the cakes and ale consecration with no more words being spoken. (B) Only the Priestess holds her seax toward the west, and there is no moment of silence. She recites:

> *Our love and happiness accompany you on your journey. We shall always remember you, and we hope that you shall always remember us. Know that you are always welcome in our Circles and our lives.*

In the second version, the cakes and ale rite is now performed. Anyone wishing to remember the deceased may do so now, then the Circle is banished.

West Country

This denomination, along with a few other rural branches, does not have its own funeral ritual. Although this fact may surprise many Wiccans, it should be remembered that the rites of the tradition have not significantly changed since their early inception at a time when witches were churchgoers. Out of a necessity to remain hidden from witch-hunters, and since most churches were built on Pagan holy sites anyway, rural denominations simply accepted the burial that the church offered.

To their credit, modern practitioners of "Country" traditions have held true to the old beliefs and have not invented a funeral ceremony. Instead, individual covens tend to adopt the burial rite of another denomination. Though some people may view this as essentially the same thing as inventing a ritual, it's actually quite different since the adopted rite is typically one that has a clear historical lineage.

GRIMOIRE

Runes, Symbols, and Rituals

At one time or another throughout history, every major religion has tried to wipe out witchcraft. But, despite torture, the gallows, and burning at the stake, the Craft survived because of the efforts of witches who went to extraordinary lengths to protect it. This protection involved the use of secret written languages, called runes. It was partially because of these secret alphabets that witchcraft was able to survive throughout the ages in a form that actually resembles its original roots.

The word "rune," like almost everything else in witchcraft, has had its meanings changed over time. Literally translated as "secret" or "mystery," the word originally referred to the symbols of magickal scripts. However, with the passage of time and the persecution of the users, these alphabets slowly became confused with the words they were used to write until the single word had two meanings. Today, the word rune is used to refer to a magickal rhyme, song, or verse, such as the Gardnerian Witches' Rune, as well as to the written characters in a particular alphabet and even to the alphabet itself.

At one time, there were scores of different secret scripts. Initially, since reading and writing were usually beyond the reach of an ordinary witch, these alphabets were used almost exclusively by Ceremonial Magicians. But as the times changed, witches were forced to master these written alphabets in order to record their customs. This increase in users caused the runic scripts to diversify and flourish in many forms.

Around the time that Celtic Britain became Anglo-Saxon Britain, a few of these so-called "witch-alphabets" were starting to break away from the pack. The Anglo-Saxon Runes (Figure 22.1) were the first of several to establish a solid foothold on the British Isles. Consisting of thirty-one different characters,[1] in many ways they are extremely similar to both the Germanic Runes and the Norse Runes.

The second alphabet to accumulate a widespread following was the Theban Runes (Figure 22.3), which were developed during the Middle

Ages. Based on the Latin alphabet, these runes took their name from a legendary magician of the period named Honorius the Theban. Consisting of twenty-five characters, it differs greatly from any of the other alphabets. Among modern witches, there is some debate about whether the Theban Alphabet can rightly be called runic or whether it should merely be classified as ancient script. This arises from the belief that the Theban was not used for magickal purposes and instead showed up only in religious texts. Because Theban Runes have been more or less adopted by the Gardnerian and Alexandrian denominations as their alphabet, they are extremely well known in the modern Wiccan community.

There are several other runes that merit a brief reference due to their historic significance. For instance, the Futhark Runes[2] are widespread throughout European, Celtic, and Britannic Wicca. Depending on the area, this runic alphabet will contain anywhere from twenty-four to twenty-nine characters; Germanic has twenty-four (Figure 22.4); Anglo-Saxon has twenty-nine; and Saxon has twenty-seven (Figure 22.5).

In addition, there's the Celtic Ogham (Figure 22.6). Often called the Druid Tree Alphabet, the Ogham dates back as early as 500 B.C. when it was originally used for everything from recording history to engraving magickal inscriptions. This system of writing uses a series of one to five straight or slanted vertical lines drawn up to, or across, a horizontal center line, with each series of vertical lines representing a letter of the alphabet.

During early times, it was commonplace for witches to use secret magickal alphabets to write down prayers, invocation, and other religious beliefs, thereby ensuring privacy from nonwitches. But this seems to have been only a minor application for runes. A much larger use appears to have been to inscribe weapons and tools. In fact, around this time in history, it was common for almost all tools and weapons to be engraved with some type of magickal inscription. This practice included knights and noblemen who regularly had local sorcerers engrave their weapons with inscriptions for protection. Placing these symbols on tools and weapons played an important role in the practices of medieval sorcerers and witches in controlling spirits, drawing upon the forces of Nature, and ensuring strength and victory over enemies. Perhaps the greatest rationale behind the use of runes was their ability to charge an object with psychic energy. This phenomenon occurs as a result of the level of dedication and concentration needed to write these difficult scripts.

The following pages are examples of the most common runes.

Included are the Theban, Anglo-Saxon, Germanic Furthark, and Saxon Futhorc. Also included are the Celestial (Figure 22.2) of Ceremonial Magick and the ancient Celtic Ogham.

ANGLO-SAXON RUNES *Fig. 22.1*

A B C D E F G H I

J L M N O P R S T

Ë U W Y Z AE EA OE NG

TH

CELESTIAL RUNES

Fig. 22.2

A B C D E F G H I,J

K L M N O,Q P R S T

U,V W X Y Z

THEBAN RUNES

Fig. 22.3

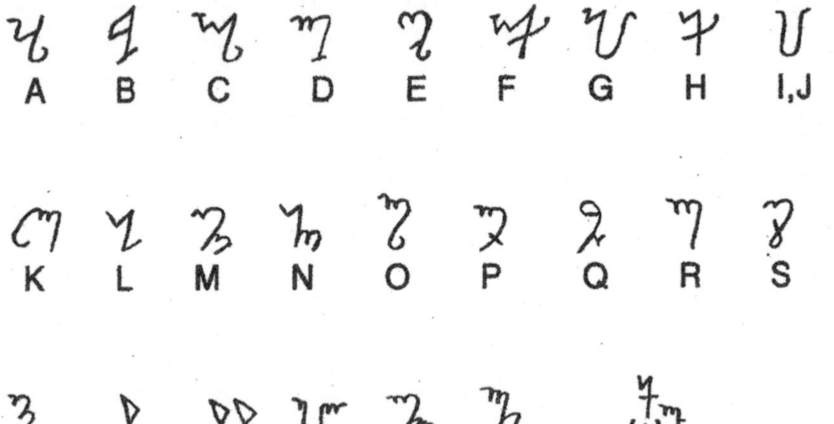

A B C D E F G H I,J

K L M N O P Q R S

T U,V W X Y Z End Sentence

GERMANIC (FUTHARK) RUNES *Fig. 22.4*

F U TH A R K G W H

N I J Ë P Z S T B

E M L NG D O

SAXON (FUTHORC) RUNES *Fig. 22.5*

CELTIC OGHAM RUNES

Fig. 22.6

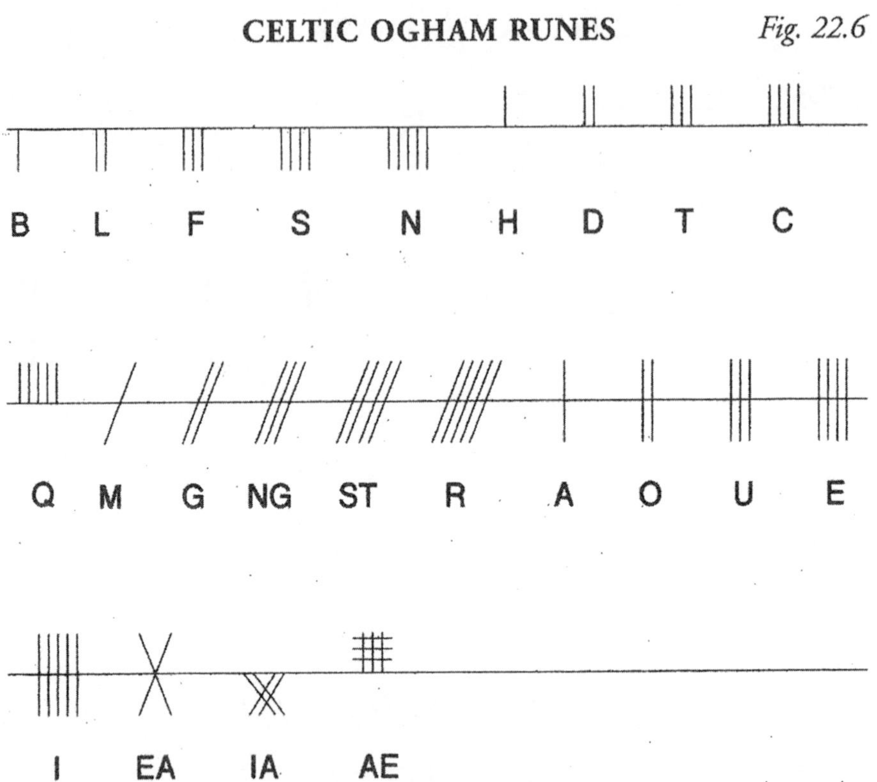

SYMBOLS AND SIGILS

Long before the alphabet was invented, pictures were used as a means of written communication. These symbols represented the basic aspects of life. But once religion crept into man's understanding of the world, a new form of written sign was needed. So, mankind began using the sigil. The sigil is an occult seal or sign that symbolizes the essence of a specific element, spirit, deity, or otherworldly being. In witchcraft and Ceremonial Magick, sigils are used for invocations and evocations, while symbols are used as emblems, designations, or to mark tools and other objects.[3]

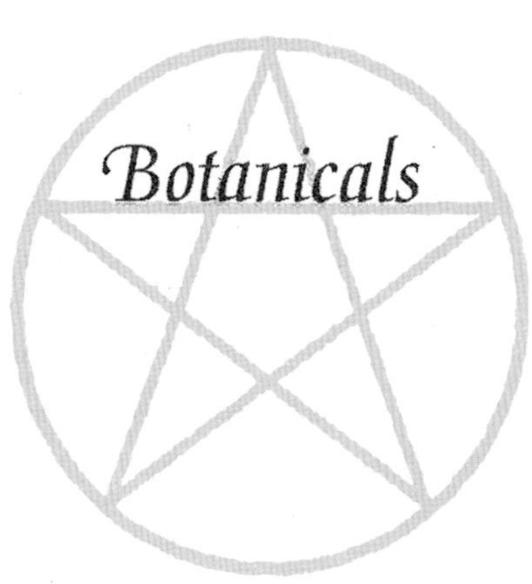

Botanicals

The use of herbs, plants, and other natural remedies in witchcraft can be dated as far back as the religion itself. For countless centuries, village witches recognized that plants had both medicinal and magickal benefits. Over time, they built up a vast amount of knowledge about the purposes of plants, to the point where it would now take several volumes to list all their uses. However, some less complicated information can be passed along quite easily.

Plants can be broken down into two basic categories: those that are used for magickal burning and those that are used for medicinal purposes. Early practitioners of witchcraft knew the difference between the two and used them quite effectively. These witches used plants for everything from healing the sick to brewing love potions. They knew the secrets of the infamous witch's flying ointments, which were in reality extremely strong hallucinogenic concoctions, and the secret of making tranquilizers and sedatives to calm the nerves or ease the pain of childbirth.

These same witches also knew how to unlock the magickal properties of plants by burning them and which ones were right to produce a desired effect. Though some of this wisdom came by way of trial and error, a good deal of all herbal knowledge came directly from Druids and Ceremonial Magicians; and all witches owe a good portion of their knowledge about plants to these teachings.

Now, when it comes to actually obtaining plants, there are a few things that all witches must know. First of all, witches believe that there is a desired method of collecting plants in order to preserve their unique properties. This is done using a tool called a boleen, which is a small knife with a curved blade. The blade resembles a crescent moon. Many witches also favor being skyclad while cutting plants, as well as cutting them at certain times of the day or night. Both of these practices are really more of a matter of choice, and the actual practices vary from denomination to denomination. For instance, Gardnerian witches feel the best time for cutting is at night during a full moon, while West Country has no such stipulation.

Since there are more plants than can reasonably be mentioned, what follows is a modest list that covers some popular topics. The first list contains plants for magickal burning, and the second contains medicinal plants.

A Final Word Of Warning: Always Consult Your Doctor For Serious Medical Needs, and Be Sure to Consult Your Doctor Before Using Medicinal Herbs, Especially If You Are Taking Prescription Medication.

MAGICKAL BURNING

To use plants for burning, begin by drying them thoroughly after collection. This can be done by hanging them in a warm, dry location. It should take only about a week for them to dry completely as long as they don't get wet. On damp days, it's important to keep the plants dry, or there's a good chance that they will mildew. If this happens, the plants are ruined and must be disposed of. Once dry, store them in an airtight container until you're ready to use them. If there's no way to grow your own, there's always a large selection for sale from various sources. However, whenever possible, purchase herbs from an occult shop or similar store, as they are more likely to carry a product that was collected in a traditional manner.

The most widely practiced method for using plants is to mix small amounts with incense, then burn this mixture in the censer. It's also acceptable to simply burn the plants by themselves, though this often presents a problem since the dried material usually burns very quickly. A way to remedy this is to spray a light mist of water over the dried plants just prior to burning. The moisture will slow the combustion process slightly while still allowing the material to burn.

Plant:	**Purpose:**
Aloe	Attract love
Althea	Attract helpful spirits
Arrowroot	Creates lust toward you
Basil	Attract success
Bayberry Leaves	Protection from harm
Betony	Protection from evil
Bloodroot	Protection against evil forces

Burdock	Cleansing
Catnip	Strength and cunning
Celery Seed	Add power to charms
Chestnut	Strength and endurance
Chickweed	Bring back a lover
Chicory	Uncover enemies
Cinnamon	Increases magical power/strength
Clover	Comfort and peace
Colicroot	Drive away enemies
Comfrey	Attract money
Coriander	Keep a lover faithful
Corn Flowers	Attract a new lover
Cowslip	Guard privacy
Daisy	Ensure a lover's faithfulness
Dandelion	Promote harmony in the home
Dog Rose	Ensure safe travel
Dogwood	Repel harmful spirits
Flaxseed	Calm discord between lovers
Ginger Root	Adventure and excitement
Golden Bough	Aid in finding love
Golden Seal	Prosperity in business
Gum Mastic	Increase power of spells
Hawthorn	Win battles
Hellebore	Gain insight
Hemlock	Cause illness in enemies
Horehound	Healing
Huckleberry	Dissipate depression; healing
Juniper	Build lust toward you
Lavender	Find a lusty lover
Lobelia	Build contentment
Mint	Happiness
Mistletoe	Repel evil
Moss	Increase success
Mugwort	Amplify magical power/perception
Myrtle	Attract money to family
Nettle	Peace and tranquility
Nutmeg	Promote good luck in difficult times
Peony	Good luck

Peppermint	Ensure a happy home life
Pine	Persuade agreement
Poppy	Overcome grief and sorrow
Primrose	Truthfulness
Pussy Willow	Keep a lover faithful and true
Rose Buds	Attract a man to a woman
Rose Hips	Attract same sex partner
Rosemary	Attract new friends/people to you
Thistle	Perceive destiny
Verbena	Create passion
Witch Hazel	Remove headaches
Wood Rose	Good fortune and success

MEDICINAL USES

In order to prepare and use plants correctly for medicinal purposes, there are a few essential points to know. Always try to adhere to the following procedures:

- Roots, bark, seeds and wood (i.e., stems, stalks) should be lightly boiled for 30-60 minutes, depending on the amount being used and the density of the material. In some cases, it might be necessary to grind or pulverize the material. A mortar and pestle are better for this than a blender or food processor because it's easier to regulate the texture by hand.
- Flowers and leaves should be steeped in hot water for 15-20 minutes. To increase potency, slightly bruise the leaves before boiling.
- Although copper cookware is traditional, it's advisable to always use glass (i.e., Pyrex) when boiling. Stainless steel cookware will also suffice. For storing mixtures, only use glass jars[1] that form an airtight seal; plastic containers (such as Tupperware) should never be used.
- Cough syrups can be made by boiling the plant material in water for 20-30 minutes, mixing in sugar or cornstarch until the mixture thickens, then slowly adding honey until properly textured.
- The average ratio of water to plant material is one cup of water to one heaping teaspoon of material. If using a prepackaged

mixture, which will usually be in powered form, simply follow the directions on the package.

- Poultices may contain astringents or emollients,[2] but not both. Also, poultices should always be covered with a clean gauze bandage and frequently changed.

Plant:	**Purpose:**
Ague Weed	Relieve common cold symptoms
Alehoof	Ease pain of rheumatism, arthritis
Alfalfa	Aid in eyesight (night vision)
Alfalfa (Raw)	Multivitamin when taken with kelp
Angelica	Cleansing—kidneys, liver, heart
Arrowroot	Relieve cough and sore throat
Ash Leaves	Ease symptoms of arthritis
Bayberry Leaves	Digestive problems
Bayberry Root	Stimulate loss of appetite
Betony	Ease strain and fatigue
Bilberry Leaves	Diuretic, ease bladder problems
Blackberry Leaves	Digestion problems, bowel disorders
Black Haw Bark	Lessen menstrual discomfort
Blue Mallow	Ease cold symptoms
Boneset	Aid in asthma
Buckthorn Bark	Laxative, ease digestive problems
Cassena Leaves	Stimulate nervous system, metabolism
Catnip	Sedative, ease stress
Chamomile Flowers	Sedative, relax nervousness
Cinnamon	Increase metabolism
Clover (Red)	Blood cleansing
Cocoa Beans	Temporary cure for mild headaches
Coffee Beans	Temporary cure for stress headaches
Coltsfoot	Relieve nasal blockage of cold
Comfrey Root	Soothe cough and sore throat
Corn Silk	Clear bladder and urinary tract
Culver's Root	Laxative, ease mild constipation
Currant Leaves	Ease coughs and sore throat
Dandelion Leaves	Source of vitamin A and E
Dandelion Root	Cure-all for internal disorders
Dandelion (Sap)	Cure warts and skin blemishes
Eucalyptus Leaves	Alleviate congestion

Flaxseed	Ease mild coughs and sore throat
Flaxseed Meal	Emollient
Garlic (Clove)	Blood and intestinal cleanser
Ginger Root	Ease symptoms of common cold
Goldenrod	Stimulate senses and alertness
Hops	Overall blood cleanser
Horseradish Root	Quicken pulse, increases metabolism
Irish Moss	Ease sore throat
Juniper Berries	Diuretic, ease urinary problems
Kelp (Raw)	Aid in weight gain and overall health
Licorice Root	Open nasal passages
Lungwort	Chest afflictions, coughs
Mandrake Root	Relieve constipation
Mayweed	Stimulate metabolism and senses
Motherwort	Ease menstrual cramps
Mustard	Quickens pulse, increases metabolism
Nutmeg	Stimulate senses and nervous system
Oatmeal	Emollient, soothe sunburn, rashes
Okra	Ease cough from common cold
Parsley Root	Diuretic, aid in passing kidney stones
Passion Flowers	Ease fatigue and stress
Pennyroyal	Relief of cold/flu symptoms
Peppermint	Arouse senses, boost metabolism
Quince	Emollient
Ragwort	Lessen symptoms of cold
Raspberry Leaves	Ease childbirth
Rhubarb Root	Laxative, ease constipation
Rue	Diuretic
Sage	Astringent
Sassafras Root	Ease common cold symptoms
Senega Root	Relieve congestion from cold
Senna Leaves	Cure mild constipation
Shepherd's Purse	Astringent
Slippery Elm Bark	Alleviate cough and sore throat
Spearmint	Arouse senses, boost metabolism
St. John's Wort	Mild astringent
Tamarind	Laxative
Tansy	Lessen morning sickness

Tea Leaves	Temporary cure for mild headaches
Valerian Root	Relax stress
Water Lilly Root	Astringent
Wheat Germ (Raw)	Overall health of bones/teeth
Wintergreen	Arouse senses, boosts metabolism
Witch Hazel	Astringent
Yarrow Root	Alleviate cramps

Divination

All religions and cultures tell of people who have the unique ability to foretell future events through psychic means. This extraordinary gift, known as clairvoyance, includes a broad spectrum of capabilities and is usually broken down into smaller categories such as precognition, scrying, and divination. In addition, there are a few disciplines, such as astrology, numerology and palmistry, that, although different from the others in many respects, are, nevertheless, still concerned with uncovering the future. In recent years, one form of divination—reading Tarot cards—has been thrust into the public spotlight due to a renewed interest in its remarkable potential. But to understand how Tarot cards work, a basic grasp of divination is needed.

Divination, often referred to as "clairvoyance with the use of tools," is the art of foretelling the future by psychic means with the aid of a physical accessory. There is a long list of items used in this practice, and this list includes things such as tarot cards, crystal balls, tea leaves, and coins. Regardless of which object is used, they all serve the purpose of triggering the intuition and acting as a focal point for the reader's intuitive awareness.

The act of divining genuine information also requires that the diviner have the ability to: (1) quiet the thinking mind; (2) blot out the distractions of the physical level; and (3) be open to the intuitive awareness of the unconscious. The intuitive awareness, in one of its many forms, is then projected onto the physical accessory being used and then interpreted.

For instance, in reading tea leaves, images are cast in the leaves for the reader to interpret. When dealing with the Tarot, the cards project a symbolic meaning, which is then interpreted by the reader. The physical aid thus offers something solid to interpret, and it also helps give the reader an added confidence. With enough practice, a seer learns to recognize the accuracy of the information being revealed to them, and this realization thereby reinforces the seer's confidence.

TAROT

Although the origin of Tarot cards is uncertain, some experts seem to have documented their first appearance sometime during the fourteenth century in India. Others, however, claim that the cards date back more than a thousand years to ancient Egypt. Since records from these times are incomplete and often inaccurate, the precise origin of the cards will likely never be known. To cloud the issue even further, there are many types of traditional and nontraditional Tarot decks used by readers.[1] Although there's no specific standard—with the exception of a few less-used versions—a typical deck of Tarot cards contains seventy-eight cards, split into two parts: the Minor Arcana and the Major Arcana.

The Minor Arcana is comprised of fifty-six cards divided into four suits—Swords, Wands, Cups, and Pentacles (or Coins)[2]—which each contain a total of fourteen cards. These four suits are then labeled Ace through Ten, plus the King, Queen, Knave, and Knight.

The Major Arcana, also known as the Trumps, consists of a sequentially numbered series of twenty-two cards, with each card bearing a symbolic figure. These symbolic figures, and their corresponding numbers, are:

#	Name	General Card Depictions
1	Magician/Juggler	Man by a table full of ritual objects
2	High Priestess	Seated woman in religious attire, often between pillars
3	Empress	Seated woman in majestic garments
4	Emperor	Man in majestic garments
5	Heirophant	Man in religious attire
6	The Lovers	Man and woman, often naked
7	The Chariot	Man in a chariot, sometimes holding spear or sword
8	Justice	Seated woman holding scales and a sword
9	Hermit/Prophet	Man with a staff and a lantern
10	Wheel of Fortune	Spoked wheel ridden by humans/animals
11	Strength/Fortitude[3]	Woman with a tamed or muzzled lion
12	Hanged Man	Man hanging upside down, usually by one foot
13	Death	Skeleton or Grim Reaper, often riding a horse
14	Temperance	Woman or angel pouring from one chalice to another

15 Devil	Horned man with goat feet; Pan
16 Tower	Circular building being struck by lightning
17 Star	Woman kneeling by water
18 Moon	Animals baying at the moon
19 Sun	Stylized or conventionalized sun
20 Judgment	Angel calling forth the dead from coffins
21 World/Universe	Androgynous figure, often dancing
0 Fool	Walking man, sometimes the Lord of Misrule

The Heirophant is also called the Priest or Pope, and there are versions that call the High Priestess the Female Pope. Also, the Fool card is often left unnumbered. Furthermore, every card of the Major Arcana can, in one way or another, be depicted in Wiccan tradition. For instance, the goat-footed Devil is certainly the Horned God, the High Priestess is surely a depiction of the Goddess of the Moon, the Wheel of Fortune and the Wheel of the Year are interchangeable, and so on throughout the deck.

Significator

A Significator is the card chosen to represent a person wishing a Tarot reading. This person is called the Inquisitor or Querent, and the card chosen should fit a general description of him/her. Before any reading can begin, this card must be established. The following are general descriptions[4] associated with each significator:

Card	**Description**
Wands	Blond/red-haired with light complexion
Cups	Moderately fair to lightly dark complexion
Swords	Moderately dark complexion
Pentacles	Very dark complexion
Kings	Men
Queens	Women
Knights	Young men
Knaves	Young women

Therefore, in order to select a significator card for a young, blonde-haired woman who has a fair complexion, the Knave of Wands would be the card chosen by the Reader: Knave = young woman + Wands = blonde hair with light complexion. If the card were for a middle-aged woman with dark hair and a slightly dark complexion, the Queen of Swords would be the card selected: Queen = woman + Swords = moderately dark complexion. Once this card is selected, the Querent shuffles and cuts the deck, then the Reader deals the cards one at a time.

Key Cards

As mentioned earlier, the twenty-two numbered key cards have varying meanings. Although these vary from discipline to discipline, a general agreement remains consistent throughout disciplines.

#	Name	Meaning
1	Magician	The Will, the Craft, cunning, skill, manipulation
2	High Priestess	The Intuition, increase/decrease, hidden knowledge
3	Empress	Creativity, success, happiness, pleasure, beauty
4	Emperor	Reason, ambition, victory, conquest; war, strife
5	Heirophant	Teaching, Divine Wisdom, morality
6	The Lovers	The Soul, impulse, inspiration, motive, power, sexuality
7	The Chariot	The Persona, victory, health, triumph; nonlasting success
8	Justice	Balance, strength, force, cosmic justice; legal matters
9	The Hermit	Philosophy, Divine Inspiration, active wisdom
10	Wheel of Fortune	Chance, fate, happiness, good fortune, evolution
11	Strength	Fortitude, courage, continuing action; obstinacy
12	Hanged Man	Transition, punishment, loss, suffering, sacrifice
13	Death	Transformation, time, involuntary change; rarely death
14	Temperance	Moderation, active action, realization, combination of forces
15	Devil	Temptation, materiality; obsession when with Lovers
16	Tower	Fighting, war, ambition; danger, ruin, fall
17	Star	Aspiration, faith, hope, help
18	Moon	Secrecy, falsity, deception, error; dissatisfaction, change
19	Sun	Growth, wealth, gain, glory; vanity, arrogance
20	Judgment	Finality, judgment, outcome, decision, rebirth
21	World/Universe	Denotes subject and depends on accompanying cards
0	Fool	Folly; stupidity spirituality, journey, thought (nonmaterial)

Majority Groupings

Besides the key cards, the other cards also have general meanings when appearing in certain suits or groupings. The following is a brief explanation of the meanings when a particular card is the majority:

Card	Meaning
Wands	Squabbling, opposition, and argument
Swords	Sadness, sickness, and even death
Cups	Pleasure, happiness, and revelry
Pentacles	Money, business, and material possessions
Key cards	Force and considerable strength
Court cards	Groups, meetings, and community

Cards also have varied meanings when in certain combinations:

#	Card	Meaning
3/4	Aces	Success, wealth; force, control, strength
3/4	Kings	Unforeseen encounters, news; speed, quickness of arrival
3/4	Queens	Power of acquaintances, influences; dominion, authority
3/4	Knights	Status, position, reputation; acquaintances of prominence
3/4	Knaves	Youth, vulnerability; invention, plans, ideas
3/4	Tens	Commerce, business transactions; responsibility, worry
3/4	Nines	Significant consistency; added responsibility
3/4	Eights	Travel, pushing on; considerable news
3/4	Sevens	Pacts, agreements; dissatisfaction, regret
3/4	Sixes	Success, financial/personal gain; pleasure, good fortune
3/4	Fives	Controversy, debate; plan, conformity
3/4	Fours	Diligence, industriousness; rest, peace
3/4	Threes	Cunning, deceit; determination, resolve
3/4	Twos	Inception, reorganization; discussion, dialogue

Numbered Cards

While there are generalized significances linked to the numbered cards when they appear in three- or four-card groupings, these same numbered cards, within a respective suit, take on new meanings that differ from their collective views. The thirty-six numbered cards and their associated values are:

#	**Meanings**
	Wands
2	Ownership, influence over another
3	Arrogance, vanity, pride
4	Compromise, understanding
5	Controversy, quarrels
6	Success, benefit
7	Opposition, resistance
8	Short messages or news
9	Health, energy, power
10	Revenge, injustice, malice
	Swords
2	Resolution, end to a fight, peace
3	Sorrow, unhappiness
4	Change (for better), healing, recovery
5	Loss, defeat, defamation
6	Travel (next card determines mode), work
7	Indecision, undependability of character
8	Petty, restricted, confining
9	Cruelty, suffering, pain
10	Death, disaster, failure
	Cups
2	Friendship, love, marriage
3	Pleasure, bounty (food and drink), gain (material items)
4	Moderated pleasure and benevolence from others
5	Divorce, loss of friendship, discontentment in love
6	Enjoyment, happiness, desire
7	Unfulfilled promises, marginal success (not long lasting), deceit
8	Tedium, lack of interest, abandonment
9	Fulfilled desire, realized potential and success
10	Good fortune, completely fulfilled wishes
	Pentacles
2	Change (for better), pleasurable travel to visit friends/relatives
3	Job, business, monetary transactions
4	Monetary gain, gifts received
5	Financial worries or trouble, loss of job or money

6 Unexpected windfall (monetary or business), material success
7 Charitable endeavors without reward, unprofitable gambles
8 Caution, prowess, mastery
9 Monetary gain, profit, inheritance
10 Wealth, fortune, treasure

Combinations

In addition to their individual and group meanings, the signification of a card is determined by other factors. A card is strong or weak, elevated or lowered, based on the card on either side of it. As a result, there are several combinations that must be noted. First, when cards of the same suit are on each side, the object card is greatly strengthened according to their nature. Second, when cards of a contrary element suit are on each side, the object card is greatly weakened. Third, when cards of complementary elements are on each side, the object card is modified, but not weakened. Fourth, when an object card falls between a card of contrary element and a card of complementary element, the object card is not weakened or strengthened as the two side cards negate each other. Air (Swords) is contrary to earth (Pentacles), while fire (Wands) is contrary to water (Cups). Complementary elements are: air is harmonious with water and fire, while fire is harmonious with air and earth.

Layout

Although there are varying layouts and spreads (Figures 24.1–24.3), there is a general format that can be followed when setting out the cards. The following is a basic formula that can be used with any spread.

Begin by discussing the purpose for the reading, then decide upon an appropriate layout pattern to answer the questions being asked. Next, the Reader should sort through the deck and select the significator. This card is then placed face up in its layout position. The deck is handed to the Querent who shuffles and cuts the cards. When the Querent finishes shuffling, they place the deck on the table, face down, and the Reader fans the cards to expose them all. Many Readers keep the cards face down, though they can be laid face up. The Querent selects a card. The Reader takes the card and places it in the first position. A second, third, fourth, etc., card is selected by the Querent and given to the Reader.

Once all the positions are filled, the Reader turns over the first card and interprets it according to its position and the meaning of the card. The Reader turns the second card and interprets it; position, significance and sequence are considered; the third, fourth, and so on are turned over. If the cards are face up, they're still interpreted one at a time.

Naturally, the points to keep in mind are the significance of each card, the position it occupies, the cards before and after it, the general sequence (all the same suit, all the same number, elemental associations, etc.). It's also worthwhile noting that if the majority of cards are from the Major Arcana, the effects will be powerful; changes will be dramatic, advancements significant, and reversals severe.

The following are four popular Tarot layout patterns.

SAXON PATH *Fig. 24.1*

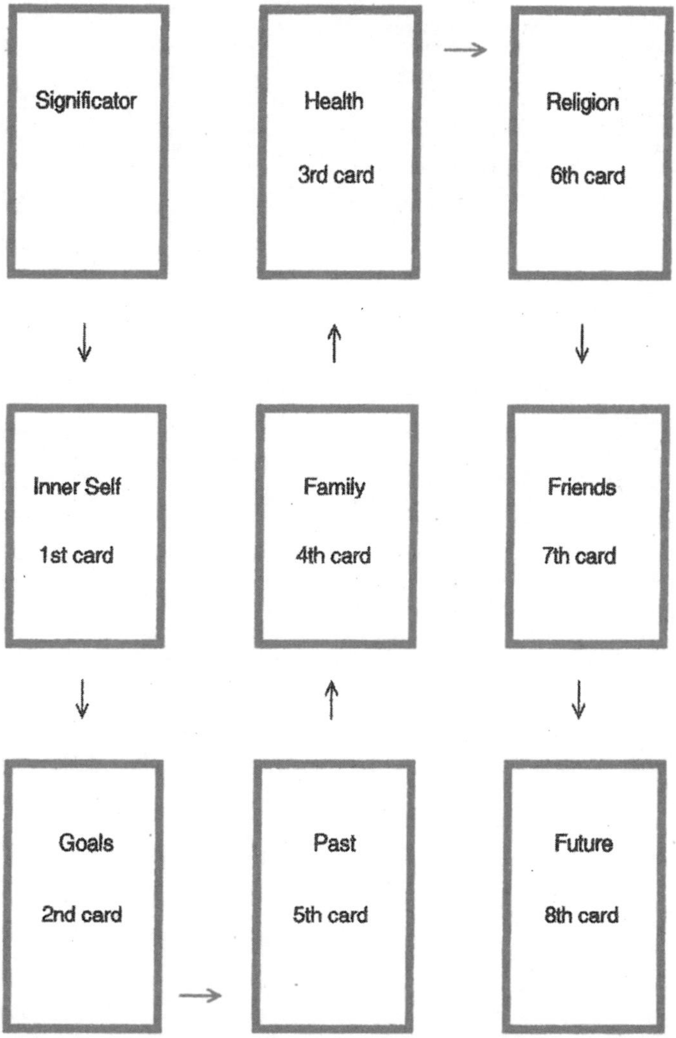

CELTIC CROSS

Fig. 24.2

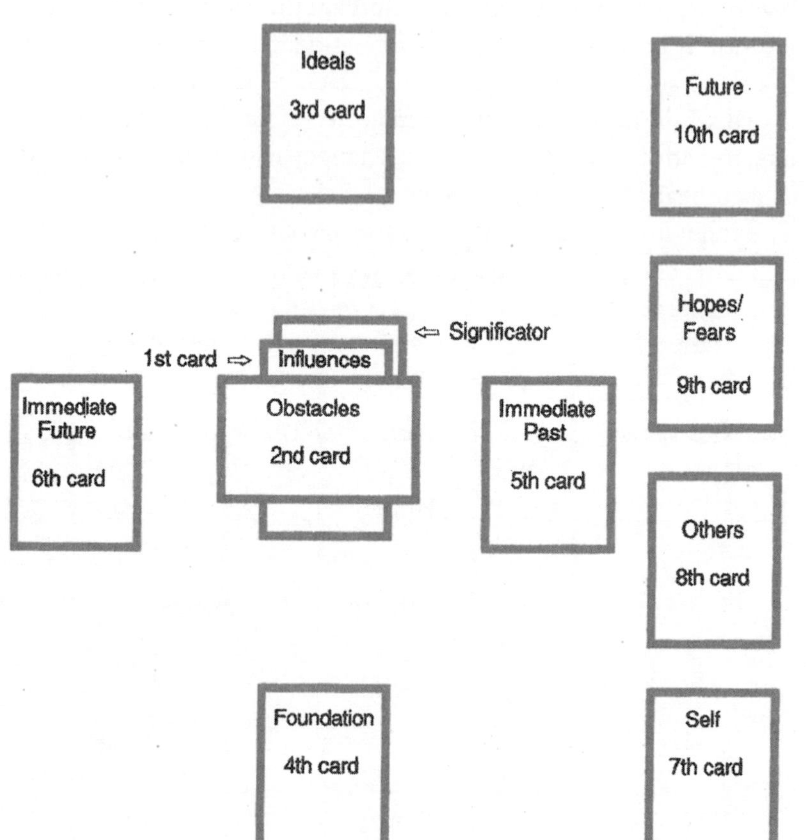

TREE OF LIFE[5]

Fig. 24.3

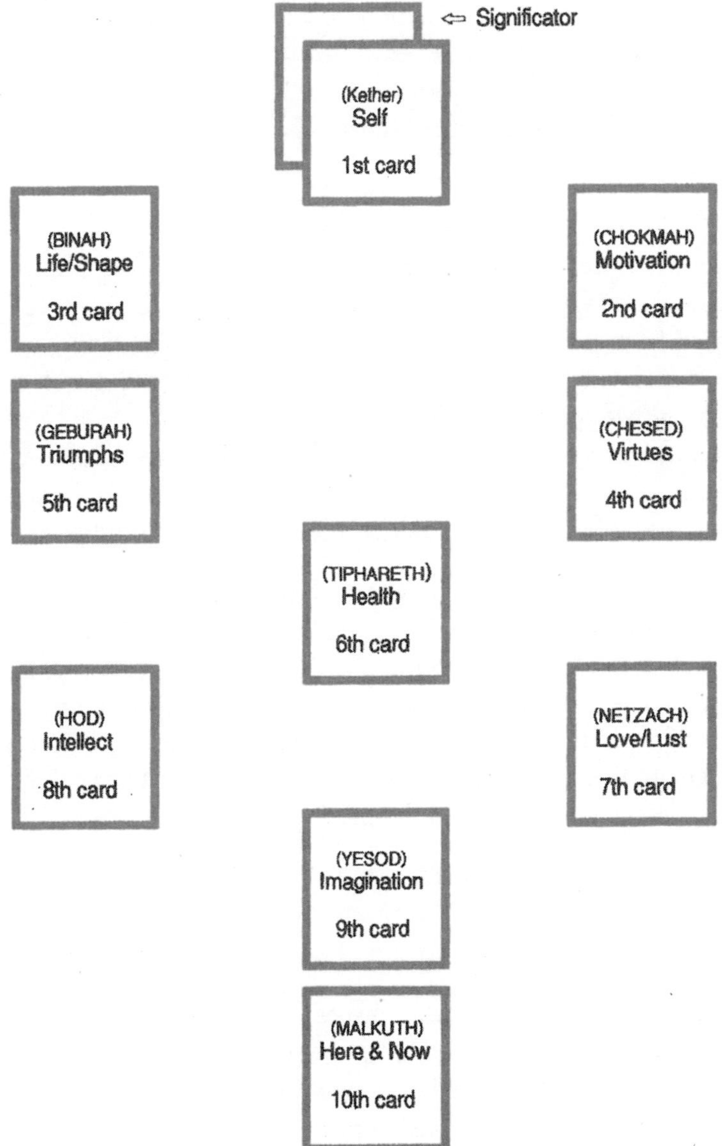

The preceding is a very basic explanation of the Tarot. For a complete breakdown of the many disciplines and methodology, there are good books available. The most suitable book for beginners is Eden Gray's *A Complete Guide to the Tarot.* To learn how to use the Tarot for advice and direction in everyday decision making rather than predictions or uncovering hidden things, Janina Renee's Tarot: *Your Everyday Guide* is one of the best on the market.

NUMEROLOGY

As its name suggests, numerology is the art of foretelling the future by using the occult value of numbers. This process can be used to forecast everything from the best time for travel to the best place to live. But perhaps the most widely recognized use for numerology is to match the compatibility of two people.

In Craft use, witches often employ this mystical art form in choosing their Craft name. This allows them to pick a name that is harmonious with their personality and in balance with their birth number.

Calculating Numbers

In order to forecast anything using numerology, the most important step is to calculate the single-digit number that represents an individual. This is known as the birth number and is derived by adding the month, day, and year of birth until a single digit is reached. For increased accuracy, the exact time of birth, if known, can also be added. The calculation for someone born on October 31, 1963, would look like this:

Birthday: 10/31/1963} 1+0+3+1+1+9+6+3 = 24
Birthday total equals 24} 2+4 = 6
Birth Number} 6

Once the birth number is established, the next step is to calculate the name number. This is done by adding the numeric value of each letter (see Figure 24.4) in a name until a single-digit number is achieved. The numeric value of each letter is listed in the following chart:

ALPHABETICAL NUMBER CHART *Fig. 24.4*

1	2	3	4	5	6	7	8	9
A	B	C	D	E	F	G	H	I
J	K	L	M	N	O	P	Q	R
S	T	U	V	W	X	Y	Z	

The formula for finding the name number for KERNUNNOS would be:

K = 2; E = 5; R = 9; N = 5; U = 3; N = 5; N = 5; O = 6; S = 1
Kernunnos} 2+5+9+5+3+5+5+6+1 = 41
Name total equals 43} 4+1 = 5
Name Number} 5

In the above two examples (birth number and name number), the first equation results in a 6, while the second is 5. If this were a witch attempting to choose a witch name,[6] the 7 would not match his birth number. The significance in matching the birth number is that the date of birth never changes and is thus a constant indicator of a person's numerical designation. As such, a name number of 5 is unacceptable. In order to rectify this situation, while still keeping the same basic name, simply substitute the "K" (value of 2) with a "C" (value of 3), thereby changing the equation total to 42; 4+2=6.

But the birth number is useful for more than figuring out a proper witch name. It can be used to choose important dates, locate a suitable place to live, or find a compatible partner.

Signs, Planets, and Colors

The numeric value of birth numbers also corresponds to an individual's planetary sign, elemental sign, and even primary and secondary colors. The following designations occur for each number:

#	Planet	Element	Color (Primary/Secondary)
1	Sun	Fire	Red / Yellow, Gold
2	Moon	Water	Orange / White
3	Jupiter	Fire	Yellow / Violet
4	Uranus	Air	Green / Blue

5	Mercury	Air	Blue / Light shade of any color
6	Venus	Earth	Indigo / Blue
7	Neptune	Water	Violet / Light Green, Yellow
8	Saturn	Earth	Rose / Purple, Blue
9	Mars	Fire	Gold / Red, Pink

When trying to decide on a compatible partner, each number also has general characteristics that make certain combinations better than others. For example: A woman with a birth number of 1 seeking a boyfriend would look for a man who has a Fire or Air sign; the numbers 1, 3, 4, 5, and 9 fall within this range. But she could go one step further by examining the general characteristics of each number and narrow down the field. This additional step would tell her that 1, 3, and 5 are her best choices. The following is a brief list of the traits associated with each number:

#	**Characteristics**
1	Self-confident and a leader. Ambitious, tending to be a driving force. Persistent to the point of being tenacious. An explorer and pioneer. Passionate, innovative, and aggressive.
2	Patient, sensitive, and emotional peacemaker who is more of a homebody than adventurer. Usually conservative and sentimental. Togetherness is a need of this person. Often talented in both music and art.
3	Friendly, lighthearted, and entertaining. Not materialistic, though very adept at gaining an edge. Self-confidence grows with age. An inquiring personality who always needs to know the finer points.
4	A practical, hard worker with exceptional patience. Often eccentric to the point of appearing unusual. Disciplined, reliable, and good with details. Very faithful and affectionate in matters of the heart.
5	An adventurous explorer who loves traveling and thrives on new experiences. Friendly and helpful as a friend, active and versatile as a companion. Sensual, provocative, and insatiable as a lover.
6	Docile, well bred, and supportive. Loving and fair, often acting as a peacemaker. Enjoys quality, comfort, and the finer things in life. Generous and sweet, usually sometimes so much that the faults of others go unnoticed.
7	Quiet, discriminating, and mysterious. Fond of outdoor activities, especially the ones that can be done alone. Motivated to seek perfection in all areas.

8 Self-sufficient, successful, and well organized. Sometimes dark and humorless owing to drive and desire to control situations. Respected for work ethic. Good manners, resiliency, and prosperity are trademarks.

9 Generous, charitable, and loyal. Lover of art, music, and travel. Under certain conditions, jealous and emotional. Afraid of the unknown and very suspicious, prefers to be surrounded by a lot of people.

SCRYING

The two most popular types of scrying involve crystal gazing and mirror gazing. But regardless of the aid used, the basic method involves clearing the mind of all thoughts in order to open it to the images that appear in the scrying medium. (A crystal is used in the following example.)

In a quiet dark room, burn a small amount of sweet-smelling incense. Clear a table of all objects except the crystal. Set a small candle where it provides light, but does not reflect in the crystal. Most witches also cast a Magick Circle, but this is more a matter of choice than a necessity. Pull up a chair that allows you to sit comfortably with your arms placed on the table.

Now it's time to begin gazing at the crystal. However, it's important to learn how to gaze. The problem is that most people tend to strain to see images. As a result, they end up staring at the crystal. Do not stare! Gaze softly, letting your eyes focus on a point inside the object. This will take practice because your natural tendency is to focus on the surface, sides, and surrounding area. For this you need to focus deep inside. At the same time, make sure that you allow yourself to blink normally, and don't think about not blinking.

After a period of time—anywhere from a few minutes to an hour—you'll begin to see subtle changes occur within the crystal. Some people describe the change by saying that it appears as if the crystal fills with smoke. This statement, however accurate it may be for some, does not apply to everyone, and the scryer should look for less predictable signs. Although these changes will initially be negligible, and almost indistinguishable, they'll slowly shape themselves into clear pictures. With time and practice, these pictures will become clearer and clearer until they resemble the pictures on a television screen.[7]

This same technique is used for black mirrors, bowls of water, smoke, fire, and any other scrying aid.

Magick

Most people have the wrong idea about magick because they invariably think of stage magic. And since everyone knows that this form of entertainment is nothing more than illusion created with smoke and mirrors, they automatically discount the possibilities offered by true magick. Yet it's the belief in the power of magick that enables a witch to perform acts that to the average nonbeliever are almost impossible to comprehend. But what is magick?

There are countless definitions for magick. French occultist Eliphas Levi offers the inaccurate opinion that it's a "traditional science of the Secrets of Nature." Aleister Crowley offers the inadequate view that magick is "the Science and Art of causing Change to occur in conformity with Will." In *The Lemegeton, or Lesser Key of King Solomon,* S. L. MacGregor Mathers defines magick as "the Highest, most Absolute, and most Divine Knowledge of Natural Philosophy, advanced in its works and wonderful operations by a right understanding of the inward and occult virtue of things; so that true Agents being applied to proper Patients, strange and admirable effects will thereby be produced. Whence magicians are profound and diligent searchers into Nature; they, because of their skill, know how to anticipate an effect, which to the vulgar shall seem to be a miracle."

However, of all the available definitions, Evelyn Underhill[1] gives one of the best, "Magic, in its uncorrupted form, claims to be a practical, intellectual, highly individualistic science; working towards the declared end of enlarging the sphere on which the human will can work, and obtaining experimental knowledge of planes of being usually regarded as transcendental."

Good and bad definitions aside, the basic concept of magick is that it's the result achieved by a person, using proper technique under the right circumstances, to cause change, either constructive or destructive. This change is brought about by manipulating the energy that flows in, around, and through all things. While the Wiccan Theories of Cause and Effect, Polarity, Gender, Motion, etc., (see Philosophy) can better explain this idea, a simplified explanation is that energy is the basic component of everything. In its raw form, all energy is neutral. A positive intent results in constructive applications while a negative use results in destructive forms. These operations are achieved through spells.

A general definition of a spell is that it's the method a witch (or coven) employs to concentrate psychic energy and direct it toward a specific task with the intention of accomplishing a predetermined objective. There are many different types of spells, along with their various components.[2] The individual parts are better defined one by one. But the bottom line is that a spell is the method used to accomplish magick.

Nowadays, "magick" is often just used in place of the word "spell." Although this is considered perfectly acceptable, there are, nevertheless, subtle differences in the actual history of the two words. For instance, the term magick, derived from the Greek "Magikê technê," was originally associated only with Ceremonial Magicians and referred exclusively to their elaborate and ornate practices. Since Ceremonial Magick was such a complicated discipline, the study of it was mainly limited to learned and wealthy men. Common folk, like witches, were therefore usually excluded due to their social and economic status combined with their inability to read or write. This forced witches to rely upon simpler forms of metaphysical conjuration for their magickal needs. However, over the years, the practices of Ceremonial Magick have been interwoven into witchcraft to the point where the two terms are now interchangeable.

There are three further points that are interesting to note. First, although the rites and ceremonies of some denominations have been heavily influenced by the intricacies of Ceremonial Magick, their basic spells are extremely uncomplicated and leave out almost all references to the complexities of Ceremonial Magick. Second, despite the fact that the ancient spelling of magick contained a "K," it's a commonly accepted belief that the modern form of the word was reintroduced by Aleister Crowley in an effort to connect it to Ceremonial Magick, as well as separate it from fraudulent stage magic. Third, it's widely believed that many aspects of Ceremonial Magick were introduced into Wicca by Gerald Gardner, and that this was the result of his association with the Order of the Golden Dawn and his friendship with Crowley.

SPELLS

Just as there are different definitions for magick, there are also varying opinions on spells. In addition to the differing opinions, there are different types of spells. And beyond that, there are divergent methods of performing the various types of spells. In other words, this is a complicated topic.

When the word "spell" is mentioned, most people, including a lot of novice witches, automatically envision something that is either negative or cartoonish. This reaction isn't their fault. Instead, it's the natural result of being exposed to countless forms of unenlightened opinions. Therefore, forget everything you know about this subject. Forget everything you've ever learned from movies, television, fictional books, and other uninformed sources. Once you've done that, you're ready to understand the reality of how spells work.

There are several schools of thought concerning the makeup and use of spells. One prominent line of thinking divides all spells into three categories—written, oral, and imagined—and holds that all spells fall into one of these basic classes. This blueprint also reasons that all spells are further broken down into parts, and it's these parts that lay the foundation upon which all spells rest. A second outlook states that spells are exclusively a product of willpower and that physical accessories are unnecessary. Another philosophy says that all spells rely upon the four elements for power and that the person casting the spell uses his or her own power to modify and direct the elemental power toward a given task.

To properly use a spell, a breakdown of its parts must first be understood. To begin with, all spells are divided into parts, or components. In their most basic forms, there are four components common to spells: specific intent, imagination, direction of willpower, and dispersal. There are also several nonessential components, such as planetary considerations, music, incense, or degrees of the Moon, which can also be factored into the spell. However, they are not absolutely necessary. These nonessential components are just that because the spell will still function without taking these factors into consideration. Nevertheless, as you become more advanced, you'll be able to greatly enhance the effectiveness of your spells by factoring in these components.

Spell Construction

The first component that must be established is the specific intent for the spell. But what does specific intent mean? Well, for starters, it means the exact problem that the spell is directed at solving. For instance, the specific intent of a healing spell would be to cure a person (or even an animal or plant) of an illness. That sounds easy, but there's more to it than that. When you're deciding what the intent of the spell is being directed at, you must be very specific about it.

Here's an example. Suppose you have a friend who gets terrible migraine headaches, and you want to conduct a healing spell. Your specific intent explicitly is to cure the headaches. Put into simple terms, you are isolating your intentions to focus on an exact idea. This is because without your intent being precise, your healing spell could easily just cure a rash. Also, the specific intent concentrates psychic energy at the intended objective rather than allowing it to weaken over a wide range of possible tasks, focusing on the headaches as opposed to any ailment. Therefore, establishing the specific intent is the first essential component of a spell.

The second component that is required for a spell to be successful is imagination. This term means just what you think it does, and there is no hidden translation. Simply stated, imagination is a clear visualization of the act or process taking place and coming to fruition. It involves forming a mental picture of what you want to happen, then mentally watching it happen.

Using the previous example, you would form a mental picture of your friend who has migraines. With the picture in mind, you might imagine a healing light coming from you and concentrating itself on your friend's head. You'd then picture the healing light soothing the headache. Finally, you'd see your friend cured. Thus, the entire process is visualized. This mental blueprint gives a step-by-step guide for the third component to follow.

The third component of a spell is the direction of psychic power. This is basically the act of sending your accumulated psychic energy to perform the task that you've chosen. This act may seem complicated at first, but it does become easier with practice. There are, however, a few things that must happen before any psychic energy can be transmitted. First and foremost, a sufficient amount of psychic energy to accomplish the task at hand must be built up and stored.[3] But in order to begin building psychic energy, you'll naturally need some way to store it as it's being accumulated. This is the main reason that all spells are always conducted inside a Circle. In this way, the Circle itself acts to contain and concentrate the energy until you're ready to direct it toward its destination. At the same time, the Circle protects you from all unwanted outside psychic interference, thereby allowing you to concentrate fully on your spell. The Circle is, therefore, both a shield from outside harm and interference, and a way to concentrate psychic energy.

Now comes the next big question: How do you actually build the psychic energy? To begin with, by working within the Circle, a certain amount of energy has already been built up during the casting. If a chant or other rite was conducted, psychic energy was also added and stored within the confines of the Circle. Therefore, before you even start raising power for your spell, you've already built up a fair amount of energy. But this is only a starting point. The spell that you work will build up a sizable amount of psychic power on its own. This will occur as a direct result of all the preparation, concentrated thought, meditation, singing, or chanting, that you use in your spell. In short, everything that you do adds a little more to the effectiveness and power of the spell that you're working.

For instance, you can sit inside the Circle and write out your spell, meditate for a few minutes, and then chant for several more minutes, and each act—writing, meditating, chanting—adds more energy. When combined with the energy already raised, you've now built up a large amount of power that you can direct at your spell. In a coven setting, this energy is multiplied by the number of witches present.

Once a sufficient amount of energy has been accumulated, it's time to use the stored power. The easiest way to explain this method is to tell you to combine the first and second components (specific intent and imagination) and direct your power at the intended task. Now remember, you've already set forth your specific intent and you've used your imagination to form a complete picture of how everything should work. You must now mentally project all your stored psychic energy to reach out to your objective. Once again returning to the previous example: You first established the specific intent to cure the headaches. Your next step was to form a picture in your mind of the entire process taking place. Now, by directing and sending out[4] the built-up psychic power, you're actually working on curing the migraines.

The final major component of a spell is the dispersal, which is itself divided into two parts. The first part is the life span of the spell, which is actually nothing more than an expiration date. In short, the spell is worked until a desired result is achieved or until a preset time has expired; then it dissipates. Having a finite life span serves to ensure that the spell doesn't serve its purpose and then after time, goes awry. Remember, a spell is always meant for a specific purpose and should never be allowed to exist simply unchecked. Since power makes no distinction between good and bad, it can be unintentionally perverted to do harm. Therefore, always set limits on your spells, and once the limit has been reached, the spell should automatically be dispersed. This is especially important for imagined spells, as opposed to material-based spells, because thoughts must be properly modified to prevent continuation.

With spells that employ material objects, there is a procedure for cleansing the energy, thus bringing a permanent end to the spell. In order to set limits, many witches use a word or phrase, much like a reverse trigger, to put an end to their spells. However, acknowledging parameters for the spell is sufficient in most cases.

The second part of the dispersal involves breaking down anything used for the spell, such as paper, candles, or other items. By breaking down these objects, the excess power that has been built up in them is released, and the spell is permanently ended. Along these lines there is the belief that material items should be disposed of using the same characteristic as the spell. For instance, the material used for a fertility spell would be cleansed in water, while items used for a passion spell would be cleansed in fire. However, while this elemental cleansing is used by almost all witches, it's not always used in such specific form. Many times, items are merely burned or washed in water. Paper would be burnt, and the ashes scattered into the wind to dissolve the energy and return it to Nature, while a glass bottle would be placed in running water to cleanse it. Both methods are equally acceptable as long as the spell's end is consciously acknowledged.

Besides the major components that go into a spell, there are a few additional factors that can be brought to bear in order to increase a spell's effectiveness. The first of these minor components is the cycle of the Moon. As you know, there are four phases of the moon—waxing, full, waning, new—and each has its own significance. When performing spells, these four phases are divided into two pairs—waxing/full and waning/new—and used for separate purposes. In simple terms, the waxing/full phases are used for "increase," while the waning/new phases are for "decrease."

For instance, a healing spell (i.e., to increase health) is most effective when done during the waxing/full phases of the moon, while a spell to stop gambling (i.e., to decrease a bad habit) should be worked during the waning/new phases. Other examples would be casting a love spell during the waxing/full phases or spells to neutralize enemies during the waning/new phases.

Similarly, astrological patterns can also play a part in the effectiveness of a spell. Since a spell is simply a projection of inner power in an attempt to bring about cosmic change, and since the Universe is connected, subtle influences of celestial bodies can make a difference. However, to use these to your advantage, you will need a good deal of astrological knowledge. Therefore, consulting a book devoted entirely to this complex subject is the only way to competently use astrological patterns to enhance a spell.

Finally, music, incense, herbs, and other things can also play a part in increasing the effectiveness and power of a spell. This is because these items have an effect on YOU. Since you are the key to success or failure, each of these items is used to add a particular quality to the working. It's the mood created by music or the scent of incense that enhances the experience for you.

Types of Spells

The three categories of spells (written, oral, and imagined) not only can be used in conjunction with each other to enhance results, but are almost always linked by a general overlapping of concepts.

Naturally, a "written spell" refers to one that is written out.[5] Now, some people might wonder why anyone would bother to write out a spell at all. Well, there are three main advantages to doing so, and only one minor disadvantage.

First, writing out the spell puts more concentrated thought into it. As the words are composed, the writer consciously thinks about what he or she wants to happen and subconsciously charges the spell with psychic energy. This process focuses thoughts on achieving results. To this end, some witches prefer to use runic symbols (see Alphabets) for this purpose, as it forces them to concentrate even more, thereby amplifying their power.

Second, writing out the spell allows time to modify and edit its wording to be precise. The benefits of this are self-evident.

The third advantage of a written spell is that it's usually easier for an inexperienced witch to perform. The ability to write it out in advance, and reword it, puts many novice witches at ease. At the same time, a written spell allows for more complexity, a feature appreciated even by experienced spell casters. Unfortunately, there is a disadvantage to a written spell. Because it is inked onto paper, a written spell removes the ability to make last-minute changes. However, since this is usually outweighed by its many advantages, it really isn't that great a drawback.

After written spells come oral spells. This type of spell is simply one that's recited out loud. The main difference, and primary advantage, between a written and oral spell is that latter can be adapted and changed on the spur of the moment. Another difference between the two spells is that an oral spell is geared toward instantaneous action, while written spells lean towards producing gradual results.

The disadvantage of this type of spell is that it requires the spell caster to be extremely precise in its wording. This can be a very challenging task, especially for a novice, and for this reason alone many witches tend to shy away from oral spells until they are more experienced. However, there's an acceptable alternative. Many witches who subscribe to this form of spell casting simply write out their spells, then recite the written spell. This allows them the security of writing the spell, yet gives them the freedom to enhance the spell's power by reciting it. Simple and effective.

The third type of spell is an imagined spell. This category encompasses a wide variety, and in actuality, almost any spell can be placed in this classification. Unlike the two previous types of spells, this form relies exclusively upon thought. It is born, nurtured, energized, and projected all from within the operator's mind.

This is also one of the chief advantages that imagined spells have over the other two types. Basically, an imagined spell allows you to form an elaborate mental picture of your spell's objective and keep it locked in your consciousness, while eliminating the distraction of writing or speaking. And, although imagination is a component of all spells, a purely imagined spell takes this concept to even greater lengths because the entire process is confined to the mind where subconscious thoughts may assist its goal.

Once mastered, this method can produce results that are astonishing in detail and complexity. However, due to the mental preparation and precision required, there are also disadvantages that come with this type of spell, especially for a novice witch. This is because these spells require strict concentration, and even the slightest distraction can have a negative impact on the results. For this reason alone, most witches use a combination of types, such as imagined/oral, to negate this disadvantage.

Cord Magick

Among both solitary practitioners and covens, cord magick is one of the most widely practiced spells because it has so many uses. Basically, this spell is a physical means to store psychic energy that is going to be used over an extended period—hours, days, weeks—for a future result. For example, you're up for a raise, and your boss is making up his mind. You perform cord magick, then gradually release the energy of the spell until you get your raise. Not only is this a very easy spell, but it's also an extremely effective one. The basic pattern that this spell follows:

Start with a cord that's nine feet long and consecrated. The ideal color for the cord is red, which is associated with life, and it should be made of natural fibers, if at all possible. Also, always work within a Circle, and it's best to pay attention to the waxing/full and waning/new phases of the moon, if possible. Since psychic energy can be stored in the cord from one lunar cycle to the next, cord magick is an extremely popular and effective spell to carry over power gained from a particular lunar phase.

To begin, follow the basic steps for a spell. Start by determining the specific intent, then imagine the full process taking place. With a mental blueprint firmly set, begin building psychic power through dancing, singing, chanting, meditating, or by whatever means are most successful. Once a sufficient amount of energy is built up, take the cord, and tie a knot at one end. As the knot is tied, mentally direct the psychic energy into it, thereby storing the power in the knot.

Resume building power until a sufficient amount is once again built up. Tie another knot, this time at the opposite end of the cord. Again, resume building psychic energy, and tie another knot. As the last knot is being tied, all the remaining psychic energy should be directed into the cord. The storing phase is now complete and the power is in the cord waiting to be released at the appropriate time. As each knot is tied, recite these words:

> *I tie this knot to bind my power, that it may work at the appointed hour.*

The pattern for tying the knots is as follows:

Knot One – right end.

———————————————— 1

Knot Two – left end.

2 ———————————————— 1

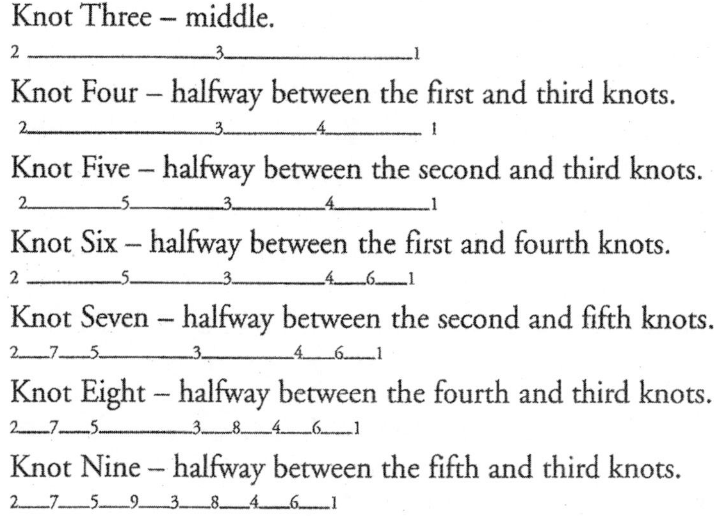

Knot Three – middle.

2 ________ 3 ________ 1

Knot Four – halfway between the first and third knots.

2 ________ 3 ____ 4 ____ 1

Knot Five – halfway between the second and third knots.

2 ____ 5 ____ 3 ____ 4 ____ 1

Knot Six – halfway between the first and fourth knots.

2 ____ 5 ____ 3 ____ 4 __ 6 __ 1

Knot Seven – halfway between the second and fifth knots.

2 __ 7 __ 5 ____ 3 ____ 4 __ 6 __ 1

Knot Eight – halfway between the fourth and third knots.

2 __ 7 __ 5 ____ 3 __ 8 __ 4 __ 6 __ 1

Knot Nine – halfway between the fifth and third knots.

2 __ 7 __ 5 __ 9 __ 3 __ 8 __ 4 __ 6 __ 1

Releasing the stored power is a simple matter, but the length of time that the spell is to encompass must first be determined. For example, if you were trying for that raise, and your boss said he'd make up his mind in a week, you'd release the power over the course of a week. If your spell was to protect a friend who was traveling, perhaps you'd release the energy hour by hour until the trip was completed. Once the time frame is determined, simply divide that time into ninths, one segment for each knot. Then, untie one knot during each of the nine time segments, and while untying the knot, imagine the spell being completed.

The thing to remember is that the first knot tied is the first knot untied. A very common mistake is to go in reverse order. Knot One was tied first, and it must be untied first for the spell to work properly. Also, there is no need to erect a Circle just to untie the knots. When the last knot is untied, all the stored psychic energy is released, and the spell is completed. As each knot is untied, recite the following:

I untie this knot at the appointed hour, and by this act, I release its power.

One final word of advice. Before untying each knot, concentrate on the intent of the spell. This act helps again to focus the released power at the objective. It's also okay to chant, sing, or meditate prior to untying the knot, thus building up a little added power. However, if the original work was done during a different lunar cycle, raising additional power may be counterproductive.

Candle Magick

Another widely practiced form of spell is candle magick. There are many, many uses for this type of spell, and these uses take several forms. As its name implies, candle magick revolves around a candle. In essence, the candle represents both the objective and the time frame in which the goal is to be accomplished. In order for this spell to be effective, the main thing needed is an understanding of the symbolism of colors. It's also useful to have a secondary understanding of astrological tables. Due to the difficulty of that subject, color knowledge will initially be sufficient. Below is a basic list of colors and the symbolism associated with each.

Color:	**Symbolism:**
Aqua	Prosperity
Black	Protection
Blue (light)	Tranquility, Healing
Blue (navy)	Empowerment
Blue (royal)	Justice
Brown	Neutrality, Repel Harm
Burgundy	Organization, Time Mastery
Gold	Persuasion, Dynamic Energy
Green (light)	Attract Nature Spirits
Green (dark)	Fertility, Fortune, Prosperity
Orange	Motivation, Inspiration
Pink	Affection, Love
Purple (light)	Attract Perfect Mate
Purple (dark)	Vision, Foresight
Red	Strength, Lust, Energy
Silver	Glamour, Beauty
White	Purity, Truth, Honesty
Yellow	Overcome Depression

To prepare for a candle spell, decide what the intended purpose is (i.e., specific intent), and select a candle with a color that matches this intent. For example, let's suppose the purpose was to find a perfect partner. A light purple candle would attract the perfect mate. If you wanted someone who was affectionate, you'd use a pink candle. For someone with a strong, lusty personality, you'd use a red candle.

You can also use two candles in order to incorporate several qualities, such as a red candle and a white candle for somebody who's strong, lusty, and honest. Nowadays, there are also two-tone candles on the market. These candles have the same properties as their single-color counterparts, but offer the convenience of using one candle to represent two qualities. When it comes to selecting a candle to represent yourself, simply use the color that best fits your personality.

In choosing colors, keep in mind that the color selection should be aimed at a "type" of person, or special characteristic, but never at a specific person. Once you've chosen a candle for yourself and your intended partner, you can also inscribe zodiac or male/female symbols on the candles to further narrow your vision.

Like all spells, candle magick takes place inside the Circle. Therefore, before beginning the spell, ready the Circle and proceed to a point where a spell will be appropriate. Don't just cast a Circle and then start the spell. At the appropriate time, start by thinking of the type of person desired. With this picture in mind, light the candle representing you. Face east and recite:

I light this candle to show my longing. As the flame burns, so do my desires.

Pick up the candle, and turn to the south, west, north, and finally back to the east. At each point, pause for a second or two, and think of the person. Replace the candle on the altar and light the candle(s) that symbolize your desired partner. Thinking of this person, recite the following:

I light this candle to bring my love to me. As it burns, so does my love.

Pick up the candle(s), and repeat the process of turning to the south, west, north, and east before placing them back on the altar next to the one representing you. When this is completed, face the altar, and recite:

As these candles burn slowly down, so does their magick draw my lover closer, and as the flames guide the way, so the hour of our meeting draws ever nearer, until the time that we both shall meet.

At this point you can allow the candles to burn completely down, or you can allow them to burn a little each day. However, if you decide to relight the candles daily, move them closer together every time they're lit. Also, take a minute to picture your intent before lighting them.

This is only one example of candle magick, and there are many, many more versions of candle spells. However, keep in mind that you can modify and develop a spell any way you like, so don't think that you have to follow any preset formula.

Crystal Love Spell

Of all the spells that witches use, love spells are among the most popular. Though cord magick, candle magick, and any number of other spells can be used to attract true love, the crystal love spell is often employed due to its simplicity. However, regardless of the ease with which it's performed, it's surprisingly effective, especially for beginners.

Before you can begin this spell, you'll first need to locate a suitable quartz crystal. These can be purchased, or if you like, you can try to find one on your own. Ideally, the color of the crystal should be clear, but there are alternatives to this. For instance, a man trying to attract a female lover might use a reddish- or rose-colored crystal, while a woman trying to attract a male lover should use a blue or aqua crystal.

Once you have your crystal, you'll also need a small bag to hold it safely or a piece of cloth large enough to securely wrap it in. The color of the bag/cloth should correspond to the personality of your intended lover. For example, red is for a vibrant lover, while white indicates a desire for a pure or honest person. Also, as was pointed out in candle magick, mixing characteristics is simply a matter of blending colors. Besides these two items, you'll also need a small bowl partially filled with water, a tablespoon of salt, and a small, white, cotton cloth.[6] Once all these items have been gathered, you're ready to begin.

As with all spells, you first have to cast a Circle and proceed to an appropriate point in the ceremony for the spell to commence. Start by placing the bowl of water on the altar pentacle and slowly mixing in the salt. After the salt is dissolved, place the crystal in the water and recite:

> *I cleanse and consecrate this crystal so I may use it to attract my lover to me.*

Pick up the crystal and dry it off with the cotton cloth. Hold the crystal in both hands and face east. Raise your hands to about shoulder high and recite:

> *O' Merciful Goddess, bless this crystal and charge it with the power to bring my lover to me. I ask for your blessings that my lover may come to me not only in my dreams, but as my true love.*

For a man, the first line will read: *O' Mighty God . . .* in place of *O' Merciful Goddess.* For someone else the wording changes to: *attract a lover for* (person's name). And the second verse should also be modified to include the person's name.

Next, turn to the south, west, north, and back to the east, repeating the verse at each cardinal point. Now face the altar again, place the crystal in the bag, or wrap it in the cloth, and tie the bag/cloth securely with a piece of colored ribbon or string. The spell is complete. If possible, keep the wrapped crystal with you until you've met that special lover, or instruct your friend to do so.

Protection Spells

Do you really need a protection spell? Well, consider these questions: Is anyone ever jealous of you? Does anyone ever just dislike your actions or the way you look? Does anyone ever misunderstand you? Odds are you answered "yes" to at least one of these questions, which means you just might need some protection.

Now, while we all know that some suffering is an inevitable fact of life, we don't have to resign ourselves to accepting all the trouble that comes our way as if it's our destiny. This is especially true when the harm is the result of a direct psychic attack caused by another person. In this type of situation, we are responsible for defending ourselves as long as we avoid causing harm to others in the process. To accomplish this task Wiccans use "active resistance," which is a method of neutralizing harmful acts or energy. While there are several methods commonly used to neutralize harmful intentions, the easiest ones are usually the most effective.

Binding Spell

A binding spell is a direct method of restraining someone from a harmful course of action. For example, you may want to "bind" a gossipmonger from spreading hateful false rumors. Or perhaps someone is planning a psychic assault, and you wish to stop it. In both cases, a binding spell is the perfect defense.

For your spell to be successful, you must always remember the main components of all spells—specific intent, imagination, direction of psychic power, and dispersal—and strictly adhere to these. Also, since all binding spells are defensive in nature, they can only be fully effective if you have a clear visualization of the person you want bound. For the novice, it's also very useful to write down your binding spell because this act will greatly aid in envisioning the spell's objective.

The procedure for conducting a binding spell is fairly simple and straightforward. First, you'll need paper, a pen or pencil, and two short pieces of string. Second, as with all spells, the binding spell must be worked inside the Circle after the Goddess and God have already been invoked. Third, take the piece of paper (or parchment), and write down exactly whom or what you want bound.

For example: You want your coworker, Joe, to stop making off-colored jokes about you every time he sees you. After you finish writing, read it aloud. When you finish reading what you've written, fold the paper into a small square. Now take the two pieces of string, and tie them around the paper so that the string covers all four sides. As you tie the string recite:

> *O' Merciful Goddess, O' Mighty God, I ask that* (person's name) *be bound from doing me any harm. With this act, I ask that the binding be done correctly, and that it shall be done for the good of all.*

The spell is now protecting you. However, when its task is finished, you must remember to disperse the spell and destroy the paper and string. Only then is the spell truly completed.

Bottle Spell

A bottle spell is another type of defensive spell that is seen throughout ancient folklore. Although similar in nature to a binding spell, the "Witch's Bottle" has as many protective uses as it has varying ingredients. However, rather than spend a lot of time on the many variations, the following is an extremely effective, yet simplified, version that employs items that are easily obtained.

To properly work this spell you'll need the following items:

- Small glass bottle or jar with a lid, such as an eight-ounce jelly jar
- One nail or screw; a small piece of white paper or parchment
- Pen with "black" ink
- Small amount of one or more of the following herbs: mistletoe, colicroot, bayberry leave, or bloodroot
- Personal article from the one to be protected; a strand of hair, nail clipping, or perspiration on a clean cotton swab
- White candle

As you already know, the spell must be worked inside the Circle after the God and Goddess have already been invoked. Begin by taking the piece of paper (or parchment) and writing:

> *I neutralize the power of anyone* (or insert specific name) *who would do me* (or name of person to be protected) *any harm.*

After you finish writing, read it aloud three times. When you finish reading, place the piece of paper, nail or screw, the herbs you've chosen to use, and the personal articles into the jar, and put on the cover. Hold the lit candle in your right hand and the jar in your left (vice versa if you're left handed). You're now going to seal the jar with wax. While turning the jar counterclockwise, slowly drip wax around the rim and recite:

> *O' Merciful Goddess, O' Mighty God, I ask that you neutralize the power of anyone who would do harm to* (person's name to be protected), *and I ask that this be done correctly, and that it shall be for the good of all.*

When the ritual is over (after you've banished your Circle), you must bury the bottle where it will not be disturbed. If it is intended to protect someone else, you must try to bury it in that person's yard or, barring that, secret it away in his or her basement, attic, or another spot where it will remain hidden. Remember, if the bottle is broken, opened, or the seal disturbed in any way, the power of the spell will be lost. Your spell is now working. As with any spell, once its intended task is finished, you must disperse the spell, destroy the paper and herbs, and cleanse the jar, lid, and nail/screw in running water. Only then is your spell permanently ended.

Protective Shield

A protective shield is simply another form of protective spell. It's a combination of an imagined and oral spell, with the main emphasis on envisionment. It is a basic, yet effective, defense against physical or psychic attack. In essence, it's like a protective cocoon wrapped around you.

Another interesting feature of this type of spell is that you can employ it to protect both inanimate objects as well as people. This means that you can protect yourself and your family, and also safeguard your house or car.

As with all spells, you must perform it while in a Circle, and it is best to be in a relaxed state before beginning. When you feel that you're ready, start by focusing your thoughts on your objective (i.e., creating an invisible force field of psychic energy that fully encapsulates the object or person). While maintaining your concentration, envision a clear, glowing bubble of energy growing stronger and stronger. Then, while imagining the shield building, face east, south, west, and north, and recite:

> *The energy of this shield protects me from all forces that come to do me harm. I ask the God and Goddess that this be done correctly and for the good of all.*

If this is intended to protect someone or something other than you, simply insert the appropriate name. The shield is now in place and will remain until it dissipates or is banished. However, in order to maintain its strength, it will have to be occasionally reinforced. Luckily, you don't need to cast a new Circle to recharge your shield. To reinforce your shield, choose a time that is quiet so you can be in a relaxed, meditative state without being disturbed. Imagine the glowing cocoon encircling the person or thing that you protected. Once you have a clear picture of this firmly locked in your mind, focus all of your energy towards reinforcing this protective sphere and recite:

> *I am protected by this shield in a good and correct way from all harm. Hateful energy and forces will have no power over me on any level.*

Naturally, the wording is changed if the shield is for someone or something, else. The spell is renewed. Keep in mind that you will eventually need to recast your shield, because like a battery, it can only be recharged so many times. However, before doing so, disperse any remnants of the old shield, and thank the Gods for all the protection. Once that's done, you may begin the process again.

At this point, you should have a good foundation about spells and what goes into proper spellcraft. Always remember the most important part of the Wiccan Rede: *An' it harm none, do what thou wilt*, and be mindful of the power of spells. If you follow these two simple guidelines, you're capable of anything.

SEASONAL RITES

Sabbats

In the Wiccan year, the eight holiest days are marked by the sabbats. These days signify changes in the seasons, the aspects of the lunar and solar cycles, the dominance or subservience of the God and Goddess, as well as a host of other ideas. And, although similar to esbats in some minor ways, they are in no way interchangeable.

In distinguishing sabbats from esbats, a few points to keep in mind are: (1) sabbats are all associated with a particular season; (2) sabbats are much more solemn occasions than monthly esbats;[1] (3) the structure of the sabbats is far more elaborate than that of an esbat; and (4) sabbats are "open" rituals, meaning that people beyond the confines of the specific coven may attend.

While this description may make it sound as if all sabbats are exactly alike, in reality, they're all very different from one another. Combined with these differences is the fact that each branch of Wicca has its own unique customs and traits. It's important to understand the separate views of each tradition in order to grasp the subtle differences in the way they worship.

Beyond the individualized beliefs of the denominations, each tradition has internal variations for such things as rituals, customs, and practices, which can be learned only through a step-by-step examination of each sabbat. But before any of this can happen, a basic understanding of sabbats is necessary.

DATES AND SYMBOLISM

The eight sabbats are divided into two categories: four Great Sabbats and four Lesser Sabbats. Like many other things in Wicca, the names of the sabbats often change from tradition to tradition. Depending on the denomination and its origins, a single sabbat may be known by two or three different names. However, even though the sabbats are referred to by different names, they're always observed at the same time of year.

The four Greater Sabbats are spread out over the four seasons as follows:[2]

- Candlemas, the first Greater Sabbat of the year, is celebrated on the eve of February 1, except in the Italian denominations, which designate it to February 2 due to a carryover effect from ancient Roman influences. Other names for this festival include: Imbolg, Imbolc, Lupercus, Oimelc, Candlelaria, the Great Spring Sabbat, the Feast of Lights, and the Feast of St. Brigid (or St. Brigid's Day). Symbolically, this sabbat marks the first stirrings of spring and returning life, as well as the beginning of the return of light.
- Beltane is celebrated on the eve of May 1 and is the second Greater Sabbat of the year. Other names for this festival include: Bealtaine, May Eve, May Day, Rudemas, Walpurgisnacht (Walpurgis Night), Tana's Day, and Celtic Summer. Symbolically, this sabbat announces the beginning of summer, the union of the Goddess and God, and the fertility of the land. According to the Celtic calendar, it's also the official end of winter.
- Lughnasadh is celebrated on the eve of August 1 and is the third Greater Sabbat of the year. Other names for this festival include: Lammas, Lughnasa, August Eve, Cornucopia, and First Harvest. Symbolically, this sabbat celebrates the first harvest (hence the name) and honors the Sun God, Lugh.
- Samhain is celebrated on the night of October 31 and is the fourth Greater Sabbat of the year although it's the first in the Wiccan calendar. Other names for this festival include: Halloween, Hallowe'en, Hallowmas, All Hallows Eve, Shadowfest, Celtic New Year, Third Harvest, and the Feast of Spirits (or the Dead). Symbolically, this sabbat signals the beginning of the Wiccan New Year, as well as the start of winter. It's a time for remembering and contacting the dead and for paying tribute to departed friends and relatives. Reincarnation and the death of the God are also themes associated with Samhain.

There are also the four Lesser Sabbats during each yearly cycle. These are broken down into two pairs, the Summer Solstice and the Winter Solstice, and the Spring Equinox and the Autumn Equinox. Aside from symbolism, and a few other factors, a major difference between the Greater Sabbats and Lesser Sabbats is that the exact dates for each of the Lesser Sabbats may vary from year to year by a few days. The disparity depends on the sun's entry into the zodiac sign associated with each festival. The four Lesser Sabbats, their zodiac signs, and their approximate dates are as follows:

- Spring Equinox, represented by the sign of Aries, is celebrated around March 21 and is the first Lesser Sabbat of the year. Other names for this festival include: Vernal Equinox, Ostara, Lady Day, Eostre's Day, and the Druidic festival of Alban Eilir.[3] Symbolically, this sabbat signifies the building power of the God and his renewed determination to mate. It's also a time of balance when the light overtakes the dark.
- Summer Solstice, normally referred to by the name Midsummer, is represented by the sign of Cancer and celebrated around June 22. It's the second Lesser Sabbat of the year. Other names for this festival include: Summer Sabbat, Litha, St. John's Day, and the Druidic festival of Alban Hefin.[4] Symbolically, this sabbat celebrates the sun at its pinnacle before entering the waning year, as well as a time of preparation for the harvest.
- Autumn Equinox, represented by the sign of Libra, is celebrated around September 21 and is the third Lesser Sabbat of the year. Other names for this festival include: Fall Equinox, Second Harvest, Mabon, Festival of Dionysus, and the Druidic festival of Alban Elfed. Symbolically, this sabbat represents the waning power and influence of the God, as well as the slowly declining cycle of life. It also signifies the dark overtaking the light, which is the opposite of the Spring Equinox cycle.
- Winter Solstice, normally referred to by the name Yule, is represented by the sign of Capricorn and celebrated around December 22. It's the fourth Lesser Sabbat of the standard calendar year, though it's the first in the Celtic calendar. Other names for this festival include: Yuletide, and the Druidic festival of Alban Arthan. Symbolically, this sabbat is recognized as the death and rebirth of the God, along with the return of the

sun and the waxing year.

PREPARATIONS

Although every denomination has its own way of celebrating the sabbats, a common practice among witches is to honor the God and Goddess by enacting renditions of ancient dramas. The death of the Holly King and his rebirth as the Oak King is one such example. In order to accomplish this in the most effective manner possible, various props are used. This method thereby incorporates a form of sympathetic magick. While many of the items (props) are self-explanatory, there are a few that should be explained.

Crowns

At different times during sabbat celebrations, most denominations make extensive use of various types of crowns—Oak Crown, Holly Crown, Crown of Lights, Crown of Flower, Sun Crown—in order to symbolize the God and Goddess in their different aspects. This is done for two reasons. First, using props makes it easier for everyone to identify the figures and follow along with the drama. This, in turn, focuses all the attention on the deity being portrayed, thereby enhancing the experience. Since the ritual is a way to connect to the Goddess and God, anything that helps accomplish this goal is useful. Second, the crowns operate along the lines of sympathetic magick. In a sense, the crowns transform the wearer into the deity being portrayed and thereby allow the deity to act through the wearer. Drawing Down the Moon and Drawing Down the Sun are ritual examples of this principle.

Decorating

Aside from the complexity of the actual ceremony, the most striking difference between a sabbat and an esbat is the amount of decorations used during the sabbats. This disparity is due to the importance of the seasonal motifs associated with the specific time of year in which each sabbat occurs, as well as the symbolism that certain items have during these times. To this end, some witches go to great lengths to incorporate seasonal facets into their rituals. This specialized preparation may include food, the altar, and Circle layouts, the color of the altar cloth, the color of candles, the types of decorations, or any number of concepts that help to enhance the symbolism of the ceremony.

Also, in regard to decorations and motifs, it's important to consider the meaning and symbolism of specific themes before passing judgment as to whether a particular item or practice is appropriate for a sabbat. For instance, twinkling Christmas lights are often used to decorate the ritual area during Yule. Since the theme of Yule is the rebirth of the God, the beginning of the waxing year, and the return of light, these items seem perfectly appropriate. They also simulate the twinkling stars. Conversely, a jack-o'-lantern would have no symbolic meaning and stick out like a sore thumb.

Cycles

An essential component of any sabbat is the status of the God and Goddess during the different cycles of the year. Although this might be a bit confusing at first, remember that the God reigns during the "dark" half (autumn/winter) of the year, while the Goddess is most active during the "light" half (spring/summer) of the year. But, this doesn't mean that the God or Goddess is completely gone during either half. Instead, the deity simply assumes his or her opposite characteristics.

For example, during the light half of the year, the God exhibits his feminine characteristics, just as during the dark portion, the Goddess exhibits her masculine characteristics. In order to put this belief into a more tangible perspective, Wiccans turn to the Wheel of the Year (Figure 26.1). The Wheel depicts the continuing cycle of life and death, and shows the transition from the light to the dark portions of the year. And, it's during these times that we see the masculine to feminine, feminine to masculine changes in the God and Goddess.[5] In short, witches use the Wheel of the Year not only to represent the continuous cycle of life, but

WHEEL OF THE YEAR *Fig. 26.1*

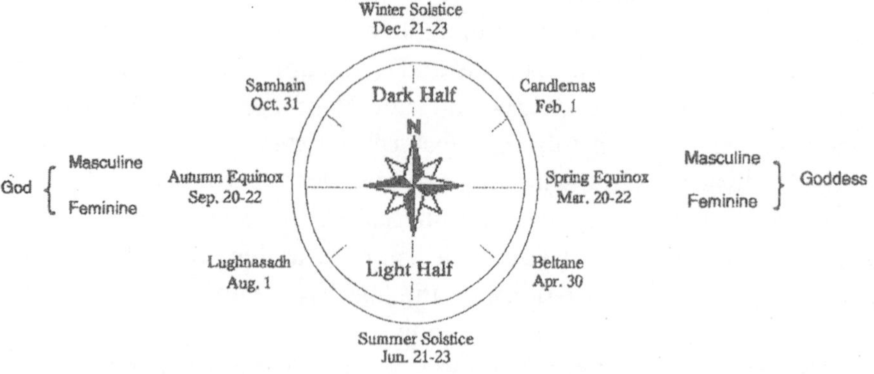

to remind them of the fact that their own duality is in direct correlation to that of the deities and the Universe.

Construction

All sabbats are basically divided into two halves: spiritual and social. In order to make this easy to understand, let's just say that the first half consists of the religious aspects (spiritual), while the second half consists of the festivities (social). Naturally, the religious half is the time where rituals are performed and tributes paid to the Old Gods. This encompasses everything from casting the Magick Circle through banishing it and includes various rites specific to the individual sabbat. Though not commonly practiced, this is also the portion that contains any workings that need to be done.[6]

The second half of the sabbat is for socializing. This portion contains a large feast in honor of the Goddess and God, plus music, singing, dancing, games, and anything else the participants feel like doing.[7] In other words, although this is still technically a part of the overall religious celebration, it's transformed into a party atmosphere.[8]

An interesting side note is that it's because of this festive atmosphere that ancient sabbats were thought to be orgies instead of religious events. This perception arose because most eyewitness accounts, from people who stumbled upon these hidden gatherings, portrayed the participants as hedonistic and sexually promiscuous. While this is a wholly inaccurate description, it's easily understood when considering it in the context of early Christians seeing naked (skyclad) witches dancing around a bonfire.

But, rest assured, a sabbat is not an orgy. Instead, it's a truly solemn occasion where witches come together to celebrate life and worship the God and Goddess, as well as a time to reconnect spiritually and give thanks.

Candlemas

Candlemas is one of the four Greater Sabbats celebrated by witches. Also known by the names Imbolg, Imbolc, Oimelc, Lupercus, the Feast of Lights, the Festival of the Goddess Brid, and Bridgid's Day, the festival itself is held on the eve of February 2 to celebrate the first awakening of spring. Like the other Greater Sabbats, Candlemas is a fire festival that stresses the earth beginning to rouse from its winter death, as well as the new light brightening the dark. It's a time of preparation for the earth to once again become fertile and a time of purifying and cleansing.

An interesting side note to this festival is that several Christian customs also fall right around this time of year. For instance, the blessing of candles in honor of St. Blaize and the blessing of throats of churchgoers against illness occur within days of Candlemas. Coincidentally, these acts introduce fire and purification into the Catholic rites. It's also from the Pagan belief in spring cleansing that the present-day habit of spring cleaning came about. In short, quite a few customs from the Candlemas Sabbat have been carried over and adapted into the practices of other religions.

Naturally, as with all things in witchcraft, there are different views on the exact historical origins of this sabbat. But regardless of how individual traditions now see the sabbat, the roots of Candlemas seem to indicate a common beginning as an early Pagan festival of spring that honored the Great Mother Goddess as she slowly turned the Wheel of the Year away from the harshness of winter. In addition to this overall view of the celebration, individual geographic locations each had their own beliefs, which coincided with the general theme.

For example, in Gaelic regions, the Goddess' hold on the local population was so strong that even the introduction of Christianity couldn't break the bond. Therefore, St. Brigid's Day became the first Catholic holy day that incorporated a strictly Pagan deity—the Goddess Brigid.

In Italy, where the major influences originally came from the Romans, the same rite became recognized as a time of personal renewal that signaled the primal awakening and a time that marked the first stirrings of the land as spring approached.[1] In keeping with this association, the Romans dedicated this sabbat to the Goddess of Love, though the month itself was devoted to Februus (God of the Dead).

Norse traditions used this day as a signal to begin preparing the fields for planting. After the sabbat, the Norse scattered ashes, magickal herbs, and salt across the fields to drive out the winter spirits and purify the land.

Despite the fact that this sabbat represents the first rays of light beginning to pierce the darkness of winter and an increased awareness in the coming spring, Candlemas got its name from the extensive use of candles during the festival. While it's considered a fire festival, in this instance, the emphasis is on the fire's light rather than its heat. The light is symbolic of the light of the moon instead of the sun's light. The basis behind this is that the moon is the symbol of the Goddess, and she is the symbol of fertility. For this reason, candles play an important role in bringing light into the ceremony. To enhance this effect, different candle customs are followed. Some denominations use a Candle Wheel (a table wreath with candles inserted into it) as a symbol of the Wheel of the Year, while others employ a Crown of Lights. In both cases, the inference is that of a full circle of light depicting the light of the full moon. This, in turn, represents the Goddess in her threefold aspect as Maiden, Mother, and Crone. It also represents the cycle of life, death, and rebirth.

Other Candlemas customs include preparing and setting out Brid's Bed (i.e., a grain dolly representing Brigid and a phallic wand representing the God). This practice is a form of sympathetic magick aimed at ensuring fertility of the land and a means for divining the prosperity of the crops. Many Celtic denominations also follow the custom of visiting magickal wishing wells at Candlemas to make a wish for the coming year. Likewise, many traditions make use of crossroads on Candlemas. Irish witches make a special point of going to the crossroads on Candlemas eve to bury adversity and negativity, while the Norse denominations go so far as to move their sabbat Circles to the center of crossroads.

SETUP

In order to properly perform this ritual, there is a fair amount of preparation that must be done prior to the actual ceremony. Since some of the setup work is time consuming, beginning a few days, or a week, in advance is advisable. For most people, the hardest part of the preparation will be designing and constructing a Crown of Lights. Although the crown is traditionally supposed to be made using candles (for the flame and light), there are many less dangerous ways to make one.

The customary method of making a Crown of Lights is, of course, to use candles. However, most witches who actually use candles have either purchased a crown that was specially made for this purpose, or they are exceptionally skilled and crafted one specifically suited to this task. The main thing to remember about using candles is the risk factor. Not only is there the hazard of hot wax dripping on the wearer's head, but the risk of exposed flames next to highly flammable hair must also be considered. This second reason alone is enough to make most witches shy away from candles. But, for those people who absolutely have to be traditional, the use of very small birthday-cake candles is probably the best bet because of their size.

It's also possible to construct a crown using small light bulbs, such as a short strand of battery-powered Christmas lights. This idea is less dangerous than candles and a preferable choice for many people, especially since the lights are inexpensive to buy, lightweight to wear, and easy to work with.

For those witches who are able to look past the apparatus and appreciate only the symbolism, modern technology has provided a safe and practical solution . . . glow sticks. Now, traditionalists may cringe at the thought of glow sticks, but the truth is that these items make a wonderful Crown of Lights. Glow sticks provide a perfectly safe source of light, are available in flexible ropelike strands, which can easily be molded into any shape, and thus make it fairly simple to construct a satisfactory crown in a minimal amount of time. And, since there is no heat given off by this substance, other material can be added to the crown without fear of fire. It can also be placed directly on the head.

Best of all, anyone can work with this material. So, before condemning this suggestion as nontraditional or unconventional, think about the intent behind using a crown, and keep in mind that it's nothing more than a symbolic tool. Since the light is the important feature to incorporate into the crown, why not use a source of light that is safe, lightweight, and easy to work with?

Along with the Crown of Lights, a flowered chaplet and a shawl are needed. These items are worn by the Mother (chaplet) and Crone (shawl). The chaplet can be a simple wreath of flowers and greenery attached to a pre-formed ring. Ribbon or other seasonal ornaments can also be added. The shawl may be an actual article of clothing or merely a large piece of cloth to drape over the wearer's shoulders.

Another item that's needed is a straw biddy. Although it's okay to buy one, this is easy to make and can be done in a relatively short time. Start with a bundle of wheat straw (any stiff, long-stemmed grass may technically be substituted) that is fourteen to eighteen inches long and three to four inches in diameter. This represents the body, head, and legs.

Tie a length of twine a few inches from the top, then wrap the twine around the bundle until it's within a few inches of the bottom. Tie it in place. Next, add a smaller crosspiece of the same substance to represent arms. Wrap and tie this crosspiece in the same manner, then tie it in place. Use a simple piece of cloth and cover the form, shaping the cloth into something that looks like a woman's dress. Clothes for a doll may also be used, or a doll-size dress may be made. (Figure 27.1.)

Along with the biddy, a phallic wand is needed.[2] This item may be as simple as a dowel or tree branch that is twelve to eighteen inches long, onto which a round or oval shaped object is fastened. A walnut, pine cone, or other similar article will suffice. (See Figure 27.1.) More elaborate or decorative additions may also be made, but a simple phallic wand will work just as well.

It's also traditional to have a bouquet of flowers and greenery on hand. If possible, select flowers that symbolize spring, such as tulips or daffodils. However, since flowers may have to be purchased from a florist, buy whatever type is available at a reasonable price.

Gardnerian

The following must be prepared before the ceremony begins. (1) The altar will need to be arranged, and it's also a good idea to have a small table set up beside it for extra items. (2) A broom should be placed next to the altar. (3) The bouquet of flowers is placed on the side table. (4) The cauldron, with a candle inside, is placed near the south cardinal point. (5) Several small evergreen branches are placed around the base of the cauldron. (6) Two unlit candles, in holders, along with the biddy and phallic wand, are placed on the table. (7) The crown, chaplet, and shawl are placed on the table. And, (8) a string of small Christmas lights is draped around the room to provide light.

BRID'S BED LAYOUT

Fig. 27.1

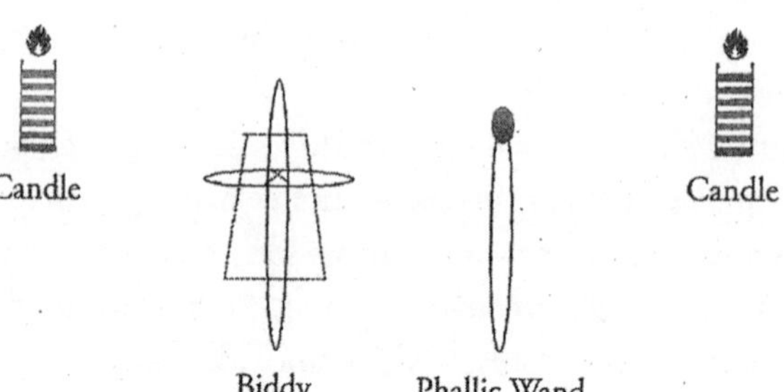

Biddy Construction

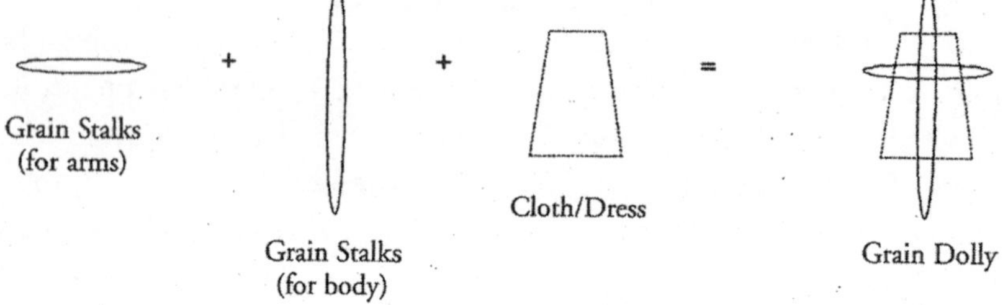

Phallic Wand Construction

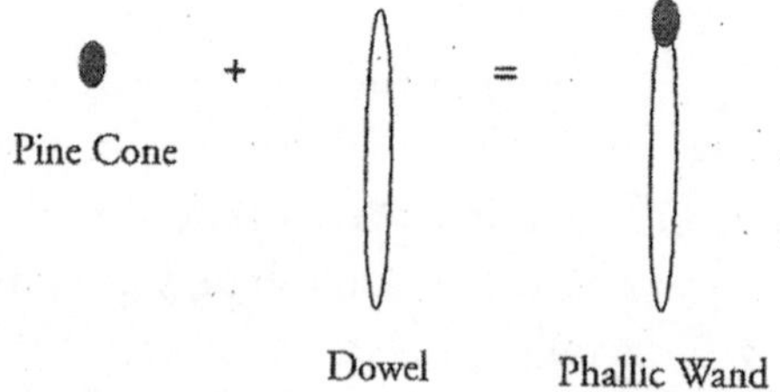

Finally, just before beginning the ceremony, lay out the biddy, phallic wand, and the two unlit candles in the arrangement known as Brid's Bed.[3] This is done by positioning the biddy and wand, side by side, on the floor in the center of the Circle, then placing one unlit candle on each side of the arrangement. The candles are lit later in the ceremony. Also, two female witches must be chosen to accompany the High Priestess. They wear the chaplet and shawl and represent the Maiden and Crone aspects of the Triple-Muse Goddess, while the High Priestess depicts the Mother aspect.[4]

The opening ritual used for Candlemas is shorter than usual. Begin by casting the Circle, then skip Drawing Down the Moon, the Charge, and the Great God Invocation; the Charge is recited later. At this point, the coven performs the Witches' Rune. Following the chant, the coven members arrange themselves facing the altar, around the edge of the Circle. Once everyone's ready, the High Priest stands with his back to the altar (facing the coven), and the High Priestess stands facing him. The pair should be close enough to touch each other. The High Priest kneels and proceeds to give the High Priestess the Fivefold Kiss. As soon as he's done, she'll reciprocate. However, slightly different wording is used for this version of the salute. The High Priest anoints both her feet and recites:

Blessed be thy feet, that have brought you down this holy path.

Anoint both knees, and recite:

Blessed be thy knees, that bend before this sacred altar.

The wording for a man and woman changes at this point. Anoint the womb (woman), and recite:

Blessed be thy womb, that is the birthplace of all life.

Anoint the groin (man), and recite:

Blessed be thy phallus, without which life would not be.

Anoint the breasts (woman), and recite:

Blessed be thy breasts, that sustain and nurture all life.

Anoint the chest (man), and recite:

Blessed be thy chest, forged in power and strength.

The wording from here on, is used for both men and women. Anoint the lips, and recite:

Blessed be thy lips, that speak the sacred names of Aradia and Cernunnos.

The High Priest assumes the Osiris Position while the High Priestess conducts the rite of Drawing Down the Sun. At the end of the rite, the High Priestess recites:

Blessed are you, O' Mighty God of Death and Resurrection, we call upon you to come to this Sacred Circle which has been cast in your honor. Fill our hearts and minds with your glory as you descend upon this Priest, your servant.

When she finishes speaking, the High Priest uses the wand to draw the Invoking Pentagram of Earth in the air above the High Priestess, then he says: *Blessed Be!* He then places the wand and scourge back on the altar while the three female witches (representing the forms of the Goddess) take up positions on three sides (east, west, south) of Brid's Bed. Once they're ready, the High Priest lights a taper from the altar candle, takes his place on the northern side of the setup, and lights the two candles beside the biddy and phallic wand.[5] He then recites:

We welcome Brid to this Sacred Circle. Welcome Brid! Welcome Brid!

At this point in the rite the Crown of Lights is lit. If candles are used, a taper lit off the altar candle (not the candles by Brid's Bed) is used to transfer flame to the crown.[6] Once the crown is lit, it's traditionally worn by the Maiden, though some covens prefer to have the Mother wear it. As long as the Maiden wears the crown, the Crone wears the shawl, and the Mother wears the chaplet of flowers. The High Priest now moves to the south, turns to face the three witches, and recites:[7]

Blessed are you, O' Merciful Goddess; Maiden, Mother, Crone. We call upon you to come to this Sacred Circle which we have cast.

A slightly altered version of the Charge is now recited, but it's done completely by the High Priest. Turning toward the coven, he recites:

Listen to the words of the Great Mother, she who of old was called among men, Artemis, Astarte, Dione, Melusine, Aphrodite, Cerridwen, Diana, Arianrhod, Isis, Bride, and by many other names. At her altars, the youths of Laceademon in Sparta made sacrifice.

Whenever ye have need of anything, once in the month and better it be when the moon is full, then shall ye assemble in some secret place and adore the spirit of she, who be Queen of all Witcheries. There shall ye assemble, ye who are feign to learn all sorceries who have not yet won her deepest secrets. To these will she teach that which is yet unknown. And ye shall be free from slavery, and as a sign that ye be really free, ye shall be naked in your rites; and ye shall dance, sing, feast, make music and love, all in her praise. For hers is the ecstasy of the spirit, and hers is also joy on earth. For her law is love unto all beings. Keep pure your highest ideals and strive ever towards them. Let none stop you or turn you aside. For hers is the secret door which opens upon the Land of Youth; hers is the Cup of the Wine of Life and the Cauldron of Cerridwen, which is the Holy Grail of Immortality. She is the Gracious Goddess who gives the gift of joy unto the heart of man. Upon earth she gives the knowledge of the spirit eternal, and beyond death she gives peace, and freedom, and reunion with those that have gone before. Nor does she demand sacrifice. For behold, she is the Mother of all things, and her love is poured out upon the earth.

Hear ye the words of the Star Goddess. She, in the dust of whose feet are the Hosts of Heaven, and whose body encircles the Universe. She, who is the beauty of the green earth, and the white Moon among the stars, and the mystery of the waters, and the desire of the heart of man, call unto thy soul. Arise and come unto her. For she is the soul of Nature, who gives life to the Universe. From her all things proceed, and unto her all things must return. Before her face, beloved of Gods and of men, let thine innermost divine self be enfolded in the rapture of the infinite. Let her worship be within the heart that rejoiceth. For behold, all acts of love and pleasure are her rituals. Thus, let there be beauty and strength, power and compassion, honor and humility, mirth and reverence within you. And thou who thinkest to seek for her, know thy seeking and yearning shall avail thee not unless thou knowest the mystery that if that which thou seekest thou findest not within thee, thou wilt never find it without thee. For behold, she has been with thee from the beginning, and she us that which is attained at the end of desire.

When the Charge is finished, the Maiden uses the besom to symbolically sweep the "old" from the Circle, making way for the "new" to take its place. She moves deosil around the inner perimeter, starting and ending at the northernmost point.[8] After the Circle is swept, the Maiden replaces the besom and joins the Mother and Crone at the altar. The High Priest retrieves the winter incense,[9] walks over to the cauldron, and kneels beside it. He then gently sprinkles incense on to the cauldron candle flame (to create smoke) and recites:

> *We bid farewell to dark of Winter, and welcome forth the light of Spring. Let this smoke carry away the time of death to make way for the coming of life, as that which is barren shall now be fertile.*

The High Priest blows out the cauldron candle, which is a signal for the three witches (Maiden, Mother, Crone) to remove the ritual costumes (crown, chaplet, shawl). These items are laid by the altar.[10] After removing the chaplet, the High Priestess stands at the altar, next to the High Priest, while the other two witches extinguish the Brid's Bed candles and place everything (candles, biddy, and wand) on the side table. The Great Rite is now enacted, and then the wine and cakes are shared. Following these two rites, the formalities of the ceremony are over. The feast may begin immediately. However, as with all the sabbats, most covens banish the Circle first to gain extra room for games, dancing, and general festivities.

Italian

This tradition celebrates the sun aspect of the God during this sabbat and places emphasis on him rather than on the Goddess. It views the earth as needing the sun's warmth to reawaken. Therefore, heat, as well as light, plays an important role in the symbolism of this rite. The Italian denominations also blend a great deal of the ancient Roman festival of Lupercalia into their ceremony. This festival celebrated the beginning of the mating season of wolves. The act of wolves mating was viewed as the union of the Wolf God and the Goddess.

In preparing for this sabbat, symbolism is extremely important. Traditionally, a cloak of wolf fur was worn by the High Priest in order to represent the Wolf God. But obtaining a real wolf pelt is likely well beyond the means of most covens. Therefore, any wolf-related fur can be used—fox, coyote. For people who are against the use of animal fur, a synthetic fake fur may be used. In addition, there needs to be a small candle for each coven member to hold and a large candle (or small torch) to represent the coming sun. Another Lupercalia adaptation is the custom of using the scourge for ritual flogging. In Roman times, this practice was believed to promote fertility in women and sexual desire in men.

Begin the ceremony by casting the Circle. Immediately after completing the casting, the High Priest lights the torch (candle) and proceeds around the inner perimeter of the Circle. This act symbolically spreads the light and warmth of the sun around the Circle. Once this pass is completed, he places the torch in the center of the Circle and returns to the altar. Turning to face the coven, the High Priest recites:

The Wheel of the Year turns, and the Lord of Light awakens from his long Winter sleep. With the coming of the Wolf God, the darkness shall once again be banished and the earth shall be renewed.

When the address is finished, the High Priestess approaches the altar and kneels before the High Priest. He assumes the God Position. She then recites an invocation to the Lord of Light:[11]

Behold the earth, which is in darkness and gloom! I will change the sister into the moon, and her brother into the sun. And so shall she ever escape him, yet will he ever catch her with his light, which shall fall on her from afar; for the rays of the sun are his hands, which reach forth with burning grasp, yet which are ever eluded.

The High Priestess stands and passes out a candle to each coven member. Once everyone has a candle, the High Priest walks to the center torch and lights his candle. He returns to the altar, and the High Priestess lights her candle from the torch. As soon as she returns to the altar, the coven members file by and light their candles. The High Priest proceeds to the east cardinal point where he leaves a small offering to the God. After the High Priest returns to the altar, the High Priestess leads the coven members in a procession to leave offerings of their own. During this, the High Priest recites:

Lord of Light, beneath the snows of winter, the Mother Earth awaits your life-giving warmth. It is through you that seeds of new life will become fertile within the womb of the earth. Shine down upon us, embrace us, and renew our strength. Know that our fires burn in your honor, that you may judge us worthy of your salvation.

As soon as the last offering has been made and everyone's returned to their positions, the High Priest dons the wolf pelt (or substitute) and retrieves the scourge. The coven, including the High Priestess, stand shoulder to shoulder in the center of the Circle while the High Priest dances around behind them. Their candles should all be held in front of their chests so the light fills the center of the Circle. While the High Priest's dancing, he uses the scourge to gently lash each member in ritual purification. During his dance, the coven chants:[12]

As the dawn was breaking the Wolf God belled
And a wolf stole back, and a wolf stole back
To carry the word to the waiting pack,
And we sought and we found and we bayed on his track
Once, twice and again!
As the dawn was breaking the Wolf-Pack yelled
Once, twice and again!
Feet in the jungle that leave no mark!
Eyes that can see in the dark—the dark!
Tongue—give tongue to it! Hark! Oh, hark!
Once, twice and again!

The scourging (and dancing) continues until every person has received several lashes.[13] The High Priest then signals an end to the chant—though he continues to dance around the coven a few more times—as he recites:

The strength of the Pack is the Wolf, and the strength of the Wolf is the Pack.

After the dance ends, the coven members return to their positions along the edge of the Circle. The wine and cakes are then consecrated by the High Priest and High Priestess and shared with the coven. This marks the end of the rite. One of two things can occur at this point. If there's enough space to hold the festivities without banishing the Circle, then this is the preferred choice. In this case, a doorway is opened to allow everyone to exit the Circle, then the feast, dancing, games, etc., begin.

When the party is over, everyone returns to the Circle and a final welcoming prayer is given to the Sun God. The Circle is then banished, and all the candles extinguished. On the other hand, if the area is too small to leave the Circle erected, simply ask everyone to say a silent welcoming prayer on their own at the conclusion of the festivities, banish the Circle, and move on to the party.

Saxon

In the Saxon tradition, Candlemas was originally called Imbolc and known as the Feast of Lights. As a fire festival celebrating the first stirrings of the earth, the cauldron (with a candle inside) is placed by the north quarter. A besom is kept near the altar for symbolically sweeping the "old" from the Circle, thus allowing the "new" life to begin. The Circle area and altar are decorated with flowers. Crocuses are favorites because they often appear through the snow. Though difficult to obtain, sheep's milk is customary since this is the time of year that ewes begin to lactate, thereby signaling the start of spring. Goat's milk, which is easier to get, may be substituted. Apple cider and honey are also traditional foods that should be added to the feast. The cauldron is ringed with evergreen boughs, and the altar cloth should be brown. Along with the altar candle, the rite requires that two additional white candles (with holders) must be set on the altar. Each member of the coven must also have a small white candle.

There are three more practices that are often incorporated into this ceremony, though they have all been borrowed from other denominations. The first is the use of a Crown of Lights. Adapted from Gardnerian practice (or perhaps Gardnerians adopted it from this tradition), the crown has the same symbolic value and is used in the same way.

The second practice is the ritual scourging of the coven to promote fertility. An obvious borrowing from the Roman Lupercalia, this act is often carried out in Saxon covens as a game during the festivities rather than as a part of the actual religious ceremony.

The third practice is known as the Procession of Torches. While there's a chance that this is original to the Saxon denomination, it's just as likely something that was borrowed from the Italian traditions.

The ceremony begins with the Circle being cast. A standard esbat rite is conducted up to consecrating the cakes and ale. If there's a full moon, the Full Moon Esbat is included. Following this, the Thegn uses a taper to transfer flame from the cauldron candle (which was lit prior to the ceremony) to the two additional candles on the altar.[14] The Priest and Priestess kiss, then the Priestess recites:

> *The Lord and Lady have been apart for too long. But the Lord's journey is nearing its end, and the Lady is on the horizon. From now*

until Beltane, the path is less dark. We welcome the Great God Woden as he casts aside the dark, and we give praise to the Goddess Frig as she renews the earth.

At the end of the address, the Priest and Priestess hold out their candles while the coven members step forward and light their candles. Female witches light their candles from the Priest's, while male witches go to the Priestess. When everyone's candle is lit, the Priest recites:

Now that the flames are lit, let the Procession of Torches begin.

With everyone lined up behind the Priest and Priestess, either in male/female pairs or singly, the procession winds (deosil) along the inner perimeter of the Circle. However, be advised that different covens follow different patterns. Some covens hold the candles in front of them at chest level using both hands. Other covens hold the candles in front of them at chest level using one hand, while holding their seaxes in the other. Still other covens hold the candles (or the candles/seaxes) above their heads. As they circle, the Priestess recites:

Woden to Frig; Dark to Light; Death to Life. As the cold of winter gives way to the warmth of spring, the flame lights our way to Beltane. And as we travel along the path, may our light renew the God and Goddess, that they may then renew our strength, love and life. So be it.

The procession continues for several passes, ending at the same (northern) starting point. It's customary to hold a chant and ring-dance at this time, though this can be excluded. With or without the chant, the coven members blow out their candles. The Priest and Priestess replace theirs (still lit) on the altar. The cakes and ale are then consecrated and shared with the coven. Following the cakes and ale rite, the besom is laid in the center of the Circle,[15] and the coven members jump over it to promote fertility. Once the last person has jumped the besom, the bell is rung three times to signal the end of the ceremony. The Circle is then banished.

Traditionally, even though the Circle is banished, the feast and games cannot begin until the Priestess recites a prayer to the God and Goddess, after which she serves each person a sip of ewe's milk. But since this is more of a cultural custom than a religious practice, it can be followed, modified, or set aside completely.

West Country

Even though this denomination has Celtic roots, the original practitioners did not celebrate the Candlemas Sabbat. In recent years, however, some West Country covens have begun holding an elaborate esbat (or a quasi-sabbat) at this time of year to mirror the celebrations of their Wiccan counterparts. Those that have adopted this custom have assumed much the same symbolism as seen in Gardnerianism and have even adopted some of the Gardnerian practices (e.g., Crown of Lights, Brid's Bed). In addition, because this sabbat is not original to the tradition, it's perfectly acceptable to include any rites into the formal ceremony.

While there is no set standard for the adopted ceremony, the basic West Country esbat rite is usually followed up to consecrating the wine and cakes. At this point, the acting coven leaders select a young woman to wear the crown, and two other female witches to set up Brid's Bed. The coven leaders then recite:

> *Welcome Brid! Come into our Circle, and into our lives. Welcome Brid!*

The crown is lit using the flame from the altar candle. Once illuminated, the wearer uses the altar flame to light the two candles by Brid's Bed. A three part ring-dance is then carried out by the coven. The sequence is: three deosil revolutions, three widdershins (counterclockwise) revolutions, and three more deosil revolutions. Symbolically, this sequence is meant to represent life, death, and rebirth.

Following the ring-dance, the coven assembles around the edge of the Circle, and the coven leaders return to the altar. A short prayer is recited to promote fertility and welcome the coming spring. The cakes and wine are consecrated and shared with the coven. After this, the Circle is banished to end the ceremony.

Spring Equinox

In a standard calendar year, the Spring Equinox is the first of the Lesser Sabbats, as opposed to the Celtic calendar where it's the second. Depending on the sun's entrance into the zodiac sign of Aries, it's held around March 21, and it's both a sun and solar festival. Since sun and solar generally mean the same thing, there's the tendency to automatically disregard the subtle differences between the two concepts. Yet, a disparity may be discerned between the terms.

At the Vernal Equinox, the two ideas exist both separately and in unison. The sun belief is represented by the young Sun God mating with the Virgin Goddess. This is symbolic of impregnating the land. Concurrently, the sabbat also celebrates a time of balance between light and dark, yet one where light is finally beginning to dominate the dark. As if this weren't enough, there's the additional symbolism of fire (a solar trait) that has been incorporated into the beliefs by way of bonfires. This complicates matters even more by drawing comparisons to the two Greater Sabbats (Candlemas and Beltane) that flank it.

Beyond the confusion created by the sun/solar/fire symbolism, there's also the theory that the Spring and Autumn Equinoxes are new additions to the contemporary Pagan religious calendar.[1] This theory holds that the current equinoxes were not originally recognized by early Celtic, Welsh, Saxon, English, or Italian witches and became part of the sabbats after their introduction by Norse invaders. But, while there may be some degree of truth to this speculation, there's also equal evidence to the contrary.

The ancient Greeks, Romans, and Egyptians all celebrated religious holy days during this time; and these civilizations were impacting the Celtic beliefs long before Norse invaders ever arrived. In either case, most modern-day witches make no historical distinction between sabbats, and all are widely accepted and celebrated.[2]

In its role as a solar festival, the Spring Equinox shares the fire and light themes with the Greater Sabbats. It also has other general themes in common with Candlemas and Beltane, because in one form or another, they're all basically associated with the renewal of life. However, because of its unique status and its much later introduction into the Wiccan religious scheme, the Vernal Equinox has taken on its own significance. On that note, it's worthwhile recognizing that the true symbol of the Spring Equinox is the Wheel of Fire, and it's partly from the symbolism of the fire-wheel that a portion of the ritual evolved. The reason that only a portion of the ritual developed from this symbolism is because the rite has a dual meaning, which owes a large part of its existence to the area where the rite is celebrated.

For example, in the colder regions, where agricultural endeavors are delayed by climate and animals mate later in the year with the arrival of warmer weather, the Spring Equinox represents a time of planting seeds and fertilizing the land—a time to sow the seeds of life. In short, it's symbolic of a time when the Mother Earth is impregnated.

However, in the areas where warmer temperatures prevail and a more temperate climate facilitates an earlier growing season, plants are already budding and sprouting at the time of the Spring Equinox. In these locations, the sabbat has evolved into a festival signifying rebirth and renewal of life rather than just a time of preparing to renew the seeds of life. And, by examining all the details associated with this ritual, it's easy to see how different factors contributed to the molding process that has produced the current version of the Spring Equinox, that's practiced today.

Along similar lines, there are several things that are common to this ritual that are also recognized by nonwitches. For example, virtually all Wiccan denominations incorporate brightly colored eggs into the Spring Equinox ceremony as symbols of new and/or eternal life. Nowadays, as a result of this Pagan practice being transformed into ordinary custom, just about everyone knows these eggs as Easter Eggs without ever realizing their origin.

Another custom adopted into modern culture through pure coincidence is that of the Easter Bunny. This belief began with the ancient witches of Europe, who honored the Goddess of Spring (often referred to by the name Eostre) by portraying her holding an egg in one hand while a rabbit sits at her feet. The way the story goes is that the rabbit wished to please the Goddess so he presented her with colored eggs. Upon seeing the beautiful eggs, the Goddess was so delighted that she commanded the rabbit to spread them around the world for mankind to enjoy—and two springtime legacies were born.

Folklore aside, the Spring Equinox illustrates the significance of all the sabbats regardless of how long each one has been formally incorporated into the religion. This can be seen in the fact that early people recognized the importance of each time of the year and made certain to pay tribute to the Goddess and God. Since it's apparent that all the seasons were celebrated in one form or another, it's likely that there were rituals for all the festivals and that some of the rites were simply lost over time. However, even if there weren't, the seasons were still appreciated. Therefore, simply because the Spring and Autumn Equinoxes were added to the sabbats later than the others does not make them any less important to Wiccan beliefs.

SETUP

To fully celebrate the symbolism and revelry of this rite, there's a fair amount of advance preparation required. However, most of this is fairly simple and can probably be accomplished within a very short period of time.

Regardless of denomination, the first item that needs to be built is a wheel symbol for the altar. This is placed in front of the figurines. There is no rule governing the complexity or composition of the piece, and the wheel may be nothing more than a plate or disc painted yellow or gold and decorated with flowers. The only requirement is that it stand upright. Therefore, using a heavy material, such as a ceramic plate, will necessitate buying or fashioning a display stand that can hold its weight. For this reason alone, a wheel made out of a lightweight wood, such as balsa or basswood, is recommended. There are several advantages to using one of these two types of wood. They are extremely light, very easy to work with, and yet durable enough to withstand being used over and over. As far as size is concerned, there is again no strict rule, and wheels range in size from about six to fourteen inches in diameter. However, simply making one that's proportional to the size of the altar is the best bet.

The second object that needs attention is the robe of the Priest.[3] Since this ritual is a sun festival associated with the God, the male coven leader's clothing is often modified to acclimate it to the symbolism of the season. This means that the Priest's robe should be bright yellow or gold so that he represents the Sun God. But, because purchasing a special garment is not cheap, less expensive ways to deal with this problem include wearing a long yellow scarf or even a yellow shawl.

In keeping with tradition, hard-boiled eggs should be colored and decorated just like regular Easter Eggs. However, since all the eggs should be eaten during the feast, only make as many as the coven can consume. There should be an extra egg to use as an offering to the Mother Earth.[4]

This sabbat, like the Winter Solstice, also features a wheel-dance. However, unlike at Yule, this version requires a separate strand of rope (cords may also be used) for each coven member. This means that there needs to be one, approximately five-foot length of rope for every two people. The ropes are tied together in the middle, and each person holds a single strand.[5] A man and woman should be at opposite ends of each rope.

At the beginning of the ceremony, the cauldron is placed in the center of the Circle. An unlit candle is placed inside it. But since the cauldron is going to be moved during the ritual, it's wise to make sure that the candle is secure. Flowers and greenery should decorate the outside of the cauldron to symbolize the renewed season. Like the candle, these need to be firmly secured.

The altar, Circle, and ritual area should be highly decorated with seasonal yellow flowers such as daffodils, but lilies or tulips will also work. A small bouquet of flowers and a Crown of Flowers for the Spring Queen are also needed. The Crown of Flowers may be a simple weave of flowers onto a wire or cardboard base, or it can be a more elaborate construction depending on your degree of talent.

Finally, the altar should be laid out in the basic pattern, except that the wheel disc should be added near the figurines. Some denominations like to follow a basic color scheme for each sabbat. This is mainly used for the altar cloth and candles. The most common color associations for the Lesser Sabbats are light green for the Spring Equinox, white for the Summer Solstice, red or burgundy for the Autumn Equinox, and purple or dark blue for the Winter Solstice.

Gardnerian

The ceremony begins with the Circle being cast and the remainder of a normal esbat rite being conducted. The Witches' Rune is sometimes omitted and used later. At the end of the esbat rite, the High Priest moves to the east side of the cauldron and the High Priestess to the west side.[6] The coven spreads out around the Circle. The High Priestess raises the wand, gestures toward the High Priest, lowers her arms, and walks (deosil) around the cauldron three times. She stops directly in front of the High Priest and hands him the wand, then proceeds to give him the silent Fivefold Kiss. At the conclusion of this blessing, the High Priest circles the cauldron three times and stops on the opposite side facing the High Priestess. The High Priestess now recites:[7]

We kindle this fire on this day, in the presence of the Mighty Ones, without malice, without jealousy, without envy, without fear of ought beneath the Sun, but the High Gods. Thee we invoke, O' Light of Fire, that which is Life. Be Thou a bright flame before us; Be Thou a guiding star above us; Be Thou a smooth path beneath us; And kindle Thou within our hearts, a flame of love for our neighbors, to our foes, to our friends, to our kindred all, and to all men on the broad earth. O' merciful Son of Cerridwen, from the lowest thing that liveth, to the name which is highest of all, Cernunnos.

The High Priestess takes the lit taper from the Maiden and lights the cauldron candle. As soon as the candle is lit, the coven members move forward, and each person picks up a rope end. The ropes are stretched taut to form the spokes of a wheel with the center knot positioned over the cauldron. (Figure 28.1.) Once everyone is ready, the High Priestess signals for the (deosil) wheel-dance to begin. If the Witches' Rune was omitted earlier in the ceremony, the wording may be used here. However, if it was already used, virtually any chant may be substituted. After reciting the chant a minimum of three times,[8] the High Priestess calls a halt to the dance, and the Maiden takes the ropes back to the altar.

WHEEL DANCE *Fig. 28.1*

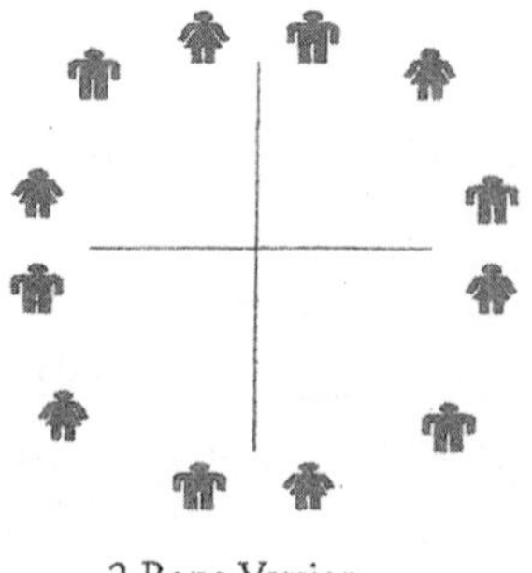

2 Rope Version

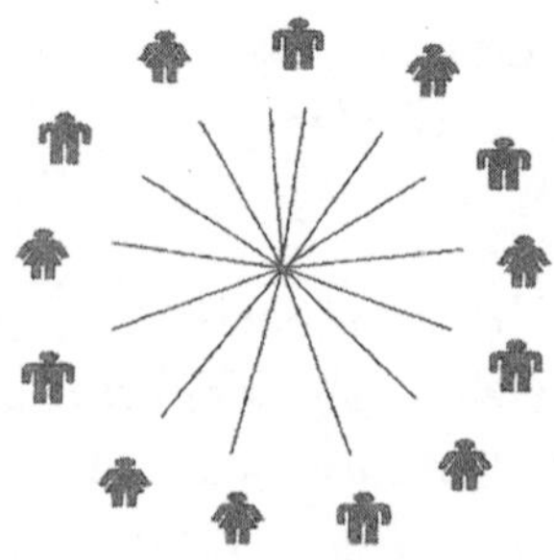

7 Rope Version

After the coven members return to the edge of the Circle, the Great Rite is performed. If the actual rite is going to be enacted, the cauldron is moved to the east quarter to clear the center of the Circle. If the symbolic version is conducted, the cauldron may remain where it is since the rite is carried out at the altar. Following the Great Rite, it's time to crown the Spring Queen. This honor is usually bestowed upon the youngest woman in the coven, though it may be given to anyone other than the High Priestess.

Crowning the Spring Queen begins with the Maiden leading the chosen woman to the altar. If the Maiden is to be crowned, the High Priest escorts her. The woman stands with her back to the altar, facing the cauldron, while the High Priestess recites:

On this holy night, we remember the Virgin Goddess in all her glory by appointing the Spring Queen. As the Maid of the Greenwood, she is honored this night by the Sun God. Behold the light that awakens the land from its long winter sleep. Come and feel the warmth of the flame, and know that life will again be born anew.

The High Priestess places the Crown of Flowers on the woman's head and embraces her with a kiss. After she steps away, the High Priest hands the Spring Queen the bouquet and embraces her with a kiss. She is then escorted to the center of the Circle by the High Priest and High Priestess, and she jumps over the cauldron. With the Spring Queen standing beside the cauldron, the coven members line up (singly or in pairs) behind the High Priestess and prepare to jump over it. However, before anyone jumps, the Spring Queen recites:

As you leap the sacred cauldron, make a wish for the coming year.

After everyone has jumped over the cauldron at least once, the High Priestess and High Priest return to the altar to consecrate the wine and cakes. As soon as these are shared with the coven, the ceremony is over. The Circle is banished, and the festivities begin.

Italian

Unlike the Gardnerian Spring Equinox Sabbat, which almost exclusively promotes the Virgin Goddess theme, this denomination's rite emphasizes the Sun God just as much as it stresses the young Goddess. In order to properly portray all the symbolism, the rite incorporates fire, earth, seeds, and the cauldron.[9]

To prepare for the ritual, the only extra items needed are a small bowl of earth,[10] a few seeds, and two candles (one red, one white). Beyond this, the Circle, altar, and cauldron are decorated with flowers and greenery. A single yellow flower should also be laid at the base of each Watchtower candle. Finally, the cauldron (with a lit candle inside) belongs in the center of the Circle.

Begin the ceremony by casting the Circle and conducting an entire esbat rite up to consecrating the wine and cakes. The High Priest picks up the unlit red candle, walks over to the cauldron, and lights the candle while reciting:

Let the flame of the Sun God glow brightly to light the world and warm the land. And let this flame guide our Lady as she returns from her long winter sleep.

The High Priestess picks up the white candle and joins the High Priest at the cauldron. She lights her candle from his and recites:

Mighty Sun God, your flame lights the path to rebirth. The young Maiden, the virginal Goddess, arises once more that new life may spring forth and be born. Welcome, Great Goddess of the Earth.

A male and female witch are summoned forward and given the candles. This pair remains at the cauldron holding the candles. The High Priest and High Priestess kiss, then return to the altar to retrieve the soil and seeds (Priestess holds the soil). Beginning at the east quarter, the pair presents the soil/seeds to the Watchtowers with a short blessing:

Lords of the Portal of the East (South, West, North) *bless these symbols of the fertility, that they may return the earth to its bounty.*

After visiting all four quarters, the pair returns to the cauldron. The High Priestess holds out the soil, and the High Priest plants some of the seeds. While this is taking place, the male and female witch raise the candles in salute. As he plants the seeds, the High Priest recites:

Blessed be the plow that tills the earth and sows the seeds of new life. Under the Moon and Sun, beneath the starry sky, all life springs forth from the Womb of the Great Goddess.

When the last seed is planted, the High Priestess lowers the dish of soil into the cauldron. Any remaining seeds are also placed inside. The High Priest and High Priestess take back the candles, and the man and woman rejoin the coven. At this point, the coven members are encouraged to come forward and place small offerings of flowers or seeds in the cauldron. Another custom is to write down a wish for the coming year on a small piece of paper, light the paper off the cauldron candle, and place it on top of the soil to burn.

Once the last person has come forward, the High Priest and High Priestess return to the altar and consecrate the wine and cakes. Although this is the end of the ceremony, the Circle is not banished yet. Instead, the pot of soil is removed from the cauldron, and the soil is watered to dissolve the ashes. This is done to ensure that the wishes are granted. After the pot is placed back inside the cauldron, the Circle is banished, and the ceremony is complete.

Saxon

The Saxon Spring Equinox ritual is very similar to the Italian rite, with both branches laying parental claim to the ceremony. But it doesn't matter whether the Saxon denomination borrowed from the Italian traditions or vice versa because the most important facet of the rite is its overall symbolism. As with the Italian rite, a significant portion of the symbolism revolves around the act of planting seeds in soil.

Preparation for the ceremony is easy. Again, a bowl of earth and a few seeds on a plate are needed, plus a phallic wand to be carried by the Priest. A very popular addition to this practice is to supply small flowerpots (filled with soil) for each coven member and enough seeds for everyone to receive a few. In place of the wand, the male coven members use their personal seaxes.

When the ceremony is over, the coven members keep the pots and watch the seeds grow as a reminder of the sabbat. The Circle area and altar are decorated with traditional flowers such as daffodils, crocuses, lilies, and tulips. Colored eggs are placed on the altar with a special green egg reserved as an offering to the earth. Small chaplets of flowers are usually worn by all the women in the coven.

The Circle is cast to begin the ceremony, and a normal esbat is performed up to the consecration of the cakes and ale. At the end of the esbat, the Priestess assumes the Goddess Position (facing the coven) while the Priest forms the Welcoming Gesture and recites:

Spring has arrived. Let us all rejoice and call to the Lady. Hear us, Great Goddess Frig, Mother of Life. We come together to celebrate the return of light and life.

The pair now reverses positions so that the Priestess is in the Welcoming Gesture while the Priest forms the God Position. She recites:

Spring has arrived. Let us all rejoice and call to the Lord. Hear us, Mighty Woden, Father of all. We come together to celebrate the time of fertility and rebirth.

Lowering his arms, the Priest retrieves the phallic wand from the altar and holds it in front of him (chest high). At the same time, the Priestess picks up the chalice and holds it in front of her. Following a signal from the Priestess, the Thegn or Scribe goes to the altar, picks up the bowl of soil and plate of seeds, and stands in front of the altar facing the coven. The Priestess recites:

As we welcome the Lord and Lady, we mark the line between the light and the dark. Thus, as the light of Spring begins its rule, we cast aside the darkness of Winter and look forward to the future. By wand and cup, seed and soil, shall the earth be reborn.

At the end of the address, the Priestess places the cup back on the altar while the Thegn/Scribe puts the bowl of soil and the plate of seeds on the ground in the center of the Circle. Still holding the phallic wand, the Priest leads a deosil ring-dance around the soil and seeds. Since the entire focus of the ring-dance is to charge the soil/seeds with energy—which is not a difficult task—it doesn't need to be too long. However, as this is a joyous time, the dance should be accompanied by a song, preferably with music, rather than just a chant.

As soon as the dance ends, the Priest, Priestess, and Thegn go to the center of the Circle where the Priestess picks up the bowl of soil and holds it in front of her facing the Priest. The Thegn picks up the plate of seeds and stands beside the Priest, but on the opposite side from the wand. If the wand is in the Priest's right hand, the Thegn stands on his left, or vice versa. During this, the coven members pair off and follow along with the Priest and Priestess.[11] Reaching out and placing the tip of the wand into the soil, the Priest recites:

As the wand is thrust into the soil, it symbolizes the union of the God and Goddess. And as the seed enters the furrow, we bear witness to the moment that the Lord impregnates the Mother Earth.

The Priest uses the wand to make one or two furrows in the soil. The men mimic this with their seaxes. With his other hand, he retrieves a few seeds and places them in the rows. Once the Priest takes seeds, the Thegn carries the plate to each pair. Together, the Priest and Priestess use their fingers to cover the seeds with soil. The coven follows along. The Priest continues the address:

And through this act of tilling and planting, we symbolize the rebirth of the Lord and Lady in their Springtime splendor. Blessed be.

The coven repeat: *Blessed be.*

All the flowerpots should now be placed on the ground around the edge of the Circle. The cakes and ale are consecrated and shared with the coven. However, rather than saving a joint offering to the earth, all coven members should take a few crumbs from their cake and plant them in their flowerpot.[12] This act symbolizes a general, and individualized, offering to the Gods. Following this, the ritual is finished, and the Circle should be banished. Before the festivities begin, everyone should eat one of the colored eggs, unless medical reasons prohibit eggs.

West Country

Because this denomination did not originally celebrate Candlemas, the Lady Day Sabbat (Spring Equinox) was the first holy day celebration after Yule. As such, it was viewed as a time of great joy because the Goddess awoke from her winter slumber. Along with the Goddess reawakening, there were other underlying reasons for the gaiety. For instance, knowing that the long winter was over and that they'd survived brought great relief to the people of the rural areas. Added to this was the fact that the sabbat marked the beginning of the growing season, which was one of the most important events of the year. The other truly significant event was the end of the harvest at Samhain. So it's easy to see why this festival was so prominent in the rural religious scheme.

The preparations for this sabbat begin well in advance of the actual day. To start with, the altar cloth and robes should be green or should include a green accessory, though the coven leaders often wear yellow (Priest) and white (Priestess). At least one hard-boiled egg per person, plus four additional eggs as symbolic offerings, must be colored. Chaplets must be made for each member of the coven; men wear greenwood chaplets while women wear chaplets of flowers.[13] If weather permits, the ceremony should be held outdoors so that a bonfire can be lit in the center of the Circle. Indoor rites require a cauldron, which should be decorated with greenery and flowers and have a large candle inside. The wand should be decorated with flowers and have a seed (acorns work best) attached to the end.[14] Some covens also keep a large bunch of long-stemmed flowers on hand to give out to the coven. Traditionally, yellow daffodils (sun) are used for the men and white lilies (moon) for the women. Finally, all the seeds that are to be planted during the entire season should be on hand to be blessed.

The ceremony begins with the coven leaders (Priest and Priestess) inside the Circle area. Coven members wait a few yards away. Prior to casting the Circle, the Priest and Priestess go to each quarter and bury one of the four eggs set aside as offerings.[15] Once that's done, the Circle is cast, and the Priest admits the coven through a doorway. He seals the gateway and returns to the altar. After positioning themselves around the perimeter of the Circle, the coven members take out their athames and hold them up in salute. At the altar, the Priestess holds up the coven athame, and the Priest holds up the wand. The Priestess recites:

> *As the Goddess returns from her long winter sleep, she brings back the fires of life that reside in all things. The Spring has come, let us all rejoice.*

Everyone now puts away their athames (the Priest places the wand on the altar), and a normal esbat rite is performed up to the point where the wine and cakes would be consecrated. The coven now conducts a ring-dance. There are several variations concerning the central figure of the dance. Naturally, the bonfire or cauldron may be used. The Priestess or Priest—she holding the flowers and he holding the phallic wand—is also an excellent choice. But the most traditional object has been the seeds for the coming year. Not only is this a way to symbolize the seasonal aspect of the rite, it charged the actual seeds with energy and blessed them. Of the numerous chants, the following verse is one of the most widely used on Lady Day:

> *Round and round the Circle,*
> *Round and round we go,*

Round and round the Circle,
Our seeds we soon shall sow.
On top of the blessed hilltops,
Our fires burn fast and bright,
They drive away the darkness,
To welcome back the light.
And as the sun shines on the land,
And warms the barren earth,
We'll use our plows to till the soil,
In this time of great rebirth.
Round and round the Circle,
Round and round we go,
Round and round the Circle,
Our seeds we soon shall sow.

When the dance ends, the Priestess retrieves the flowers and hands them out to the coven. This can also be done before or during the dance. Following this, the Priest and Priestess meet in the center of the Circle. He must have the wand with him. As they face each other, the Priest taps the Priestess three times with the wand (right breast, womb, left breast), then the two embrace and kiss. The Great Rite is now enacted. Although original custom dictates that this be an actual rite, modern practice permits otherwise. If a symbolic rite is performed, the coven may remain. However, for the actual version, the coven leaves the Circle area until summoned back.[16]

After the Great Rite, the wine and cakes rite takes place. The colored eggs are consecrated at the same time, and then everything is shared with the coven. Once this is done, the Circle is banished, and the ceremony is over.

Beltane

Beltane is the third overall sabbat in the standard Christian calendar year and the second Greater Sabbat. Celebrated on the eve of April 30 or May 1, it is often called the May Eve Great Sabbat or May Day. In Germany, May Eve is known by the name Walpurgisnacht, which is derived from the Christianized name for the old Teutonic Earth Mother. Other names include Rudemas, Bealtaine, and Bhealltainn.

In early Celtic custom, Beltane and Samhain were thought to be the two most important sabbats of the year, as they were viewed as the festivals that marked the beginnings of summer and of winter. It was at the Beltane Sabbat that the "Bel" fires were lit in honor of the male deity. In agricultural areas, these Bel-Fires, which were nothing more than bonfires that were built on the top of a hill, were lit to purify the land to ensure a good harvest. There was also a custom of lighting two bonfires and driving cattle between them to purify the herd of winter spirits and insure good milk production. Today, since most witches don't have livestock to protect, this custom has been modified into one where witches themselves walk between the twin bonfires to assure their own good health.

Due to the connection with fire, it's only natural that this sabbat, like all of the Greater Sabbats, is a fire festival. However, Beltane is also associated with the sun, which makes it a sun and fire festival. This duality comes from the Celtic tradition, which held Bel as the God of Light and the God of Fire. While it gave Bel all the attributes of the sun, it never considered him to be a true Sun God. The Celts weren't alone in this belief. For instance, the Norse lit Balder Fires in honor of their own Sun God, thus combining the fire/sun aspects. The Norse, however, had a more true Sun God than the Celts.

In Druidic (and Celtic) belief, this sabbat also marked the beginning of fertility of the land, which in turn marked the end of the Pookas' reign over the fields. After Samhain, the Pookas had claimed the fields as their own, destroying all crops that had been left unharvested. At May Eve, however, the Pookas relinquish the fields for another growing season. In other words, Beltane signaled the start of spring planting, with all eyes turned toward ensuring a successful harvest during the coming season. Part of this effort consisted of taking the ashes from the Bel-Fires and scattering them over the fields to bless and purify the land. But this process only worked when a proper ceremony was held. Therefore, the Beltane celebration was an important transition point between winter and summer.

Beyond the fire/sun symbolism, there are other historical interpretations of Beltane that are very interesting. Beyond the fact that this sabbat is a fire festival that's connected to the sun, the principal traits most often associated with May Eve are sex, birth, and new life. It's also worth noting that this is the time when the king and queen of the magic woodlands come together and unite, thereby making Beltane a "lusty" time of sexual union.

Naturally, with all this going on, there is a great deal of symbolism that accompanies this multifaceted sabbat. For instance, the Maypole is a phallic symbol, and dancing around the Maypole was at one time considered to be such lewd behavior that it was publicly outlawed. There are several other similarly symbolic activities associated with May Eve that focus on the sexual aspect of the sabbat. Back-to-back dancing, jumping over the cauldron, and the love-chase game are but a few examples.

Nowadays, however, regardless of any symbolism or past intentions, the main thrust of the Beltane Sabbat is the fun and festive atmosphere linked to the rites. This is clearly a ritual of celebration and a time to have fun. Furthermore, while all the sabbats are enjoyable and fun, since they all have dancing, singing and games, Beltane is even more festive than the rest. This stems from the sexuality and gaiety of the occasion interwoven throughout the ritual, thereby enhancing its overall celebratory atmosphere.

SETUP

The preparation will depend on the tradition, and some require more than others. There is not as much work required to prepare for this sabbat as was needed for the preceding two, but there's still enough to warrant some advance preparation. Bear in mind that the items used will vary from denomination to denomination, so the following descriptions will be generalized.

Although the symbolic use of a crown is not universal, it's, nevertheless, a very popular custom among many denominations. Depending on the tradition, there are two types of crowns used during this sabbat; the

Oak Crown or the Crown of Flowers. The difference between the two crowns results from the views of the different denominations toward the symbolic aspects of the season. For instance, Gardnerian and Alexandrian covens revere the God and Goddess, while the Italian denominations honor only the Goddess. Therefore, the individual denomination will determine the crowns to use.

Because it may be the most difficult to fashion, the first thing to work on is an Oak Crown, which will be used to represent the Oak (or May) King. This item can be very simple in design and can be made either by interweaving oak branches into a circular crown or by attaching oak twigs to a pre-formed crown made from any material (leather, wire, etc.) that is easy to work with.

Something to keep in mind is that this Oak Crown will also be used during the Yule Sabbat, so any time spent constructing it won't be wasted. For this reason, it's a good idea to make one that is durable enough to last, another one won't have to be made for Yule. If at all possible, oak leaves should be added to the crown. Only use new, green leaves, as this is a sign of new life, and omit them altogether if you can't find green leaves. If green oak leaves are available, it's also advisable to collect a few small branches with leaves attached, and use them to decorate the altar area. In constructing the Crown of Flowers, a simple chaplet can be made by weaving flowers around a leather or wire base. Silk or plastic flowers may also be used.

This next suggestion is going to be difficult for most people, and it's understandable if it can't be followed. However, if at all possible, it's customary to collect a few small branches from a hawthorn tree to decorate the altar. On the off chance that you're lucky enough to find hawthorn, try to get a tree that's blossoming. Use the blossoms to decorate the altar and some for the crown. Special chaplets are also made for the women using the hawthorn flowers, but related species, such as blackthorn, work just as well. Although they do not have the exact same symbolic value, these substitutes will suffice. It's also worth noting that, according to custom, the hawthorn should not be gathered until May Eve, but this can be overlooked for reasons such as a busy schedule or difficulty accessing the hawthorn.

Nuts should be used in the cakes for this ceremony.[1] Walnuts, pecans, or hazelnuts are all traditional nuts for this festival and excellent choices for use in the cakes. It's also customary to have a bowl of nuts on hand for this rite. These can even be substituted for the cakes.

Besides nuts and cakes, there are other foods linked by custom to this feast. For example, honey is a traditional food that was served, and many times a honey mead or beer was prepared specifically for the Beltane Sabbat. Goat's milk or cheese was also usually served because of the goat's association with the God, while rabbit (associated with the Goddess, as well as prolific breeding) was the main meat served.

For those witches who cannot bring themselves to use goat's milk, pitchers of cow's milk also embody the new season, while a green salad represents the land coming into bloom. In northern areas, maple syrup became a favorite of many witches. It also symbolizes the Earth's juices (sap) rising to renew life. The point is that there are many foods to choose from, both traditional and nontraditional, and the goal is simply to pick things that correctly symbolize the season.

You will need to place the cauldron in the center of the Circle, and a candle (in a candleholder) should be placed inside the cauldron. When lit, this flame will represent the Bel-Fire. Obviously, if the ritual is going to be conducted outdoors and a bonfire is going to be lit, the cauldron with the candle isn't necessary. Keeping a fire extinguisher on hand is highly recommended whenever a bonfire is used. Also, even with a bonfire, a single candle (preferably in a glass lamp to shield it from any wind) to represent the Bel-Fire is still needed. This is because there's a point in the ceremony where the Bel-Fire will be extinguished for a short time, and this is much easier to do with a candle than with a bonfire.

Finally, set up the altar as usual. Decorations may also be added, such as wrapping yellow and white cloth (representing the colors of the sun and moon) around the handles of the tools. Omit the censer for fire-safety reasons. Small swatches of these fabrics may also be placed under the pentacle, the altar candles, the figurines, and any other altar item. Some covens even go so far as to have altar cloths that are specialized for each sabbat. Beltane colors would include yellow, white, red, and green.

Gardnerian

Both an Oak Crown and Crown of Flowers will be used for the rite. Hawthorn, blackthorn, or oak branches, with buds or new greenery, are used to decorate inside the Circle. The altar is set in the north, and the cauldron is set in the center of the Circle. Flowers decorate the altar, Circle, and cauldron. A Maypole may be set up inside or outside the Circle. Depending on the number of people attending the sabbat, the Circle may be enlarged to eighteen feet, instead of the usual nine feet, to make added space for extra participants.

Begin by consecrating the water and salt, then casting the Circle. Slightly different wording is used to invoke the Watchtowers. After completing the four passes around the Circle (athame, water, incense, candle) return to the eastern cardinal point. Face east and recite:

Lords of the Watchtowers of the East, Lords of the Air, I summon you to bear witness to these rites, that your winds may blow gently across the Earth as the Goddess comes to renew the land.

Take the athame, and draw the Invoking Pentagram of Earth. Kiss the tip, and press it to your heart. Close your eyes for a moment, and visualize the pentagram. Walk over to the south, and recite:

Lords of the Watchtowers of the South, Lords of Fire, I summon you to bear witness to these rites, that you may bring forth warmth across the Earth as the Goddess comes to renew the land.

Walk over to the west, and recite:

Lords of the Watchtowers of the West, Lords of Water, I summon you to bear witness to these rites, that you may send your glistening waters to flow forth across the Earth as the Goddess comes to renew the land.

Finally, walk over to the north, and recite:

Lords of the Watchtowers of the North, Lords of the Earth, O' Merciful Goddess Aradia, O' Mighty God Cernunnos, I summon you to bear witness to these rites, and watch over this sacred Circle.

With the Circle cast, conduct Drawing Down the Moon and/or Sun, recite the Charge in its entirety, and then perform the Witches' Rune.[2] Once the chant ends, the coven spread out around the Circle. The High Priest dons the Oak Crown and stands next to the cauldron facing east. He recites:

O' Glorious Goddess of the Moon, look down upon the woods and meadows and see the land begin to bloom. As did our ancestors before us, we cast forth our words of praise.

A love-chase sequence is now enacted by the High Priest and High Priestess.[3] The High Priest picks up the scarf and holding it between both hands, chases the High Priestess around the Circle. They are walking at a deliberate, but controlled, pace. When he catches her, he wraps the scarf around her, pulls her to him, and kisses her.

Immediately after the kiss, the High Priest lays (or kneels in a crouched position) on the ground between the cauldron and the altar. The High Priestess covers him with the scarf. Sometimes one or two female witches cover him while the High Priestess looks on. The Maiden blows out the altar candle[4] while the High Priestess kneels facing the cauldron. The coven members follow her lead and kneel facing the cauldron, too. After a moment of silence, the High Priestess blows out the Bel-Fire candle and recites:

As the flame of the Bel-Fire has been extinguished, so the Oak King is dead. He who was once the consort of the Great Mother is no more; He who was the God of the Waning Year is dead.

Pause here for a few seconds.

But if the Oak King is dead, all is dead. The Earth cannot bear fruit, the animals cannot bear young, and the Great Goddess has no mate. All is lost without the Oak King. What shall we do?

The coven responds: *Rekindle the Bel-Fire that the Oak King may be awakened.*

The High Priestess answers: *Rekindle the Bel-Fire. So mote it be.* She lights a taper off the north Watchtower candle and returns to the cauldron where she relights the Bel-Fire candle.[5] She hands the taper to the Maiden, who goes to the altar and relights the altar candle. The High Priestess removes the shroud (scarf) from the High Priest and recites:

O' Mighty Oak King. The Bel-Fire has been rekindled. Come back to us that the Earth may once again be fertile. (Alternate verse: *O' Mighty Oak King, with this flame of the Earth, the Bel-Fire is rekindled that you may once again awaken into life, and that the land may again be fruitful and alive.*)

The High Priest stands, and the High Priestess embraces him. The pair now leads a ring-dance around the cauldron (Bel-Fire). While they dance, everyone sings:

O' do not tell the Priest of our Arts,
Or he would call it a sin;

But we will be out in the woods all night,
A-conjuring Summer in.
And bring you news by word of mouth,
For women, cattle and corn;
For the Sun is coming up from the south,
With oak, and ash, and thorn.[6]

At this point, different covens follow different paths. Some covens keep singing this verse while pairs of witches break away from the ring-dance and jump over the cauldron. Once everyone else has jumped the cauldron, the High Priestess and High Priest jump over, then the entire coven sit around the Bel-Fire. Other covens move on to the "Bagahi laca bachahé" chant (normally conducted during the esbat), and the ring-dance is prolonged throughout the verse. Jumping over the cauldron may follow this chant or be done during it. The following two chants are sometimes used in place of the "Bagahi laca bachahé" chant:

Oak King Chant
I am the Mighty Oak King, the God of the Waxing Year;
I am the lover of Mother Earth, the Goddess you hold so dear;
I am the Sun that shines in the sky, the light of each passing day;
I am the flame of the fire, that lives to keep death away.

May Eve Chant
In woods and meadows, by sacred rite,
We dance and sing, on this magickal night;
For as winter departs, and summer arrives,
Good fortune abounds, and revelry thrives;
With joyous praise to the moon and sun,
We sing this song, that our will be done.

The Great Rite is now performed. When this is completed, the feast is enjoyed. If more than one coven is present, the Circle may be opened, but not banished, to create adequate room. Try to remember that this is a festive night, and you might want to liven things up from the normal sabbat festivities. Including a Maypole, both for symbolic and festive purposes, is a good way to accomplish this. While some witches go to the expense of having an elaborate Maypole specially made out of oak with silk ribbons, a long wooden dowel, or broom handle, with a base, onto which colored ribbons are attached at the top, is more than sufficient.

The basic game involves nothing more than having everyone take hold of a ribbon and dance around the Maypole until the ribbons are wrapped tightly, at which point the participants kiss. The ribbons are unwound, and the dance starts over. Normally, a song or chant is sung by the dancers during the dance. The Oak King Chant and May Eve Chant are both used. While this may seem a little silly or childish, it's a fun way to add symbolism and sexuality to the rite. When the festivities end, the High Priest and High Priestess return to the Circle and facing the altar, kneel before the cauldron. The others need not reenter the Circle, though they should all face the cauldron. The High Priestess recites:

I end this rite and disperse the Bel-Fire, that it may fill the land with its warmth and its light. Blessed Be!

All respond: *Blessed Be!*

The High Priestess leans forward and blows out the Bel-Fire candle. The ritual is complete once the Circle is banished. If the ceremony was held outdoors and a bonfire was lit, make absolutely certain that it's fully extinguished before leaving. Also, if the sabbat was not held on your land, make sure to clean the area thoroughly.

Italian

The Italian traditions refer to this sabbat as Tana's Day. As such, exclusive emphasis is placed on the Goddess, with little or no recognition given to the Stag God.[7] Much of this is due to the outlook on the fertility of the fields being the domain of the Goddess.

Prior to the ceremony, the ritual area should be heavily decorated with flowers, and a bowl of grapes should be placed on the altar. If possible, grapevines should be added to the decorations. A plain white candle should be on hand for each coven member and guest in attendance. Traditional colors are red (fire), yellow (sun), white (moon), and green (renewed life). No crowns are used, but the women may wear floral chaplets. And although a Maypole is often added as a festival game, it's not as prominent as in other denominations.

The ceremony begins with the Circle being cast following the usual steps. After the Watchtowers have been set, the High Priestess holds a white candle, which will later be lit from the altar candle. The High Priest leads her to the south cardinal point and performs the rite of Drawing

Down the Moon. Once finished, he uses a taper to transfer the altar flame to the candle that the High Priestess is holding. He blows out the taper and addresses the coven:

In the presence of the Goddess, we gather to welcome forth the new cycle of life. The long winter has passed, and the time of rebirth is upon us. Let us show tribute to Tana, that she may bless us with her bounty in the coming year.

One by one, the coven members (who are all holding unlit candles)[8] approach the High Priestess, light their candles, and recite:

Blessed be, O' Great Tana, Queen of Heaven. Welcome.

As soon as everyone's candle is lit, and the coven members have returned to their places, the High Priestess lifts the sword and recites the Charge of Aradia in its entirety. When she finishes, she lays down the sword, and the High Priest places the Crown of Flowers on her head. At this point, there are two distinctly different versions. The first involves the coven moving to the east quarter while the High Priest and High Priestess share the wine with them. In the second version, the High Priestess recites the wine invocation to the Goddess[9] as a blessing to seek fertility (of the vine). Assuming the Goddess Position, she recites:

I drink, and yet it is not wine I drink,
I drink the blood of Diana,
Since from wine it has changed into her blood,
And spread itself through all my growing vines,
Whence it will give me good return in wines,
Though even if good vintage should be mine,
I'll not be free from care, for should it chance
That the grape ripens in the waning moon,
Then all the wine would come to sorrow, but
If drinking from this horn I drink the blood
The blood of Great Diana, by her aid,
If I do kiss my hand to the new moon,
Praying the Queen that she will guard my grapes,
Even from the instant when the bud is born
Until it is a ripe and perfect grape,
And onward to the vintage, and to the last

Until the wine is made, may it be good.
And may it so succeed that I from it
May draw good profit when at last 'tis sold,
So may good fortune come unto my vines,
And into all my land where'er it be.
But should my vines seem in an evil way,
I'll take my horn, and bravely will I blow
In the vinevault at midnight, and I'll make
Such a tremendous and a terrible sound
That thou, Diana fair, however far
Away thou may'st be, still shall hear the call,
And casting open door or window wide,
Shalt headlong come upon the rushing wind,
And find and save me, that is, save my vines,
Which will be saving me from dire distress;
For should I lose them I'd be lost myself,
But with thy aid, Diana, I'll be saved.

In this second instance, the wine is shared after the invocation. Following either version, the High Priestess (as the Goddess) blesses each coven member with an embrace and kiss, beginning with the High Priest. Each person retrieves his or her candle and stands facing the center of the Circle. The High Priestess recites:

Blessed be the Goddess, she who brings fertility and life back to the land. Hail, O' Goddess of the Earth.

The ceremony is concluded with the wine and cakes being shared, then the Circle is banished. The Circle may also be banished before the wine and cakes are shared. Following the Circle being banished, the celebration begins. Dancing should be very sexually suggestive, as should any games, and kissing and embracing should be a prominent part of both.

Saxon

This denomination, like Gardnerian Wicca, leans heavily on symbolism. Crowns are used for both the God and Goddess. While the God's crown is oak, the Goddess' crown may be either flowers or a plain metal circlet with a silver crescent moon. Flowers ring the Circle and decorate the altar. The cauldron (if used) is placed at the north quarter and holds a candle.[10] A Maypole is placed along the east quarter.[11] The altar cloth is green.

Although not mandatory, if at all possible, the Priest should wear a red or yellow robe, the Priestess a white or silver robe, and the coven members wear green robes. To the Saxon denominations, food is an important part of Beltane. Honey mead, apple beer, and sweet ale are staples, as are milk and cheese, acorn bread, eggs, and domestic fowl.

The ceremony begins with the Circle being cast and the coven members taking their places facing the altar. The Priest and Priestess are at the altar. A normal esbat rite is now enacted up to the cakes-and-ale consecration. At this point, the Priestess, standing at the altar, takes a step forward, and addresses the coven. She recites:

We come together on this night to witness the end of the dark time and the beginning of the light, and to join in worshipping Woden and Frig. Let us give thanks to Woden.

The Priestess steps back. The Priest steps forward and takes over the recitation:

Woden has reached the end of his long journey. The time has come to light the Beltane Fires to renew our Lord.

The coven responds: *Light the fires to honor our Lord.*

A moment of silence follows while each witch gives silent thanks to Woden. The Thegn uses a taper to transfer flame from the altar candle to the Beltane candle in the cauldron. Once the candle is lit, the silence ends. A seasonal play, or other activity, is enacted here with the only requirement being that the design must highlight a sexual or purifying aspect. Dancing around the Maypole is one possibility, but many covens prefer to conduct a ring-dance and jump over the cauldron. The Priest and Priestess go first and then break away, allowing the coven members to continue on their own. After a few more minutes, the bell is rung three times to signal the end of the dance. The Priest puts on the Oak Crown and kneels (head bowed) in the center of the Circle facing the altar while the Priestess recites:

The Wheel of the Year turns without end. Where it was once the cold and dark of the Oak King, so it turns again to the warmth and light of the Springtime Goddess. The Lord, Woden, shines down, whilst our Lady, Frig, breathes new life into the land. As the Wheel turns, the Lord and Lady become the Lady and Lord, whilst the bud and twig become the leaf and branch. The reign of Winter has ended and the abundance of Spring has begun. Welcome Frig.

The coven responds: *Welcome Frig.*

With the Priest still kneeling in the center of the Circle, the Thegn lights a taper from the cauldron and passes it over the Priest, saying: *Let the fires of Beltane renew you.* The Priest stands and walks to the altar where he picks up the Crown of Flowers and places it on the Priestess while reciting:

Lovely Lady, we welcome you. As the time of Woden draws to a close, the time of Frig moves forward. Let these flowers be your crown as you guide us and guard us throughout the coming months.

The Priest moves forward and kisses the Priestess. She then recites:

As your Beltane Fires drive away the long, dark winter night, I hear your calls and come to light the path to summer. From the dark I will guide you to the light. From the cold I will guide you into my warmth. Know that Love is the spark of life, and that my love is always there for you. As the wheel continues to turn, so shall we move ever forward with it.

The coven responds: *Farewell to our Lord, Hail to our Lady.*

As soon as her speech is done, the Priestess kisses the Priest again, then turns to greet each witch with a kiss as they go by in a single file. Unless it has already been performed, the Maypole dance is conducted now. If it was done previously, then the coven members jump over the cauldron. The Thegn (who may or may not be participating) rings the bell three times to end the dance, which signals the coven to move on to the cakes and ale rite. Once this is completed, the Circle may be banished, and the sabbat feast begins.

West Country

This denomination is different from the others in a few respects. First, because West Country witches only celebrate five major sabbats, each one takes on more importance. As one of the two great fire festivals, Beltane enjoys a special place in the West Country calendar. Second, since May Eve is such a lusty time, rural people naturally placed a great deal of significance in a ceremony that promoted fertility of the fields, animals, and clan. Therefore, in times past, even nonwitches appreciated the symbolism of the May Day celebrations.

In setting up a West Country Beltane ceremony, oak branches with new greenery or pine boughs are used to decorate the inside of the Circle area. A path leading into the Circle may also be laid with the branches. Garlands of flowers are used to dress up the altar area. A Maypole is set up outside the Circle, and the ribbons are decorated with flowers.[12] The altar is set in the north, and a bonfire site is fixed in the center of the Circle. Furthermore, the Circle for the sabbats will be eighteen feet, instead of the usual nine feet, in order to make added space for extra participants. The robes for the sabbat are green to celebrate the renewed earth. A Crown of Flowers is kept on the altar for the May Queen.

The ceremony begins with everyone standing outside the Circle area (arranged in male/female pairs), except the Priest and Priestess. They cast the Circle in the usual way, then exit the Circle to lead the others in. Once inside, the coven members take up position in an arc along the edge of the Circle, facing the altar. Nonwitches are required to stand behind the coven. As soon as everyone is settled, the wine and cakes are consecrated, but the rite is altered slightly for the sabbats.

The Priest starts by filling the ceremonial goblet with wine. He then empties this into a container[13] and refills the goblet a second (and possibly third) time with a sufficient amount of wine to accommodate all the extra people in attendance. There should be enough wine for each person to take more than just a little sip. The implication behind this act is that by consecrating the goblet wine, the wine poured from it gets consecrated at the same time.

At this point the Great Rite takes place. Since an actual rite requires the coven to leave the Circle, a symbolic version is much easier. In either case, the following sequence is performed even though it is similar to the symbolic Great rite. The Priest holds the goblet in front of him while the Priestess dips her athame into the wine. The Priestess recites:

Blessings be upon this cup of wine, that has flowed from the seed planted in the earth. As we drink, we give thanks for what we have received.

Each takes a sip from the goblet. The Priest puts down the goblet and picks up the plate of cakes. The Priestess pushes the tip of her athame into one of the cakes and recites:

Blessings be upon this food, which has come from the earth's bountiful womb. As we eat, we give thanks for what we have received, and we ask the Lord and Lady to grant us fertility and reward for the coming season.

The Priestess puts down the athame, breaks off a piece from one cake, and eats it. She then takes the plate from the Priest. He eats the rest of the broken cake. He picks up the goblet, and the wine and cakes are shared with the congregation.

Once everyone has partaken of the wine and cakes, a dance is held around the fire. Dancers may either hold hands and perform a normal ring-dance or they stand back to back and conduct the more customary spiral dance. Since the mood is supposed to be very jolly, the tempo of the music should be fast. During the dancing, individuals should be encouraged to break away and jump over the fire. This continues until the Priest/Priestess decides it's gone on long enough and calls an end to the dance.

When everyone settles down, a female coven member or guest[14] is brought forward by the Priest. He positions her facing the coven. The Priest picks up the Crown of Flowers and places it on her head while the Priestess recites:

We crown the May Queen, we bless the earth, and we pray to the Lord and Lady that fertility will spring forth from the earth's bountiful womb. Hail the May Queen. Hail the Lord and Lady.

The coven responds: *Hail the May Queen. Hail the Lord and Lady.*

In modern practice, the Circle is now banished and the feasting begins. This differs from traditional activities because the feast was withheld until the following morning (May Day). During the feast and party, the Maypole dance is performed. When the festivities are over, the bonfire is extinguished, and the ceremony is complete.

Summer Solstice

The Summer Solstice, also known as the Midsummer Sabbat, is the first solstice and second Lesser Sabbat, during a standard calendar year. Depending on the sun's entry into the zodiac sign of Cancer, it's celebrated around June 22. A unique aspect of Midsummer, which is also the key to much of its symbolism, is that it occurs on the longest day of the year, which, in turn, produces the shortest night. And, it's because of this long-day/short-night phenomenon that the sabbat is primarily identified with the Sun God image of the male deity. The sun is at the peak of its annual cycle, and it's on this day that the year changes course from waxing to waning. Because of this changeover, many denominations hold this sabbat as the day when the Oak King (God of the Waxing Year) dies and is replaced by the Holly King (God of the Waning Year).

The transformation is reversed at the Winter Solstice, with the Holly King being supplanted by the Oak King, thereby bringing the cycle of life into a full circle. Yet, even with all of the God-oriented symbolism, the sabbat is not strictly a celebration of the God, nor is it, as many people think, solely a sun and fire festival. The truth of the matter is that the Summer Solstice is both a fire and water festival that represents the God and Goddess aspects of the season. But, in order to celebrate both deities, the symbolism of the rite must be viewed in two separate ways.

The God aspect of this festival is derived from the phases of the sun, with the most notable symbolism showing up in the Oak King to Holly King transference, and the waxing to waning life cycle. Fire also plays a key factor in the Midsummer ritual, very much as it did during Beltane, appearing most prominently in the form of ritualistic cleansing bonfires.

For instance, it's a common practice for witches to light twin bonfires and walk between them in order to purify themselves. Although this obviously evolved from the ancient custom of driving livestock between the fires for purification, the fire once again symbolizes spiritual cleansing and establishes a direct link to the God.

Water also plays an important role in the symbolism of the ceremony. The water aspect of the rite is a representation of the Goddess in her dual life/death role. She presides over the death of the Oak King and the rebirth of the Holly King. In addition, the impregnated Goddess, symbolizing the lush abundance of the earth and the coming bounty of the harvest, is honored during this sabbat. This veneration draws focus to the previously performed fertility rites (conducted during Beltane) and validates their worth, without taking anything away from the overall theme. In order to represent this aspect of the Goddess, it's common practice to fill a cauldron partially with water to symbolize her as the wellspring of life.

This sabbat also represents fertility. By borrowing a great deal of imagery from the classical pregnant Goddess concept, this rite became closely tied to conception. As a result, ancient customs held fast to the belief that a woman who wanted to conceive a child should walk skyclad through the vegetable fields (or even a vegetable garden) during the Summer Solstice.[1] Coincidentally, or perhaps just because the weather is so nice at this time of year, this is one of the sabbats most often performed skyclad, even by covens that normally work robed.

Yet, regardless of the complexities of the symbolism, the main thing to remember about Midsummer is that it's a God and Goddess ritual, as well as a fire and water rite. It's the peak of the Oak King's glory before his death at the end of the waxing year and the start of the Holly King's reign at the beginning of the waning year. The entire event is overseen by the Goddess.

SETUP

Depending on the denomination and the customs being followed, the preparation for this ceremony is fairly elaborate. This is because of the different characters that need to be symbolically portrayed during the ceremony.

The first things that need to be prepared are the four crowns representing the Goddess and the phases of the God. The crowns are (1) Sun Crown; (2) Oak Crown; (3) Holly Crown; and (4) Crown of Flowers. Assuming the Oak Crown was saved,[2] the Holly Crown can be constructed using a pre-formed wreath onto which holly is interwoven. Since the only requirement for the Sun Crown is that it be yellow or gold, it can also be fashioned out of rolled-up cloth and be similar in design to the Holly Crown. Also, to enhance the symbolism of each crown, consider adding decorations to represent the individuality of the deity associated with each one. Even though the Crown of Flowers represents the Goddess, it doesn't need to be elaborate.[3]

Since there is so much symbolism to contend with, decorating becomes a very significant part of the preparation for this sabbat. As a result, a great deal of time and energy is spent on gathering appropriate materials and properly arranging them into a seasonal motif. And because everything should blend into an interconnected theme, the decorating should begin on the perimeter of the Circle area and move inward toward the center. Summer flowers, such as Queen Anne's lace and goldenrod, are some of the best choices for this sabbat because they symbolize the beauty and bounty of the season, while also representing the colors of the sun and moon. In addition to flowers, long-stemmed ornamental grasses and potted plants[4] are acceptable. Everything from the Watchtowers to the cauldron should be adorned with decorations.

Two candles with holders are needed to represent the twin bonfires. These are set approximately three to four feet apart in the center of the Circle. If the ritual is held outdoors and actual bonfires are to be lit, one of two things will have to be done. The Circle will have to be expanded to accommodate the bonfires, or the bonfires will have to be very small in order to leave enough room inside the Circle for movement and dancing.

The cauldron is placed directly in front of the altar, then decorated with flowers. Once in position, it's partially filled with water. Since it's customary in some denominations to use a small branch to sprinkle the cauldron water onto the coven, this branch should be placed beside it. Among the denominations that follow this practice, the white varieties of heather, fir, spruce, or birch are all recommended.

A dark-colored scarf, or a large piece of dark material, is needed to represent a death shroud. However, the fabric should be slightly translucent, like cheesecloth or lace. This item will be used with the crowns, so it should be kept near the altar.

Finally, all tools should be laid out on the altar just prior to the start of the ceremony. In selecting incense, the best choices are those scents that have a flowery fragrance. For a mild bouquet, rose or lilac are excellent choices, while jasmine or lavender offer stronger alternatives.

Gardnerian

Prior to the ceremony, a single red candle should the placed in the center of the Circle (between the two bonfire candles). It's lit to represent the Sun God. At the same time, the High Priestess must select three men to portray the Oak King, Holly King, and Sun God. The High Priest is normally chosen as the Holly King. She must also delegate the role of the Goddess, though she usually assumes this for herself. If not the High Priestess, the Maiden is the next likely candidate. The men may not wear their crowns during any portion of the opening ritual, though the High Priestess may don the Crown of Flowers immediately after the Charge.

The ceremony begins with the Circle being cast and proceeds through the Witches' Rune. Following the chant, the coven members take up positions along the perimeter of the Circle. The High Priestess and Maiden stand at the altar, the High Priest (soon-to-be Holly King) at the west cardinal point, and the male witch (soon-to-be Oak King) at the east cardinal point. Once everyone is settled, the High Priestess motions for the Maiden to give the Oak Crown to the witch portraying the Oak King, who immediately puts it on. She then recites:

> *At Yule, thou did slay thy brother, the Holly King, and since then thou hast ruled as the Oak King, God of the Waxing Year. Yet as the Wheel turns, your time slowly comes to an end.*

The Oak King walks to the center of the Circle and faces the coven. The red candle should be in front of him. Assuming the God Position, he recites:

> *I am the Oak King, God of the Waxing Year. I have reigned as the consort of the Goddess throughout this time of light, and I shall continue until I am deposed by the dark.*

As soon as the Oak King stops talking, the High Priestess motions for the Maiden to give the Holly Crown to the High Priest. He immediately puts it on. She then recites:

> *Thou art the Holly King, God of the Waning Year. As the Wheel turns, your time approaches.*

The Holly King walks to the center of the Circle, stands on the other side of the red candle, and assumes the Slain God Position.[5] As soon as the Holly King is set, the High Priestess recites:

We have come together at this sacred time of the year to witness the coming of the darkness. Our Lord, the Sun God, is at the height of his power, signaling the start of the waning year. As it begins, so shall the Light soon begin to fade, and the bounty shall once again lay dormant in the womb of the Great Mother.

The Midsummer Dance is now performed. However, there are variations as to how the dance takes place. Some covens like to have everyone, except the Oak King and Holly King, participate in the dance, while others relegate the dancing specifically to the Goddess. This version, however, involves the Goddess and the Sun God. After receiving the Sun Crown from the Maiden, the Sun God retrieves the red candle from the center of the Circle, while the Goddess retrieves her athame. Incorporating upward hand movements into the dance as a gesture to the sun, the pair dances around the Oak King and Holly King. As the pair dances, the coven chants:

O' blessed Lady of pale moonlight,
Dance and sing, this Midsummer night;
The Oak King is dead, gone to his tomb,
His life is done, 'til reborn from the womb;
O' blessed Lady of pale moonlight,
Dance and sing, this Midsummer night;
The Holly King comes, his time is here,
And light will fade with the waning year;
O' blessed Lady of pale moonlight,
Dance and sing, this Midsummer night;
As the life of the Oak King fades away,
The reign of the Holly King begins today;
O' blessed Lady of pale moonlight,
Dance and sing, this Midsummer night;
But after the Winter covers the Earth,
The cycle will turn to celebrate birth;
O' blessed Lady of pale moonlight,
Dance and sing, this Midsummer night.

The dancers come to a halt at the end of the chant. The High Priestess goes to the altar, while the Sun God places the red candle back in the center, lays the Sun Crown around it, and returns to his place with the coven. Once everyone is settled, the Oak King extinguishes the Sun God candle, and the High Priestess recites:

The sun is in decline, and with it the reign of the Oak King, God of the Waxing Year, comes to a close. Behold, the time of the Holly King, God of the Waning Year, is upon us.

As soon as the High Priestess finishes speaking, the Holly King comes out of the Slain God Position. There are two different versions of the drama play that can take place at this point in the rite. The Holly King pretends to slay the Oak King, or the Oak King just pretends to die. Either way, the Oak King ends up kneeling in the center of the Circle.[6] The Maiden comes forward and drapes the scarf over the Oak King's head. The Holly King then recites:

The reign of the Oak King is over, and the reign of the Holly King has begun. With the Sun God at his pinnacle, the waxing year gives way to the waning year, and the warmth and bounty of Summer shall slowly give way to the cold death of Winter. Only when the Oak King is reborn shall the cycle reverse. The spirit of the Oak King is gone from this Sacred Circle. I, the Holly King, rule in his stead, and shall do so until his rebirth. When the Wheel of the Year has turned, and the seasons once again change, I shall die so that the Oak King shall be reborn, thus fulfilling the never-ending cycle of life. Farewell O' Oak King; Blessed be the Holly King. So mote it be.

The coven repeats: *Farewell O' Oak King; Blessed be the Holly King.*

It's customary for the Oak King to be led to the west quarter by the High Priest and High Priestess before the shroud is removed by the Maiden. Once this is done, the male witch and Maiden join the coven. However, there is still the problem of what to do with the Oak Crown. Since the Oak King is dead, his body (the Oak Crown) is supposed to be buried. At Yule, this is done by placing the crown inside the cauldron, which is symbolic of returning it to the womb. But since the cauldron is filled with water, this is impossible. Simply keeping the crown covered with the shroud is sufficient.

After bringing the crown to the west quarter, the pair returns to the altar where they symbolically enact the Great Rite to celebrate the joining of the Goddess and God. The wine and cakes are consecrated and shared with the coven. Following the wine and cakes, the High Priest resumes his Holly King role and assumes the Osiris Position facing the altar. The cauldron should be between the High Priestess and him. The High Priestess raises the athame toward the Holly King, draws the Invoking Pentagram of Earth in the air above the cauldron, and recites:

O' bright and shining Sun God, we invoke thee to come and spread thy warmth on the land. Heed our call, and fill us with thine light, that it may drive away the dark; and guide us along a path, that we may walk in the footsteps of the Old Gods.

The Holly King dips the wand into the cauldron to symbolically join the God with the Mother Earth. He then recites:

As the Lance joins the Grail, spirit joins flesh, man joins woman, and Sun joins Earth, so do I, by this act, join the God with the Goddess, that there may be light and dark, life and death. So mote it be.

It's now time for another dance, but the goal of this one is purification. Therefore, it's time to set out the twin bonfire candles. Place them equidistant along a line between the east and west candles. When they're in place, the Maiden lights the candles using a flame taken from the altar candle. The High Priestess then recites:

The Midsummer fires are lit, and the Cauldron of Cerridwen is filled with the consecrated Waters of Life. Come forth, that you may be blessed.

Beginning with the High Priest, the entire coven passes by the altar while the High Priestess uses the branch to sprinkle water on them. After everyone's been blessed, she sprinkles a few drops of the water toward each cardinal point while reciting:

Blessed be the East (South, West, North) *that this Water of Life, which has been touched by the God, and filled with his spirit, shall fall upon you.*

After putting down the branch, the High Priestess leads the coven through the bonfire candles. Besides being purified, it's also customary to make a wish while passing between the bonfires. However, there seem to be three schools of thought on the topic of the wish. First, some witches feel that it's only appropriate to make a wish in regard to the current year. But since Samhain is the end of one year and the beginning of the next, a wish made at Midsummer for "this year" only lasts for slightly more than four months. The second belief is that the wish must be for the coming year. Unfortunately, this means that the wish doesn't start until Samhain since the "next year" does not begin for four more months. Finally, there are some witches who don't impose an imaginary time limit on the wish.

Once everyone has been blessed and purified, the ceremony is over. However, before banishing the Circle, the High Priest should remove the Holly Crown. He should then extinguish the bonfire candles, or at least move them onto the altar. Only when this is done is the Circle banished.

Italian

The Summer Solstice, or Summer Feast, is one of the least complicated of all the Italian sabbat ceremonies. Although this is surprising, especially given the fact that the Winter Solstice can be very complicated, it's nevertheless the same throughout the various branches of the denomination.

A simple ceremony means easy preparation. After placing the altar on the northern edge of the Circle and the cauldron on the southern edge, a large red candle is placed inside the cauldron and lit just before the ceremony. The ritual area, altar, and cauldron should then be decorated. Summer flowers and greenery are used for the decorations, and chaplets are usually made for the women. Finally, extra flowers should be stripped of their petals until there is enough to give each coven member a small handful. Other than this, nothing special is required.

The ceremony begins with casting the Circle and proceeds through a complete esbat rite. At the point where the wine and cakes would normally be consecrated, the esbat format is abandoned, and the sabbat rite takes over. The High Priestess, standing at the altar beside the High Priest, recites:

> *We gather on this sacred night to bid farewell to the Sun God. He is the Lord of Light, who begins his journey downward into the Realm of Shadows until his eventual rebirth at Yule. Yet, as the Wheel of the Year ever turns, the God will again be reborn.*

The High Priest, with his back to the altar, assumes the God Position while the High Priestess walks over to the cauldron and blows out the candle. She turns to face the altar and recites:

> *Behold, the flame in the womb of the Mother Earth is extinguished. On this night we consign the God of Light, Lord of the Waxing Year, to his long winter sleep. Let it be known that the spirit of the Lord of*

the Waxing Year must now depart to make way for the Dark God, Lord of the Waning Year.

At the end of her address, the High Priest transitions from the God Position to the Slain God Position. The High Priestess then recites:

O' Mighty God of Darkness, Lord of the Hunt, with each passing day the Light grows dimmer and you grow stronger. As the darkness and cold overtake the land, we pray that you provide the bounty of the harvest. Protect us, O' Lord, through the coming months. Blessed be.

The coven responds: *Blessed be.*

Coming out of the Slain God Position, the High Priest kisses the High Priestess on the lips and embraces her. This is symbolic of the God's blessing. He then goes around the coven and delivers the same blessing to each person. When he finishes, the High Priestess accompanies him to the altar, and the pair consecrates the wine and cakes. As each coven member is given the wine and cakes, the High Priest recites:

Receive this gift in honor of the reborn God.

After sharing the wine and cakes with the coven, the High Priest and High Priestess take an offering to each Watchtower.[7] At each quarter, the wine and cakes are offered to the spirits with the following words:

O' Mighty Spirits of the Earth (Air, Water, Fire*) at this time of balance, when the Lord of Light submits to the Lord of Shadows, we offer these sacred gifts and ask that you bestow your blessings upon us.*

After all four quarters are addressed, the coven gathers in the center of the Circle to conduct a slow widdershins ring-dance to symbolically usher out the Sun God. Once this is over, the Circle is banished, and the festivities begin.

Saxon

This denomination has a very modest sabbat ceremony for Midsummer. However, although there's a simple approach taken to the ritual, an enormous amount of time and energy is dedicated to the festivities. This situation arose from the Saxon outlook on the season, combined with the outside forces that influenced the culture. Since the Summer Solstice signaled the decline of light and the harshness of winter was just around the corner, it became customary to hold a grand celebration as a means of bidding farewell to the Sun God. But, beyond saying good-bye, the main reason behind staging such an extravagant event was that the early Saxons hoped that the lavishness of the festivities would make the Sun God anxious to return, thereby shortening the winter.

As a result of the party theme, an important facet of this sabbat is the amount of work that's put into decorating and the attention paid to the feast itself. To start with, the entire ritual area (both inside and outside of the actual Circle) should be heavily decorated with flowers and greenery. Yellow flowers should adorn the altar and cauldron. If possible, it's customary to use sunflowers and daisies on the altar, a large sunflower at each quarter. There should be one sunflower (fully destemmed) on hand that can be placed inside the cauldron.[8] In addition to decorating with flowers, chaplets of white flowers should be made for all the women and greenery circlets for all the men.

A decision must also be made regarding the cauldron because, depending on the way it's used, there are two completely different symbolic values attached to it. Prior to placing it in the southern quarter, a choice must be made between putting a large candle inside or filling it with water. Although either is acceptable, the water version seems to be more widely used in modern practice. If this is the method used, then a single red candle is placed in the center of the Circle. In the other method, the candle goes inside the cauldron. Smaller red candles can also be handed out to the coven, though this is really more of a Winter Solstice custom.

A final note about the Saxon celebration centers on the feast. Though the religious portion of the rite is an important aspect of the sabbat, the feast—and the singing, dancing, and gaiety that accompanied it—were the cornerstones on which the early Saxons rested their hopes that the Sun God would return quickly. Therefore, the foods for the feast should be as lavish as finances allow. Early fruits, such as strawberries and blueberries, should be plentiful. Sweets, pies, and cakes are another customary food, as are cheeses, milk, honey, and greens.

Once everything's set, the ceremony begins with the Circle being cast. The red candle in the center is lit immediately after the casting with the same flame that was used to light the Watchtowers. The Priest and Priestess proceed to the altar while the coven members spread out along the perimeter of the Circle. A normal esbat rite then takes place up to the beginning of the cakes and ale rite. At this point, the Priestess starts the sabbat ceremony by reciting:

The time of balance is upon us. Gather around and witness the end of the Light and the beginning of the Dark. The wheel has turned and the Sun begins its descent. Soon, the harshness of Winter shall return to the land.

The Priest goes to the center of the Circle, picks up the candle, and holds it high in the air while the Priestess recites:

O' Mighty Lord, Woden, as the sun slips away, and the harshness of winter approaches, we ask that you guide us along the path of Life and watch over us as we journey through the coming months of darkness. Bless us with your love, O' Mighty One.

When this address ends, the Priest lowers the candle and extinguishes the flame. He returns to the altar.[9] The Priest and Priestess now take the sunflower and together, place it in the cauldron. It doesn't matter whether it floats or sinks. Dipping their fingers in the cauldron water, they bless each other. One by one, the coven members approach the pair to be blessed, men by the Priestess, women by the Priest. Once the blessing is done, the Priest and Priestess lead a ring-dance around the Circle. After the dance ends (with a minimum of three complete revolutions), the coven members drop down. The Priestess recites:

Let this feast made in honor of Woden and Frig, and may our love for them shine brightly through the days ahead. So be it.

The coven repeats: *So be it.*

Because the feast is so important to this sabbat, the cakes and ale rite becomes connected to it. Therefore, just before banishing the Circle, the Priestess and Priest consecrate the cakes and ale, but they don't share them with the coven yet. This is the end of the religious ceremony. The Circle is banished, then the cakes and ale are shared with the coven, followed by the feast and festivities.

West Country

This denomination uses the tale of the wren slaying the robin as a way of symbolizing the waning year overtaking the waxing year. The reverse is used during Winter Solstice. To get ready for this sabbat, the drama play requires advance thought and preparation. Since the wren and robin need to be distinguishable from one another, costumes must be made. Dual crowns (one red and one brown) are the easiest way to accomplish this—they can also be reused for Yule—but more elaborate costumes are just as appropriate.

Because this denomination originated in rural areas where the land was already lush and in bloom, decorating was not that important to this rite. However, as the denomination spread to more urban areas, the ritual area required more attention. The result is a combination between old and new. Nowadays, the Circle and altar are heavily adorned with flowers. But, other than that, not much else is done.

The ceremony opens with the Circle being cast by the coven leader. In this instance, the Priestess casts the Circle because the Priest will most likely be dressed to portray a character in the drama that follows. During the casting, the coven members remain outside the Circle area. They are then admitted to the Circle through the doorway cut by the Priestess. When all the coven members are inside, the Priestess returns to the altar, The doorway is left open. Facing the coven, she narrates the drama as it's acted out in the middle of the Circle. She begins:

As the wheel turns and the seasons change, we must give thanks for the sacrifice that is made. Many months ago, at Yule, the light conquered the dark, and the Robin Redbreast came to rule the land.

The May Queen (representing the Goddess) enters the Circle and stands in front of the altar. Next, the person portraying the robin enters through the doorway, makes one pass around the Circle, then stands in the center facing the coven. As he passes the altar, the Priestess (or May Queen) hands him a single red candle that was lit from the altar flame. The Priestess continues:

The robin watched the darkness of winter lose its hold and give way to the light. He watched as the fields were plowed and planted. And, as the sprouts grew, he cast the light down upon them.

The robin blows out the candle, and the May Queen bows her head. This is the signal for the wren to enter. After making a pass around the Circle, the wren joins the robin in the center. The May Queen raises her head and acts surprised. The Priestess again continues:

But, as is always so, the Wheel of the Year turned, and the Little Wren King once again returned to preside over the harvest.

The robin, chased by the wren, dances around the Circle until caught. A mock fight ensues before the robin is defeated. He then lies at the wren's feet. Once the robin is dead, the May Queen moves forward and places a flower on the body as a symbolic burial. The Priestess concludes the story:

> *The robin was buried; the wren reigned supreme; and the dark is free to return once more. Let all be safe in the knowledge that though the death of winter shall soon be upon us, it is but the next step in the cycle of life.*

Now that the drama is over, the May Queen and male witch (the robin) rejoin the coven while the Priest joins the Priestess at the altar. The wine and cakes are consecrated by the pair and shared with the coven, marking the end of the ceremony. The Circle is banished.

Lughnasadh

The Lughnasadh Sabbat is the third Greater Sabbat of the standard calendar year. And like all of the other Greater Sabbats, it's a fire festival. Depending on the denomination, Lughnasadh is often referred to by its Gaelic name Lammas, which literally translates to "loaf mass." Lammas is also known as First Harvest, since the month of August is normally the time that many crops begin to ripen. The same holds true for the Italian traditions, where the festival is known as Cornucopia in reference to the bounty of the harvest. By custom, the sabbat is usually celebrated on July 31 or August 1. However, due to a connection with the slaying of the Pagan King (William Rufus), quite a few witches insist that it shouldn't be held until the eve of August 2.[1]

Another reason for the discrepancy of dates centers on the dispute over the name itself. There is an Old Irish word, Lúnasa, which means August. It's argued that this is the origin of the name Lughnasa, which is a shortened version of Lughnasadh. Although this is a logical assumption that probably has some degree of merit, the true source of the name comes from the close association that the sabbat has with the Celtic God, Lugh. And, in fact, Lughnasadh literally means "the commemoration of Lugh."

Because there are several different versions of the God to choose from, the problem of determining who Lugh really is often arises. A quick lesson on the God is required. Now, regardless of the name used (and "Lugh" will be used from here on), Lugh is both a Fire God and a Light God. He's the Celtic Sun God worshipped by the Druids at the beginning of August in honor of the harvest, as well as the male deity that represents the consort of the Goddess during the harvest.[2] In one way or another, Lugh has also been linked to an assortment of other God names—Baal, Balor, Beli, Llew, and Lucifer—which are all interconnected in the rite through mythology and the particular denomination that worships them.

For instance, in Celtic lore, Lugh was the ruler of the Tuatha Dé Danann, and the rite focused on him, while the Anglo-Saxon sabbat observes the death of the Corn King[3] at the harvest. Though this connection is just a harvest-time interpretation of the Holly King. In short, there are multiple versions of the Lughnasadh theme to go along with the multiple Gods.[4]

In conjunction with the God being associated with the harvest, there are sexual rituals that are closely tied to the fields. With fertility being so important to survival, several ancient customs held that the best way for a woman to prepare to conceive a child was for her to dance naked in a cornfield on this night or for a couple to have sex in a cornfield. This relationship added to the significance of this sabbat and mirrored the Goddess/God connection.

Without getting into great detail, there are three main points that must be understood in order to appreciate the theme of the celebration. These are: (A) the mating of the Holly (Corn) King with the Goddess; (B) the death of the Holly (Corn) King; and (C) his eventual rebirth. All three of these aspects play important parts in the ritual itself, and they are the only concepts that must be understood in order to comprehend the significance of this Sabbat. As long as these phases are recognized and acknowledged, in combination with the sexual-sacrificial aspects, the symbolism of the festival will not be lost.

SETUP

The preparation for this festival isn't particularly easy, but it's nothing that will require great skill or craftsmanship. In fact, the bulk of the work consists of decorating. Other than that, the remaining preparations do not require much advance prep work.

As with the Midsummer Sabbat, two different crowns—Holly Crown and Crown of Flowers (with grain added)—will be used. However, there are a few minor alterations to each of these. To begin with, the Holly Crown can be made in the same manner as it was for Midsummer (i.e., by intertwining holly branches into a circular wreath), onto which kernels of corn are added. A suggestion is to intertwine cornhusks and/or corn silk into the wreath as it's woven, then use glue to attach kernels of dried corn along the top edge of the wreath. This crown then represents the dual Holly/Corn King facets. Another suggestion is to make two separate crowns (one corn and one holly) to represent the individual God themes.[5]

If deciding upon two crowns, the Corn Crown can be made by simply attaching cornhusks, silk, and kernels to a pre-formed framework.

The same idea lends itself to the Crown of Flowers. While putting together this crown, simply intertwine small stalks of grain with the flowers. Wheat, barley, oats, and rye are all types of grains that can be easily added; and all of these are traditional choices. At this time of year, it's also customary to use a lot of yellow flowers to make the crown, as the yellow flowers represent the sun at its strongest point.

As with Midsummer, this ritual requires the use of a large scarf or a large piece of material. Since this item is used as a death shroud, the most appropriate color is dark green or brown to represent both death and the earth. However, any dark tone will suffice.

A small loaf of bread is also needed. If at possible, the preferable choice is fresh-baked bread, but, bakery bread, or even rolls, may be substituted. If the bread is going to be baked for the sabbat by a member of the coven, a natural, unrefined flour should be used. The other ingredients should be as natural as possible. In place of regular bread, cornbread is a popular (and traditional) substitute. The only problem with using cornbread is that, because of its consistency, it can be difficult to work with during the ceremony.

Music is another item that demands advance thought. While there is music at all sabbats, the music for this ceremony is of greater importance than in other instances. Select music for the following: (A) The main ceremony requires music that has a soothing background theme; (B) the Corn Dance music should be totally instrumental and have a rhythmic beat; and (C) the festival music can be anything that you feel is appropriate, but it should be very jubilant to portray the excitement of the bountiful harvest. A coven member should also be selected in advance to make sure the music is changed at the appropriate times.

When laying out the Circle area, the cauldron is placed near the east candle, which is the quarter that represents rebirth. Also, the outside of the cauldron should be carefully decorated with flowers, stalks of grain and/or corn. A final touch that's become increasingly popular is to fill the cauldron with stalks of grain or corn. This has come to signify the bounty of the harvest season coming forth from the womb of the Great Mother.

Four ears of corn may also be used during the ceremony. These can be fresh corn from the local grocery store, but dried ears of decorative corn (referred to as Indian corn) are recommended. However, the use of this nonessential item is determined more by individual coven practice than along denominational lines.

Now this next suggestion is not required, and it's included merely for the sake of thoroughness. Depending on the tradition or the outlook adopted concerning Lugh, it's customary to wear clothing with an "athletic" theme. This is because Lugh was viewed as a Warrior God, so ancient custom was to hold athletic contests/games as part of this festival. It is also possible that the Romans introduced the athletic theme to the sabbat, and it simply carried over. Either way, in keeping with this custom, many witches still wear this type of clothing.

Finally, lay out the altar tools in the usual manner. Remember, the topic of this ritual is the bounty of the harvest, so the altar should be decorated with grains, corn, flowers, and any other seasonal motif that's appropriate.

Gardnerian

The opening for Lughnasadh progresses as a normal esbat through the water/salt consecration and casting of the Circle. After the Circle is erected, the ceremony moves right into the Fivefold Kiss. Once this is completed, the High Priest puts on the Holly Crown and the High Priestess dons the Crown of Flowers. If a separate Corn Crown was made, the male witch chosen to be the Corn King puts on his crown, too. When everyone is ready, the High Priest gives an altered version of the Charge. Turning toward the coven, he recites:

> *Listen to the words of the Great Mother, she who of old was called among men, Artemis, Astarte, Dione, Melusine, Aphrodite, Cerridwen, Diana, Arianrhod, Isis, Bride, and by many other names. At the altars, the youths of Laceademon in Sparta made sacrifice.*
>
> *Whenever ye have need of anything, once in the month and better it be when the moon is full, then shall ye assemble in some secret place and adore the spirit of she, who be Queen of all Witcheries. There ye shall assemble, ye who are feign to learn all sorceries who have not yet won her deepest secrets. To these will she teach that which is yet unknown. And ye shall be free from slavery, and as a sign that ye be really free, ye shall be naked in your rites; and ye shall dance, sing, feast, make music, and love, all in her praise. For hers is the ecstasy of the spirit, and hers is also joy on earth. For her law is love unto all beings. Keep pure your highest ideals and strive ever towards them. Let none*

stop you or turn you aside. For hers is the secret door which opens upon the Land of Youth; hers is the Cup of the Wine of Life and the Cauldron of Cerridwen, which is the Holy Grail of Immortality. She is the Gracious Goddess who gives the gift of joy unto the heart of man. Upon earth she gives the knowledge of the spirit eternal, and beyond death she gives peace, and freedom, and reunion with those that have gone before. Nor does she demand sacrifice. For behold, she is the Mother of all things, and her love is poured out upon the earth.

Hear ye the words of the Star Goddess. She, in the dust of whose feet are the Hosts of Heaven, and whose body encircles the Universe. She, who is the beauty of the green earth, and the white Moon against the stars, and the mystery of the waters, and the desire of the heart of man, call unto thy soul. Arise and come unto her. For she is the soul of Nature, who gives life to the Universe. From her all things proceed, and unto her all things must return. Before her face, beloved of Gods and of men, let thine innermost divine self be enfolded in the rapture of the infinite. Let her worship be within the heart that rejoiceth. For behold, all acts of love and pleasure are her rituals. Therefore, let there be beauty and strength, power and compassion, honor and humility, mirth and reverence within you. And thou who thinkest to seek for her, know thy seeking and yearning shall avail thee not unless thou knowest the mystery that if that which thou seekest thou findest not within thee, thou wilt never find it without thee. For behold, she has been with thee from the beginning, and she is that which is attained at the end of desire.

When the Charge is finished, the High Priestess leads the coven in the Witches' Rune. After a few revolutions of the Circle, the High Priestess and High Priest break away. The coven may continue for another few passes. Once the dance is done, the coven returns to the edge of the Circle.

There are two versions that can occur here. One version calls for the High Priest and High Priestess to perform the love-chase procession using the scarf. Then they allow the paired coven members to enact it. A second version omits the love-chase and simply moves on to the death enactment of the God. The Holly King (and/or Corn King) goes to the center of the Circle and kneels facing the altar, while the High Priestess, with the help of the Maiden, takes the scarf and lays it over the Holly/Corn King. This mimics a death shroud.[6] The Maiden retrieves the loaf of bread (still on its plate) from the altar and brings it to the High Priestess, who recites:

O' Mighty Mother, bringer of all fruitfulness, give us fruit and grain, flocks and herds, and children for the tribe, that we may be mighty. By thy rosy love, do thou descend upon the body of thy servant here.

Symbolism is very important here. The Goddess was just invoked into the loaf of bread, which is now recognized as a symbol of her essence. Since her spirit was invoked into the bread, the bread also represents the food of life. An interesting side note is the similarity between this Wiccan practice and that of Catholic communion. The Catholic rite obviously being an adaptation of an early Pagan practice. The Maiden now begins a slow deosil dance around the Holly/Corn King. The High Priestess sometimes performs the dance, as well. This is known as the Corn Dance, or the Harvest Dance, and it's similar to the Midsummer Dance. However, since there is no chanting during this dance, the tempo follows the music. The tempo of the music should increase as it goes on in order to increase the speed of the dance. As the Maiden dances, she gradually increases her speed to match the music until she is moving fairly fast, then she comes to a halt with the Holly/Corn King between her and the altar. The Maiden and High Priestess each take hold of the plate and extend it over the kneeling Holly/Corn King. The women recite:

Alas, the Holly King, God of the Waning Year, is dead. As it has been since time began, the Corn King, who has embraced the Great Mother as her consort, is no more. He has returned to the womb of the earth from whence he came, and remains in eternal sleep. But if there is no Holly King, there can be no Oak King, and the earth shall never again be bountiful. Thus, the Holly King must be reborn.

The coven asks: *What shall we do?*

In response, the Maiden says: *We shall eat the bread of life.*

Turning to face the coven, the High Priestess answers: *So mote it be.* She takes the plate and breaking off a small piece of the loaf, begins giving a piece of bread to each coven member. They each hold their pieces and wait. The High Priestess returns to the center of the Circle, where she and the Maiden lift the scarf off the Holly King. If there's a separate Corn King, he remains covered. The High Priest accompanies the High Priestess and Maiden to the altar. Each takes a piece of bread. The rest is set on the altar.[7] The High Priestess recites:

Eat of the bread of life, that the Holly King shall be reborn.

Everyone eats their piece of bread, then the High Priest steps forward and recites:

> *I am the reborn Holly King, God of the Waning Year. I am the consort of the Great Mother Earth. Fear not, for as I have been reborn, so too shall the Oak King come again. But now, let the earth enjoy the fruits that the Goddess has made, and let all creatures share in the bounty. So mote it be.*

The coven repeats: *So mote it be.*

At this point in the ceremony, another ring-dance is sometimes performed. But more often than not, the coven simply moves on to the Great Rite. After the Great Rite is finished and the wine and cakes are shared with the coven, the ceremony is concluded by banishing the Circle. Since this is the time of the first harvest of the season, the feast should include a wide variety of fruits and vegetables. As a showing of thanks, coven members should at least taste each food. Also, the music for the festivities should be upbeat and have a fast tempo. Finally, if the coven has younger members, athletic games or contests should be performed.

Italian

In the Italian denominations, the sabbat is called Cornucopia, which is a reference to the bounty of the first harvest. The seasonal abundance theme is emphasized by grandly decorating the ritual area with flowers, fruits, vegetables, and any other item that exemplifies the bountifulness of the season. To strictly follow custom, grapes and nuts are excluded because they don't ripen until the Autumn Equinox. It's also customary to decorate the altar and cauldron with flowers, stalks of ripe grain, and fruit. Flower chaplets, intertwined with stalks of grain, are usually made for all the women of the coven. And a freshly baked loaf of bread is placed on the altar.

For an outdoor ceremony, a small bonfire is set up in the center of the Circle and the cauldron is placed in the south. For an indoor ritual, the cauldron is placed in the center and a large candle is placed inside it. In addition, each coven member should be given a kernel of corn, or stalk of grain, which they will use as an offering.

When everyone's ready, the ceremony begins with the Circle being cast. A traditional esbat is conducted up to the point where the wine and cakes would normally be consecrated. At this stage, the coven forms into a single-file line with the High Priestess in the front and the High Priest at the end. The High Priestess leads the procession to the western quarter where she presents her offering. She steps to the side, and one by one, the rest of the witches present their offerings. They then return to their places along the southern edge of the Circle. While the offerings are being made, the High Priestess recites:

Great God and Goddess, Rulers of the Earth and Sky, receive these offerings as a sign of our love and devotion. Let these gifts show that we are thankful for the bounty that has been given to us; and with your wisdom we pray that your guidance will see us through yet another cycle of life.

A chant and ring-dance are performed around the center of the Circle, after which incense is sprinkled onto the fire. The dance proceeds until the High Priestess calls for it to end. Taking the loaf of bread in her hands, she holds it up and recites:[8]

I conjure thee, O' Meal! Who art indeed our body, since without thee we could not live, thou who at first as seed before becoming flower went in the earth, where all deep secrets hide, and then when ground didst dance like dust in the wind, and yet meanwhile didst bear with thee in flitting, secrets strange!

And yet erewhile, when thou wert in the earth, even as a glittering grain, even then the fireflies came to cast on thee their light and aid thy growth, because without their help thou couldst not grow nor beautiful become; therefore thou dost belong unto the race of witches and fairies, and because the fireflies do belong unto the sun . . .

Queen of the Fireflies! Hurry apace, come to me now as if running a race. Bridle the horse as you hear me now sing! Bridle, O' bridle son of the king! Come in a hurry and bring him to me! The son of the king will ere long set thee free; and because thou forever art brilliant and fair, under a glass I will keep thee; while there, with a lens I will study thy secrets concealed, till all their bright mysteries are fully revealed, yea, all the wondrous lore perplexed of this life of our cross and of the next. Thus to all mysteries I shall attain, yea, even to that at last of the grain; and when this at last I shall truly know, Firefly, freely I'll let thee go! When Earth's dark secrets are known to me, my blessing at last I will give to thee!

The bread is placed back on the altar (to be shared with the coven later), and the wine and cakes are consecrated by the High Priestess and High Priest. After the consecration rite, the coven members form a single-file line and approach the altar. Each person receives the following: a piece of bread from the High Priest, a sip of wine,[9] a cake from the High Priestess, and a second sip of wine. When the last witch has been given bread, cakes, and wine, the High Priestess recites:

The seed that was planted in the spring has grown, and the fruits have begun to ripen into the bounty of the harvest. Let us give thanks to the Great God and Goddess for all that we have received; and all that we shall receive. Blessed be.

The coven repeats: *Blessed be.*

This is the official end of the rite. However, before the Circle is banished, custom dictates that pregnant women (and those trying to become pregnant) should be presented to the four quarters. Starting in the east, the High Priest and High Priestess position the women (one at a time) in front of the cardinal points and recite:

May the new life that springs forth from the womb be strong, healthy and loved; and may the blessings of the East (South, West, North) *ever be upon this child. Blessed be.*

The Circle is now banished, and the festivities begin.

Saxon

Surprisingly enough, although this is a Greater Sabbat celebrating both the first harvest and the death/rebirth of the God, this denomination does not hold an overly elaborate ceremony. Instead, the overall atmosphere of the ritual is dignified with just a hint of relaxed exuberance.

Decorations for the rite include yellow (or summer) flowers for the altar and Circle. Sunflowers are especially appropriate. The altar cloth and candles should be yellow or gold. Besides the regular cakes, an offering of food is needed to share with the coven. Although a loaf of bread is normally used for this, any fruit or vegetable can be substituted. Also, chaplets of flowers are customarily worn by the women, with circlets of ivy being worn by the men. Flower necklaces (similar to Hawaiian leis) are sometimes worn, too.

The ceremony begins with the Circle being cast with the coven members either in the ritual area or just outside it. If they remained outside, they're led in by the Thegn and Scribe as soon as it's cast. With the coven arranged in an arc along the southern edge, the High Priest and High Priestess perform a normal esbat rite. They stop before consecrating the cakes and ale. At this point, the Thegn rings the bell three times. This is the signal for the High Priest, standing with his back to the altar, to recite:

We come together on this night to mark the start of the season of the First Harvest. Now is the time when the fruits of our labor begin to ripen; and the bounty of the land is everywhere. As the Wheel of the Year has turned, so the seed has given way to the stem, the stem to the flower, and the flower to the fruit. Let us honor the God and Goddess for all they have given us.

The High Priest takes a step backwards, and the High Priestess steps forward. She picks up the address where he left off and recites:

Great Goddess Frig, Mother of life and love, in the spring we planted the seeds in the earth. Under your guidance, we nurtured them with love and protected them from harm. And, now that the fruits of our labors have grown forth from your womb, we give thanks and praise for the bounty that you have bestowed upon us.

As she finishes speaking, the High Priestess steps back, and the High Priest again steps forward. He now picks up the address where she left off by reciting:

Mighty God Woden, Lord of Light, without you the seed would not grow. You have shone your light down upon the earth, giving warmth to our crops. For this we give thanks and praise to you.

The High Priestess, followed by the High Priest, Thegn, Scribe, and coven, leads a slow deosil ring-dance. This is more of a welcoming gesture than a power-raising dance. After three passes, everyone returns to their original places. A death drama is now performed.[10] This can be carried out by the High Priest, High Priestess, and one other male witch, or three participants (one woman and two men) may be chosen to enact the whole play.[11]

When everyone is prepared, the drama begins with the woman playing the Goddess standing a few steps back from the center of the Circle.

Her back should be toward the altar. The first man stands at the east quarter and the second at the west quarter. To differentiate symbolically between the two, the man in the east carries a flower and the other an ear of corn (or any fruit/vegetable). Once everyone is in the proper place, the woman assumes the Goddess Position (Figure 31.1) and recites:

Hear now the words of the Earth Mother, and heed the message that she brings. For the time of death and rebirth is at hand.

The eastern man comes forward and presents the woman with his flower. He takes a step back and waits. The western man comes forward and presents the woman with his ear of corn. He then steps back, too. Both men now face each other, and the coven begins a slow rhythmic chant. Alternatively, the coven claps instead of chants, or music is played. The two men dance around the Circle—one moving deosil and the other widdershins—until they've made thirteen complete revolutions, one revolution for each lunar cycle. Following the last pass, two men lie down in the center of the Circle. The eastern man is on the bottom with the western man draped over him.[12] The woman, having retrieved the loaf of bread, holds it over her head and recites:

The God is dead. But, by the power of this sacred bread of life, he shall again be reborn.

A second ring-dance is held. This time the tempo is more upbeat, and the purpose is to raise power. The power is then directed into the bread. The dance continues until the woman calls for it to stop, and the coven members return to their places. When everyone is settled, the woman lowers the bread and presents it to the High Priestess. Ripping a small piece off the loaf, the High Priestess gives it to the woman, then goes around the coven giving each person a small piece of bread. saving enough for herself, the High Priest, and the other participants. Once the High Priestess is finished, she returns to the altar, and the woman recites:

May this fruit of the harvest give strength and life to the body. And may the promise of the fruits to come, give hope for a bountiful year.

She then eats her bread with everyone following her lead. Both men stand up. The High Priestess comes forward and gives each a piece of bread, which they eat. Following this, the western man stands to the side of the High Priest and the woman to the side of the High Priestess. The Thegn rings the bell three times. This is the end of the death drama. However, the two participants (man and woman) remain at the altar for the rest of the ceremony. Facing the coven, the High Priestess and High Priest recite:

> *As the Sun mirrors the Moon, the Lord mirrors the Lady. And we, as the children, mirror the God and Goddess. Help us in our quest to love and honor you, Woden and Frig, and give blessings to your children, that we may truly know the peace, joy and love that come from the bounty that you bring. So be it.*

The coven repeats: *So be it.*

With the help of the man and woman, the cakes and ale are now consecrated and shared with the coven. An offering of the cakes and ale is then made to the earth. Once the Circle is banished, the formal rite is over. Dancing, games, and the feast take place.

West Country

Despite the fact that this is a Greater Sabbat in most traditions, the West Country denominations do not even celebrate it. Although there could be any number of reasons for not commemorating this seasonal event, the most likely is that the rigors of the harvest overshadowed the need for spiritual celebration.

In recent years, however, many West Country witches have observed this sabbat in much the same way as other traditions. They've accomplished this by adopting various bits and pieces of the rites of other denominations and adding aspects of their own tradition which they feel fits the spirit of the festival. This method of constructing new rites has, in effect, molded the adopted practices into true West Country fashion.

Because this sabbat was only recently added, decorating is a matter of personal choice. Still, as a rural-based tradition, greenery, flowers, fruits, and vegetables should be present in abundance. The altar and each cardinal point should be decorated with colorful fruits, vegetables, and flowers. A loaf of bread (preferably cornbread) is needed, as are four ears of corn. The ears of corn represent the seed of life, and four are used to point to the four quarters. The broom should also be kept close to the altar for easy access, and a candle should be placed in the center of the Circle area, unless a bonfire is in the middle.

With the altar set up in the north, the ceremony begins with the coven leader lighting the center candle. The Circle is cast, and a normal esbat rite is conducted up to consecrating the wine and cakes. The coven should be positioned along the southern edge of the Circle. The coven leader (usually a Priestess for this sabbat), standing in front of the altar facing the coven, assumes the Goddess Position and recites:

We gather together to celebrate the turning of the Wheel of the Year. As the Wheel turns, it brings with it season after season. And now, the season of harvest is upon us. Welcome all who have come to praise the Goddess and thank her for the bounty of the earth.

The coven responds: *Blessed be the Goddess.*

Picking up the loaf, the Priestess holds it slightly above her head and recites:

Blessed be the bounty of the Mother Earth. From the womb of the Goddess, we receive the bounty of the harvest. Let us give thanks and praise for all that we have received; and for all that is still to come. Blessed be the Mother Earth.

The coven repeats: *Blessed be the Mother Earth.*

It's now time to share the bread with the coven. The assistant coven leader (usually a Priest), carrying the chalice of wine,[13] accompanies the Priestess as she approaches the coven. Moving from one member to the next, she hands each person a piece of bread, which they dip into the wine before eating it. An alternate version is to allow each coven member to rip off his or her own piece of bread. Once everyone has been given bread and wine, the Priestess and Priest return to the altar. A coven member steps forward and blows out the center candle. The Priest, carrying the four ears of corn, begins a slow widdershins spiral. His goal is the center candle. As he walks, the Priestess recites:

Though the Great Mother lives on, the Harvest God is no more. And, without him, the bounty of the Goddess cannot continue. Yet, as one generation dies, another is reborn. And so the Wheel turns.

When the Priest reaches the center, he positions the four ears of corn so that they point to the four quarters. The Priestess brings the broom and lays it on top of the corn. The Priest has removed the center candle and gone back to the altar. As soon as the Priest departs, the coven members line up and follow the Priestess in jumping (east to west) over the broom/corn. After the last person has jumped over, the Priest relights the candle from the altar candle. He returns to the center and jumps over the broom. Once he's jumped over, the Priestess removes the broom, and he places the candle in the middle of the four ears of corn. Everyone returns to his or her original place, and the Priestess recites:

> *Great Mother, Goddess of all Creation. In this time of plenty, you have taught us the secrets and the true meaning of life and death. It shall guide us along the path of eternal peace, joy and love. Marked by the living seed and bounty of the earth, we give praise to the God and Goddess for this bounty, and to ensure that a fruitful harvest is to come.*

A deosil ring-dance is performed by the coven while the Priest and Priestess consecrate the wine and cakes. The dance can also be done separately if the coven leaders wish to join in. After this, the Circle is banished, and the rite is over. The feast can now take place, but fruits and vegetables should be the main course.

Autumn Equinox

The Autumn Equinox, or Fall Lesser Sabbat, is the second equinox of the Wiccan calendar year, as well as the second equinox of the Christian calendar year. Known by the Celtic name Mabon, and the Greek Festival of Dionysus, this equinox is celebrated around September 21, which makes it the third Lesser Sabbat of the year when following the standard calendar. However, as with all Lesser Sabbats, the exact day on which the festival is celebrated depends upon the time the sun enters its zodiac sign.

The symbolism associated with this sabbat is one of balance and harmony. It's a time when light and dark run parallel with each other, and for a brief time, day and night are proportionally equal. Therefore, it's appropriate that the Autumn Equinox is associated with the zodiac sign of Libra, which itself is the sign that represents balance and harmony.

Because the Autumn Equinox signifies the waning power and influence of the God and his slow decline toward the end of the cycle of life, there's also a declining-life theme associated with this sabbat. Though this decline is indicated in several ways, the two most telling signs are the degree to which the sun's power wanes in both its length of duration and intensity, as well as the declining fertility of the land.

Another important aspect of the sabbat depends on the area where you live. In olden times, most regions would have already harvested the summer crops by this time, thereby earning a brief respite from the hardships of daily life. For this reason, the Fall Lesser Sabbat is known as a time of relaxation and slowing down. Ancient Pagans viewed this as a rest period after the rigors of the harvest and a time to savor the bountiful fruits of their labors. For early people, there were other benefits produced at this time of year, too. Along with the bounty of the harvest, the relaxation time and slowed pace of life, this was the first real chance for socializing and renewing friendships, alliances, and family ties. This also holds true for the Samhain Sabbat, which shares some common traits with the Autumn Equinox. This renewed socializing was important to these early people for survival during the coming months, as well as for emotional and spiritual harmony.

When it comes to the actual sabbat, this is probably the least complicated ritual of the entire year, which is again a reflection of the underlying theme of slowing down and relaxation. Even though this is a leisurely time of year, it's essential to understand and appreciate the need to balance your inner Self. Up until now, all the deities, seasons, themes, and rituals have been climbing toward the pinnacle of Lughnasadh. Now, however, everything enters a time of balance, which will then gradually lead into decline. Yet, before this decline begins, it's extremely important for every person to realign their inner equilibrium so that the descent into the doldrums of winter will not adversely impact their spiritual harmony.

Although Samhain is the sabbat most often associated with the dead, the Autumn Equinox is actually the first time that departed ancestors are remembered.[1] This remembrance was carried out as either part of the ceremony or by way of a separate act and was done because it was believed that by paying tribute to departed souls during this sabbat, it ensured that when they returned at Samhain, they were predisposed toward peacefulness. To accomplish this, offerings were made to the spirits, burial mounds and cemeteries were visited, and graves were decorated to honor the dead.

SETUP

The preparation for this sabbat is extremely simple. In fact, the most time-consuming part will be decorating the altar, the Circle, and the cauldron. One quick point about decorating that must be completely understood is that there is a recurring "balance" theme. This is important for the harmony of the ritual and cannot be ignored. Therefore, when selecting decorations, remember that it's essential to intermix "light" with "dark." An example of this would be to use a yellow flower set against a dark green leaf—the symbolism in this example pattern is that of the sun/day (the yellow flower) against the night (the dark leaf).

The altar should be decorated with symbols of the harvest. Recommendations include using ears of corn and stalks of wheat, vines laden with grapes,[2] small branches filled with acorns or chestnuts, or any other plant that bears fruit. It's also advisable to add some color to the altar. Fall flowers or leaves that have turned color are perfect for this purpose.

While decorating the altar, it's also a good idea to add a little ambiance to the Circle itself. One suggestion that's very appealing is to wrap stalks of wheat around the candleholders of the Watchtower candles. This makes a very pleasing decoration and at the same time, presents a small offering of the harvest to the Watchtowers of the Circle. Make sure the stalks cannot be touched by the flame.

The final project will be to decide on how to decorate the cauldron. This, like the altar, should be adorned with items that represent the season and the harvest. Grapevines or thin leafy twigs are particularly useful as they can easily be wrapped around the cauldron. Once decorated, the cauldron is placed near the west quarter as a sign of the waning cycle of power and the waning cycle of the year.

After the decorating is finished, the rest of the preparation is very easy. A small bunch of leaves (about as many as can be held in one hand) should be placed in a bowl on the altar. These leaves can be from any type of tree, but oak or chestnut are best because they are nut-bearing trees. Hazelnut, walnut, pecan, or almond are also excellent choices, but they tend to be harder to find. Custom holds that leaves should be collected on the eve of the rite. However, in a warm climate where the leaves never turn color, green leaves can be collected in advance and colored with spray paint.[3]

While not a specific requirement for the rite, most denominations tend to follow a general pattern regarding clothing and usually dress in autumn colors. Red, yellow, and orange, are all excellent choices. Furthermore, flowing attire, or even something that is just loose fitting, is a highly recommended type of clothing used to symbolize the relaxation theme. At the same time, it's also advisable to dress in a manner that symbolizes the balance between light and dark. Some witches accomplish this be dressing in a two-scheme pattern, whereby they wear bright clothing on their upper torso and dark clothes from the waist down.

In the last twenty years or so, many Gardnerian and Alexandrian covens have added a grain tribute to their rites.[4] To follow this, a single stalk of wheat with the ear still attached should be put on a plate or dish and placed on the altar. Though wheat is recommended, any grain will suffice. In the event that a full stalk of grain can't be located, an ear of corn may be substituted.

Finally, set up the altar. Make sure to include the besom with the tools. A rule of thumb is that the broom should be placed to the east of the altar. Along with the decorations and the leaves, a dish containing fruit should be placed on the altar. If performing the grain tribute, the plate with the ear of grain is also placed on the altar. Everything else on the altar will be the same as always.

Gardnerian

The first step in this ceremony is the same as that in all the previous sabbats. Begin by consecrating the water/salt and casting the Circle. The opening should progress as usual and culminate with the Witches' Rune. However, it's only appropriate to recite one verse of the Witches' Rune because of the balancing aspect associated with this ceremony.

The ceremony now takes two different paths. The first is a traditional rite celebrating equilibrium, while the second is the Grain Tribute rite. If following the traditional path, the High Priest stands to the west side of the altar and the High Priestess to the east side. Taking the scourge, the High Priestess purifies the High Priest by lightly scourging him, in pairs of lashes, while reciting:

> *At this time of perfect equilibrium, I give you one lash for light and one lash for dark; one lash for balance and one lash for harmony; one lash for life and one lash for death. And in doing so, I purify you in the name of the Goddess Aradia and the Great God Cernunnos.*

As soon as the High Priestess finishes, the High Priest takes the scourge and repeats the same process on her. He uses the same wording, but reverse the order of the pairs:

> *At this time of perfect equilibrium, I give you one lash for dark and one lash for light; one lash for harmony and one lash for balance; one lash for death and one lash for life. And in doing so, I purify you in the name of the Great God Cernunnos and the Goddess Aradia.*

Once both coven leaders have been purified, the coven pairs off (male/female) and the members of each pair purify each other with the scourge. A variation calls for the High Priestess to scourge all the male witches and the High Priest to scourge all the female witches.

If performing the Grain Tribute, the Maiden takes the dish containing the wheat from the altar and places it in the center of the Circle. She returns to stand with the coven. The High Priestess faces the center of the Circle, arms spread in the Position of Power (minus the tools), and recites:

As it has been since the beginning of time, Day and Night, Light and Dark are now an equal part of the year. But this delicate balance will be broken soon, and the Dark will overpower the Light. Give thanks and remember what has been, for it shall be a long time before Light returns. Until then, the Earth shall remain barren, and Dark shall reign supreme. But fear not, for as the Wheel of the Year turns, the Light shall once again return to banish the Dark.

The Procession of the Harvest is now conducted. To perform this dance, the High Priestess and High Priest go to the edge of the Circle (at the east quarter) and with the coven behind them in male/female pairs, begin a slow ring-dance that spirals widdershins inward toward the center of the Circle. The path will lead the dancers to the dish with the wheat. The High Priestess and High Priest stop so that they're facing west. They kneel within reach of the dish (the coven fan out into an arc behind them), and the High Priestess recites:

In this seed lies the bounty and rebirth of the new year. Now that Light is waning, and the Dark is waxing, it is a time to reflect upon the end of the yearly cycle.

At this point, the ceremonies converge. The High Priestess stands at the west quarter facing the center of the Circle and the High Priest at the east. The coven members position themselves along the southern edge of the Circle, unless the Grain Tribute was performed, at which point they kneel in the center facing the altar. The High Priestess recites:

Farewell, O' Sun, ever-returning Light,
The hidden God, who ever yet remains;
Who now departs to the Land of Youth,
Through the Gates of Death,
To dwell enthroned, the judge of Gods and men,
The horned leader of the Hosts of Air.
Yet, as he stands unseen about the Circle,
So dwelleth He within the secret seed—
The seed of new-reaped grain;
Hidden in earth, the seed of the stars.
In Him is Life, and Life is the Light of man,
That which was never born and never dies.
Thus, the Wicca weep not, but rejoice.

The High Priestess and High Priest go to the center of the Circle (whether or not the Grain Tribute was performed) and lead the coven in an outward spiral ring-dance (deosil). During the dance, the Maiden takes the leaves and slowly scatters them as she walks. She should be the last in the procession. Keep in mind that the leaves float when they fall, so do not allow them to break the Circle! In order to ensure this, the Maiden should drop the leaves with the hand (her right) nearest the center. The Great Rite is then conducted. Following the Great Rite, the wine and cakes are shared. Blackberry wine is a Celtic specialty, and most Gardnerian covens substitute this for their normal ritual wine. The Candle Game is then held.[5]

To begin the game, all the men sit in a ring, facing inward, in the center of the Circle, and the women take up positions behind them. A lit candle is passed (deosil) from man to man while the women attempt to blow it out. A woman is only allowed to try blowing it out while it's in the hands of the man in front of her. Whenever a woman blows out the candle, she uses the scourge to give the man three light strokes. Then he turns and gives her the Fivefold Kiss (without the words). The candle is lit again, and the game resumes. It's customary for the game to continue until all women have succeeded in blowing out the candle at least once.

After the Candle Game, an offering is made to the aging Goddess. The High Priestess takes the chalice and pours wine onto the ground (or a libation dish) while reciting:

> *As darkness overtakes the land, we wait for the Goddess to return, knowing that Earth shall again be reborn when the light once again graces the sky. Blessed Be.*

The Circle is now banished and the feast, singing, dancing, and festivities begin.

Italian

This denomination celebrates the equinox by enacting a play in honor of the Lord of Light as he begins his slow departure into darkness. There are many different forms of this play in the various branches of the tradition. The following version relates the Stag God and the Wolf God theme.[6]

The altar is set up in the north, the cauldron in the west, and a candle (representing the Lord of Light) in the east. An uncut loaf of bread is placed on the altar along with a bowl of oak leaves. The altar and Circle are decorated with grapevines, leaves, fruit, nuts (especially acorns or chestnuts), and stalks of grain (wheat, oats, rye, or corn). If possible, a mask with antlers (Stag God), a mask with fur (Wolf God), and a crown (Moon Goddess) should be prepared in advance.[7] Assuming the High Priest will represent the Wolf God or Stag God, a male covener must be chosen to portray the other. The High Priestess plays the Goddess. If the High Priest or the High Priestess is not taking part, more participants will be required for the roles.

The ceremony begins with the Circle being cast and proceeds through the Charge of Aradia. At this point, the coven moves to the south and forms an arc along the edge, facing the center of the Circle. The High Priestess dons the crown in representation of the Moon Goddess, Diana. The High Priest, wearing the Stag God mask, stands at the east cardinal point, and the male witch, wearing the Wolf God mask, stands at the west quarter. The High Priestess recites:

We have come together on this holy night to bear witness to the turning of the Wheel of the Year. And in doing so, we shall bid farewell to the Lord of Light.

The Stag God leaves his place in the east and comes to the center of the Circle, where he bows to the Goddess. The High Priestess picks up the chalice from the altar, extends it outward in front of her with both hands towards the Stag God, and recites:

Great God of the Forests, Lord of Light, the seeds have come to fruit, the abundance of the harvest has been gathered, and the fields are bare. As your light slowly fades, the earth will again enter its long winter sleep. But with all life, there is death, just as with death, there is surely life. And so the Wheel turns.

The Stag God moves to the west, and the Wolf God chases him around the Circle as a symbol of the dark of the coming winter chasing after the light of the departing summer. After a few passes around the Circle, the Stag God is caught by the Wolf God (in the center of the Circle) and vanquished. The Stag God lies at the feet of the Wolf God. The Wolf God then recites:

I am the Lord of Shadows. Ruler of the Realms of Death and the Underworld. As the light of summer fades away, and the death of winter spreads over the land, know that the time of the Stag God has come to an end, and the time of the Wolf God has begun.

The Maiden goes to the altar, retrieves the bowl of leaves, and passes them out to the coven members. She returns to the altar and stands next to the High Priestess holding out the plate with the loaf of bread. Once everyone has their leaves and the Maiden is in place, the Wolf God returns to the west quarter and spreads his arms. This gesture is meant to symbolize the Gates of the Underworld being opened. The High Priestess recites:

The time of abundance is upon us. But ahead lie the lean times; the dark of winter when the land is barren. Let us partake in the celebration as we bid farewell to the Lord of Light, and pray that when the time is right, he is again reborn to drive the dark away. Come forth and pay tribute to our departed Lord.

One by one, the coven members file past the Stag God and drop their leaves on him. They should approach from the side the Maiden is on. After dropping the leaves, each person approaches the Maiden, breaks off a piece of bread from the loaf, and eats it. He or she then moves to the High Priestess, takes a sip of wine,[8] and returns to his or her original place along the edge of the Circle. The Maiden and High Priestess walk over to the Wolf God so that he can take a piece of bread and a sip of wine. Then they return to the altar. The High Priest removes the Stag God mask and places it in the cauldron. He joins the Maiden and High Priestess at the altar, and the three eat the bread and drink the wine.

Once everyone has had bread and wine, the remainder of the loaf is placed in the cauldron and an offering of wine is added (the wine can be poured onto the bread so that the bread absorbs it). After the offering is made, the Wolf God walks over to the east quarter and blows out the candle representing the God. He returns to the altar and faces the coven while the High Priestess (still representing the Goddess) recites:

Behold, the reign of the Light is no more, and the Dark shall rule until the Light returns. Hail and Farewell, Great Lord of Light. Hail and Farewell.

The coven repeat: *Hail and Farewell.*

This ends the drama. The Wolf God mask is removed, and the male witch returns to stand with the rest of the coven. The Maiden also rejoins the coven. The High Priestess and High Priest consecrate the cakes and wine, but do not share them with the coven at this point. Instead, they take a small offering of the cakes and wine to the west quarter, and they place it in the cauldron.[9] After returning to the altar, they offer a moment of silence for all to give thanks for the bounty of the year. The Circle is then banished, and the feast begins.

Saxon

This denomination holds a simple Autumn Equinox rite. Other than a few decorations, no special preparations are required. The altar is usually set in the center of the ritual area, but depending on its size, it can be placed in the north to create more room for dancing. Red is the traditional color for the altar cloth, but orange, brown, or black will also work. The colors to avoid are green and yellow.

Decorating is an important part of this rite. The Circle area should be ringed with fall flowers, acorns, pine cones, or grain stalks. Colored leaves are often scattered on the floor, and ears of corn are laid at the four cardinal points. A bowl of fruit (one piece for each person present, plus an extra piece as an offering to the Gods)[10] is placed on the altar alongside a bowl of nuts.

The ceremony begins with the Circle being cast and the Temple erected. The coven remains outside the Circle area. Once the Circle is cast, the Thegn rings the bell three times to summon the coven members, who enter through the gateway. The Priest greets them and then closes the gateway. The coven assembles along the southern edge of the Circle, the Priest stands beside the Priestess at the altar, the Thegn stands to the west, and the Scribe stands in front of the Priest/Priestess facing the coven. The Scribe then recites:

> *As the season of plenty draws to a close, we come together to celebrate the bounty of the summer, and prepare for the coming of winter. Listen now to the words of the Goddess.*

After his speech, the Scribe takes his place among the coven, and the Thegn again rings the bell three times. The Priestess (representing the Goddess)[11] then speaks to the coven:

> *In the spring, you sowed the seeds and planted the fields. And, with the Lord of the Greenwood by my side, I watched over them until the land was rich with life. As the fruits of your labors ripen, and the*

bounty of the earth is reaped, do not forget what we have given. For the light will soon give way to the dark, death will overtake life, and Woden will be with you throughout the dark months. But know that I do not forsake you, and when light returns I shall again fill the earth with my bounty. Hold fast my blessings for the coming months, as I hold fast to yours.

The Priest holds the bowl of consecrated water for the Priestess to dip her fingers in. She sprinkles a few drops of water on the Priest and recites:

To the seasons that have passed, and those as yet to come, the Lord Woden, and Lady Frig grant you their blessings in peace and happiness, love and joy.

In response, the Priest says: *And I grant them mine.*

The Thegn leaves his place and leads the coven past the altar so that the Priestess can bless each member. She uses a shortened blessing: *The Lord and Lady grant you blessings.* Each witch responds: *And them mine.* The Thegn rings the bell three more times, then the Priest and Priestess consecrate the cakes and ale. Hard cider is often substituted for the ale. Once the coven has shared in the cakes and ale, the Priestess gives a final blessing:

Blessed Lord and Lady, we thank you for the gifts that you bestowed upon us. Now that the bounty of the harvest is stored, we bid you farewell until the earth warms and the light returns. So be it.

The coven repeats: *So be it.*

This is the end of the ceremony. The Circle is banished, and the feast begins. As in other Celtic lands, blackberry wine/brandy is a traditional drink. Another staple of the Autumn Equinox is the baked apple.

West Country

The Autumn Equinox is another sabbat that this denomination did not celebrate in the past, but one that modern West Country witches have adopted. The most logical reason behind the tradition's failure to observe this day may be the very theme of the celebration—that of harvest. Since the harvest is an extremely busy time of year for rural areas, a festival would consume valuable time and energy that could be put to use in the fields gathering crops. But now that the season isn't filled with work, many modern West Country witches see no reason not to observe this sabbat.

Because of its lack of history, the ritual itself is a piecemeal adaptation from the rites of other traditions. Yet aside from this aspect, the West Country covens that celebrate the Fall Lesser Sabbat put just as much spirit into it as they do for their traditional holy days. Therefore, it's nearly impossible to tell that this is not an original West Country sabbat.

In decorating for this sabbat, the pastoral nature of the denomination is highlighted. Colored leaves are used for both decorations and ritual purposes. Leaves are used to decorate the altar. A colored leaf is placed under each cardinal point, and leaves are strewn around the Circle. The altar is also decorated with stalks of grain, ears of corn, grapevines, and fall flowers. If space permits, a Horn of Plenty is placed on the altar. If no space is available, it can be placed on a small side table or simply used as a centerpiece for the feast. The symbolism behind this is that the Horn is a phallic symbol of the God, and when it's filled with the fruits of the harvest, it represents the womb of the Goddess spilling forth the bounty of the earth. If the ceremony is held outdoors, cornstalks are bundled together into freestanding pillars and placed (outside the Circle) at the four quarters. The broom should also be kept close to the altar for easy access, and a candle should be placed in the center of the Circle area.

To begin the ceremony, the coven leader lights the center candle (representing the sun at its pinnacle). The Circle is cast and a normal esbat rite conducted up to consecrating the wine and cakes. The coven members position themselves along the southern edge of the Circle. The coven leader (usually a Priestess for this sabbat), standing in front of the altar facing the coven, recites:

Goddess of the Earth, as Light departs to unseen realms, and Darkness overtakes the land, comfort us with the knowledge that Light shall again return, and that the land shall again be reborn.

The assistant coven leader (usually a Priest) walks over to the candle in the center of the Circle and kneels beside it. He blows it out while the Priestess recites:[12]

Farewell, O' Sun, ever-returning light,
The hidden God, who ever yet remains.
He now departs to the Land of Youth,
Through the Gates of Death
To dwell enthroned, the judge of Gods and men,

The Horned Leader of the Hosts of Air.
As the swan flies south, and the leaves fall,
Let the seed sleep in the womb of the Great Mother,
Until the land is no longer covered under a blanket of darkness.

After this address, the Priest picks up the candle and returns to the altar. The Priestess (or a female witch who was selected in advance) takes the broom and, moving deosil, sweeps the leaves (which were scattered around the Circle floor) into a pile in the center of the Circle.[13] When all the leaves are collected, the broom is laid on top of the pile of leaves. Then, going from east to west, then west to east, the Priestess jumps (or steps) over the broom and leaves. This act symbolically represents the life/death cycle of the Light giving way to the Dark, then the cycle being reversed. Once the Priestess has jumped both ways, the Priest leads the coven members through the act. When everyone has taken a turn, the coven returns to the edge of the Circle, and the Priestess and Priest return to the altar. The Priestess recites:

As the Wheel of the Year turns, may the fading Light depart slowly, and keep the Dark at bay until at last it slowly overtakes the Earth. Yet even then, we shall ever be content to wait for the Light, for we know that it shall once again be reborn, and in doing so it shall reawaken the seed that sleeps in the womb of the Great Mother. So be it.

The coven repeat: *So be it.*

If this is an outdoor ceremony that has a bonfire, the leaves (or at least a handful of them) are thrown onto the fire. For indoor rites, a leaf should be burnt in a fireplace, censer, incense burner, or a dish. Symbolically, this practice has its roots in cremation, an act meant to return the body to the Mother Earth. In this case, the leaf represents the body, which is the bounty of the harvest.

After the leaf (or leaves) is burned, the wine and cakes are consecrated and shared with the coven or saved for the feast. Following this, the Circle is banished, and the ceremony is complete. The feast takes place with the usual dancing and singing. Another custom that modern West Country witches have adopted is the naming of a Harvest Queen. This female witch presides over the festivities of the Fall Sabbat and if of appropriate age and experience, is allowed to act as honorary coven leader until Samhain.

Samhain

The Samhain Greater Sabbat, which everyone today recognizes as Halloween, is certainly the most well-known of all the Wiccan holy days. As a matter of fact, it would probably be hard to find anyone who hasn't heard of Halloween. But of the countless people who think they know all about this day and its customs, how many of them really know what it represents? Learning about its roots is the first step in understanding the significance of the celebration.

Since all witches know that Samhain is celebrated on October 31, it's surprising that so many of them prefer to cite the "eve of November 1" as the official date of the sabbat. But, since this is technically the same night, most people naturally assume that this is just another play on words—and they're wrong. The difference in the wording of the dates is because Samhain marks the beginning of the Celtic calendar year. It is, in effect, Witchcraft's New Year's Eve. As such, many witches believe that to say the sabbat falls on October 31 is to abandon it to the old year, when it rightly belongs to the new year. Therefore, in this instance, the play on words has a very significant meaning, which is often overlooked.

The second most contemplated point is the origins of the name, of which there are two schools of thought. The first contention is that Samhain is derived from the Gaelic "Samhraidreadh," which translates to "summer's end." Since Samhain marks the dividing line between the end of summer and the beginning of winter, this seems the most likely origin. The second is that it's named after Samana (God of Death). As the beginning of the winter, a time of death, this theory also has distinct possibilities. But both concepts are theoretically equal, and the exact origin is of less importance than the symbolism connected to the sabbat.

Samhain is probably filled with more customs and symbolism than any other sabbat. It's therefore understandable that this is one of the most beloved, and famous, of all the Wiccan holy days. It is the first Greater Sabbat of the Celtic calendar year, making it the fourth and final of the standard calendar year. Known by the names Halloween, Hallowmas, Hallowe'en, All Hallows Eve, Celtic New Year, Celtic Winter, and the Third Harvest, it resembles all Greater Sabbats in that it's acknowledged as a fire festival. However, unlike the rest of the Greater Sabbats, the significance of most of the customs and folklore associated with this festival are commonly misunderstood. Beyond that, the misunderstandings are even more interesting given the fact that it was because of them that Halloween became so popular with nonwitches. And, in a bizarre twist of irony, these customs—trick-or-treating, costumes—are the same things that outrage many witches at the mention of the commercialized holiday. Yet, most of their misplaced feelings are simply the result of a lack of understanding surrounding the historical roots behind the festival; and a negative outlook on the benefits that commercialization has given to the overall image of Wicca.[1]

One of the most interesting bits of folklore associated with Samhain has to do with the veil that separates the living from the dead. Often referred to as the Feast of the Dead, Samhain has always been considered a special time to commune with deceased friends and relatives. In perpetuation of this belief, ancient lore proclaimed this night as the time when the spirits of the departed could easily enter the realm of the living because the veil that separates the two planes was easily transgressed. Since the spirits were those of friends and relatives, offerings of food, known as soul cakes, were left for the souls. However, if no offering was made, the spirits were said to become mischievous and harmful, feeling that they'd been overlooked or forgotten. Today, this custom of presenting offerings of food to those who show up on the doorstep is affectionately known as trick or treat.

Another ancient custom that has been transformed into popular usage is the practice of celebrating the sabbat by lighting magickal bonfires on the top of sidh-mounds. This Celtic practice allowed the spirits to enjoy the warmth of the Samhain fires, thereby encouraging the deceased to commune with friends and relatives in a peaceful manner. For those people who did not participate in this ritual, but still wanted protection from the spirits, the only alternative was to carve hideous faces in pumpkins, gourds, and turnips to frighten away the spirits. Over time, the bonfire and the carved pumpkin were combined into the famous "jack-o'-

lanterns" of today.[2] These were also carried by witches on their way to sabbat in order to drive away evil spirits.

There are also many other traditional legacies that have been carried over from Samhain and transformed into modern practices. And, although many people don't realize it, there is always a great deal of symbolism associated with these acts. For instance, the popular game of bobbing for apples developed from the belief that the apple symbolized the spirit of the Goddess Pomona and grabbing the apple ensured the good will of the Goddess until Yule.[3]

When this custom found its way into Celtic lands, the apple assumed a more general representation of the soul. By placing apples in a tub (originally a large cauldron, which symbolized the womb of life), early Celts believed that extracting the apple from the cauldron was equivalent to pulling a soul through the veil that separates life and death—symbolism that again went back to the Roman belief that the Goddess Pamona and the Goddess Fortuna were able to bring souls back from the Land of the Dead on this night. In other words, bobbing for apples became a symbol of rebirth and reincarnation.

Another legacy that has evolved into a present-day custom is the practice of wearing masks and costumes. This ancient tradition goes so far back in time that scholars are not sure of its original meaning, though it's believed that the mask symbolized a form of sympathetic magick. Ceremonial costumes have always been a part of the religion, but were further refined during the Inquisition to hide the identities of witches, much like hooded cloaks. In short, time and time again, many age-old practices from the Samhain Sabbat have been accepted into common usage.

For Wiccans, however, Halloween is about more than just fun and games. This holy day is a sacred occasion that represents one of the best times of the year for communing with the souls of the departed. Unfortunately, when it comes to communing with the dead, a great many people—even many that are involved in witchcraft, spiritualism, or the occult—think that spirits are invoked whenever it's convenient for us. Just to set the record straight, spirits are invited to join us; they're not commanded to appear. They're not the family dog that comes running when called in the hope of being petted or fed. They're not employees who fear losing their jobs. And they're definitely not slaves. They're the spirits of departed friends and relatives, and they deserve the same respect that they enjoyed while alive. So, anyone with the notion that holding a séance allows the dead to be controlled, think again. Remember, always be respectful of spirits, and they'll always be respectful and helpful to you. Enough said.

The final tradition that needs to be examined is the feast itself. Now, some witches may think that this is just the social part of the festival, as it is with many of the other sabbats. If this were true, then the feast would rightly take second place to the actual ritual. However, during Samhain, the feast is just as important as the religious rites. This is because the eating, drinking, and festivities in general represent a symbolic challenge to the coming darkness of winter. By celebrating in such dramatic fashion, witches are openly defying the harshness and death of the coming season, while proclaiming their belief in life and the future fertility of the land.

SETUP

The preparations for this sabbat are very time consuming, but they're also fun. Since there are a few items that need to be constructed, which will probably take some time, it's a good idea to begin a week or two in advance. Also, when it comes to decorating and celebrating, try to enjoy both the Wiccan Samhain and the ordinary Halloween at the same time, rather than taking offense at the modernized version of this holiday. Granted, the commercially recognized symbols of Halloween are not especially flattering to witches, but the popularity and lighthearted attitude of the season is what really matters. Try to carry this spirit over into the celebration.

Samhain is a festival in which the decorations should convey a very lighthearted attitude. Remember, the underlying theme is defying the coming death of winter. In order to accomplish this, incorporate some of the bounty of the harvest and some traditional items such as jack-o'-lanterns. Even adding some commercial Halloween decorations such as paper ghosts or skeletons is fine. In keeping with the ancient use of jack-o'-lanterns, it's possible to use small pumpkins (so as not to break the Circle) as the Watchtowers. This is done by simply carving out the pumpkins and placing the Watchtower candles—which should be red for Samhain—inside to help guard the Circle from unwanted spirits.

The cauldron should be heavily decorated with colored leaves, stalks of corn, or grapevines. It's placed in the center of the Circle, and an incense burner, or dish, upon which incense can be burned, is placed inside. An open-faced plate is usually recommended over an enclosed burner or covered censer as it will be easier to sprinkle incense onto the open plate without interrupting the ceremony. Also, do not light the charcoal ring until just before casting the Circle. In conjunction with the incense burner, a subject that is often overlooked is the incense itself. Since this occasion is all about showing contempt for death, soothing spirits, and promoting good will, the incense should have a sweet scent. This is also a perfect time to burn magickal herbs for special devotional purposes.

As Samhain is governed by the Lord of Misrule,[4] a special wand needs to be constructed for his use. Nowadays, this can be either a wand or a staff, though it likely originated from a walking staff. Bear in mind that this item is used only once a year, during the Lord's six-week rule from Samhain to Yule, so the amount of time and effort put into making it is a matter of personal preference. To get some ideas for constructing this item, remember that it eventually became the court jester's staff, which found its way into history amusing royalty. Copying this popularized design is a good starting point.

The following method of construction can be applied to either implement. (1) For a wand, use a sixteen- to eighteen-inch dowel. For a staff, use a five- to seven-foot broom handle. Paint the shaft one or more bright colors, and add pictures or symbols. (2) Fill a piece of cloth with dried beans or plastic beads to form a small head. Secure this onto the top of the wand/staff. (3) Add a ruffled collar at the point where the wood and head come together to hide the junction. (4) Add a floppy, four-cornered, multicolored hat, and attach bells to the hat and/or around the collar. Also, a lot of covens go to the added trouble of making a Crown of Mischief, too. This is nothing more than a court jester's hat. It should match the hat on the wand/staff. While this really isn't necessary, it does liven up the ceremony. However, the quality of the items themselves is insignificant, and the symbolic value is all that matters.

Aside from the altar, the most important part of the setup preparation will involve the food and drink for the feast. This should be as elaborate as possible, and there should be a large assortment of fruits and vegetables from which to choose. Also, with the exception of vegetarians, it's important to have meat for this feast. Samhain is the end of the harvest season and the beginning of the hunt. It's a time when ancient people stored meat for the coming months, and a time when the herds were culled of the weakest animals, making meat plentiful. It has thus become customary to serve meat at Samhain. Along with the meat, things such as fruit, nuts, bread, and ale (or beer) are all standard fare. Green salad, and summer vegetables should be excluded.

Because this is considered one of the best times for contacting spirits, it also enjoys a reputation as a perfect time for divination. Therefore, it's customary to have a crystal ball, scrying mirror, or other divinatory tool on hand. Some covens prefer to use a large, dark-colored, water-filled bowl, or even the smoke from incense, as this allows the entire coven to participate at the same time.

Finally, the altar is laid out in the usual fashion. No special tool layout is needed, but the broom, staff and/or crown for the Lord of Misrule should be close at hand. There should also be fruit (especially apples) and nuts on the altar. Corn, wheat, colored leaves, vines with grapes, branches with nuts, pumpkins, gourds, and squash should be all around the altar and Circle.

Gardnerian

The ritual begins with the Circle being cast, paying particular attention to setting the Watchtowers. A traditional esbat is then conducted all the way to the end of the Charge. The High Priest gives the High Priestess the Fivefold Kiss, but she does not reciprocate.[5] Normally, the Bagahi laca bachabe verse would now be recited. However, for Samhain, it's recited after the Invocation to the Great God. This occurs because the Bagahi laca bachabe verse is added to the beginning of the Witches' Rune, as part of the chant, for two reasons: (A) to increase the length of the dance in an effort to build more power; and (B) to be more inviting to spirits. After the chant ends, the sabbat ceremony begins. The consecration of the wine and cakes, and the Great Rite, are put off until later in the ceremony.

With the coven in an arc along the southern edge of the Circle, the High Priestess faces the cauldron (in the center of the Circle) with the sword raised slightly above her shoulders using a two-handed grip.[6] The coven members have their athames out and follow her movements. While drawing the Invoking Pentagram of Earth[7] in the air, the High Priestess recites:

> *Glorious Goddess Aradia, let this sign mark the entrance to the magickal Portals between the Worlds.*

The High Priestess lowers the sword and places it back on the altar. The coven members put away their athames. She then walks to the south side of the cauldron and sprinkles incense on the burner—a sufficient amount so that it burns for several minutes, but not so much that it becomes overpowering. With the coven behind her, she turns to face the altar, raises her arms over the cauldron, and recites:

O' Mighty God, Lord of the Underworld, on this holy night we bid thee to fling open the Gates of the Realm of the Departed Souls, that we may be free to commune with our ancestors who no longer walk in this world. Come to this sacred place, O' Great God of Life and Death, and allow us this night for remembrance.

As the High Priestess lowers her arms, the High Priest leaves the altar and stands on the west side of the cauldron. The High Priestess moves to the east side so that she's facing him. The Maiden now goes to the altar and retrieves the altar candle and a little more incense. She returns to the cauldron, but remains on the north side. When everyone is positioned, the Maiden sprinkles a little more incense onto the cauldron burner. The High Priestess recites:

Dread Lord of Shadows, God of Life, and Bringer of Death; Yet is the knowledge of thee, the knowledge of Death. Open wide, I pray thee, the Gates through which all must pass. Let our dear ones, who have gone before, return this night to make merry with us. And when our time comes, as it must, O' thou the Comforter and the Consoler, the Giver of Peace and Rest, we will enter thy realms gladly and unafraid. For we know that when rested and refreshed among our dear ones, we will be reborn again by thy grace, and the grace of the Great Mother. Let it be in the same place and the same time as our dear ones, that we may meet, and know, and remember; and love them again. Descend, we pray thee, on thy servant and priest.

The High Priestess walks (deosil) around the cauldron until she's standing in front of the High Priest. He's taken a step backwards to provide her with a little more space. She now proceeds to give him the Fivefold Kiss. Immediately following this salute, the Maiden goes to the altar and walks in a slow (widdershins) spiral around the Circle until she is back in the center of the Circle. This should be done in three passes. Once the circling is completed, the High Priest gives a signal for the coven members to move to the west quarter. They stand shoulder to shoulder, alternating male/female, to form a pathway leading to the center of the Circle where the Maiden, High Priest, and High Priestess have taken up positions on the east side of the cauldron. Facing west, the High Priestess recites:[8]

Listen and hear these words, all who have come to this world. We open the Western gateway, and welcome you forth, that we may freely and peacefully commune with you on this blessed night. For on this sacred night, the Lord of the Dead allows the veil between the worlds to be easily breached, that our dear ones may visit the land of the living. Come! Follow the Maiden on her spiral path, and she shall lead you into the warmth of the light.

All three people now perform a different task. The High Priestess moves to the other side of the cauldron, directly in front of the pathway, and assumes the Welcoming Gesture. She also sprinkles a little more incense into the cauldron. At the same time, the High Priest walks down the pathway and ritually opens a doorway in the Circle so that the spirits can enter. He also steps out of the way so as not to block the doorway. As soon as the doorway is cut, the Maiden (having followed the High Priest) begins another slow spiral to the center of the Circle. The High Priestess resumes reciting the greeting:

Welcome spirits! Come and share in the feast that we have laid in your honor. May you remain with us in peace. For on this most holy night, all of our thoughts and prayers are for you.

As soon as the Maiden reaches the center of the Circle, the High Priest seals the doorway by retracing the original cut. The High Priestess then recites:

Now is the time for true welcome. May the spirits that have come to this sacred spot be at peace, and may they share in the bounty of the feast that we have laid. Make known to us your mysteries, that they may aid us in strengthening our own lives.

If the incense smoke in the cauldron has died down, recharge it. There are now a few different events that can take place: (1) divination; (2) offerings to the spirits; (3) a power raising ring-dance; or (4) meditation. These can be carried out separately, combined, or omitted completely. Whichever path is chosen, the High Priestess must call an end to it after she feels that it's gone on long enough. The coven moves to the eastern side of the Circle[9] and forms another pathway. The High Priest walks to the end and waits while the High Priestess returns to the west side of the cauldron and faces down the pathway. The Maiden retrieves the altar candle and goes to the west side of the cauldron. Since the High Priestess is there, the Maiden stands directly behind her. Once the Maiden is settled, the High Priestess recites:

At this time, which is like no other, in a place that does not exist except where we have created it, on this most sacred night of Samhain, in the presence of the spirits of our ancestors, we give thanks and praise in honor of the Goddess and her Consort, the Horned God.

The Maiden now walks in a deosil outward spiral, leading the spirits in an outward procession. Just before she begins, the High Priest cuts a doorway for the spirits to exit. As the Maiden walks, the High Priestess recites:

O' Merciful Goddess, Mother of the Earth, O' Mighty God, Guardian of the Portal between the Worlds, bless the flames of this world, that although the light is swallowed by the dark, it shall again be reborn to burn brightly and renew the flame of life.

As soon as the Maiden reaches the doorway, the entire coven observes a moment of silence, at the end of which, the High Priest seals the doorway. It's now time to conduct the Great Rite. However, because there is so much symbolism at this time of year, the Great Rite should be done with extreme care in order to emphasize the true meaning that it holds.[10] When the rite is over, another moment of silence is observed to think about the meaning of the ritual and to affirm the belief in life and reincarnation. The wine and cakes are consecrated and shared with the coven. This marks the official end of the ceremony.

It's now time for the festivities. But before you begin the party, it's time to crown the Lord of Misrule. This involves a small ceremony where the person being appointed as the Lord is crowned and given his wand/staff. He's then allowed to make a pass around the Circle so that each coven member can playfully bow or curtsy to him. Back at the altar, he recites:

I, having been named the Lord of this night, hereby decree that mischief and merriment shall be the law until the fire dies. So mote it be.

The formal ceremony is over, and it's time to eat, drink, and rejoice. Before this, however, the Circle must be banished. As always, once the Circle is banished, singing and dancing are encouraged.

Italian

Shadowfest is one of the names that this denomination uses for Halloween. And judging by the extreme importance that's placed upon the aspect of death and rebirth, this name is very appropriate. In addition to the normal esbat layout, there are two red candles placed on the altar, the Watchtower candles are black, and there must be a white candle for each coven member. The altar can be set up by the north quarter or center of the Circle.[11]

The ceremony begins with the Circle being cast. Immediately following the casting, the High Priest moves to the west quarter where he stands in the Slain God Position.[12] The coven members arrange themselves around the perimeter of the Circle, while the High Priestess stands in the center of the Circle facing the High Priest. The cauldron is in the east quarter. The High Priestess recites:

> *Blessed Goddess and God, on this night of beginning and end, bless this sacred gathering of your children, and protect us as we honor you.*

The Myth of the Descent of the Goddess is now recited or performed. If it's to be acted out, the following roles must be assigned prior to the ceremony: Narrator, Goddess, Lord of the Underworld, and Guardian of the Portals. On the other hand, if the Myth is simply recited, the High Priest and High Priestess change places, and the High Priestess recounts the tale. But since reciting the story is rather anticlimactic, the theatrical version is the one most often chosen. This is the version given below.

Before the story can be acted out, everyone must be provided with the props needed for their roles.[13] The Goddess receives a necklace and a veil. The Guardian receives a single red or black cord, which he loosely ties around his waist. The Lord holds the coven sword, plus he's given a crown and a black or red scarf (which he wears like a cape). When everyone has their accessories, the participants take the following positions: The Narrator stands to the east; the Lord of the Underworld stands in front of the west quarter; the Goddess stands to the north; and the Guardian of the Portals stands in the center of the Circle facing the Goddess. The coven sits around the southern edge of the Circle, facing the center. Once everyone is prepared, the Narrator begins:

> *In ancient times, the Dread Lord of the Shadows was lonely. But our Lady, the Goddess, would solve all mysteries, even the mystery of*

death. So she journeyed to the Underworld upon the Sacred River of Descent, where she came upon the seven gates. And at each of the gates, the Guardian of the Portals challenged her . . .

The Goddess steps forward, and the Guardian challenges her:

Strip off your garments, and lay aside your jewels. For you may bring nothing with you into this, our realm.

The Goddess removes her necklace and lays it at the feet of the Guardian.[14] The Guardian removes the red/black cord from his waist and binds the Goddess with it. Her arms are behind her back, and the cord is tied around her wrists, then the ends are draped over her shoulders and tied around her neck with the loose ends hanging down over her chest. The Narrator continues:

So she laid down her garments and her jewels and was bound, as all living things must be who seek to enter the realms of Death and the Mighty Ones. By the seventh gate, the Goddess was naked and bound. And then was she presented to the Lord.

Taking the ends of the cord, the Guardian leads the Goddess forward until she is facing the Lord. Although she's facing west, she's still close to the center of the Circle. The Guardian then releases her and steps aside. The Narrator continues:

Such was her beauty that the Lord himself knelt, bowed his head, and laid his sword and crown at her feet . . .

The Lord kneels and lays the sword at the feet of the Goddess, then removes the crown and lays it with the sword. He kisses the feet of the Goddess and says:

Blessed are your feet, that have brought you down this path. I beg of you to stay here with me, and let me touch your heart.

Standing up, the Lord places his hands on the Goddess' chest (above her heart). She responds:

No, for I love you not. Why do you cause all the things that I love, and take delight in, to fade and die?

The Lord moves his hands away from the Goddess and says:

My Lady, you speak of age and fate, against which I am helpless. Age causes all things to wither; but when men die, at the end of time, I give them rest, peace, and strength. For in time, they may return to the living. But you are so lovely that I ask again that you not return, but stay and abide with me.

Taking a half-step backwards, the Goddess says:

No. For I love you not.

The Lord picks up the scourge (which should be close by). He faces the Goddess and says:

If you refuse my love, then you must kneel to Death's Scourge.

The Goddess responds: *It is fate, and better so.* She kneels before the Lord as he gives her several light lashes. After the last stroke, the Goddess says:

I now know your pain, for I know the pain of love.

Laying down the scourge, the Lord helps the Goddess to her feet. He then kneels at her feet and says: *Blessed are you.* He gives her the Fivefold Kiss (no words are recited) and says:

Thus may you attain to joy and to knowledge.

At this point, the Narrator takes over the story:

And he taught her all the mysteries and gave her the necklace, which is the circle of rebirth.

The Lord picks up the necklace and puts it on the Goddess. She picks up the crown and puts it on his head. The Narrator continues:

And she taught him the mystery of the sacred cup, which is the cauldron of rebirth.

From here on, the Narrator may merely read the rest of the story. But this is a little boring, so the remainder of the play is usually acted out as follows: The pair moves to the altar. The Goddess should be on the left (west) and the Lord on the right (east). The Goddess picks up the chalice, the Lord puts his hands over hers, and the Narrator says:

They loved and were one, for there be three great mysteries in the life of man; and love controls them all. To fulfill love, you must return again at the same time, and at the same place, as those you loved before; and you must meet, and know, and remember, and love them again.

After putting down the chalice, the pair faces the coven. The Lord assumes the God Position, the Goddess assumes the Goddess Position, and the Narrator continues:

But to be reborn, you must die and be made ready for a new body. And to die, you must be born; and without love you may not be born. But our Goddess is inclined to love, and joy, and happiness; and she guards and cherishes her hidden children in this life and the next. And in death she reveals the way to her communion, even as in life she teachs the mystery of the Magick Circle, which is placed between the worlds.

This is the end of the Myth, though the Lord (i.e., the High Priest) remains where he is for the time being. The Guardian and Narrator rejoin the coven. The High Priestess moves to the west quarter and recites:

Death moves ever forward. And, for a time, the Goddess dwells in the Realm of the Shadows. But this time will pass, and the seasons will ever change once more. Let us therefore embrace the Lord. Blessed be O' Mighty Horned One.

The High Priest assumes the Slain God Position as the High Priestess approaches him. When she's standing directly in front of him, she marks the Invoking Pentagram of Earth[15] on him and recites:

O' Mighty Lord of Death, we welcome you to join us. Your time of power is at hand, and we desire your presence that we may know you, love you, and honor you. O' Mighty Lord, come now, to be among us.

Following the invitation, the High Priestess kisses the High Priest on the lips. Then he walks over to the east quarter. Facing the center of the Circle, he recites:

I am the Lord you seek. The Great God of the Hunt; the Wolf God; the Lord of the Realm of Shadows. I have come in answer to your call, that you may know that I do not forsake you. Look upon me and know that I am always with you, as you are always with me; for we are one.

Each coven member now comes forward, and the High Priestess gives each one a white candle. They take the candle and light it from the altar candle. Once everyone's candle is lit, they stand and wait along the west side of the Circle. The High Priest joins the High Priestess at the altar, and the pair consecrates the wine and cakes. In consecrating the wine, they perform a symbolic mating of the God and Goddess (think symbolic Great Rite). When the wine and cakes are consecrated, the coven approaches the altar in a single-file line. The High Priestess offers each person a sip of wine. The High Priest then offers a piece of the cakes. After each coven member accepts the cake, the High Priest blows out his or her candle. This symbolizes the end of light. As soon as the candles are all extinguished, the coven members toss them into the cauldron. This represents the light sleeping in the womb of the Great Mother. The coven returns to the south, and the High Priestess recites:

The dark times are beginning, and the light sleeps until the turning of the Wheel reawakens it. But fear not for we are protected. Therefore, let us be loving and joyful, and let this feast proclaim our faith in the promise of that which is to come.

The coven responds: *Blessed be.*

At this point, it's appropriate for the coven to file by the High Priest and High Priestess, where each member receives a hug and kiss; females from the High Priest, males from the High Priestess. This concludes the ritual. The Circle is banished, and the feast begins.

Saxon

This denomination holds to the same general symbolism as the others (i.e., the summer Goddess giving way to the winter God), but constructs its ritual in a slightly different way. Instead of having the Priestess and Priest take turns throughout the ceremony, the Saxon rite mirrors the seasonal symbolism by dividing the ceremony into two halves. The Priestess conducts the first half, and the Priest conducts the second. Other than that, and a few minor accessories such as a simple crown for the God and a chaplet of flowers for the Goddess, the ceremony is very uncomplicated.[16]

As with all sabbats, the Circle is cast, and an esbat rite is conducted up to the consecration of the cakes and ale. The Priest moves to the center of the Circle and kneels facing the Priestess as she recites:

The summer draws to a close, and the winter shall soon begin, much as the Goddess Frig gives way to Woden, her Consort. Praise be to the Goddess Frig.

Coven responds: *Praise be to Frig.*
The Priestess raises the sword (or seax) and recites:

O' Glorious Goddess, we give thanks to you for the bounty of the summer; for the warmth, the harvest, and the new life that was bestowed upon the land. And as this time marks the end of your reign, we pray that you shall return again next year when your time is once again upon us. Until then, with love we bid you farewell, and we pray that your Consort shall guide us safely through the dark. Praise be to the Goddess Frig.

Coven responds: *Praise be to Frig.*
The Priestess lowers the sword and places it back on the altar. She picks up the crown, walks over to the kneeling Priest, and holds out the crown. As she places it on his head, she recites:

This is the symbol of Woden, God of Life and Death, the Lord who guards us through the hardships of the coming winter. While you wear this, you speak, act and lead us for the Lord. Guide us through the darkness, that we may again revel in the return of our Lady Frig.

The Priest stands and kisses the Priestess, then turns to face the coven. She backs away until she's standing by the altar. He recites:

As the Lord of Life and Death, I will protect you from the winter until the coming of spring. Know that while I am with you, there is always light, hope, life, and the promise of the coming year. So be it.

Coven members respond: *So be it.*
The Priest joins the Priestess at the altar. They kiss and embrace. One by one the coven members file past the Priest and Priestess, who kiss and embrace them. Some covens have Priest and Priestess kiss each member, while others have the Priestess kiss the men and the Priest the women.

Once the last person has returned to the edge of the Circle, the Priest removes the crown, holds it outward above his head, and recites:

The time of celebration is upon us. Let us honor the Lord for what he has given us, and what is yet to come. Let us welcome forth our ancestors, that they may join us as we feast in this time of plenty. And let us be joyous and merry, that we may show that we are unafraid of the coming of winter. This task I charge the Lord of Mischief. So be it.

Again, the coven responds: *So be it.* There's now a choice. Some covens appoint the Lord of Mischief first, then consecrate the cakes and ale second, while others do it the opposite way. Either is acceptable. Whoever was chosen to be the Lord of Mischief steps forward and is given the crown and staff by the Thegn.[17] The Lord recites:

Having been appointed Lord of the sabbat, I hereby proclaim that mischief and revelry shall be my law. But the night is fleeting, so abandon yourself in dance and song and merriment.

The Priest and Priestess consecrate the cakes and ale. This is the end of the ceremony. As soon as the Circle is banished, the reign of the Lord of Mischief begins, as do the festivities.

West Country

The November Eve Sabbat, or Samhain, is the fourth festival (according to a standard calendar) celebrated by this denomination. And because there are only five recognized sabbats, each one takes on an importance beyond that of other traditions. In the rural regions where this denomination originated, this sabbat marked the first opportunity for people to relax and enjoy the fruits of their spring/summer labors. Because of this, they went to great lengths in their Samhain preparations. Abundant decorations were prepared as was an elaborate Circle complete with bonfires at each quarter. Food and ale were plentiful, and the atmosphere reflected a sense of relief that the crops were safely harvested for winter. In fact, the merriment was so great that nonwitches were even encouraged to attend the festivities. This promoted good will with the Gods and local residents.

The Circle is eighteen feet with a bonfire in the center. The altar is heavily decorated with fruits, vegetables, nuts, fall flowers, and garlands. Apples, wheat, rye, potatoes, and corn (which were extremely important crops to early West Country people) are placed around the perimeter of the Circle. Potatoes and corn were often baked in the quarter bonfires. Another custom, though usually not followed today, calls for the men to carry their grain scythes or sickles and the women to carry small hand-baskets.[18] The May Queen (crowned at Beltane) and Priestess (coven leader) preside over the ceremony, while the assistant coven leader (the Priest), representing the God, remains outside the Circle until the very end of the rite.

The ceremony begins with the Circle being cast and the wards set. But then, instead of a normal esbat being performed, a male witch comes forward and assists the May Queen in consecrating the wine and cakes. Holding the chalice, the May Queen recites:

The Wheel of the Year turns, the fruits of the fields have been reaped, and the season of plenty draws to a close. We now give thanks to the Great Mother for the bounty of the harvest.

The Priestess takes a cake and crumbles it onto the ground. Then the May Queen pours out an offering of wine on top of the cake. The Priestess recites:

What was once grown in the earth, is now returned. Let this offering sustain the Goddess during her long winter sleep.

Two chants follow. The first is a ring-dance performed by the entire coven in honor of the Goddess. Any rhythmic chant may accompany the dance, but the wording should incorporate reference to the bounty of the harvest and the changeover of the seasons. A popular verse follows:

Apples and nuts and colored leaves,
The time draws near, it's November Eve;
Honey and barley and lots of corn,
We sing and dance, 'til the Dark God is born;
Fields and meadows and orchards grow cold,
Praise be to the Goddess, and the Gods of old.

Immediately following this chant/dance, the women go to the center of the Circle and stand around the bonfire (or cauldron),[19] the men dance (deosil) around the perimeter of the Circle, and everyone chants:

Welcome to our Mighty Lord,
Who comes in answer to our word;

Herne the Hunter, Dark of night,
Guard us while we wait for Light;
God of Winter, guide the way,
Until the Goddess, again can stay;
And while we wait, for what shall be,
We call the Lord, for all to see;
The Earth will sleep, while fires burn,
Give praise to Herne, that the Wheel will turn;
For as we laugh and dance and sing,
The time is now, come join our ring.

Once the chant ends, the Priest enters the Circle. He makes one pass around the Circle, then he goes to the altar and replaces the May Queen. She joins the rest of the coven. The Priest and Priestess then silently exchange the Fivefold Kiss. This is the normal end of the ritual. As the new coven leader,[20] the Priest banishes the Circle, and the feast begins.

Winter Solstice

The Winter Solstice, or the Yule Sabbat, is the fourth Lesser Sabbat of the year according to the Christian (standard) calendar, though it's the first when following the Celtic calendar. Regardless of the method of measurement, Yule is celebrated as close to December 22 as possible, depending on the sun's entry into Capricorn.

An important feature of Yule is that it represents the point where the year changes from waning to waxing. During Midsummer, the year changed the opposite way, from waxing to waning. In the Northern Hemisphere, Yule is the time when the sun reaches its southernmost position in its yearly rotation, thereby creating the shortest day (and longest night) of the year. Early witches knew that after this point the days would gradually lengthen as the sun journeyed to its northernmost point during Midsummer.

Thus, this is the time of year when the Holly King (God of the Waning Year) dies and gives way to the Oak King (God of the Waxing Year). This dual deity is also represented in some traditions by the wren (waning) and robin (waxing).[1] This renewed God theme is, therefore, one that symbolizes the rebirth of light and the renewed fertility of the land.

However, the God is not the only deity that's associated with this sabbat. The Goddess is represented during Yule, too, and she is also identified with rebirth. In fact, it's at this time of year that she not only becomes the mother of the God, but also his lover. The God is usually portrayed in a son/lover concept with the Goddess. This theme emerges at the Winter Solstice when she gives birth to him. Then he impregnates her with the seed of life. Yule logs are a Celtic depiction of this concept. This theme is not limited to Wicca. There are many versions of it throughout the various religions of the world—from the Christian Christmas Nativity to the Ancient Greek Festival of Dionysos—that all occur around this time of year. It's because of these details that this ritual is such an important milestone in the yearly cycle of life when the solar cycle reverses course and the days begin to lengthen. Symbolically, it's the death of the dark and birth of the light, along with the transformation of the Goddess into her life-bearing form.

Another fact that's often overlooked is that witches celebrate Christmas. Now, some people are probably perplexed by the notion that a Pagan would celebrate a Christian holiday. However, Winter Solstice was a Pagan holy day long before Christianity existed. Further, since the entire Christian Christmas concept (i.e., the son of God transformed to Savior) is based on the Wiccan son/God theme, Christmas itself must be considered a direct spin-off from Paganism. Under these circumstances, it's perfectly logical for witches to enjoy it, too.

In case this information isn't convincing enough, a little research into the subject of Christmas discloses that Old Saint Nick, or Santa Claus as he is now known, is obviously a Christianized version of Nik. Digging even more will further unearth the fact that Nik was a name used for Woden, who was associated with the God of the Waning Year. Thus, the Christianized symbol of holiday gift giving (Santa Claus) was originally a Pagan deity.[2] In case this still isn't enough, just remember that this is a time of great joy, love, and generosity, which by itself should be sufficient encouragement to accept Christmas. In short, there is no reason for witches to shut themselves off from the seasonal festivities. Most importantly, though, this is a season of peace and goodwill. Whether Christian or Wiccan, these ideals should always be celebrated.

Beyond the general symbolic associations of these sabbats, there are numerous customs and practices that highlight specific themes and beliefs. For instance, mistletoe, holly, and pine are all Druidic influences that have been widely adopted into the season. The custom of kissing under mistletoe evolved from the Druid handfasting rite whereby the marriage vows were sealed with a kiss underneath a sprig of mistletoe. Christmas trees developed from the Druidic practice of decorating pine trees with images of things that they hoped the new year would hold for them.[3]

But the Druids weren't the only ones to contribute to this cultural phenomenon. Celtic and Norse customs, such as lighting fires to lure back the sun or ringing bells to herald back the light after the long season of dark, have all been incorporated into the modern festivals. Wreaths were also commonplace at ancient Yule celebrations to represent the Wheel of the Year, and the Yule log has always been a phallic symbol of the Oak God. In other words, although Christmas may have become a Christianized holiday, its roots and symbolism belong to the various Pagan religions.

SETUP

The preparation for this sabbat is fairly lengthy. But since some of the items were constructed for other ceremonies, a few of the articles may already be made. If not, there are a few things that need to be assembled for the ritual.

The three crowns—Oak Crown, Holly Crown, and Crown of Flowers—are first and foremost. The first two were made for Midsummer and Beltane and can be reused. Otherwise, construct the crowns as follows.

To build the Oak Crown, take thin twigs from an oak tree and interweave them into a circular wreath to form a chaplet. An alternative is to attach oak branches to a solid base that's easy to work with. Wire wreaths are a good bet for this type of foundation because they are pre-formed. It's also advisable to attach green oak leaves as a sign of new life. But because these are almost impossible to find in most areas at this time of the year, it's okay to paint a few leaves green to add the symbolism.

The Holly Crown is just as simple to make. The same directions apply, except holly is used in place of the oak branches. Also, since holly is very supple, it should be much easier to weave into a circular wreath without the need for an underlying support.

The Crown of Flowers is nothing more than a simple interwoven circlet of flowers formed into a light chaplet.[4] Remember, it's the symbolism, not the object, that matters.

As with Midsummer, a dark-colored scarf or a large piece of dark material is needed. This will again be used as a shroud, but this time for the Holly King. For convenience, this item should be placed near the altar or wherever your accessories are stored.

As a symbol of the womb and rebirth, the cauldron occupies a prominent place during this sabbat and thus should be decorated. The first thing that needs to be added to the cauldron is a candle. This may be a seasonal Yule candle that's purchased especially for the rite or a common ceremonial candle that's been garnished with pine needles. The cauldron itself should be adorned with Yuletide seasonal decorations, such as ivy, pine boughs, mistletoe, or even Christmas ornaments. Also, keep in mind that commercial accessories such as garland or tinsel will work nicely. Once decorated, the cauldron should be placed beside the south quarter.

A Yule log is an indispensable item because it adds a touch of symbolism and ancient custom to the ceremony. But because this item has been passed down through the ages, there are a lot of different views concerning it. The log itself is a phallic symbol that is almost always cut from an oak tree.[5] Early practice was to decorate the log with intertwined mistletoe, holly, and evergreen to represent the Triple-Goddess and God uniting. The adorned log was then placed on the fire in an attempt to entice the light and warmth to return to the land—a form of sympathetic magick. Others used the Yule log as an ornamental object on the hearth or altar. This version still had the holly, evergreen, and mistletoe attached to it, but three candles were added to represent the Goddess.

Modern denominations have gotten away from burning the log and have instead moved toward the decorative form. To make an ornamental Yule log, drill three (candle-size) holes into a twelve- to fifteen-inch oak log, then plane the underside until it sits flatly. Insert three decorative candles into the holes, and attach mistletoe, holly, and evergreen to the wood. In the event that the log is going to be burned, the candles are removed just before the log is placed on the fire.

Decorating also plays a big part in this celebration. Where space permits, some witches like to have a Christmas tree in the same room as the Circle, although it's always kept outside the Circle perimeter. Others, however, seem to think that this is too much a symbol of commercialism and deem it inappropriate for the worship area. Likewise, some witches keep the lights on the Christmas tree switched on during the ceremony, while others firmly believe that they should be kept off. Since opinions vary so much on this subject, it's best left up to personal judgment or coven practice.

Besides the Christmas tree, the altar and Circle area are decorated using traditional trimmings of pine boughs, pinecones, mistletoe, and holly. Also, if at all possible, adding poinsettias to the altar arrangement is highly recommended. These plants display flowers in the God-color (red), bring living greenery to the rite (a symbol of the coming spring), and are aesthetically pleasing since they naturally brighten up the area.

Along these same lines, the use of small Christmas lights, strung around the room, has become a popular practice among modern Wiccans of all denominations. Whether multicolored or single colored, twinkling or not, these will add a festive atmosphere to the room and mimic the stars in the night sky. However, if you are using lights, remember that they must not break the plane of the Circle.

Another decorative item is the wreath. Made of evergreen, holly, mistletoe, or almost any natural material, the wreath is a seasonal symbol of the Wheel of the Year.[6] Though most commonly seen hanging on doors, the wreath now occupies a place on many Wiccan altars. Often, the wreath is placed around the altar candle, but it can also encircle the God/Goddess figurines.

Finally, before setting out the tools on the altar, it's appropriate to decorate both the altar and Circle area. These are usually adorned with pine boughs, pinecones, holly, and mistletoe, but other creative ideas include oak branches, candles, garlands, or Christmas ornaments. In short, any item that promotes the Yuletide spirit may be introduced into the decorating scheme. Once the ritual area is finished, the tools are laid out on the altar. This is also the best time to decide on which fragrances of incense are to be used. These should be placed by the censer. Of all the different scents, frankincense is one of the few traditional incenses of the season, but pine and jasmine are also common.

Gardnerian

Prior to the ceremony, a single red candle should be placed in the center of the Circle. It remains unlit to represent the dormant Sun God. At the same time, the High Priestess must select two men to portray the Oak King and Holly King. The High Priest normally assumes the Oak King role. She must also delegate the role of Goddess, though she usually reserves this for herself. If not the High Priestess, the coven's Maiden is the next likely candidate. The men may not wear their crowns during any portion of the opening ritual, although the High Priestess may don the Crown of Flowers immediately after the Charge.

The ceremony begins with the Circle being cast and proceeds through the Witches' Rune. Following the chant, the coven take up positions along the perimeter of the Circle, leaving a gap in their ranks at the cauldron. The High Priestess and Maiden stand at the altar, the High Priest (soon-to-be Oak King) at the east cardinal point, and the male witch (soon-to-be Holly King) at the west cardinal point. When everyone is set, the High Priestess motions for the Maiden to give the Holly Crown to the witch portraying the Holly King, who immediately puts it on. She then recites:

At Midsummer, thou did slay thy brother, the Oak King, and since then thou hast ruled as the Holly King, God of the Waning Year. yet, as the Wheel turns, your time slowly comes to an end.

After the speech, the Holly King walks to the center of the Circle and faces the coven. He should be next to the unlit red candle. Assuming the God Position, he recites:

I am the Holly King, God of the Waning Year. I have reigned as the consort of the Goddess throughout this time of darkness, and I shall continue until I am deposed by the light.

Next, the High Priestess motions for the Maiden to give the Oak Crown to the High Priest. He immediately puts it on. She recites:

Thou art the Oak King, God of the Waxing Year. As the Wheel turns, your time approaches.

Walking to the center of the Circle, the Oak King stands on the other side of the red candle from the Holly King, and assumes the Slain God Position.[7] As soon as the Oak King has gotten into the position, the High Priestess recites:

We have come together at this sacred time of the year to witness the rebirth of the Light. Our Lord, the Sun God, lies dead. Unless he is reborn, the Light shall not return to warm the land and fertilize the seeds that lay in the womb of the Great Mother. Return to us, O' Mighty Sun.

The coven members file past the altar, and each person receives a red candle, which is lit from the altar candle. Once everyone has a lit candle, they join hands, and the Maiden leads a deosil ring-dance around the Circle. Each person should have a hand on two candles at the same time. The speed of the dance increases as the High Priestess recites:

Queen of the Moon, Queen of the Sun,
Queen of the Heavens, Queen of the Stars,
Queen of the Waters, Queen of the Earth,
Bring us the Child of Promise!
For it is the Great Mother who gives birth to him;
And it is the Lord of Life who is born again;

Darkness and tears are set aside, when the Sun comes up again.
Golden Sun of hill and mountain,
Illumine the land, Illumine the world,
Illumine the seas, Illumine the rivers,
Sorrows be laid, and joy be raised.
Blessed be the Great Mother!
Without beginning, without ending,
Everlasting to eternity.
Io Evo! He! Blessed be!
Io Evo! He! Blessed be!
Io Evo! He! Blessed be!

The High Priestess calls the dance to a halt, and the coven members return to their places. The Maiden returns to the altar. Lighting a taper from the altar candle, the Maiden then returns to the center of the Circle where she lights the red (Sun God) candle. She goes to the cauldron and lights the candle inside it before returning to the altar. The High Priestess recites:

The sun is reborn, and with it, the reign of the Oak King, God of the Waxing Year, begins.

As soon as the High Priestess finishes speaking, the Oak King comes out of the Slain God Position. There are two different versions of the drama play that can take place here. The Oak King may pretend to slay the Holly King, or the Holly King just pretends to die. Either way, the Holly King ends up kneeling in the center of the Circle.[8] The Maiden comes forward and drapes the scarf (or material) over the Holly King's head. The Oak King recites:

I am the Oak King, God of the Waxing Year. I am the God of Light; Son and Lover of the Great Mother. I have come to drive away the dark, that the land shall again be fertile, and I shall reign until the Wheel turns again at Midsummer, and the Holly King is reborn.

The coven recites: *Farewell, O' Holly King; Blessed be the Oak King!*

It's customary for the Holly King to be led to the west quarter by the High Priest and High Priestess before the shroud is removed by the Maiden. Once this is done, the male witch and Maiden join the coven. However, there is still the problem of what to do with the Holly Crown.

Since the Holly King is dead, his body, symbolized by the Holly Crown, is supposed to be buried. Even in an outdoor ceremony, this is usually impossible or impractical. Therefore, the crown may be symbolically returned to the womb by laying it inside the cauldron. This is done by the High Priestess and High Priest before they return to the altar.

After returning to the altar, the pair symbolically enacts the Great Rite to celebrate the joining of the God and Goddess. The wine and cakes are then consecrated and shared with the coven, after which the Circle is banished.

Although the religious portion of the ceremony has ended, there is still a custom that occurs before the feast. In order to promote fertility, the cauldron is moved into the center of the Circle. With the High Priestess and High Priest going first, everyone jumps over the cauldron. The coven leaders are followed by the Maiden and ex-Holly King, then the coven in pairs. When this is finished, the feast begins. At the end of the festivities, remember to blow out the candle in the cauldron. Also, if a Yule log was burned, the ashes should be gathered after they cool and scattered onto a field.

Italian

This denomination has quite a few versions of the Winter Solstice ceremony. Though it's not uncommon for slight differences to occur within a tradition, it rarely happens to the degree seen here. One explanation for this extreme diversity could be that the rites of some regions were influenced by the Romans and Greeks, while other sects remained more closely tied to their original Tuscan roots. Another possible explanation is that the rites were incorrectly translated into English and concepts that were difficult to understand were merely substituted with existing Wiccan practices. In either case, it must be acknowledged that there is no set standard for this sabbat. The following version is the simplest form used in Italian Wicca.[9]

About the only special preparation is that the altar is set along the northern edge of the Circle, the cauldron is placed in the center, and a large red candle is placed inside it. An evergreen wreath traditionally hangs from the altar, with a smaller version (or just a few pine branches formed into a circle) placed around the God figurine or the God candle. However, neither is absolutely required. If space permits, a Yule log is placed on the altar or laid next to the cauldron. Though it is not essential, the Circle, cauldron, and altar are usually adorned with garlands, pine boughs, holly, mistletoe, and other seasonal decorations.

When everything is in place, the ceremony begins with casting the Circle and proceeds through a complete esbat rite. At the point where the wine and cakes are to be consecrated, the esbat format is abandoned, and the sabbat rite takes over. The High Priestess stands at the altar, beside the High Priest, and recites:

We gather on this sacred night to welcome back the Sun God. He is the Lord of Light who has dwelt in the Realm of Shadows since his death at the Summer Solstice. Yet, as the Wheel of the Year ever turns, the God must be reborn on this night to drive away the dark.

Remaining where he is, the High Priest assumes the God Position while the High Priestess moves to the center of the Circle. Before leaving the altar, she lights a taper from the altar candle (or God candle) and uses this to light the cauldron candle. She blows out the taper, turns to face the altar, and recites:[10]

Behold, the flame in the womb of the Mother Earth burns brightly on this night to welcome forth the God of Light, Lord of the Waxing Year, who has arisen from his long sleep. Let it be known that the spirit of the Dark God, Lord of the Waning year, must now depart.

At the end of her address, she motions for the High Priest to join her. He remains in the God Position, but moves to her side. She now recites:

O' Mighty Sun God, Lord of Light, bringer of Life, with each passing day you grow brighter and stronger. As you drive away the darkness and cold, we pray that you restore the warmth and fertility to the land. And, as you send your light, we ask that you grace us with your blessings. Protect us, O' Lord, throughout the coming months. Blessed be.

The coven responds: *Blessed be.*

Coming out of the God Position, the High Priest kisses the High Priestess on the lips and embraces her. This is symbolic of the God's blessing. He then goes around the coven and delivers the same blessing to each person—he may kiss the men on the cheek. When he finishes, the High Priestess accompanies him to the altar, and the pair consecrate the wine and cakes. However, instead of merely sharing these with the coven, the High Priest individually gives out cakes to each person with the following words:

Receive this gift as a sign of the renewed season and the reborn God.

After receiving this gift, each person should break off a small piece of cake and make an offering by placing it in the cauldron. This marks the end of the ritual. The Circle is now banished so that the feast can begin. At some point during the festivities, coven members should pair up and take turns jumping over the cauldron. Also, since this sabbat occurred during the dead of winter, a traditional food was smoked or dried meat (hard sausage, beef jerky, etc.). Before the cauldron candle is extinguished, the High Priest should make an offering of this meat by searing a small piece in the cauldron candle flame.

Saxon

The complexity of this sabbat will depend on a number of factors that affect what can or cannot take place during the ceremony. For instance, if the rite is held outdoors and a bonfire can be lit, a new dimension is added to the ritual. This also holds true for an indoor ceremony if there's a working fireplace in the room. Under either scenario, tapers or small candles should be passed out to each coven member. These are thrown into the fire at a specific point in the ritual. Another facet that lends to the intricacy of the ceremony is the amount of work put into decorating, because some of the decorations may be incorporated into certain practices.

A perfect example of this is the Christmas tree. Having a Christmas tree in the house is believed by some to have originated as an early Saxon custom. The Saxons were also thought to be the first people to place candles on the branches, as well as gifts underneath it. They also held ring-dances around it to celebrate the season and pay homage to the forest spirits. Therefore, adding a Christmas tree to the ritual area increases the ceremonial potential of the rite by providing the opportunity to include many traditional customs.

The Saxons also held various beliefs related to the wheel and its relationship to the cycle of life during the Winter Solstice. Some of these ideas eventually were transformed into the modern wheel-dance.[11] Although this addition requires only minor preparation, it's still something that must be done in advance. A decision must also be made regarding the cauldron. If one is to be used, it should be placed in the southern quarter[12] and have a large candle inside.

A final note about the Saxon celebration centers on the feast. Its most important aspect involves the principle of "giving and receiving."

Traditionally, there was one table filled with the foods of the feast—fowl, red meat, dried fruits, nuts, wine, and ale—while another table on the opposite side of the room had nothing but an empty bowl sitting on it. This second table was set aside to collect gifts for the poor—in other words, to invoke the Wiccan threefold Law of Return. Legends say that anyone who eats from the first table without leaving an offering on the second will have bad luck for the coming year.

After choosing which seasonal customs will be included or excluded and setting up the area, the ceremony begins with the Circle being cast. The Priest and Priestess then go to the altar while the coven spreads out along the perimeter of the Circle.[13] A normal esbat rite takes place up to the beginning of the cakes and ale rite. At this point the Priestess starts the sabbat ceremony by reciting:

> *Gather around and witness the end of darkness. Through the long winter months, the sun was lost. But the Wheel has turned and the sun can begin its return. Let us now light the way, that we may help guide the Lord back from the beyond. And let the fires that we kindle give him strength and show that our love for him burns brightly. So be it.*

The coven repeats: *So be it.* The Priestess and Priest each picks up a red candle and light them from the altar candle. At the same time, the Scribe and/or Thegn pass out tapers or small candles to the coven. Holding the candles in front of them, the pair recites:

> *We offer this flame to Woden, our Mighty Lord, that it may light his path and guide him along his journey as he returns to drive away the harshness of winter.*

When this address ends, the Thegn leads a procession (deosil) past the altar during which each person lights his or her taper/candle from the candles held by the Priest and Priestess. Men light theirs from the Priestess, women from the Priest. Once the last taper has been lit, the Priest and Priestess take the lead in the procession. The rest of the coven stay single file even though the Priest and Priestess are side by side. After the third pass around the Circle, the Priest and Priestess stop beside the cauldron while the coven continues to file by them. As the witches pass, they place their tapers into the cauldron[14] and then return to their previous position along the Circle perimeter. Once the last witch has passed the cauldron, the Priest and Priestess return to the altar. If there's no bonfire in the center of the Circle, the Thegn and Scribe move the cauldron there. The Priestess places her candle on the altar. The Priest continues holding his while he recites:

The darkest days of winter are behind us. Although there are still lean times ahead, with each passing day the light will become longer and the Lord will become stronger, until he once again reaches the height of his power. Let us rejoice at the return of our Lord.

A wheel-dance is conducted around the center of the Circle. Keeping the middle of the wheel (the point where the ropes join) directly over the center of the cauldron (or bonfire) is the key to the symbolism of this dance. In a coven of thirteen, twelve people link hands to participate in the dance. The Priest remains at the altar, but the Priestess joins in. This allows eight people to hold the four ropes (wheel spokes), while the four remaining people link the spokes together. (See Figure 28.1.) The group dances in a circle and chants:

A light for the winter, to brighten this ring,
A light to guard us, as we wait for the spring,
We kindled the fires, and let them burn,
With love as the key, may the Great Wheel turn.

After the wheel-dance ends (minimum of three complete revolutions), the coven members drop down where they are. Their hands should remain linked, and the wheel should remain intact.[15] The Priest raises the candle that he's holding and recites:

Let this flame light the way for our Lord, that he may guard us and guide us through the days ahead. So be it.

The coven repeat: *So be it.*

As the Thegn collects the ropes and puts them away, the Priestess joins the Priest at the altar. The pair now conducts the cakes and ale rite. This is the end of the ceremony. However, if any of the ancient customs are going to be performed—Christmas tree wishes, wreath light, etc.—they should be carried out before the Circle is banished. When all the ceremonial aspects are completed, the Circle is banished, and the festivities begin.

West Country

In order to express the symbolism of the God of the Waxing Year vanquishing the God of the Waning Year, this denomination turns to the story of the robin slaying the wren. These legendary characters are carried over into the ceremony and memorialized through a brief drama play.

The only real difference in preparing for this sabbat is that the robin/wren theme requires a little advance thought. For instance, how elaborate will the costumes be? Dual crowns (one red and one brown) are the easiest way to convey the legend. But a point to consider when deciding on costume design is that the denomination sprung from rural areas and during the harshness of the winter, the emotional value of the rite was extremely important to these people. For this reason, the original costumes were quite elaborate in an effort to enhance their symbolism and as a form of sympathetic magick. Therefore, why be simple? With a little advance preparation, fancy costumes can be made for both wren and robin participants.[16]

Another authentic custom is the placement of a Yule log on the bonfire at the beginning of the ceremony. Since the majority of sabbats are now held indoors, this usually isn't possible unless the room has a fireplace. To compensate for this, modern witches have resorted to using a miniature version of the Yule log.[17]

Decorating is also very important to the rites of this denomination. The ritual area is heavily adorned with evergreen boughs, pinecones, holly, and mistletoe. A sprig of mistletoe should be hung over the spot where the entrance to the Circle is going to be cut.[18] For an outdoor ceremony, pine branches (with green needles) should be on hand for the bonfire. For indoor rites, a small handful of green pine needles will suffice. Nuts and dried fruit should be on the altar, as well as a large red candle.

Although this is a rite to call back the male deity, which would normally mean a Priest would act as coven leader, in this instance, a Priestess assumes this distinction since the Priest will most likely be dressed to portray a character in the upcoming drama. Once everything is set, the Circle is cast by the coven leader. During the casting, the entire coven remains outside the Circle area until they are admitted to the Circle through the doorway cut by the Priestess. Instead of entering in pairs, they file in one at a time so that they can be greeted by the Priestess (under the mistletoe) with a kiss. When all the coven members are inside, the Priestess returns to the altar with the doorway left open. Facing the coven, the Priestess narrates the drama as it's enacted in the middle of the Circle. She begins:

Gather around and listen to this Yuletide tale, for as the Wheel turns and the seasons change, we must give thanks for the sacrifice that is made. Many months ago, at Midsummer, the light began to dim, and the Little Wren King came to rule the land which was covered by the bounty of the Goddess.

The May Queen (representing the Goddess) enters the Circle and stands in front of the altar. Next, the person portraying the wren enters through the doorway, makes one pass around the Circle, and stands in the center facing the coven. As he passes the altar, the Priestess (or May Queen) hands him a single red candle, which was lit from the altar flame. The Priestess continues:

The wren watched the crops ripen and fade away. He watched the light slowly give way to the darkness of winter. And the Goddess could do nothing but watch with him.

As the wren blows out the candle, the May Queen bows her head. This is the signal for the robin to enter. After making a pass around the Circle, the robin joins the wren in the center. The May Queen raises her head and acts surprised. The Priestess continues:

Yet, in time, the Wheel of the Year turned, and the robin redbreast once again returned. And when he looked around and saw that the land was cold and barren, and in the grip of winter, he knew that he must defeat the wren before the light could fill the sky. But the wren had hidden in the holly so that the robin could not find him.

The wren holds a piece of holly (or any greenery) in front of him as if hiding. After pretending to search in vain, the robin recites:

Where art thou, Little Wren King? The Wheel has turned, and your time has passed. Come out from your hide.

Dropping the holly, the wren briefly struggles with the robin before he's defeated. He then lies down at the robin's feet, and the robin takes the red candle from him. Once the wren is dead, the May Queen moves forward and places a pine bough over the body as a symbolic burial. She uses a flame from the altar candle to light the candle the robin is holding. The Priestess concludes the story:[19]

The wren was buried; the robin redbreast reigned supreme; and the light was free to return once more. Let all rejoice in the knowledge that the death of winter shall soon give way to the life of the coming spring.

Now that the drama is over, the May Queen and the male witch (the wren) rejoin the coven while the Priest (still in costume) joins the Priestess at the altar. The wine and cakes are consecrated by the pair and shared with the coven, marking the end of the ceremony. The Circle is banished.

APPENDICES

Notes

1. History

1. Some witchcraft historians argue that there are people of more importance than Gerald Gardner. For instance, Charles Godfrey Leland published *Aradia: Gospel of the Witches* in 1899; James G. Frazer published *The Golden Bough: A Study in Magic and Religion* in 1890; Margaret A. Murray published *The Witch Cult in Western Europe* in 1921 and *The God of the Witches* in 1933; and, even Aleister Crowley's name has been brought up as a prominent contributor. However, Gardner's efforts are still the most well-known, and the denomination bearing his name is the most widespread.

2. The Canon Episcopi has been attributed to the Church Council of Ancyra, which met in 314 A.D., and was thereafter made part of Church canon law. Although some modern scholars have doubted this, in his book, *The Geography of Witchcraft*, Montague Summers credits Regino (c. 906 A.D.) with including the Canon Episcopi in his *De Ecclesiastica Disciplinis*. In the twelfth century, it was incorporated into the *Corpus Juris Canonici*, where it officially became a part of canon law.

3. Papal bulls on witchcraft were still being written long after the 1484 bull of Innocent VIII. For instance, Pope Alexander VI published two bulls on the subject of witchcraft; Julius II wrote a scathing bull condemning the black mass; Leo X issued a bull on witchcraft in 1523; Clement VII wrote two bulls; and, in 1586, Pope Sixtus V denounced astrologers as practitioners of black magic. But these paled in historical comparison.

4. Although fewer than 1,000 people were officially listed as executed for witchcraft, many more died in prison. During the fifteenth, sixteenth, and seventeenth centuries, the bubonic plague was rampant in English prisons, and many one-year sentences were shortened by death. However, these deaths are not included in official witchcraft execution estimates.

5. A popular technique for deciding whether a person (usually a woman) was a witch was to bind her arms and legs and throw her into water to see if she would sink or float. This random method was later replaced by the "dunking stool." If the person didn't drown, the accused was judged to be a witch. If the person did drown, he or she was judged not to be a witch and posthumously acquitted.

6. Many accounts credit Tituba with making the witch cake. But, during a sermon on March 27, 1692, the Reverend Parris mentions that Mary Sibley had instructed his "Indian man" to make the cake. Of equal interest is the fact that Indian John was Tituba's husband. He was also accused as a witch, and suffered from being bewitched.

7. As early as May 1692, a decision was made not to execute witches who confessed so that they could provide testimony against those who refused to confess. Yet, at no time did the authorities intend to spare the lives of those who confessed. Instead, they planned to secure the convictions, then execute everyone at a later time when their testimony was no longer needed.

8. The "inner circle" girls all lived in a specific section of Salem Village, while "outer circle" girls came from an area of Salem Town. Although the geographical significance is not readily apparent, the proximity of each group to contaminated grain fields shows that many of the girls may have been faking their illnesses.

9. There are historical accounts claiming that prior to the 1692 witch hysteria, the accusing girls had formed a "circle"—which would loosely equate to a coven—in order to dabble in witchcraft themselves. During these meetings, they received tutoring from Tituba in areas such as palmistry, divination, and even spell-casting.

10. Court of Oyer and Terminer, translated literally, means "to hear and determine." This term was applied to courts set up to deal with specific or unusual circumstances.

11. Giles Corey refused to stand trial because he realized that his land would not be taken from his family as long as he was not convicted of witchcraft. Therefore, disregarding his own fate, he willingly accepted the torture of being pressed under stones. And to show his contempt for his accusers, Corey's last words were "more weight."

12. In witchcraft prosecutions, "witch law" was not the same as criminal law. Any accused witch who escaped prison and fled Massachusetts was safe since witches were not pursued into other jurisdictions.

13. In his book, *Salem Witchcraft, with an Account of Salem Village and a History of Opinions on Witchcraft and Kindred Subjects* (Boston, 1867), Charles W. Upham asserts his belief that the witch-hunts were based on conscious fraud and conspiracy. This theory is partially supported by the actions of Increase Mather and Cotton Mather. As early as August 1692, Cotton Mather privately suggested releasing some accused witches on bail. Then, on October 3, 1692, Increase Mather made a direct challenge to the court by proclaiming that "It were better that ten suspected witches should escape, than that one innocent person should be condemned."

14. Once the witchcraft hysteria died down, the General Court set aside a public fast day to atone for the scandalous events of 1692. On this day in 1697, Samuel Sewall, one of the judges who sat on the Court of Oyer and Terminer, gave a public apology for his part in the witchcraft cases. In 1707, Ann Putnam also confessed to unwittingly being deceived into falsely accusing innocent people as witches, but claimed that it was due to the "great delusion of Satan."

15. Bridget Bishop was not well liked by many people in authority because she ran an unlicensed tavern and a gambling house.

16. Several sources maintain that Gerald Gardner was initiated into the Craft by "Old Dorothy Clutterbuck," a practicing witch from a coven in New Forest, England. According to Doreen Valiente, this woman is also rumored to have presided over the rites that took place against Adolf Hitler in the New Forest in 1940.

17. Doreen Valiente was initiated by Gerald Gardner in 1953. Over the years that followed, she helped him create the *Gardnerian Book of Shadows* and write many of the passages that formed the basis for the denomination.

2. Philosophy

1. The Theory of Mentalism and Theory of Rhythm are the sixth and seventh laws. Mentalism states that all creation and knowledge exist in, and are composed of, the Divine Mind. Rhythm states that everything is in a constant circular change and motion and that reality is composed of opposites. Neither of these will be explored.

2. There's a somewhat controversial hypothesis that says that because of the natural makeup of homosexuals and lesbians, it's often easier for them to become attuned to the dual nature of their psyche because their opposite gender component is more prevalent in their consciousness than it is in someone who's trying to suppress theirs.

3. Nobody knows exactly where these laws originated. Some believe they're an ancient text while others believe they're a fairly modern collection of rules; some have even attributed them to Gerald Gardner. Whatever their origin, these are the basic tenets that all Wiccans should follow. There are slightly different versions contained in *The Book of Shadows of Lady Sheba* (Llewellyn, 1971) and *King of the Witches* (Davies, 1969). These versions, however, tend to enumerate each law separately.

4. These two lines are shunned by denominations that hold the God/Goddess as equals or those who exalt the God.

5. Gay and lesbian witches regard this portion of the law as a reference to the mother/son formula rather than a biased statement against same-sex practices.

6. Avalon is also known as Tirnan-Og, the Land of Youth, the Land of Apples, and several other names depending on the specific Celtic denomination.

7. It is acceptable to charge for some services. Witches who read the Tarot, grow herbs for sale, or even those who write books are perfectly capable of charging for their services.

3. Deities

1. Christianity follows the male/female pattern, with the Virgin Mary held in a subordinate role to Jesus Christ. In recent years, a few Wiccan traditions have begun to adopt the view that the God and Goddess are on completely equal footing.

2. The sun became a masculine symbol after Roman and Christian influences altered the landscape of religious views. With this change, the acceptance of women in leadership roles also declined, thereby creating a patriarchal dominance of society and modifying the role of the God-figure.

3. For purposes of clarity, the area where the name is believed to have originated has been added whenever possible. However, many times a deity was generalized as "Celtic" due to the vast usage of the name throughout many of the Pagan denominations. Also, this is only a sampling of the names most commonly used by witches. Although there are occasional Greek/Roman deities provided, the list primarily consists of Wiccan Gods and Goddesses or names used by modern Wiccan paths.

4. Although the various Wiccan Gods are referred to as "woodland" Gods, or Gods of the "hunt," they are nevertheless always equated with the sun. The daily and yearly cycles of the sun and moon, the seasonal changes, the love/chase aspect, and the mother/son/consort beliefs all revolve around the God as the sun and the Goddess as the moon.

4. Otherworldly Beings

1. The four elements are represented by the arms and legs of the upright Pentagram, along with a fifth element—the Element of Spirit—which incorporates them all into one. All witches recognize these as categories of Nature, as well as the basis of all existence.

2. A ceremonial magician commands spirits to do his magick. This is not to say that witches don't summon otherworldly beings, because they do. In fact, witches regularly request the presence of spirits, and the God and Goddess, through methods known as invocation and evocation. However, they do so in order to commune with these beings, not to force them to perform tasks.

3. A male Folletti spirit is called a Folletto, while a female spirit shares the same name, Folletti, as the whole group.

4. In some Celtic Wiccan traditions, the four portals between the worlds are called the Wards and are the same as the Watchtowers of the Circle.

5. Since the topic of Faeries is so diverse, this is only an abridged listing. For a complete discourse on Faeries, there are two must-have books, *World Guide to Gnomes, Fairies, Elves & Other Little People* by Thomas Keightley and *A Dictionary of Fairies*, reprinted as the *Encyclopedia of Fairies*, by Katharine Briggs.

6. Hobs are also known as Hobgoblins. However, since Goblins are malicious spirits who enjoy hurting humans, negative connotations often become attached to the term Hobgoblins.

7. Of all the Nymphs, the Dryad is the only one that is not immortal. This Nymph dies with its tree, which is why the Dryad is so focused on protecting its host.

8. Pixies are also called Pigsies and Piskies. However, these magickal entities should not be confused with Pikeys, Yellow-Bellies, or Diddikais, who were an actual race of short, forest-dwelling people who lived in the forests of rural England.

9. This spirit was also called the "Little Washer at the Ford."

10. It's believed that a Boggart is simply a Brownie that has been so teased or misused that it has become uncontrollably mischievous. This being is not to be confused with Bogies, Bogles, Bug-a-boos, or Bogey-beasts, which are all frightening and dangerous entities.

5. Traditions, Structure, and Offices

1. Of all the traditions that specifically practice Ceremonial Magick, the Hermetic Order of the Golden Dawn is the most widely known. At one time or another, Aleister Crowley, Dion Fortune, W. B. Yeats, A. E. Waite, and S. L. MacGregor Mathers were counted among the members of the Golden Dawn. These individuals have all had an impact on the Wiccan and Neo-Pagan religions. Founded in 1887 by Dr. William Westcott, this path has spawned numerous other sects such as the Argentinum Astrum of Aleister Crowley and the Inner Light Group of Dion Fortune.

2. The requirement of a 100-year-old family tree is usually accepted because this extends the family history to a pre-Gardnerian time. However, some people feel the family history of a true hereditary witch must go well beyond that requirement and usually expect a minimum Craft lineage of 200 to 300 years.

3. The "Left Hand Path" includes all the forms of Black Alchemy, Black Magick, Demonic and Devil worship, Necronomiconism, and Satanism.

4. More information about the Science Tradition can be found in Laurie Cabot's book, *Power of the Witch* (Delta, New York, 1989).

5. A complete discourse on Seax-Wicca can be found in Raymond Buckland's book, *The Tree: Complete Book of Saxon Witchcraft* (Weiser, New York, 1978). This book is out of print and difficult to find, though used copies occasionally turn up. Copies may be available directly from the publisher.

6. Many Pagan traditions take the stance that while they have titles and offices, they are not a structured religious hierarchy. A few actually become offended when this insinuation is made. Other denominations go so far as to claim that they don't even have titles or offices. Although all of this is true to a certain extent, even the most loosely organized paths have some type of internal foundation that serves as a type of hierarchy, whether they like to admit it or not.

7. The High Priest/ess and Maid(en) are described in the context of mixed gender circles, clans, covens, and groves. A single-gender male group would naturally be run by a High Priest, while a single-gender female group would use a High Priestess. Instances where both genders are required for a ritual (e.g., Drawing Down the Moon), but a group is single gender, will be explained in a later chapter.

8. In God-oriented traditions, the High Priestess becomes the assistant and the High Priest assumes the leader role.

9. It's customary in Saxon witchcraft that, prior to becoming a Ceorl, a person starts off as a "Theow" (pronounced "Thou"). A Theow attends ritual meetings by invitation in order to become acquainted with the tradition. Later, if the Theow so desires, he or she may request to become a Ceorl.

6. Tools of Witchcraft

1. Although the word "tools" is used, some items such as the broomstick, bell, attire, etc., are really best described as accessories. However, since most of these items are as important for ritual use as some tools, they've been included in this category.

2. I have heard of cases where the athame has been used for engraving inscriptions. Whether this is accurate or merely a mistake, I can't be sure. I've never seen the athame used for anything other than ritual use, nor have I ever personally encountered any witch who has used it otherwise. However, just because I haven't done it or seen it done, doesn't mean that it isn't so.

3. Bune Wand is the old Scottish term used for a witch's flying broomstick.

4. Keep in mind that pine boughs, flowers, etc., will quickly dry up and lose their needles/petals. Therefore, if any of these are used for the brush, they will have to be replaced on a regular basis.

5. The cauldron, as well as several other tools (bell, broom, drum, censor, scissors, etc.), is not immediately needed and a substitute can be used. However, depending on your denomination and whether you join a coven, you should eventually acquire a complete complement of tools.

6. This view of trees and wood was used for all tools that had wooden parts, i.e., the broom, scourge, wand, and even wooden knife/sword handles. Also, although a wooden

bowl seems relatively insignificant, its effectiveness can be enhanced by selecting one made of fruit-bearing wood like cherry.

7. Virgin trees are those that have never fruited, flowered, or those that are still too immature to reproduce.

8. The Handfasting Rite is the only time that the sword can be used for actual cutting.

9. Some forms of Ceremonial Magick use more than one type of sword. In *The Key of Solomon the King*, there are two different swords shown: the straight-bladed sword that is most commonly used by witches (plate XIV, figure 70); and the scimitar, which is a curved-blade sword with Persian or Middle Eastern origins (plate XIII, figure 63). There is also mention of a third sword that is to be used by the Disciples (page 98), but no description of this one is given.

10. Unlike Pagan traditions, Ceremonial Magick often uses a wand that is much shorter than the average forearm measurement. In fact, it's not uncommon for some magicians to have wands that are ten inches long. (See *The Golden Dawn*, page 320.)

11. Some Celtic traditions call the white-handled knife the bolline. This should not be confused with the curved-blade boleen used to cut herbs.

7. Altars

1. In Saxon Wicca the altar is usually round. However, an oval, square, or rectangular altar will suffice.

2. This assumes that the ceremony is being held indoors. For outdoor ceremonies, simply clear the area of any large items that may break the Circle.

3. In traditions that use Watchtowers as part of their ritual Circle, when the altar is set up on the northern edge the North Watchtower candle usually sits directly on the altar rather than on the floor, and the same holds true for setting up on the eastern edge.

4. Only the Gardnerian and Saxon layouts show a place to set down the *Book of Shadows* on the altar. Although the other traditions do not give it a permanent resting place, it can be put anywhere that's convenient.

5. The Science Tradition was founded by Laurie Cabot in the early 1970s. This tradition incorporates elements of several Wiccan and Pagan paths with Ceremonial Magick and the latest developments in theoretical physics. Or, as Laurie Cabot states, it blends "new science with the old laws of magic." (*Power of the Witch*, page 149.)

6. Being right-handed, I keep my athame on the right, which makes it easier for me to reach; if left-handed, I'd move it to the left. Again, this is more a matter of convenience than anything else. In the Italian altar layout the handle would face the right/left.

7. In the Saxon tradition candles are not used as Watchtowers. Instead, candles are placed around the Circle for illumination only, and as many as seven may be used.

8. Some denominations (e.g., Science, West Country) have designated places to put burning herbs and incense on the altar.

9. When a libation dish is used, the contents are taken outside and poured onto the Earth after the ceremony. This completes the offering process.

8. Magick Circle

1. Some traditions, like West Country, also employ an eighteen-foot Magick Circle

for larger gatherings. However, regardless of the size, symbolically the Circle represents infinity and eternity, as it has no beginning and no end.

2. Many well-established covens have a special room that they use exclusively as their temple area, and this may have a Circle permanently painted or marked on the floor. When it's impossible, or impractical, to permanently mark the floor, it's common to use an area rug with the Circle inscribed on it. The important thing to remember is that any markings just represent an outline and are not the actual Magick Circle.

3. Although some witches use a dual Circle and place candles at the cardinal points, you should always remember that this practice is strongly rooted in Ceremonial Magick and differs from simply employing Watchtowers. Before attempting this dual Circle version, its uses and restrictions should be carefully researched.

4. Gerald Gardner adapted the general structure of his rite from the Circle casting ritual described in *The Key of Solomon the King*, Book I, Chapter III, pages 17–21; and Book II, Chapter IX, pages 99–100.

5. Gerald Gardner took the wording for these passages directly from *The Key of Solomon the King*, Book II, Chapter V, pages 90–91.

6. Some witches prefer to light the Watchtower candles after erecting the Circle. In such a case, a taper is lit from the altar candle and used to light the Watchtowers.

7. Denominations heavily influenced by Ceremonial Magick sometimes use specific invoking pentagrams for each cardinal point, i.e., Invoking Pentagram of Air for east (Figure 8.4), Invoking Pentagram of Fire for south (Figure 8.5), Invoking Pentagram of Water for west (Figure 8.6), and Invoking Pentagram of Earth for north. The sequence of strokes for each pentagram is: Earth = 1, 2, 3, 4, 5, 1; Fire = 1, 5, 4, 3, 2, 1; Air = 3, 4, 5, 1, 2, 3; Water = 4, 3, 2, 1, 5, 4. *The Golden Dawn*, Volume III, Book Four, pages 280–286, provides a complete explanation.

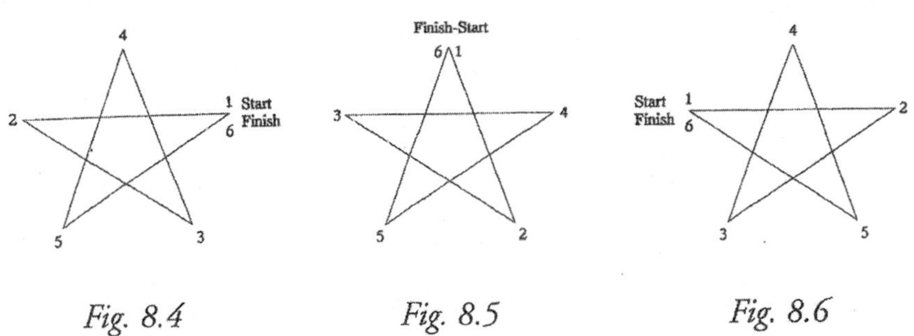

Fig. 8.4 *Fig. 8.5* *Fig. 8.6*

8. Italian covens have adopted the Catholic practice of keeping consecrated (holy) water on hand at all times; thus, they already have some ready at the beginning of the rite. The water is stored in a consecrated bottle and refilled during each ceremony.

9. All the candles may be lit at once, or they may be lit one at a time.

10. If only one altar candle was used, the Priest/Priestess take turns with it.

11. Given the fact that Raymond Buckland was a trained Gardnerian long before

he introduced Saxon, the phrase "So be it" is most likely a modified version of the Gardnerian, "So mote it be."

12. Technically, witches need to be initiated before casting a Circle, but they also need to be initiated inside a Circle in order to become a witch. Without contact with an initiated witch or coven, the only way to accomplish this is to venture forth and cast a Circle before becoming a witch. This brings up a second problem—consecrating tools. Again the problem arises for the uninitiated: Without being a witch, there's no Circle to consecrate tools in, so there's obviously no consecrated tools to use. Therefore, the first Magick Circle will be cast using little more than imagination and a willingness to enter into Wicca.

13. Insert the Goddess and God names of your choice or of the denomination you intend to follow.

14. Regardless of whether or not the Circle will be used again in the near future, it's unthinkable to leave the Circle erected and unsupervised. The steadfast rule is that the Circle must be banished at the conclusion of each ceremony. The only exception to this rule is that a doorway can be cut in the Circle without banishing it. This is done by cutting a doorway in the Circle using your athame. Make a cut that starts at the floor and extends to your full height, then arch it over and back down to the floor. Some traditions use side-to-side cuts rather than up and down. Upon reentering the Circle, close the hole by retracing the cut with the athame, then draw a pentagram with the athame to seal the breach. Just remember, if the Circle is opened all work must stop until it's closed again.

15. The person carrying the newly consecrated items, or offerings, stands behind the coven.

16. In the Gardnerian tradition, this duty usually falls upon the Maiden. However, any witch may be assigned this task.

17. Although the Gardnerian tradition uses only the Banishing Pentagram of Earth, denominations heavily influenced by Ceremonial Magick sometimes use specific banishing pentagrams for each cardinal point, i.e., Banishing Pentagram of Earth for north, Banishing Pentagram of Air for east (Figure 8.7), Banishing Pentagram of Fire for south (Figure 8.8), Banishing Pentagram of Water for west (Figure 8.9). The sequence of strokes are also different as stroke 1 begins from the lower left arm to the tip; in the Invoking Pentagram the strokes work from the tip to the lower left arm. The series of strokes for each banishing pentagram: Earth = 1, 2, 3, 4, 5, 1; Fire = 3, 2, 1, 5, 4, 3; Air = 4, 5, 1, 2, 3, 4; Water = 5, 4, 3, 2, 1, 5. *The Golden Dawn*, Volume III, Book Four, pages 280–286, provides a complete explanation.

BANISHING PENTAGRAM OF AIR

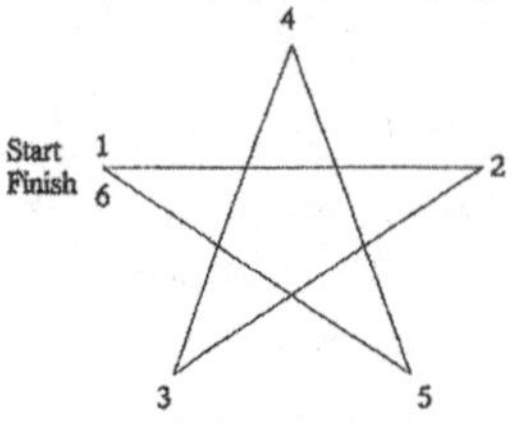

Fig. 8.7

BANISHING PENTAGRAM OF FIRE

Fig. 8.8

BANISHING PENTAGRAM OF WATER

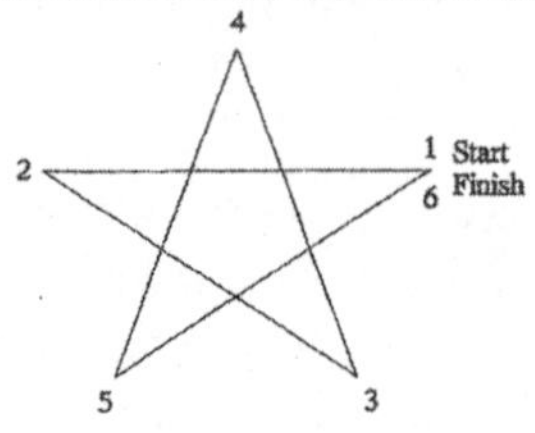

Fig. 8.9

18. If the north Watchtower is the altar candle or if it's the only source of light in the room, it can be kept lit until the room lights are turned on.

19. The Aridian tradition refers to this stance as the Gesture of Power.

20. In some covens, the members kiss the blades (sword, seax) before lowering them.

9. Invoking the Gods

1. In an all-female coven, another High Priestess would assume the role of the High Priest and invoke the Goddess. In an all-male coven, a High Priest would assume the High Priestess' place, and the spirit would be invoked into him. However, this second instance requires preparation because, as the recipient, he must "gender switch" in order to accept the "female" spirit.

2. In the event that the coven doesn't have a scourge, an athame can readily be substituted as an alternative.

3. The Osiris Position was adapted from the practices of the Golden Dawn. See "Sign of Osiris Risen," *The Golden Dawn*, Volume II, Book Two, page 134.

4. The Fivefold Kiss is also known as the Fivefold Salute. It consists of a series of eight kisses (or blessings).

5. There's also a Gardnerian (and an Alexandrian) version that has the Priest touch the Priestess in the following pattern: right breast, left breast, womb, and right breast. This series is repeated three times. Either form is acceptable.

6. Gerald Gardner wrote an entirely different recitation that he originally adapted from an Aleister Crowley poem. Although it was accepted for a long time, in recent years a large portion of Gardnerians have moved away from Gardner's original text and have instead adopted this new passage as more suitable for invocation. The origin of this new text is unknown, but it's believed to have been written by Doreen Valiente, Alex Sanders, or possibly Stuart Farrar.

7. This is also new wording. The original verse, written by Doreen Valiente, went as follows: "Of the Mother darksome and divine; Mine the scourge, and mine the kiss; The five-point star of love and bliss; Here I charge you, in this sign." While this passage is still widely used, the newer version is gaining popularity because it tends to fit into the invocation process better than the original.

8. The Italian pattern is similar to one of the Gardnerian versions. The difference is that the Gardnerian High Priest uses his hand instead of a wand, and the triangle is formed three times.

9. Most denominations that invoke the God into the Priest do so through the ritual of Drawing Down the Sun. However, in the West Country tradition, the Priest performs this act silently just prior to invoking the Goddess.

10. If a dish of water is used for a Full Moon Esbat, the dish should be placed at the feet of the Priestess.

11. Although the pattern of kisses closely follows that of Gardnerian Wicca, the wording is condensed so that only one verse is recited to cover the entire sequence of kisses. It's also worth noting that a "salute" usually refers to a kiss and embrace, which may or may not be accompanied by a verbal blessing.

12. If this ritual is performed by an all-female coven, a High Priestess assumes the

role of the High Priest and the God is invoked into her. However, this requires preparation because the High Priestess must mentally "gender switch" in order to accept the "male" spirit. In an all-male coven, a High Priest performs the invocation in place of a High Priestess.

13. Since the athame usually has a short handle, the dominant hand must be on it. If a witch is right-handed, the right hand is on the handle and the left should be resting on top of the right. If left-handed, the hand positions are reversed.

14. The position of the hands against the chest depends on the length of the athame. Lower them as needed to keep the tip from touching the neck or chin. (This is the reason that the sword is not used.)

15. The "area above the pubic region" means anywhere below the navel. Because this is only a symbolic gesture, wide latitude is given to placement.

16. This is the first instance where the wording changes between man and woman. The wording for a woman would be womb rather than phallus. The second instance occurs in the next line, which now reads ". . . formed in strength."

17. There's also a Gardnerian (and an Alexandrian) version that has the Priestess touch the Priest in the following pattern: right breast, left breast, pubic area, and right breast. This series is repeated three times. Either form is acceptable.

18. At sabbat ceremonies, a bonfire (or candle) is usually lit as the High Priest says "Let there be light."

10. Declamations

1. The Gardnerian Charge was adapted from several sources. Parts were taken from Leland's *Aradia: Gospel of the Witches*; parts were taken from Aleister Crowley's *Book of the Law*; and parts were written by Gardner and Doreen Valiente.

2. This last sentence is from Gardner's original text, but it's often omitted in contemporary versions of the Charge as being inappropriate. Nevertheless, it can still be found in use simply because it was part of Gardner's original wording. Cf. *The Book of Shadows* by Lady Sheba, (Llewellyn, 1971).

3. The Charge is a prime example of Craft custom having somewhat of an adverse effect on Craft practice. It's customary for a new witch to copy, by hand, his or her denomination's *Book of Shadows*. But over the years, constant recopying has unintentionally altered the wording of the original and produced slightly different variations. Although the variations aren't detrimental in this example, that's not always the case.

4. The Charge of Aradia appears in *Aradia: Gospel of the Witches*, (Chapter 1, pages 4–7; Chapter 2, page 14).

5. This speech is normally divided between the esbat and Full Moon Esbat rituals, though it can be used as a whole during the sabbats or other special occasions.

6. This is where the "Charge" portion begins. The preceding two verses were almost identical to those found in an esbat, but from this point on, the wording becomes Goddess oriented. In a normal esbat ceremony, the following lines are simply inserted in the appropriate places.

7. There's no question that this portion of the address is very similar to the Gardnerian and Italian Charges. Though unconfirmed, this is most likely a modern addition that was adopted after the Gardnerian version became popular. While this is usual-

ly the end of the esbat speech, many Saxon covens like to add the next few lines.

8. This is one of many prayers to Woden. There's also a version that takes its wording from the esbat rites, another that borrows wording from the Gardnerian Invocation to the Great God Cernunnos, and still another that's in the form of a rhyming chant.

9. Certain traditions place the invocation of the God first and the Goddess prayer second.

10. Unlike the Charge, which uses established wording, this is the name given to any of the prayers used for the God.

11. The Horned God Sign is formed by keeping the forefinger and little finger raised while folding the middle and ring fingers into the palm and wrapping the thumb over them. This sign is usually made with the right hand.

12. The following passage was taken from *The Key of Solomon*, Book I, Chapter V, (pages 25, 28). This is only one of many versions used.

13. This is a version of *The Conjuration of Cain*, as it appears in *The Sabbat: Treguenda or Witch-Meeting—How to Consecrate the Supper*, of *Aradia: Gospel of the Witches*, (page 12).

14. A second version of a prayer to Woden.

11. Consecration

1. The process for consecrating water and salt has already been described in the Circle casting rite.

2. Some denominations believe that the item must be kept with you at all times, if possible, for the entire month.

3. The sword is consecrated using the same process as the athame/seax.

4. The Gardnerian tradition prefers that a man and woman work together to consecrate an item, especially the athame/sword. Although this is not essential, when the practice is followed, each person should perform half the tasks.

5. This is known as the First Conjuration. Gerald Gardner took the wording for this passage directly from *The Key of Solomon the King*, Book II, Chapter VIII, page 97.

6. This is known as the Second Conjuration. Once again, Gerald Gardner took the wording directly from *The Key of Solomon the King*, Book II, Chapter XIX, page 115. Because the original contained "God the Father Almighty" and "Angels," Gardner altered the wording slightly.

7. The sword is consecrated when a coven is first formed, and the rite is performed by the Priest/Priestess forming the coven.

8. The pentacle itself is also consecrated, and this technically should be the first item done after the athame.

9. As with the athame consecration, Gerald Gardner took the wording for this passage directly from *The Key of Solomon the King*, Book II, Chapter VIII, pages 97–98.

10. Elemental tools will be presented to the quarter to which they correspond. For example: wand = air = east; chalice = water = west. The wording of the passage that follows will also be appropriately amended.

11. Custom dictates that this should occur at midnight. But any time after ten o'clock is acceptable.

12. The Saxon ceremony is called Cakes and Ale, as ale is used instead of wine. This

stems from the belief that the original Saxon witches wouldn't have had wine and would have, therefore, used the only alcoholic beverage (ale) readily available.

13. This holds true unless the Great Rite is held, at which point the consecration of wine become an important part of the ritual. (See Great Rite.)

14. This does not need to be performed by the coven leaders. In fact, when a High Priestess/Priest other than the coven leaders are chosen to perform the Great Rite, this pair will automatically be the ones to consecrate the cakes and wine.

15. There are two different patterns that can take place at this point. The first dictates that the chalice be passed around and that each person takes a sip. The second says that the cakes are consecrated first, then the wine and cakes are shared together. Either version is correct.

16. During the months that the God reigns as the primary deity, the Priest handles the blessing. During the months that the Goddess reigns, the Priestess performs the blessing.

17. If the owner of the item is a man, the High Priestess conducts the rite with him. If it's a woman, the High Priest conducts the consecration with her. The point is to have a man and woman participating. It's also permissible for the owner to place the item on the pentacle, then allow the High Priest and High Priestess to conduct the rite.

12. Wiccan Chants

1. A simple fact is that although they all had their own chants, most traditions never bothered to give their versions a name. But once they saw what a great term the Gardnerians had, they adopted it.

2. Once cast, the Magick Circle forms a cone. As psychic energy builds up inside this cone, the combined energy force is known as the Cone of Power.

3. These four lines are repeated three times both times they're used.

4. At the beginning of the chant, the tempo is slow and drawn out so that the words sound like "Looorrrd aaand Laaady, Laaady aaand Looorrrd." But with each set of words, the tempo accelerates until its pace reaches a quickened tone. Also, though Woden and Frig are used in this example, any deity name may be inserted.

13. Great Rite

1. The ritual is known as the Great Rite in Gardnerian and Alexandrian practice, but other denominations call it the Rite of Joining, the Crossing Rite, or the Ridencrux Rite. Here, it will always be called the Great Rite.

2. In its most basic form, the Great Rite is a way of channeling the unification of the Goddess and God into an appreciable concept.

3. Couples that are engaged, or longtime lovers, can be allowed to perform this rite. But, these people should always be partners who are committed to each other.

4. In single-gender covens that choose to perform the Great Rite, this is the form that they usually use. All that's required is for one partner to symbolically adopt his opposite gender trait.

5. The Great Rite is usually enacted only at the sabbats. Although it may be performed on other occasions, its magnitude seems a little much for an ordinary esbat.

6. This version is based on the symbolic rite that is popular today. While it contains

Gardner's original wording, the athame/chalice portion is new. The traditional version is contained in the chapter on Third-degree Initiation.

7. Consecrating the wine plays an important part of the symbolic rite. The cakes are consecrated separately after the rite is over.

8. Custom dictates that these two witches stand even with the hips of the High Priestess and just beyond her fingertips. In reality, the attendants only need to be close enough to hand the chalice/athame to the High Priest/ess and take the veil once it's removed.

9. This portion of the recitation was adapted from Aleister Crowley. See *Magick* (London, 1973).

10. Boaz ("In it is strength") and Jachin ("He shall establish") are the twin pillars that flanked the entrance to the Holy of Holies in Solomon's Temple. See *Bible*, Kings, VII:21 and Chronicles III:17; and *Thompson Chain-Reference Bible* (pages 1626–1627). In Ceremonial Magick, Boaz (Black Pillar) equals strength, severity, while Jachin is the White Pillar of Mercy. See *The Golden Dawn*, Volume I, Book One (page 81). In the Great Rite, the outstretched legs of the Priestess represent the twin pillars; right leg is Boaz, left leg is Jachin.

11. In an "actual" ceremony, this is the point at which the coven leaves.

12. Thrusting the athame into the chalice is the symbolic act of joining the God and Goddess.

13. It is most likely going to be the female witch who's holding the athame. If she hasn't set it down, she can momentarily hand it to the High Priest or another male witch.

14. In covens that have a Maiden, she cuts the doorway. Otherwise, any female witch may do so.

15. If the ceremony is being held outdoors, members of the coven should go to a place where they cannot see or hear anything that happens in the Circle. If the outdoor areas make this impossible, the coven should stand as far away as possible and keep their backs to the Circle.

16. The West Country Great Rite is given in the section on Second-degree Initiation as this is the only time it is ever used.

14. Esbat

1. The difference between the Full Moon Esbat and New Moon Esbat concerns the waxing/waning power of the moon, which in turn affects the workings that can be conducted during each phase.

2. This is not a steadfast rule, and there may be reason to admit nonmembers to the esbat. However, these times are normally few and far between for most covens, especially those that worship skyclad. This is also true of traditions that worship clothed, but prefer neophytes to be skyclad during initiation.

3. In years that have thirteen full moons rather than twelve, the thirteenth is called the Oak Moon.

4. The reason behind placing the Goddess figurine in a more prominent location is that the full moon is a representation of her, and she is the principal deity associated with this ritual. If at all possible, try to arrange the altar so that moonlight entering the room

falls on the figurine.

5. Through accident or error, midnight simply became known as the traditional time when rituals were conducted, hence the term the "witching hour."

6. Drawing Down the Sun is also performed on certain occasions, such as an initiation. At those times, this is the point at which it's conducted.

7. If there is an initiation taking place, the order of the Charge and Witches' Rune are reversed and the initiation takes place after the Charge.

8. These first four lines are also used at the beginning and end of the Witches' Rune. The Bagahi laca bachabé verse is from a thirteenth century French play, *Le Miracle de Théophile*, written by a troubadour named Ruteboeuf. See Michael Harrison, *Roots of Witchcraft* (London, 1973).

9. This is the spot where the Great Rite is conducted, though it's not always performed.

10. During an initiation, this is when the newly initiated witch consecrates his/her tools.

11. This chant is similar to the Gardnerian Witches' Rune chant and is aimed at raising power. However, the energy raised is focused at the chalice of wine rather than simply allowing the power to build within the Circle.

12. Originally a Tuscan custom of fireside chats, in the Italian tradition today, the Veglia is a short speech giving the oral history of the denomination.

13. This is not the consecration rite, but merely a blessing. The consecration rite takes place after the working portion of the ceremony is completed.

14. The Charge of the Goddess used by Italian denominations is very similar to that used by Gardnerians. This resulted from the Gardnerian Charge being adapted from Leland's *Aradia: Gospel of the Witches*.

15. The opening and closing prayers vary greatly from coven to coven. The only requirement for the prayers is that they stress the virtues of the Goddess and give thanks. It's also important to incorporate reference to the phase of the moon (full or new) and the effect this will have on the rite.

16. The New Moon Esbat is similar in design. The difference between the two rites parallels the difference between the waxing/waning phases of the moon. The new moon signifies the phase where death and rebirth meet, and this is the theme transferred to the ritual.

17. This entire section is similar to, if not an adaptation of, the Gardnerian Charge.

18. There's a subgroup within the Saxon tradition that inserts a modified version of the second half of the Gardnerian Charge at this point.

19. West Country makes no clear distinction between a Full or New Moon Esbat. Though they recognize the significance of each lunar phase, there is no major modification made to the ritual.

20. The pan of water, which reflects the moon, is used to bring the moon into the Circle only during the Full Moon Esbat. Since this will be the focus of a ring-dance, it needs to be placed in (or moved to) a spot that allows the dancers to circle it. This may create a problem for indoor rituals where window placement may make reflecting the moon impossible. In such cases, the pan of water is abandoned completely.

21. This first chant is usually nothing more than a few simple lines or a rhythmic prayer. Its purpose is to infuse the newly cast Circle with an initial burst of power in anticipation of the Goddess and God being called.

22. The chant (with ring-dance) is the equivalent of the Gardnerian Witches' Rune. The dance centers around the bonfire, pan of water or the altar. Unlike the first chant, the goal of this chant is to build sufficient power to facilitate working.

15. First-Degree Initiation

1. The time for taking this name will depend on the tradition. Gardnerian witches wait until they become second-degree witches before adopting a witch name, while West Country witches do it immediately.

2. The Gardnerian and Alexandrian traditions also have a fourth designation known as Witch Queen. Only a coven leader can be elevated to this position and only after two new covens are formed from the coven she leads. Some covens have a formal initiation for this, while others merely acknowledge the new title.

3. Most denominations use the nine-foot cord. Gardnerian, however, uses all three cords, while Alexandrian uses two. Particular colors are not required, but different traditions do have preferences. Gardnerian prefers three red cords, though green, blue, or black are acceptable. Alexandrian uses two cords; a red cord for the wrists and neck and a white cord for the ankles. West Country uses a single cord. White is preferred, but any color will suffice.

4. The Horned Helmet is a Saxon custom that was adopted from the Norse traditions. This can be almost any type of headgear from a horned Viking-style helmet to an antlered hat.

5. With the exception of one or two relatively minor differences, the Alexandrian rites virtually mirror the Gardnerian practices.

6. If for some reason the initiation must take place later in the ceremony, the Novice should be asked to wait in a separate room. At the very least, the Novice should wait in an area outside the Circle.

7. Gardnerian custom dictates that the witches performing the binding and the High Priest/ess acting as the Initiator should be of the opposite sex from the Novice. But this is not a steadfast rule, and exceptions are common.

8. A common practice is to tie the cords so that they drape over the shoulders and hang down over the chest. They are then called cable-tows. Some covens use these cable-tows to lead the Novice around.

9. This sentence is used by Gardnerians, yet for some reason, it doesn't usually appear in printed versions of the rite. It is, however, contained in Gardner's *High Magic's Aid*, which verifies its authenticity.

10. Gerald Gardner borrowed the Cabalistic Cross passage, literally word for word, from *The Golden Dawn*. See *The Golden Dawn*, Volume I, Book One (page 53).

11. If the coven has a Maiden, this is the woman he calls. If not, he usually motions to the most senior female witch.

12. The lashes given to the Novice are nothing more than light, symbolic strokes.

13. Except for the first three rings, all the other counts are optional.

14. For convenience and practical reasons, the bowl and cup do not necessarily have to be ceremonial items.

15. "Swear my allegiance to the Old Ways" is a passage that relates back to the Inquisition and implies that the witch will not reveal the secrets of the Craft.

16. A person wishing to enter the Saxon tradition must first be schooled in the basics of the Craft. While some covens ask a prospective candidate to submit to extensive training, others merely require that they understand the basic aspects of the religion.

17. There is also the philosophy that says the Priestess initiates a man and the Priest a woman. In this case, the Priestess would speak saying: *I am the one who speaks for Frig.* She would also handle the remaining initiation.

18. In reverse-gender initiation, the Priest/ess kisses the Ceorl on the lips. There is also a version where the Priest/ess kisses the Ceorl on the lips, then on the three points that were anointed.

19. A "Gesith" is the Saxon term used for a witch (male or female). The Priestess and Priest are selected and elevated to coven leaders by the rest of the coven.

20. There are various versions of this. The Inductee crawls through the spread legs of the other witches; the Inductee is first turned around several times to make him/her disoriented, etc. The main goal seems to have been to make the entrance process fun.

21. This represented the elements of water and fire, the fire having warmed the mixture. Crawling on the ground had subjected them to earth and air.

16. Second-Degree Initiation

1. With the exception of one or two relatively minor differences, the Alexandrian rites virtually mirror the Gardnerian practices.

2. A half-mask is used in West Country initiation to hide the identity of the Priest/Priestess, and as a symbolic representation of the God/Goddess. The nature of each mask should suggest the deity it represents.

3. A veil and jewelry are needed if the (Gardnerian) Magickal Legend of Aradia is enacted. Otherwise, a veil is necessary during the West Country initiation only if a man is being initiated.

4. Gardnerian custom dictates that the witches performing the binding and the High Priest/ess acting as the Initiator, should be of the opposite sex from the Initiate. But this is not a steadfast rule, and exceptions are common.

5. For a woman the wording is Priestess and Witch, then High Priestess and Witch Queen. Though the use of Witch Queen seems odd, this is Gardner's exact wording.

6. Gardner prescribed that the coven circle only "3 times." However, recent practice has been to conduct the Witches' Rune in its entirety.

7. The lashes given are nothing more than light, symbolic strokes.

8. Except for the first three rings, all the other counts are optional.

9. This position is known as the Magick Link. Its purpose is to allow the Initiator, whether High Priest or High Priestess, to transfer psychic power to the Initiate, thereby proliferating the psychic flow within the Craft.

10. This is an Americanized version of the Sigil of Second Degree. Gardner used the Inverted Pentagram, i.e., pubic area, right breast, left hip, right hip, left breast, pubic area (Figure 16.2). But, since the inverted pentagram unfairly receives negative connotations from being associated with Satanism, it's seldom used today. There's also a third version,

SIGIL OF SECOND DEGREE (Inverted)

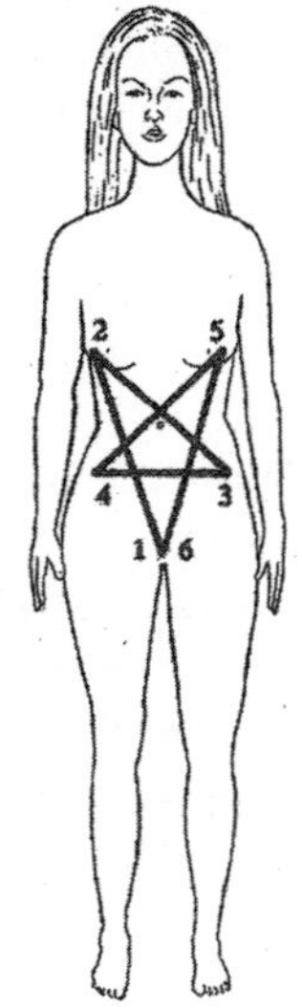

Fig. 16.2

SIGIL OF SECOND DEGREE (European)

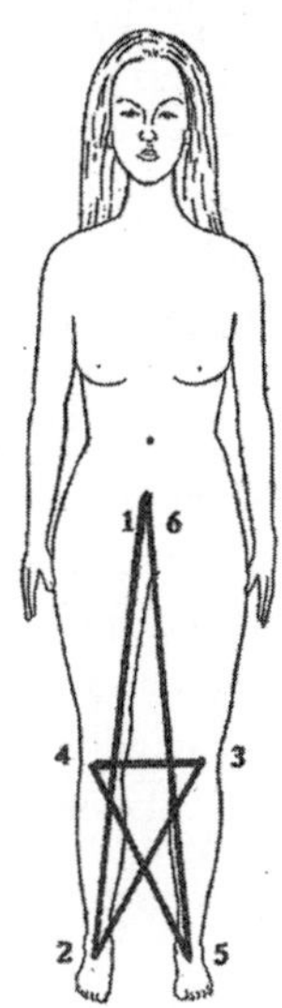

Fig. 16.3

pubic area, right foot, left knee, right knee, left foot, pubic area (Figure 16.3), but again, this isn't that popular.

11. The candle is normally inscribed with a pentagram and then kept by the witch as a sign that he/she has progressed to an advanced stage within the Craft. If the witch ever founds a coven, this candle is the first one placed on the altar.

12. This part of the rite is added to teach the Wiccan Rede principle that all acts, good or bad, return threefold.

13. The Magickal Legend of Aradia is also known as the Legend of the Descent of the Goddess (*Witches' Bible Complete*), and The Myth of the Goddess (*Witchcraft Today*). The versions are all similar with only minor wording changes.

14. By today's moral standards, this is a highly questionable practice. However, in the rural areas where West Country developed, there were no such sexual hang-ups. Sex was equated with life, and the idea of promiscuity never entered into the formula.

15. Custom dictates that quartered apples are used in place of the cakes.

17. Third-Degree Initiation

1. The Initiate is labeled "Priestess," while the Initiator is labeled "High Priest." This is simply done for clarity. However, in order to initiate someone to the third degree, the Initiator must be a third-degree witch.

2. The Magickal Legend of Aradia begins here. If it was used at the end of the second-degree initiation, it should be omitted. In that case, move forward in the rite to the point where the Priestess is in the Osiris Position receiving the Fivefold Kiss.

3. The participants are distinguished as follows: The Goddess dons the jewelry and

veil; the Lord of the Underworld wears a crown and holds the sword; the Guardian of the Portals ties a red cord around his waist and holds the athame.

4. Unless the participants can remember all the words, it's impractical to have everyone recite his or her own verses. Therefore, the Narrator narrates while the participants perform the rite.

5. In this instance, "magic" means love.

6. The Crowned Pentagram is the Sigil of Third Degree.

7. If the Great Rite is actual, the coven exits at this point.

18. Handfasting

1. The Wand of Flowers can be as simple as a bunch of flowers wrapped with string to give them rigidity or an actual wand that is covered with flowers.

2. Since this rite can be used for same-sex unions, a broomstick, which is a fertility symbol, may seem inappropriate or offensive to a gay or lesbian couple. But the exact opposite is true. Failing to have this item at a gay or lesbian Handfasting is viewed as inconsiderate of the couple's feelings, as well as ignorant of ritualistic custom. Omitting a fertility symbol is the equivalent of saying that the couple, whether gay or straight, should not be allowed children. For this reason alone, there is always a fertility symbol at all Handfasting ceremonies.

3. The Maiden, if there is one, can take the place of the High Priestess and lead the groom into the Circle, though only the High Priest should lead the bride. In either case, the High Priestess and High Priest should not be out of the Circle at the same time.

4. This passage normally follows the Fivefold Kiss.

5. Even if only one person is a witch, the couple still consecrates the wine and cakes together with the witch leading the other partner. If neither is a witch (something that happens from time to time), the couple still performs the consecration, but the High Priest and High Priestess lead them through the rite.

6. The pairs should be arranged: man/woman, woman/man, man/woman, etc. This arrangement ensures a male/female sequence of pairs and columns.

7. Any non-Wiccan guests follow behind the coven.

8. The altar candle is used for the fire. However, since passing the rings through flame may damage them, they're merely passed over it.

9. The "poem" is usually something specifically prepared for, or by, the couple. It may also be a favorite literary work. The poem, "Love and the Witches," written in 1891 by Mary E. Wilkins Freeman (1852–1930) is often used.

It was a little, fearful maid,
Whose mother left her all alone;
Her door with iron bolt she stayed,
And 'gainst it rolled a lucky stone-
For many a night she'd waked with fright
When witches by the house had flown.

To piping lute in still midnight,
Who comes a-singing at the door,-

That showeth seams of gold light,-
"Ah, open, darling, I implore"?
She could not help knowing 't was Love,
Although they'd never met before.

She swiftly shot the iron bar,
And rolled the lucky stone away,
And careful set the door ajar-
"Now enter in, Sir Love, I pray;
My mother knows it not, but I have watched
For you this many a day."

With fan and roar of gloomy wings
They gave the door a windy shove;
They perched on chairs and brooms and things;
Like bats they beat around above-
Poor little maid, she'd let the witches in with Love.

10. The only passage that's common to all West Country Handfasting rites seems to be a line spoken to the bride and groom by the presiding Priest/ess: *Ever remember that ye are the Hidden Children of the Goddess.*

19. Handparting

1. If either party answers "no," the ritual ends immediately. Handparting can only take place with unanimous agreement.

2. The significance of this arrangement is the interruption of the male/female bond.

3. Although this is not legally a responsibility of the High Priest/Priestess, it's still a moral obligation that the High Priest/Priestess assumes when he/she conducts the initial Handfasting.

4. As with Handfasting, this is not a steadfast requirement due to the possible presence of non-Wiccan guests.

5. The "Law" refers to the Craft principles of not harming others.

20. Wiccaning

1. This custom is carried out only when it's possible to plant the tree after the rite. During winter months, when it's impossible to plant a tree, the custom is abandoned because the tree would die.

2. If the coven has a Maiden, she may wait with the parents instead of the High Priest.

3. Covens in all denominations often have the High Priest, High Priestess, Maiden (or godparents if they use them) hold the child during the ceremony. However, this is a totally discretionary practice that must be decided on a case-by-case basis. It should never be mandatory.

4. After being consecrated, the wine is set aside at this point. It'll be used to anoint the child and shared later with the cakes.

5. The "womb" refers to the cauldron. The cauldron is a feminine symbol, and in

this context, it refers to the Celtic "Cauldron of Cerridwen," which is the "Sacred Cauldron of Inspiration and Knowledge."

6. Mother/father's legal name is used here, and their "witch" name is used later. If either, or both, is not a witch, their legal names are used throughout.

7. There's also a version of this rite, made popular by Janet and Stewart Farrar, that calls for the use of godparents. If this variation is used, it begins here. The basic addition is that the godparents are asked to promise loyalty to the child.

8. Italian anointing oil is usually "extra virgin" olive oil.

9. This act replaces the sharing of wine and cakes.

10. Saxon Wiccaning, also called the Birth Rite, can take place as part of a normal esbat or as an individual ceremony.

11. This process is meant to cleanse the child of impurities.

21. Funerals

1. Although seldom practiced by witches any longer, there is an old Celtic custom of binding a corpse with cords. These cords were then removed from the body and used in "learning second sight." (See *Witchcraft Today*, page 159, n.2.)

2. The version described is the second form held without the body of the deceased.

3. If the body were present, the Circle would be arranged so that the deceased was in the west quarter.

4. The High Priest/Priestess should be the same gender as the deceased.

5. As the witches touch the candle, a transfer of energy links the entire coven. In order to assist (power) the soul as it departs, this energy is released when the candle is burned.

6. The "funeral pyre" refers to the black candle.

7. The participants are distinguished as follows: the Goddess dons the jewelry and veil; the Lord of the Underworld wears a crown and holds the sword; the Guardian of the Portals ties a red cord around his waist and holds the athame.

8. Unless the participants can remember all the words, which is unlikely, it's impractical to have everyone recite his or her own lines. Therefore, the Narrator narrates all the verses.

9. The altar cloth is usually included only when the person is a coven leader. If used, it's folded and placed on the chest of the deceased or draped over the body like a shroud.

10. If the deceased's body is present, it's placed on the western edge of the Circle and the coven members arrange themselves on either side.

11. The Myth of the Descent of the Goddess is the Italian version of the Magickal Legend of Aradia.

22. Runes, Symbols, and Rituals

1. Over the course of history, the Anglo-Saxon Runes have varied in number from a low of twenty-eight characters to a high of thirty-three. However, the thirty-one characters used today are the most widely accepted number.

2. This rune derives its name from the first six letters ("th" is one letter) listed in the sequence. The Saxon version is known as "Futhorc" instead of Futhark, due to a repositioning of the "o" and "c" in place of the "a" and "k" symbols.

3. Examples of sigils can be found throughout *The Key of Solomon*. Examples of some symbols used on tools can be found on pages 96–97 (plates XIII and XIV).

23. Botanicals

1. Glass jars do not release material into the mixture and prevent contamination. However, airtight jars will also hold pressure. If hot liquid is added to a jar, the pressure must be released after the liquid has cooled.

2. An "astringent" is something that tightens or contracts the skin. A rash would be treated with this. An "emollient" is something that softens or soothes the skin. A bee sting or sunburn is treated with this.

24. Divination

1. There are several hundred different Tarot decks on the market. Of these, the Rider-Waite deck, designed for A. E. Waite, is very popular. Another fairly popular version is the Thoth deck, developed by Aleister Crowley, and defined in Crowley's *Book of Thoth*. The following is a list of other specialized decks.

Classic: Rider-Waite, Aquarian, Thoth, Marseilles
Esoteric: Golden Dawn, Masonic, Royal Fez Moroccan
Symbolism/Mythology: Norse, Celtic, Jungian
Historical: Visconti-Sforza (15th century), Tarot Vieville (17th century), Vandenborre Bacchus (18th century), Oswald Wirth (19th century).

2. The names of the four suits of the Minor Arcana match the Elemental tools used in witchcraft.

3. Some decks transpose Justice (8) and Strength (11).

4. The descriptions are only suggestions. Significators should be chosen to match a person's profile. This may mean selecting a card with a different description simply because it more closely fits the person.

5. The Tree of Life spread is divided into three pillars. The left-hand path is known as the Pillar of Judgment and represents the feminine/passive/negative side; the right-hand path, the Pillar of Mercy, is the male/active/positive side; and the middle path, the Pillar of Mildness, is the balance of the two opposites.

6. Most denominations frown upon taking the names of deities for witch names.

7. The pictures will usually be symbolic and require interpretation.

25. Magick

1. Evelyn Underhill, *Mysticism*, (1930; twelfth edition), page 152.

2. Some books refer to the different components of a spell as its "elements." While this terminology is acceptable, it often causes confusion with the Four Elements.

3. A solitary witch building psychic power to a point where it's sufficient to fulfill the goal of a spell has a more difficult time than a coven simply because a coven has more witches combining their psychic energies. But at the same time, a solitary practitioner does have the advantage of directing all of his/her psychic power at a single purpose rather than a broad spectrum. The wide intent is a drawback of coven spell casting.

Therefore, a solitary witch can usually achieve singular results as often as a coven can achieve group results.

4. It's a common practice to use a "trigger" word to release the psychic energy. Any word or phrase will work just as long as you know that by saying it, you are sending the accumulated energy on its way.

5. It's a steadfast rule never to use recycled material, simply because there might be energy left over on the recycled paper. For ecologically conscious people, using recycled material is possible by cleansing it first.

6. Whenever possible, use spring water and sea salt, since these items are to cleanse and consecrate the crystal, or simply use the salt/water from the altar.

26. Sabbats

1. It's common practice for a sabbat to follow a denomination's esbat ritual up to a certain point before moving on to the actual sabbat rite.

2. The sabbats are listed in reference to the Christian (standard) calendar that is in use today. This differs from the Wiccan calendar, which recognizes Samhain as the Celtic New Year.

3. The names for the Druidic Lesser Sabbats differ from their Wiccan counterparts, though the Druidic Greater Sabbats share the same Celtic names.

4. In a few old (or poorly researched) books, this sabbat is sometimes erroneously referred to as Beltane. This error is due to the early Beltane-like practice of lighting bonfires on hilltops. However, the two festivals should not be confused, especially since Beltane is a Greater Sabbat.

5. These changes can be further explained by the Law of Polarity and Law of Gender.

6. Sabbats aren't normally the time for a coven to conduct healings or perform spells, though exceptions are sometimes made if the task requires an inordinate amount of power or is extremely urgent.

7. It's important to remember that the singing and dancing associated with this portion of the sabbat has a different goal than the chants and dances in the first part. These activities are for entertainment purposes while the others have a religious objective.

8. Mardi Gras in New Orleans, Louisiana, and Carnivale in Rio de Janeiro, Brazil, are two grand examples of similar religious festivals where a party atmosphere exists in conjunction with a religious theme.

27. Candlemas

1. This sabbat should not be mistaken for the ancient Roman holiday of Lupercalia, which was observed on February 15.

2. It's better to make a special phallic wand than to adapt a personal or coven wand.

3. Although this Irish custom is very common throughout Gardnerian practice, its placement within the ceremony differs. Some covens like to set it up at this point, while others like to wait until after Drawing Down the Sun.

4. If possible, a woman younger than the High Priestess should be chosen for the Maiden and a woman older than the High Priestess for the Crone.

5. There are far more elaborate Brid's Bed rites, but this one is both quaint and wide-

ly used throughout Gardnerian and Alexandrian practice.

6. It's also allowable to use the flame from the cauldron candle or, if outdoors, the flame from a bonfire.

7. A modified version of the Charge is part of this address.

8. The Mother and Crone may either follow behind the Maiden or remain at the altar while she sweeps the Circle.

9. Traditionally, "winter" incenses are frankincense, myrrh, and evergreen, though holly, mistletoe, and rosemary are also acceptable. In addition, many occult shops sell special blends of incense specifically for individual sabbats. A small twig of evergreen (with green needles) may be substituted for the incense.

10. If glow sticks are used for the crown, there is no way to extinguish the light. Therefore, the only way to douse the light is to place the crown in a bag (a cloth bag, large purse, etc.) that blocks the light until the ceremony is finished.

11. This passage appears in *Aradia: Gospel of the Witches* (chapter 14, page 87).

12. A modified version of verses 2 and 3 of the "Hunting-Song of the Seeonee Pack" from Rudyard Kipling's *The Jungle Book.*

13. This entire sequence—wearing the wolf pelt, dancing, scourging—is adapted from the Roman festival of Lupercalia.

14. These candles first appear at the Yule Sabbat and remain until after this ceremony.

15. Instead of the besom, the cauldron may be moved into the center. Also, the Lupercalia fertility scourging may be inserted in place of jumping the besom or cauldron.

28. Spring Equinox

1. The Spring and Autumn Equinoxes are considered "new additions" because they first appear post-Christianity while the traditional sabbats existed pre-Christianity.

2. There's a very small minority of witches who refuse to accept anything other than Celtic or European witchcraft, believing that these were the areas where true witchcraft originated and that anything else is nontraditional.

3. This doesn't necessarily hold true for all denominations, but it does include covens that practice skyclad. For this rite, a skyclad coven will dress the Priest in a special ceremonial garment.

4. The egg may be buried to infuse the land with fertility, or it can simply be shelled and crumbled onto the ground as an offering.

5. If thirteen people participate (seven women/six men), the High Priest holds a strand in each hand while the other ends are both held by women. When there's an extra man, the High Priestess holds two ends. (See Figure 28.1.)

6. The High Priestess holds the phallic wand, which she gives to the High Priest after circling the cauldron.

7. During the speech, the Maiden goes to the altar and lights a taper from the altar candle. When she leaves the altar, she brings the ropes for the wheel-dance with her.

8. This is based on the length of the Witches' Rune. Shorter chants will require more renditions, while longer chants may require fewer than three.

9. The Aridian branch of this denomination has an entirely different Spring Equinox rite than any listed here. Though it incorporates most of the same symbolism,

it adds an interpretation of the ascent of the Goddess from the Realms of the Underworld. (See *Italian Witchcraft*, pages 146-147.)

10. A ceramic pot is ideal because the seeds can be planted in it and left to grow.

11. Ideally, the pairs consist of a male and female. Each man should hold his seax while each woman holds two flowerpots, her own and her partner's. If there are more men or women, the pair shares the responsibilities by holding the seax and pot together.

12. Because an egg is buried after the ceremony, the normal offering of cake is not required.

13. The "greenwood" chaplets for the men can be made of any greenery, including ivy, stalks and branches with new leaves, or even long-stemmed grasses. Short branches are sometimes added to resemble horns.

14. Attaching a seed makes it a phallic wand and symbolizes the planting season.

15. For an indoor ceremony, the eggs are simply placed at the base of the Watchtower candles.

16. If an actual rite is going to be held and the coven leaders are not an intimate couple, the honor may be designated to another couple.

29. Beltane

1. Anyone allergic to nuts should substitute sunflower seeds or fruit.

2. There is a great difference between a solitary practitioner and a coven at this point in the Beltane ritual. This is because a coven has several individuals participating in the rite and can enact a symbolic courtship between the Goddess and God, while a solitary witch doesn't have that luxury. A solitary practitioner will thus miss out on some of the gaiety and sexuality of this ritual.

3. There are several versions of this love-chase sequence. In this version, only the High Priest and High Priestess perform the chase. Others, however, have each pair of witches take a turn. Also, some versions have the coven rhythmically clap during the chase.

4. Do not blow out the altar candle if it's also the north Watchtower candle.

5. Blowing out the Bel-Fire symbolized the death of the God of the Waning Year, which the Oak King represented. Relighting the Bel-Fire symbolizes the reborn Oak King. It's important to gain a rudimentary understanding of this symbolism because it will be further complicated during Lughnasadh and Winter Solstice when both the Oak King and Holly King are part of the rite.

6. A Gardnerian adaptation of verse five of Rudyard Kipling's poem, "A Tree Song," from "Weland's Sword," which is part of his book, *Puck of Pook's Hill*. In borrowing this verse, Gardner made two minor changes in the first and third lines of the original text.

7. The Italian Stag God is the equivalent of the Oak King, while the Wolf God is the equivalent of the Holly King.

8. Traditionally, the candles should not be extinguished until the rite is over. However, it's often awkward and impractical to hold them throughout the entire rite. Therefore, when candles are used there should be a place to set them down where they can be left burning, but where they will not be in the way or do any harm.

9. The wine invocation is given in *Aradia* (Chapter 8, pages 44-47). Though Leland titled it, "To Have a Good Vintage and Very Good Wine by the Aid of Diana," he later acknowledges it has a relation to a good harvest for the coming year (page 48).

10. Some people put kindling in the cauldron and create a controlled bonfire. This is fine, but it will require cleaning the cauldron afterward.

11. Due to size restrictions, this is often placed outside the Circle to be used after the ceremony. Enlarging the Circle to accommodate the Maypole is also allowable.

12. In a village setting, the Maypole would not be used at the sabbat, but would be saved until the next day's festivities. However, modern West Country Wiccans have incorporated the Maypole into their rites.

13. This container may be an ordinary pitcher. Its only purpose is to hold the wine. A funnel may be used to pour the wine back into its bottle, though this may be a bit messy or cumbersome.

14. The female is selected in advance to become the May Queen. Traditionally, she was supposed to be a virgin, and she wasn't allowed to attend the May Eve celebration. But this custom has been dispensed with, and any deserving girl/woman may be chosen for this honor.

30. Summer Solstice

1. It's also interesting to note that there are several old beliefs that regard the act (of a woman walking naked through the fields) as a way to ensure a successful harvest.

2. An Oak Crown was made for Beltane.

3. Because many parts of this sabbat are predominantly male oriented—the death of the Oak King and birth of the Holly King—a simple chaplet will be more than sufficient for the Crown of Flowers.

4. An emerging trend is to use potted strawberry plants as decorations. These are inexpensive, very easy to grow, and they offer perfect symbolism. The fruit on most varieties of strawberries ripens in mid to late June.

5. The Holly King assumes the Slain God Position because technically he has not been reborn yet. However, some covens view the relationship as sibling rivalry and insist both kings exist simultaneously.

6. The Sun God candle may be moved out of the way to make room in the center of the Circle to finish the drama.

7. If the ceremony is not held outside, a libation dish and offering plate need to be placed at each quarter.

8. When the sunflower is placed inside the cauldron, it symbolizes the Sun God returning to the womb of the Great Mother.

9. If candles were given to the coven, the Thegn now leads a procession (widdershins) past the altar, during which each person extinguishes his or her candle.

31. Lughnasadh

1. King Rufus, often called the Red King, was, by all accounts, a Pagan. As such, he was loathed by the Christian clergy, but adored by the common people. According to legend, Rufus saw himself as a sacrificial king, in the image of the Corn King, and this may have led him to actually sacrifice himself. On August 2, 1100, while in New Forest (where Gerald Gardner was initiated), he was felled by the arrow of Sir Walter Tyrell. Whether a coincidence or planned, his death occurred in the thirteenth year of his reign. See *The God of the Witches* and *The Witch-Cult in Western Europe*, both by Margaret A. Murray.

2. It's worth noting that the Goddess is portrayed in her Triple-Goddess image at this time of year, and this ties in the sexual/sacrificial aspect of the rite. The sexual aspect to the ritual is derived from the mating of the God/Goddess, while the sacrificial aspect appears in the death of the God.

3. The God being closely linked with corn is probably not the original interpretation. The initial association was probably of a more common grain such as wheat, oat, or rye.

4. In his book, *The White Goddess*, Robert Graves gives an interesting translation of both Lugh and the Lughnasadh Sabbat.

5. The making of two crowns gives another witch the chance to participate in the rite, which is a very important feature to many covens.

6. If a male witch is chosen as the Corn King, then both men go to the center of the Circle. Otherwise, the High Priest will represent both deities.

7. A piece of bread should be saved as an offering to the earth.

8. This verse is "The Conjuration of Meal," as it appears in *Aradia: Gospel of the Witches* (pages 10-11).

9. An assistant needs to be chosen to hold the chalice. This person is either given bread, wine, and cakes before or after the coven.

10. The version listed is only one of many ways that this drama is carried out. Other versions include candles to represent the God.

11. Offering roles to three people, especially younger members, is a good way to further involve the coven in the ritual.

12. This is the symbolic death of the God. When the men rise, the eastern man will rejoin the coven while the other will continue to represent the God.

13. Although the wine is in the chalice, it's not consecrated. This wine is symbolic of the lifeblood of the harvest.

32. Autumn Equinox

1. The Autumn Equinox is the first time that death has shown itself on a wide scale, leaves turning color and falling from trees, frost killing crops and insects, etc.

2. Rather than trying to locate vines with grapes still attached, simply take sections of a grapevine and fasten bunches of grapes to them with twine.

3. If spray-painted leaves are too gaudy, there are other ways to accomplish the objective of adding color. Leaves can be made out of colored paper; but green leaves should be mixed with the fakes in order to add the natural symbolism.

4. This trend is often attributed to Janet and Stewart Farrar, the authors of *Eight Sabbats for Witches* (London: Robert Hale, 1981).

5. The Candle Game is also a popular Gardnerian custom during Candlemas.

6. The Stag God is a pre-Pan deity of summer, crops, and the forest, while the Wolf God is the hunter deity of winter.

7. In preparing a flower crown, use only white lilies. If these are not available, make a silver or white crescent-moon crown using other materials.

8. An alternate version practiced by many covens is to break off the bread and dip it into the wine before eating it.

9. If the ceremony is held outdoors, both offerings (bread/wine and cakes/wine) can

be made directly onto the ground. The cauldron is only used indoors to symbolize the earth.

10. To save space, grapes can be used. One or two bunches will supply plenty of fruit.

11. Although not required, some Saxon covens have the Priestess wear a silver or crescent-moon crown when she delivers this address.

12. Much of the beginning portion of this passage originates in the Gardnerian Autumn Equinox invocation, while a portion of it is from a popular solitary rite.

13. If the coven broom is delicate, a household straw broom can be used to sweep the leaves into the pile, then the coven broom is used for the rest of the rite.

33. Samhain

1. Whether witches like it or not, the commercialization of Samhain (Halloween) has thrust witchcraft into the spotlight on a grander scale than anything done by any witch. And though present-day Halloween is not exactly an accurate picture of the holy day, it has, nevertheless, given true witches a voice to spread the Wiccan word. Proof of this occurs in Salem, Massachusetts, on every October 31 as nearly one million visitors flock to the town where they mingle with the many resident Wiccans.

2. These jack-o'-lanterns were also used to frighten evil spirits and nonwitches away from sabbat meetings.

3. The belief was that the old God died at Samhain and that the Goddess mourned him for the next six weeks until he was reborn at Yule.

4. Various cultures know the Lord of Misrule as the Lord of Mischief, the Jester, the Master of Merriment (or Merry Disport), and the King of the Bean. He has also been linked to the Norse God, Loki, who was seen as a prankster.

5. In some covens, the High Priestess wears a veil throughout the ceremony.

6. There is a major divergence at this point in the rite. Some witches (especially those from Europe, Ireland, Scotland, and Britain) entrust the lead aspect of the rite to the High Priest, while American witches tend to relegate the duties to the High Priestess.

7. A more elaborate practice is to draw the entire series of invoking pentagrams—air, earth, fire, water, spirit—to make the ritual area as inviting as possible for spirits.

8. This speech is addressed to the spirits that have gathered outside the Circle.

9. The spirits entered from the west (death), but exit to the east because the east quarter represents rebirth. Some covens move the cauldron to the east quarter prior to cutting the doorway, but doing this makes it difficult to cut and seal the doorway.

10. Samhain is one of the few times that the actual Great Rite is recommended.

11. Altar placement will normally depend on the Myth of the Descent of Aradia. If it's to be acted out, space is needed, and the altar goes in the north. Otherwise, the center of the Circle is fine.

12. The Slain God Position is basically the same as the God Position (see Figure 17.1), except the High Priest's head is bowed.

13. The props can all be simple. Any necklace and veil (or scarf) will work, but they should both be white, if possible. The Lord's crown can be made from any material.

14. Along with removing the jewelry, some covens have adopted the use of a veil to represent clothing being shed, while others require that the Goddess actually strip off her ceremonial robes and remain skyclad during the play.

15. Some Italian witches use the inverted triangle instead of the invoking pentagram because they feel the invoking pentagram is too Gardnerian.

16. The crown may be plain, though most Saxon covens use a horned helmet. The chaplet should be fall flowers, but stalks of grain may replace the flowers or be mixed in.

17. These items are the same ones used by other traditions, which means this is likely a newer addition to the ceremony.

18. The scythes, sickles, and baskets represent the tools of gathering the harvest.

19. Mirroring the Goddess, the May Queen's rule is waning as this sabbat marks the first time that she is in decline, meaning she's been in office for more than six months. As such, she stands on the west side of the altar while the Priestess stands on the east side.

20. Unlike the Gardnerian and Alexandrian denominations, West Country has no truly permanent coven leaders. However, this denomination does decree that a Priest act as coven leader during the dark half of the year, while a Priestess assumes the duties during the light half. This mirrors the aspects of the God and Goddess.

34. Winter Solstice

1. Some denominations view the struggle between the Holly King (wren) and Oak King (robin) as a battle where one deity kills the other—the Oak King kills the Holly King at Yule, then the Holly King kills the Oak King at Midsummer. In other traditions, the belief is simply that one deity dies when the other is reborn and that no actual battle occurs. Under either scenario, the deities remain two parts of the same whole.

2. Further evidence of Santa's connection to Yule is found in the following. Red clothing is a reference to the robin or Oak King. Eight reindeer represent both the number of sabbats and an animal sacred to Celtic and Italian custom. The sleigh refers to a Germanic custom against using the wheel on this night. And gift giving is a Druidic practice during Yule.

3. Pine trees, or evergreens, were respected because of their ability to remain green during the winter. To Druids, this was symbolic of eternity since the tree never lost its leaves. Deciduous trees were believed to die when they lost their leaves and were then reborn in the springtime.

4. This crown started out as a simple evergreen wreath, evolved into a wreath with candles, then transformed into a flowery chaplet.

5. The log may also be maple, cherry, walnut, or hazelnut. However, oak is by far the premier choice.

6. In another example of sympathetic magick, fruits and nuts were added to wreaths as a way of wishing for a bountiful harvest in the coming season, and candles were sometimes added to call back the light. These augmentations were eventually transformed into Christmas decorations.

7. The Oak King assumes the Slain God Position because he has technically not been reborn yet. However, some covens view the relationship as sibling rivalry and insist that both kings exist simultaneously.

8. The red (God) candle may be placed on the altar to make room in the center of the Circle to finish the drama.

9. An excellent example of a longer version of the Winter Solstice Sabbat is found in Raven Grimassi's book, *Italian Witchcraft: The Old Religion of Southern Europe.*

10. Once in the God Position, the High Priest remains at the altar until summoned.

11. The wheel-dance is merely another form of ring-dance. Two six-foot lengths of rope are tied together at the center to represent the spokes of a wheel. Another version has seven ropes used. (See Figure 28.1.) In this version, four dancers take the ends, then they hold hands with the other coven members to form a wheel.

12. Though the normal Circle layout has the cauldron placed in the south and a bonfire in the center, incorporating a fireplace presents location problems. Since the fireplace can't be moved, the only solution is to reorient the Circle layout. If the fireplace is in the east or west, the altar may remain in the north and the cauldron in the south. If the fireplace is in the south, the altar may remain in the north with the cauldron set on the hearth. If the fireplace is in the north, northeast, or northwest, the altar moves to the south, and the cauldron goes next to it.

13. The actual goal is to have the coven simulate a wheel. However, since it's impractical to have people stand along the northern side (the altar's in the way), simply having them spread out around most of the Circle is sufficient.

14. If there's a bonfire or fireplace, the tapers/candles are tossed into the fire instead of the cauldron. Even with a separate fire, the Priest and Priestess still take up positions beside the cauldron.

15. A bonfire presents the problem of lighting the ropes on fire. The coven members may raise their arms over their heads to keep the ropes above the flames or remain standing.

16. The same costumes may have already been made for Midsummer. If so, they may be reused.

17. Instead of a log, a short segment of tree branch is decorated and used. The piece should be small enough to burn safely in a cauldron or open incense dish.

18. Even indoors, this needs to be hung from a freestanding fixture that does not break the cone of power of the Circle. A solution is to hang it from the end of a slender stick and have someone hold it above the gateway.

19. There's often a ring-dance after the drama concludes. It's usually performed by the coven while the Priest and Priestess consecrate the wine and cakes, but it may also take place before this rite if the coven leaders wish to participate in it.

Glossary

AIRTS, FOUR: The Gaelic word meaning the four cardinal points. Important to witchcraft and Ceremonial Magick to properly align the Magick Circle. Also corresponds to the four elements.

AMULET: A consecrated object worn to protect the wearer from evil or other similar harm by repelling or blocking the evil/harm from reaching the wearer. Differs from a talisman, which is worn to attract something of benefit to the wearer.

ANKH: An ancient Egyptian symbol that resembles a cross with a loop on top. Symbolic of life and cosmic knowledge, it has found its way into Wiccan practice as a symbol in spells and assorted other uses.

AQUARIUS (Jan. 21–Feb. 19): The eleventh sign of the zodiac in astrology, known as the sign of the Water Carrier. Recognized as an air sign in witchcraft, it is ruled by the planet Uranus. The energies associated with this sign are masculine-yang-positive-active, and its opposing sign is Leo.

ARIES (Mar. 21–Apr. 20): The first sign of the zodiac in astrology, known as the sign of the Ram. Recognized as a fire sign in witchcraft, it is ruled by the planet Mars. The energies associated with this sign are masculine-yang-positive-active, and its opposing sign is Libra.

ASTROLOGY: The study of the stars, planets, and other heavenly bodies for the purpose of divination or prophecy. Often called stargazing.

BANISHING: This term has three meanings in witchcraft. (1) It relates to banishing the Circle or dispersing the power that constitutes a Magick Circle after the ritual purpose is completed. (2) It is the act of repelling a troublesome spirit or harmful entity. (3) It means to expel a witch from a coven for an offense that cannot be overlooked. While this is almost never necessary, when it becomes so, the witch must be expelled at once in order to maintain harmony in the coven.

B.C.E. (Before Common Era): A nonreligious abbreviation used by non-Christians and scholars in place of B.C. Similarly, C.E. (Common Era) is used in place of A.D.

BEL-FIRE: In ancient custom, this was a bonfire lit on a hilltop during Beltane to celebrate the return of fertility to the earth.

BIDDY: A straw doll used to represent the Goddess figure in creating Brid's Bed. A form of poppet used in witchcraft for ritual purposes. Also known as a Corn Dolly.

BLESSED BE: A phrase used by witches as a blessing and often used as a formal ending to a letter or similar writing. The term "Amen" would be its closest Christian equivalent.

BOOK OF SHADOWS: A handwritten diary of magick spells and practices kept by a witch and/or coven.

BURNING TIMES: The Inquisition. Generally referring to the mid-fifteenth to early-eighteenth centuries, during which time witches were hunted down and executed.

CANCER (June 22–July 23): The fourth sign of the zodiac in astrology, known as the sign of the Crab. Recognized as a water sign in witchcraft, it is ruled by the Moon. The energies associated with this sign are feminine-yin-negative-passive, and its opposing sign is Capricorn.

CAPRICORN (Dec. 22–Jan. 20): The tenth sign of the zodiac in astrology, known as the sign of the Goat. Recognized as an earth sign in witchcraft, it is ruled by the planet Saturn. The energies associated with this sign are feminine-yin-negative-passive, and its opposing sign is Cancer.

CARDINAL POINTS: The four points of the compass—east, south, west, north. In witchcraft and Ceremonial Magick, these points correspond with the Watchtowers of the Circle and the four elements and are key to properly orienting the Magick Circle.

CELTIC: The name may refer to the Celtic tradition of witchcraft or the races of northernmost Europe and the British Isles. Celtic Wicca, which is Goddess oriented, forms the basis for many modern versions of witchcraft.

CEREMONIAL MAGICK: An extremely disciplined and exact form of magick, originally only practiced by priests and scholars. It has strong roots in Christianity, Judaism, and Hebrew and is therefore much younger than witchcraft. Basically, this form of magick is a method of harnessing and controlling the forces of Nature through ritualistic words and actions. The Ceremonial Magician uses many of the same tools as a witch, but in a far more elaborate way. Further, whereas witchcraft views the forces of Nature as neutral, Ceremonial Magick categorizes them as black or white (good or bad) and employs them according to this predetermined status. Today, some aspects of Ceremonial Magick have been blended into witchcraft, especially since the birth of Gardnerian Wicca.

CHARM: A magickal object, similar to an amulet or talisman, that can also be used as an object of bewitchment.

CHRISTIAN (GEORGIAN) CALENDAR YEAR: The standard calendar year in use throughout the world, which begins on January 1 and ends on December 31. It differs from the Celtic (or Wiccan) calendar, which recognizes the new year as beginning at the Samhain Sabbat.

CLAIRVOYANCE: The awareness of an unknown or unseen object or future event through psychic means; one of several types of extrasensory perception (ESP).

COLLECTIVE UNCONSCIOUS: The part of the unconscious that is inherited and common to all members of a species; accumulated and inherited memories from past generations.

CONE OF POWER: This term refers to the combined psychic energy that is built up within the Magick Circle during a ceremony. Its base is the interior perimeter of the Circle, and its apex is above the center, forming an invisible cone. It is often associated only with a coven, but this is a mistake since it is equally present when solitary witches work. The only true difference is that a coven produces more psychic energy.

CONSECRATION: The ritual act of purifying and making sacred. Most often used in reference to the ritual water and salt mixture used to cleanse the Circle, tools, or other objects of negative energies or unwanted influences.

CORN DOLLY: Similar to a biddy, but made exclusively from the last sheaf of corn from the harvest, which is then fashioned into a figure representing the Goddess.

COWAN: A nonderogatory word often used by witches to refer to nonwitches.

CRAFT: A general term used in place of Wicca, the Old Religion, the Craft of the Wise, or any other name meaning witchcraft.

CROWLEY, ALEISTER (1875–1947): Once denounced as the "Wickedest Man in the World" by the Italian press, Crowley was a member of the Hermetic Order of the Golden Dawn before forming his own order, the Argentinum Astrum (Silver Star). A flamboyant Ceremonial Magician with notoriously warped ideas, Crowley, nevertheless, became widely known in many circles. He is best known for his *Book of Law*, which set forth ideas, as well as prophecies, that he claimed were given to him by a nonhuman entity. Although not a witch in the normal sense of the word, he is still noteworthy in this book for his alleged contributions to Gerald Gardner, which took place near the latter part of Crowley's life.

CRYSTAL BALL: A transparent globe used for divination and meditation. In reality, most crystal balls are made of common glass, which is primarily due to the expense of true crystal.

DEOSIL: A clockwise movement, or moving with the sun, that symbolizes life and positive energy. This type of motion is associated with movement within the Magick Circle and most often used in reference to casting the Circle or during the ring-dance.

EKE-NAME: The Wiccan word for the secret witch name taken during Initiation.

ELEMENTALS: Primitive spirits or entities derived from the four elements. Witches and practitioners of the occult believe that elementals assist them in magical tasks. The elementals of air and fire are associated with masculine-yang-positive energies, while those of earth and water are linked with feminine-yin-negative energies.

EXORCISM: The psychic process of banishing an unwanted (usually evil or malevolent) entity from a person or place.

EVOCATION: The summoning of spirits, demons, or other nonphysical entities that are of the lower order. Higher order spirits and the Gods are not evoked. Also, an entity is evoked into the Magick Triangle, not the Magick Circle. The "triangle" is a symbol of manifestation and is drawn outside the Circle.

FAERIES (FAIRIES): The tiny mythical forest-dwelling spiritual beings of folklore said to live in enchanted lands and possess magical powers. Over time, theories have been advanced claiming that faeries were an actual race of small people who lived on the English Isles. Also referred to as Pickeys, Elves, Little Folk, or any number of other subdivisions, faeries have been the subject of much lore. Notable in witchcraft from ancient times when the Enchanted Realm of the Faerie was believed to be closely associated with witches and the Craft.

FAMILIAR: Usually thought of as the animals kept by witches and said to provide psychic assistance. Some think the animals act as a kind of early-warning device against harmful psychic activity. Naturally, whenever people think of a familiar, they think of the traditional black cat. However, dogs, horses, ferrets, weasels, crows, and even toads are mentioned in ancient folklore. There are actually two other types of familiars, but these are less well-known. The first is the spirit of a human being, more accurately described as a ghost. The second is a nonhuman spirit, or elemental, and is usually associated with an inanimate object.

FLAGELLATION: In common usage, this term refers to the practice of whipping a person as a means of punishment. In the context of witchcraft, this symbolic practice involves using the scourge to gently whip a person with the intent of producing an altered state of consciousness.

FLYING OINTMENT: A legendary salve that was said to enable witches to fly, become invisible, or shape shift. In reality, this ointment is a combination of potent poisonous plants, such as belladonna or other members of the nightshade family, lard or fat, and other herbs, that produce a hallucinogenic state after being rubbed on the body and absorbed through the skin.

GARDNER, GERALD BROSSEAU (1884–1964): Undoubtedly one of the most famous witches of all time, he is credited with bringing Wicca out into the open and informing the general public of its true message. The founder of Gardnerian Wicca and father of the Gardnerian Revival, he was also a celebrated author, writing many books on the subjects of witchcraft and Magick. Though he was often criticized for inventing his own brand of witchcraft, the rituals on which Gardner based his tradition are said to owe a great deal to Masonic practice and to Aleister Crowley. Whether this is indeed true is not known. However, it is a commonly held belief that Gardner built his tradition's beliefs by adapting ancient texts, such as the Key of Solomon the King, and modifying beliefs of other occult pursuits to suit his own ideas of how witchcraft should be practiced.

GEMINI (May 22–June 21): The third sign of the zodiac in astrology, known as the sign of the Twins. Recognized as an air sign in witchcraft, it is ruled by the planet Mercury. The energies associated with this sign are masculine-yang-positive-active, and its opposing sign is Sagittarius.

GENDER SWITCHING: The act of portraying a character that is of a different sex than oneself. A method of role playing that allows a female to represent a male deity or a male witch to represent a female deity for ritual purpose. Usually only used by solitary witches and single-gender covens.

GOLDEN DAWN, ORDER OF THE: Occult order based on Ceremonial Magick and founded in 1887. Noteworthy here in reference to Aleister Crowley, as well as the numerous Wiccan practices that were adopted from Ceremonial Magick sources.

GRIMOIRE: A book containing magical rituals and spells. It is very often associated with, or mistaken for, a *Book of Shadows*, although the two are quite different. A witch may at times use a grimoire, and many witches have a section of their *Book of Shadows* that contain a grimoire. The two, however, are by no means interchangeable.

HEXAGRAM: A six-pointed star formed using two interconnected triangles and symbolizing the Hermetic principle "as above, so below." The Jewish Star of David is a perfect example of a non-Pagan hexagram.

HIGH MAGICK: Another name for Ceremonial Magick. In contrast, country, practical, or folk magick, which is the basic foundation of witchcraft, is considered Low Magick.

HOLLY KING: From ancient folklore, it's the name given to the God of the Waning Year. With the Oak King, he plays an integral part in the cycle of life, death, and rebirth. The dual-king aspect is seen in many sabbat rituals.

HOROSCOPE: Also known as a Natal Chart, it is a chart interpreting the positioning and movements of planetary bodies and the effect these have on a person. In order to construct an exact chart, three things must be known: (1) the day, month, and year of birth; (2) the geographical place of birth; and (3) the time of birth—as exact as possible. Many believe that a person's horoscope is a map of past and future events in an individual's life.

IMAGE MAGICK: A powerful form of sympathetic magick that operates on the principle that an object resembling a person (or other object) can exert power over the person. Dolls, figurines, straw and wax images, or any number of things can be used.

INCANTATION: The use of special words, phrases, chants, or speeches, often rhymed or rhythmically set to produce a magickal effect. The Gardnerian Witches' Rune is an example of an incantation.

INVOCATION: The summoning of higher-order spirits and the Gods. In this case, think of summoning as an invitation rather than a command. At the beginning of most rituals, the God and/or Goddess are invoked into the Magick Circle to lend aid in workings. Drawing Down the Moon and Drawing Down the Sun are two examples of rites to invoke the essence of the Goddess and God into the body of a High Priestess and High Priest.

KABBALAH: Also known as the Cabala, Cabbala, Kabala, and Qabbalah, an esoteric occult interpretation of the Hebrew scriptures that sets forth an elaborate system for achieving union with God. Although based on monotheistic teachings and strict codes of behavior that are unacceptable to witches, the basic tenets are consistent with many Wiccan beliefs and practices.

KARMA: Cosmic result, or consequence, of one's life and actions, which manifests itself during future incarnations. One of the most important beliefs of the Wiccan religion is reincarnation.

KEY OF SOLOMON THE KING: A famous grimoire allegedly written by King Solomon and originally translated into English by S. L. MacGregor Mathers from manuscripts in the British Museum containing a list of instructions, prayers, exorcisms, incantations, invocations, and other magickal information. A careful study of this manuscript reveals the origins of many modern-day Wiccan practices.

LEFT-HAND PATH: The name used for black magick or Satanic worship. Wicca has absolutely no connection to these practices.

LEO (July 24–Aug. 23): The fifth sign of the zodiac in astrology, known as the sign of the Lion. Recognized as a fire sign in Witchcraft, it is ruled by the Sun. The energies associated with this sign are masculine-yang-positive-active, and its opposing sign is Aquarius.

LIBATION: An offering of consecrated water, wine, or other liquid that is poured on the ground or into a libation dish as a ritual gift to the Gods.

LIBRA (Sept. 24–Oct. 23): The seventh sign of the zodiac in astrology, known as the sign of the Scales. Recognized as an air sign in witchcraft, it is ruled by the planet Venus. The energies associated with this sign are masculine-yang-positive-active, and its opposing sign is Aries.

LORD OF MISCHIEF: A representation of the mischievous aspect of the Samhain Sabbat. In folklore, this figure is also called the Lord of Misrule and is portrayed as a court jester carrying a fool's staff. Represented in tarot cards as the Fool.

LOW MAGICK: Often referred to as Natural Magick, Folk Magick, or Practical Magick, it encompasses all magickal practices employed by witches. A much less formal or ceremonious discipline than High Magick.

MAGICIAN: A practitioner of the ceremonial magickal arts who is not a believer in the religious aspects of Wicca and does not celebrate sabbats, esbats, or other Wiccan religious practices.

MAGICK: The art, science, or practice of producing metaphysical, transcendental, or supernatural effects through the use of words, actions, gestures, spells, or formulas.

MAYPOLE: A tall, flower-wreathed pole with long colored ribbons attached to the top and hanging to the ground. Participants hold the ribbons and dance around the pole in a circle. Also a phallic symbol with fertility implications.

MERRY MEET, MERRY PART: A shortened greeting and departing phrase used by many witches. The original saying was "Merry Meet, Merry Part, Merry Meet Again." It symbolizes the joyousness of gatherings or being in the company of another witch. Such greetings originally came into use during the time of the witch-hunts so witches could tell a witch from a nonwitch.

NIK (OLD NIK): In pre-Christian times, a name used for the Saxon God, Woden, or the Holly King. It was perverted over time by Christianity to refer to the Devil. However, in Pagan strongholds, it also came to refer to Saint Nicholas, or Santa Claus, despite Christian efforts to the contrary.

NUMEROLOGY: A form of divination that uses numbers and their corresponding meanings to foretell future events or other information.

OAK KING: From ancient folklore, the name given to the God of the Waxing Year. With the Holly King, he plays an integral part in the cycle of life, death, and rebirth. The dual-king aspect is seen in many sabbat rituals.

OCCULT: Of or relating to the effects, knowledge, or even practice of, Magick, witchcraft, or any number of supernatural ideals. It may also mean "secret," "mysterious," or "not revealed."

PAGAN: Originally meaning "country dweller" and used as a derogatory term by early Christians to refer to a follower of the Old Religion, now most commonly used to describe a believer of witchcraft or any of the earth-based religions. The word has been used in reference to Druids, Wiccans, and even American Indians.

PALMISTRY: The art or practice of reading the lines of the hand to divine a person's past, future, character, or aptitudes; a form of divination.

PENTACLE: A word having three distinct meanings. (1) A five-pointed star, usually within a circle, used in witchcraft. The upright symbol represents a human being with arms and legs extended or the four elements ruled by the fifth Element of Spirit. The inverted symbol is often viewed as a sign of Black Magick or Satanism, but this is merely a perversion of the symbol created by early Christianity and has nothing to do with witchcraft. (2) A flat disc, plate, or dish displaying the five-pointed star, used in rituals to represent the earth element and feminine energy. (3) The coins suit of the Minor Arcana in the Tarot.

PENTAGRAM: A written, drawn, or scribed five-pointed star; a pentacle symbol. The upright pentagram symbolizes power, protection, life force, and a number of other beliefs. It is often used to invoke or banish spirits when used during a ritual.

PHALLIC WAND: A wand used to symbolize the male aspect of fertility.

PHILOSOPHER'S STONE: In folklore, a substance believed to be the way an alchemist turned other metals into gold. Sought after throughout history, everyone from kings to clergy dreamed of learning the secret.

PISCES (Feb. 20-March 20): The twelfth sign of the zodiac in astrology, known as the sign of the Fishes. Recognized as a water sign in Witchcraft, it is ruled by the planets Jupiter and Neptune. The energies associated with this sign are feminine-yin-negative-passive, and its opposing sign is Virgo.

POLYTHEISM: The belief in and worship of more than one deity. Wicca, which worships both a God and Goddess, is a polytheistic religion.

POPPET: A doll used in sympathetic magick.

PRECOGNITION: Of or relating to a foreknowledge of future events or states.

QUARTERS: (*See* Cardinal Points.)

QUERENT: In the Tarot, astrology, or divination, the person seeking answers.

REINCARNATION: A main belief held by witches, and others, that the human soul is reborn time and time again after death.

RING-DANCE: A deosil circular dance within the Magick Circle for the purpose of raising power or directing a working around a certain object or point. There are several dances (Midsummer, Corn, Harvest) that follow this pattern.

RUNES: Meaning "secret" or "mysterious," any of the symbols (letters) in the traditional alphabets of witchcraft. Runes serves two purposes: to hide the writing from the uninformed; and to make the writer concentrate more on the text, thereby increasing the thought going into the writing. Not to be confused with the Witches' Rune, which is a rhythmic chant for raising power.

SAGITTARIUS (Nov. 23–Dec. 21): The ninth sign of the zodiac in astrology, known as the sign of the Archer. Recognized as a fire sign in witchcraft, it is ruled by the planet Jupiter. The energies associated with this sign are masculine-yang-positive-active, and its opposing sign is Gemini.

SCORPIO (Oct. 24–Nov. 22): The eighth sign of the zodiac in astrology, known as the sign of the Scorpion. Recognized as a water sign in witchcraft, it is ruled by the planets Mars and Pluto. The energies associated with this sign are feminine-yin-negative-passive, and its opposing sign is Taurus.

SCRYING: The practice of foretelling the future by interpreting images that are seen in a scrying mirror or crystal ball.

SCRYING MIRROR: Also called a Black Mirror, any smooth, dark-colored surface resembling a mirror used for divination or meditation. The object, whether a scrying mirror or crystal ball, is known as a speculum.

SEANCE: A gathering aimed at communicating with the spirit world.

SHAPE SHIFTING: The process of transforming from human to animal (or other) form. This can occur in one of two ways. First, a physical transformation takes place. The belief that witches can become cats, bats, etc., is based on this principle. The second transformation occurs only to the astral body. This form is restricted to the astral plane and only associated with Shamanism.

SIGIL: An image or symbol that represents a specific spirit, deity, or other preternatural being. An occult seal or sign.

SKYCLAD: The practice of being naked for ritual purposes. The term literally translates to "clad by the sky." Many witches and covens, especially in Europe, prefer to conduct their rituals in this manner.

SOLITARY: A witch who is not part of a coven and for one reason or another, practices witchcraft alone. A solitary witch may from time to time associate with a coven or other witches, but they are primarily loners. Some witches who are coven witches also practice as solitaries from time to time.

SO MOTE IT BE: A phrase used extensively in witchcraft rituals and blessing, it has evolved to more or less mean "according to (my) our will."

SOUL CAKES: An offering of food left for the spirits of the dead to placate and/or commemorate them while they are in the Realm of the Living.

SPIRITUALISM: The belief in communication with the dead and/or use of a person acting as a medium to communicate with the spirits of the dead.

SUMMERLANDS: In Wicca, the afterworld where the soul goes after physical death.

SYMPATHETIC MAGICK: (*See* Image Magick.)

TALISMAN: An object, similar in design to an amulet, worn to attract positive influences or forces to the wearer, rather than repel negative influences or forces.

TAPER: A long wax-covered wick used for lighting candles or transferring flame.

TAURUS (Apr. 21–May. 21): The second sign of the zodiac in astrology, known as the sign of the Bull. Recognized as an earth sign in witchcraft, it is ruled by the planet Venus. The energies associated with this sign are feminine-yin-negative-passive, and its opposing sign is Scorpio.

TELEPATHY: The awareness or knowledge of someone else's thoughts or feelings by psychic means; one of several types of extrasensory perception

(ESP).

TEMPLE: The usual meeting place of a coven or sacred place for a solitary witch. The temple will usually be a room set aside for ritual purposes only and may have a Circle permanently marked on the floor. However, since a Magick Circle can be cast anywhere, permanent temples are not required.

UNDERWORLD: The Realm of the Dead. In ancient mythology, the place in the earth where the souls of the dead go after death. Similar to the Summerlands as a resting place for souls, though usually depicted as dark and fiery. The Christian heaven and hell are derived from the different views of the Summerlands and Underworld.

VIRGO (Aug. 24-Sept. 23): The sixth sign of the zodiac in astrology, known as the sign of the Virgin. Recognized as an earth sign in witchcraft, it is ruled by the planet Mercury. The energies associated with this sign are feminine-yin-negative-passive, and its opposing sign is Pisces.

WANING: To decrease in size, strength, or duration. A term used in witchcraft applied to the lessening light and influence of the moon and sun or to the degree of the Goddess/God associated with it.

WATCHTOWERS: The four cardinal points around the Magick Circle where candles are placed. These represent the Guardians of the Circle and are one of many practices borrowed from Ceremonial Magick. Also known as Wards or Quarters.

WAXING: To increase in size, strength, or duration. A term used in witchcraft applied to the growing light and influence of the moon and sun or to the degree of the Goddess/God associated with it.

WICCA: The catchall term used by witches to describe various denominations of the Craft. Though the word itself is widely accepted, its origin is hotly contested. Likely sources include the Old English word for witch—wicca (meaning male witch) or wicce (meaning female witch). Other possibilities include the Old English word wiccacræft (witchcraft) or wiccian (meaning to practice wiccacræft). In addition, words such as wiccedom (witchdom or witch-kingdom), wiccian (to bewitch), and the Middle English wicche (a plural form of witch) help to confuse the issue.

WICCAN REDE: The moral code that all Wiccans strive to follow. Although a longer version is often used, the most widely known portion is "An it harm none, do what thou wilt."

WIDDERSHINS: A counterclockwise movement, or moving against the sun, most often associated with movement within the Magick Circle and used in banishing. Symbolic of negative energy, death, or decline.

WITCHES' LADDER: A tool of sorcerers to bring misfortune or nightmares. This magickal object consists of a triple-knotted rope with a feather stuck in each knot.

WIZARD: The name given to a male witch by most nonwitches, though some male witches actually prefer this title. A wizard (meaning "wise man") should not be confused with warlock, as the latter is an ancient derogatory Scottish term meaning traitor.

YIN-YANG: The principal belief of Taoism that states that cosmic energy is either feminine-passive-negative (Yin) or masculine-active-positive (Yang). The two energies are complementary to, but opposite from, each other.

ZODIAC: The imaginary belt in the heavens that consists of the paths of the planets, divided into twelve signs or constellations; the symbols of the zodiac that are used in astrology.

Bibliography

Adler, Margot. *Drawing Down the Moon*. Boston: Beacon Press, 1981.

Bell, Jessica W. *The Book of Shadows*. St. Paul, MN: Llewellyn, 1971.

Boyer, Paul, and Stephen Nissenbaum. *The Salem Witchcraft Papers: Verbatim Transcripts of the Legal Documents of the Salem Witchcraft Outbreak of 1692*. New York, 1977.

Bromwich, Rachael. *The Welsh Triads*. Cardiff: University of Wales Press, 1961.

Buckland, Raymond. *The Tree: The Complete Book of Saxon Witchcraft*. New York: Samuel Weiser, Inc., 1974.

Bulfinch, Thomas. *The Age of Fable*. Cambridge, MA 1855; reprint 1987.

Cabot, Laurie. *The Power of the Witch*. New York: Doubleday, 1989.

Carmichael, Alexander. *The Sun Dances*. Scotland: Floris Books, 1977.

Crowley, Aleister. *Book of Thoth*. California: Shambala Publications, 1981.

Crowley, Aleister. *777 Revised*. London: 1952.

Davidson, Gustov. *A Dictionary of Angels, Including the Fallen*. New York: Free Press, 1967.

Falassi, Alessandro. *Folklore by the Fireside: Text and Context of the Tuscan Veglia*. Texas: University of Texas Press, 1980.

Farrar, Janet and Stewart. *A Witches' Bible*. Custer, WA: Phoenix Publishing, 1981.

Farrar, Janet and Stewart. *Eight Sabbats for Witches*. London: Robert Hale, 1981.

Fortune, Dion. *Moon Magic*. London: Aquarian Press, 1956.

Fortune, Dion. *The Mystical Qabala*. London: Benn Press, 1935.

Fortune, Dion. *The Sea Priestess*. London: Aquarian Press, 1957.

Frazier, Sir. James George. *The Golden Bough: A Study of Comparative Religion*. London 1890; reprint New York, 1981.

Gardner, Gerald B. *High Magic's Aid*. London: Houghton, 1949.

Gardner, Gerald B. *Witchcraft Today*. London: Rider, 1954.

Graves, Robert. *White Goddess, The* (3rd ed.). New York: Faber and Faber, 1966.

Gray, Eden. *Complete Guide to the Tarot.* New York: Bantam, 1988.

Grimassi, Raven. *Italian Witchcraft: The Old Religion of Southern Europe.* St. Paul, MN: Llewellyn, 1995.

Johns, June. *King of the Witches: The World of Alex Sanders.* New York: Coward-McCann, 1970.

Kipling, Rudyard. *The Jungle Book.* London: MacMillan, 1905.

Kipling, Rudyard. *Puck of Pook's Hill.* London: MacMillan, 1906.

Kittridge, George Lyman. *Witchcraft in Old and New England.* New York: 1920.

Knight, Sirona. *Celtic Traditions.* New York: Citadel Press, 2000.

Kramer, Heinrich, and Jacob Sprenger. *Malleus Malificarum.* Original 1484; Trans. by Montague Summers in 1928.

Leek, Sybil. *The Complete Art of Witchcraft.* New York: Signet, 1971.

Leland, Charles Godfrey. *Aradia: Gospel of the Witches.* London: 1899.

Leland, Charles Godfrey. *Aradia: Gospel of the Witches.* New Trans. by Pazzaglini and Pazzaglini; Phoenix Publishing, 1998.

Leland, Charles Godfrey. *Etruscan Roman Remains.* First published 1892; reprint Custer, WA: Phoenix Publishing, 1999.

Leland, Charles Godfrey. *Legends of Florence.* New York: MacMillan, 1896.

Lethbridge, T. C. *Witches.* New York: Citadel Press, 1962.

Macfarlane, Alan. *Witchcraft in Tudor and Stuart England.* New York: 1970.

Markale, Jean. *The Celts.* Rochester, VT: Inner Traditions International, 1993.

Mathers, S. Lindell MacGregor. *The Key of Solomon (Clavicula Solomonis).* Originally published 1889; reprint Weiser, 2000.

Matthews, John. *The Elements of the Arthurian Tradition.* London: Element Books, 1989.

McCoy, Edain. *Witta: An Irish Pagan Tradition.* St. Paul, MN: Llewellyn, 1993.

Murray, Margaret A. *The Witch-Cult in Western Europe.* London: 1921; reprint Oxford University Press, 1970.

Rees, Alwyn and Brinley. *Celtic Heritage: Ancient tradition in Ireland and Wales.* London: 1961; reprint New York: 1978.

Regardie, Israel. *The Golden Dawn* (6th ed.). St. Paul, MN: Llewellyn, 1989.

St. Clair, David. *Pagans, Priests and Prophets.* New Jersey: Prentice-Hall, 1976.

Starhawk. *The Spiral Dance.* California: Harper and Row, 1979.

Stewart, R. J. *The Living World of Faery.* Glastonbury, U.K.: Gothic Image, 1995.

Thorsson, Edred. *Northern Magic: Mysteries of the Norse, Germans and English.* St. Paul, MN: Llewellyn, 1992.

Underhill, Evelyn. *Mysticism* (12th ed.). New York: 1930.

Upham, Charles W. *Salem Witchcraft, with an Account of Salem Village and a History of Opinions on Witchcraft and Kindred Spirits.* Boston: 1867.

Valiente, Doreen. *An ABC of Witchcraft.* Custer, WA: Phoenix Publishing, 1973.

Valiente, Doreen. *Witchcraft for Tomorrow.* New York: St. Martin's Press, 1978.

Waite, Arthur Edward. *The Pictorial Key to the Tarot.* New York: Weiser, 1973.

Weinstein, Marion. *Earth Magic: A Dianic Book of Shadows.* Custer, WA: Phoenix Publishing, 1986.

Index